Flexible Applications of Cognitive Processing Therapy

Evidence-Based Treatment Methods

Flexible Applications of Cognitive Processing Therapy

Evidence-Based Treatment Methods

Tara E. Galovski
National Center for PTSD, VA Boston Healthcare System and Boston University School of Medicine, Boston, Massachusetts, United States

Reginald D. V. Nixon
College of Education, Psychology & Social Work, Flinders University, Adelaide, SA, Australia

Debra Kaysen
Department of Psychiatry and Behavioral Sciences, Stanford University, Stanford, CA, United States

ELSEVIER

ACADEMIC PRESS
An imprint of Elsevier

Academic Press is an imprint of Elsevier
125 London Wall, London EC2Y 5AS, United Kingdom
525 B Street, Suite 1650, San Diego, CA 92101, United States
50 Hampshire Street, 5th Floor, Cambridge, MA 02139, United States
The Boulevard, Langford Lane, Kidlington, Oxford OX5 1GB, United Kingdom

Library of Congress Cataloging-in-Publication Data
A catalog record for this book is available from the Library of Congress

British Library Cataloguing-in-Publication Data
A catalogue record for this book is available from the British Library

ISBN: 978-0-12-816715-1

For information on all Academic Press publications
visit our website at https://www.elsevier.com/books-and-journals

Publisher: Matthew Limbert
Acquisitions Editor: Nikki Levy
Editorial Project Manager: Barbara Makinster
Production Project Manager: Paul Prasad Chandramohan
Designer: Matthew Limbert

Typeset by Thomson Digital

Contents

4. Emerging as an effective therapy: CPT is put to the test

Part II
Flexible Administrations of the CPT Manual

5. Challenges to optimal therapy outcomes

6. Therapy is hard: Improving patient engagement and working through avoidance

Part III
Dissemination and Implementation of CPT

11. Applications of CPT in diverse populations and across cultures

12. Administering CPT across health care systems and clinical settings

13. Future frontiers

About the authors

We (Drs. Galovski, Nixon, and Kaysen) all began our CPT journey at the birthplace of CPT—the Center for Trauma Recovery (CTR) at the University of Missouri—St. Louis. Dr. Kaysen was the first of us to be introduced to CPT as Dr. Resick's graduate student in the very early days when CPT was being compared to PE in the first randomized clinical trial. Dr. Nixon was also mentored by Dr. Resick at the CTR during his postdoctoral fellowship. Dr. Galovski next joined the CPT family as a research professor and served as project director of the CPT dismantling study just as Dr. Nixon was leaving to return to Australia and Dr. Resick left CTR to take the position of the Director of Women's Health Sciences Division of the National Center for PTSD. Since those early days participating in the development of CPT in the first clinical trials establishing its, efficacy, all three of us have gone on to develop, test, and practice CPT across a wide variety of settings and patient populations.

Between us, we have conducted 15 CPT trials as coinvestigators, served as consultants on an additional 15+ trials, published over 225 peer-reviewed papers and chapters on CPT and related topics, and forged new paths and improved overall outcomes for more survivors of trauma by developing 8 additional CPT trials as principle investigators. We have been funded by NIH, DoD, VA, NHMRC, SAMHSA, DVA, ARC, USAID foundations, and local-funding agencies. All three authors were among the original team of CPT investigators to develop the large-scale CPT dissemination effort within the United States. VHA that serves as a model for additional rollouts in which we participated or led across the US DoD, at the state level (TX, MO, CO) and we continue to disseminate CPT as national and international trainers.

Between three of us we have worked clinically with, or conducted clinical trials across, numerous trauma populations including survivors of sexual assault, torture, veterans (combat and military sexual trauma), active duty military, sexual minority women, first responders, MVA/accidental injury, and acute survivors. This work has been conducted within the US populations as well as with Iraqi's, Congolese, native Americans, and Australians. We have served as consultants for well over 1000 practicing clinicians in a variety of contexts and as primary mentors for over 30 trainees at the undergraduate, graduate, and postdoctoral levels and secondary mentors for countless other. Readers can always google us to see what we are up to next! Individually, we thought we would each speak to what specifically drive us to this type of work.

Dr. Galovski's story: As an eternal optimist but also a firm realist, I do believe that people can move through truly horrific and almost unspeakable events and get to the other side. After doing this work as a practicing clinical psychologist and scientist for nearly 20 years, I have had the privilege of seeing lives change for the better. We all know that we cannot undo the past, but we can make our worlds big enough to hold even the worst of experiences and still live our best lives. As therapists, we have the honor to accompany our patients on this journey, but the journey is theirs. I can honestly say that I have been awed by the strength and fortitude of the survivors who found the courage to walk through the doors of the CTR in St. Louis and do this difficult work. It was an extremely difficult decision to leave the remarkable CTR and come to Boston, but I felt compelled to give back to the Veterans who have served us so well, and particularly to our women Veterans, and can do exactly that in my current capacity as the Director of the Women's Health Sciences Division of the National Center for PTSD and as an Associate Professor at Boston University School of Medicine. There is much work to be done and I am excited to continue to tackle this challenge of moving the needle ever further toward recovery from PTSD.

Dr. Nixon's story: I am often asked how I came to work in the area of trauma and why. I completed one of my clinical training placements at a specialist PTSD unit (St John of God Hospital, North Richmond). There I was inspired by the determination of those who had received the worst deck of cards that life could throw at them. Yet they, as well as the people I have worked with since, have shown me that with the right environment and help, incredible amounts of recovery is possible. I was also fortunate enough to be mentored early in my career by two leaders in our field, Dr. Richard Bryant and Dr. Patricia Resick, seeing firsthand the quality of their work and dedication to improving our knowledge of how best to help those after trauma. It is this background that drives my desire to further contribute to the traumatic stress field, a contribution that will not just reduce suffering but results in people having the opportunity to live and enjoy the lives they deserve.

Dr. Kaysen's story: I come from a large, diverse, opinionated, and loving family scattered all over the world. On top of that I have added in an equally large chosen family. That family also had an ethos of service. Within that beautiful network I have also seen people I love dearly touched by traumatic events, how it has affected them, and how they have made it through. Those stories helped pull me into the trauma field. When I entered graduate school and discovered the CTR and my graduate school mentor, Dr. Patricia Resick, I knew I had found my clinical and research home. That passion for helping facilitate recovery, respecting people's natural resilience, and embracing the knowledge and diversity of people across the globe has driven my own work and has led me from the University of Washington to Stanford, where I am honored to help support the next generation of clinicians and researchers in the trauma field.

Foreword

"Flexible Applications of Cognitive Processing Therapy," is a lovely companion to the treatment manual "Cognitive Processing Therapy for PTSD: a Comprehensive Manual." It is authored, not only by researchers and CPT trainers, but by three therapists who have extensive experience in conducting CPT in varied practice settings: Tara E. Galovski, Reginald D. V. Nixon, and Debra Kaysen. All three of these skilled clinicians and researchers have added to the evolution of CPT to new formats and populations while keeping the heart of the therapy intact. Although the original treatment manual says "comprehensive," by that we meant the basic CPT manual for different populations and formats and all of the materials needed to complete individual, group, or variable length treatment (without or with the trauma account). It could not cover in detail all of the various additional problems that individual patients bring to the therapy room (or refuse to) that could undermine treatment. This volume adds to that manual by providing rich information on clinical considerations that can arise with a population that not only has PTSD, but life circumstances and comorbid symptoms that can stymie therapists and affect their ability to complete this evidence-based treatment with fidelity.

The first few chapters review the symptoms of PTSD, what CPT consists of, and the theoretical background. The research supporting CPT follows and then the book moves into dealing with specific challenges such as dealing with avoidance and managing common problems that are encountered with patients. Then the book moves into more difficult client situations such as conducting CPT with those with complex trauma histories, managing emotional dysregulation from extreme numbing and dissociation to the opposite pole, such as strong anger. There is a chapter on comorbid disorders and how to decide which to treat first, the PTSD or other disorders and how to manage treating both simultaneously when called for. There is a chapter on dissemination including working within agencies and systems. Finally there are chapters on diverse populations and cross-cultural adaptations as well a peek into the future of CPT.

This book is not a replacement for the treatment manual—it does not explain how to implement CPT—but devotes entire chapters to topics that were given only a paragraph or two in the treatment manual, due to page limitations. It also updates the research findings that have emerged to guide treatment since the treatment manual was published. For those who do not have ongoing access to consultation by experts, answers to typical situations, and more in-depth discussion of possible strategies for handling common and less common problems, when to deviate from the protocol without losing fidelity, and adaptations that have been made that maintain the crucial elements of CPT are all included. Throughout the book, several case study examples are followed to add richness to the explanations and suggestions for possible interventions.

"Flexible Applications of Cognitive Processing Therapy" demonstrates well that an evidence-based brief manualized treatment for PTSD need not be rigid and disregarding of client needs. The authors do an excellent job of providing advice to therapists about how to adjust the protocol to the ongoing circumstances of the patients' lives and then how to return to treating PTSD with CPT without meandering off course. This book is very clear and a helpful addition to the implementation of CPT in clinical practice and should sit on the shelf next to the treatment manual for easy access to expert guidance.

Patricia A Resick, PhD, ABPP
Professor of Psychiatry and Behavioral Sciences
Duke University Medical Center

Acknowledgments

Tara E. Galovski sends much love and thanks to Jim, Saige, Hope, and Sam. Above all else, you are my Team G'lov and my future self is really quite jealous of my current self.

To Mark Rider, how many people get to name their dad as both their hero and their best friend? I am forever honored to be your daughter. I miss you.

And to Adrienne, your light continues to shine in ways that are unimaginable and indescribable. Too soon, too short, but so powerful. You inspire me to do this work better, every day, truly.

Reginald D. V. Nixon would like to thank his family—Julie, Anna, and Will—for their support and tolerance, especially when he is busy "with that work stuff." He would also like to thank his mentors, colleagues, and students who have over the years either given sage advice, been valued collaborators, or simply kept him on task.

Debra Kaysen would like to thank first and foremost her partners, Carter and Karla, and her son Evan for their seemingly endless patience and support. She would like to thank the Sacred Journey Community and the Healing Season's Community for including her in the work we have done together. To the brilliant women of the Trauma Recovery Innovation Program (Drs. Stappenbeck, Lindgren, and Bedard-Gilligan), I adore you all and am eternally grateful for the inspiration, wisdom, and giggles you have brought to my life.

All three authors would like to acknowledge that none of this work could be done if Patti Resick had not written this beautiful therapy. We want to thank the larger CPT family as well the trainers, scientists, and clinicians around the globe. We learn so much from you and always appreciate your support and wisdom. We also want to acknowledge the various institutions, which have housed and supported our projects as well as all of the agencies that have funded our studies, allowing this work to continue and grow. Finally, and perhaps most importantly, we want to express our appreciation and gratitude to all of the trauma survivors who participated in our studies. You have paved this path and made the journey to recovery possible for so many more to follow.

Part I

Cognitive Processing Therapy: Supporting Evidence

Chapter 1

The face of PTSD

Chapter outline

What is PTSD?

You may have heard the adage, "If you've seen one, you've seen 'em all!" This saying could not be further from the truth when considering clinical presentations of posttraumatic stress disorder (PTSD). The unique nature of each individual trauma and the nuances of the context in which that trauma occurred, coupled with prior trauma history and comorbid disorders and conditions, all contribute to the unique and variable clinical presentations that clinicians will grapple with when treating trauma survivors suffering from PTSD. The diagnostic criteria for PTSD was recently expanded in the Diagnostic and Statistical Manual, 5th Edition (DSM-5: American Psychiatric Association, 2013) to include 20 symptoms distributed over four clusters. The sheer number of symptoms and the number of possible combinations of symptoms that can result in the diagnosis of PTSD attests to the variability in clinical presentations that a therapist may observe across patients presenting with the exact same diagnosis. For example, one patient suffering from PTSD may appear withdrawn and emotionally numb or shutdown while another may present as quite emotional and have difficulty containing that emotion throughout the therapy sessions. A third patient may exhibit a significant fearful and anxious demeanor and may dissociate frequently when presented with reminders of the trauma while a fourth patient may become angry and even volatile during and outside the session. Given the heterogeneity in the diagnostic criteria and the variability that therapists observe across clinical presentations, it may be difficult to imagine how one single therapy can possibly be effective across all of these different manifestations of one disorder.

Flexible Applications of Cognitive Processing Therapy. http://dx.doi.org/10.1016/B978-0-12-816715-1.00001-7

Clinical complexities

Adding to the clinical challenges inherent in treating this disorder, PTSD rarely occurs in isolation, meaning that it is quite common for multiple additional disorders to co-occur with PTSD, including substance use disorders, insomnia, major depression, and/or personality disorders. Indeed PTSD is less likely to present as a sole diagnosis than it is to present with one or more comorbid conditions (Bradley, Greene, Russ, Dutra, & Westen, 2005). It can be quite challenging for the treating therapist to first differentially diagnose various disorders, which often present with overlapping symptoms, and then develop a cohesive treatment plan. This treatment planning could involve decisions about prioritizing which disorder to treat first or deciding to treat multiple disorders simultaneously. Similarly, there are often additional necessary considerations as to what types of comorbid presentations are likely to interfere with successful engagement in CPT or whether these conditions could lead to CPT being iatrogenic. Conversely, the therapist might consider whether the treatment of PTSD may actually alleviate the symptoms of other comorbid conditions. For example, a typical conundrum faced by PTSD therapists is comorbid PTSD and substance use disorders. A patient might be using alcohol or substances to diminish the pain of the PTSD symptoms. In this case, the PTSD symptoms may be a clear cause of alcohol misuse. Treating the PTSD symptoms as the primary target of care should then logically not only decrease the PTSD symptoms, but also decrease the need to use the substance. However, a therapist could also grow concerned that by engaging with the trauma memory, the patient's distress could increase and, in turn, increase the need for even more self-medication through substance misuse. These and other clinical conundrums will be discussed in detail later in this book.

In addition to comorbid psychiatric conditions, a host of other complicating factors can also contribute to the challenges inherent in treating PTSD. For example, many trauma survivors sustain injuries during their traumatic event (e.g., assaults, combat, motor vehicle accidents) and lingering physical limitations, such as traumatic brain injuries or reproductive health complications, chronic pain, scarring, and other related health difficulties can serve as additional stressors warranting clinical attention—as well as constant reminders of the trauma triggering PTSD symptoms.

Likewise, trauma survivors' functioning can be significantly impacted by the traumatic event and these impairments in functioning can, in turn, have detrimental effects on relationships resulting in the crumbling of support systems. PTSD can interfere with trauma survivors' ability to secure and keep gainful employment; traumatic events such as car crashes and natural disasters can include property loss and damages—all resulting in financial difficulties. Financial difficulties are not only a constant source of additional stress, but can prevent people from accessing resources such as therapy. Living with PTSD symptoms, and the additional stressors that surround PTSD, can create significant stress on existing relationships, further depleting the trauma survivors' resources and supports. In sum, PTSD can interfere with just about every aspect of people's lives. We see the worlds of trauma survivors suffering from PTSD grow smaller and smaller as they work hard to avoid anything that reminds them of their traumatic event. We see our patients struggle with PTSD-related fears for their own safety and that of their loved ones to the extent that it prevents them from living the lives they want to live. And we see these struggles expand to encompass all aspects of individuals' functioning, further increasing their overall traumatic stress burdens.

The toll of PTSD

PTSD, by definition, presents significant challenges to patient engagement and retention. In order to be successful, trauma-focused therapy must break through the avoidance inherent in the diagnosis of PTSD and include an element of accessing the trauma memory. In essence, we are asking patients to do precisely what they most adamantly do not want to do—think about the worst thing that ever happened to them. In fact, it is not unusual for the therapist to be the first person to whom trauma survivors disclose their traumatic experience. It is also not uncommon for patients to initiate treatment for traumas that had occurred on average a decade and a half ago (Resick et al., 2008; Galovski, Blain, Mott, Elwood, & Houle, 2012). While studies report the average number of years from index trauma to treatment, it is also important to note the substantial range of time since trauma across patients. While trauma survivors certainly seek treatment secondary to fairly recent events, it is not uncommon for patients to seek treatment decades after his/her trauma. Living with PTSD clearly impairs functioning and, as years of suffering with the disorder go by, the chronicity can contribute to significant personal and community costs as trauma survivors struggle with the burden of PTSD symptoms.

Treating PTSD is clearly complicated from the therapist perspective. Engagement in PTSD treatment is immensely challenging from the patient perspective. Fortunately, we have excellent psychological interventions that can effectively treat PTSD. These therapies are manualized and accessible, well researched, and well taught.

Cognitive processing therapy

Over the last several decades, the research on Cognitive Processing Therapy has burgeoned, earning it top ratings and designations as a first line treatment for PTSD across national and international clinical guidelines and evidence reviews (U.S. Department of Veteran Affairs and Department of Defense, 2017; American Psychological Association, 2017; UK National Institute for Health and Clinical Excellence, 2005; Australian Centre for Posttraumatic Mental Health, 2013; Bisson et al., 2019; Foa, Keane, Friedman, & Cohen, 2008;

Institute of Medicine, 2007; Forbes et al., 2007). The updated CPT manual recently published (Resick, Monson, & Chard, 2017) has enhanced previous iterations, increasing the accessibility of the therapy for clinicians from all types of health care systems. The process of training in CPT has also been manualized and the training workshop, developed by national experts in CPT, has been refined over the years, leading to the widespread dissemination of CPT (Karlin et al., 2010). Best practices of learning CPT include a 2-day workshop (with an option of a third day to include a group CPT training) followed by a period of regular (weekly) consultation with a CPT expert, providing CPT trainees to ask questions on individual cases in real time as they administer the protocol to their patients. The consultation process has been found to be particularly effective in increasing therapist skill in administering the therapy (Monson et al., 2018). Meta-analytic study has quantified the effectiveness of CPT and results show that CPT emerges as one of the most effective therapies of PTSD (Steenkamp, Litz, Hoge, & Marmar, 2015; Cusack et al., 2016). Suffice it to say, we can conclude that CPT is a very effective therapy for PTSD.

However, we also know that CPT is far from perfect. We know that, despite its success, approximately one-third of patients do not lose their PTSD diagnosis after completion of therapy (Schottenbauer, Glass, Arnkoff, Tendick, & Gray, 2008) and that these numbers may be even higher in specific populations such as veterans engaged in VA healthcare (Steenkamp et al., 2015). We know that our premature dropout rates are far too high and that dropout from treatment may even be higher in clinical practice settings (Schottenbauer et al., 2008). The burning question then becomes, why is a therapy that is clearly so effective for the majority of patients suffering from PTSD not effective for a sizable minority? And what can we, as clinicians, do to help move that needle further toward recovery for more of our patients?

This book seeks to expand on the session-by-session instruction provided in the CPT manual and enhance the contributions of the CPT consultation process by acknowledging and addressing clinical complexities and psychosocial stressors that can create challenges to optimal therapy outcomes (COTOs). By leveraging the available research on successful modifications of the CPT protocol to meet patients' needs, we hope to provide clinically relevant guidance to clinicians as they grapple with attending to COTOs while administering CPT.

Balancing patient needs with fidelity to the treatment manual can feel akin to walking a tightrope. A slip in the direction of a more flexible protocol administration can jeopardize the effectiveness of the intervention; however, maintaining rigid fidelity may result in increased patient dropout or poorer, less holistic outcomes. Most of us do not have the time or bandwidth to stay abreast of every new research paper that is published on CPT. This book seeks to provide guidance on flexible approaches to the administration of CPT by relying on the literature on CPT modifications as well as leveraging our own years of experience as CPT therapists and clinical supervisors for hundreds of PTSD patients, as clinical trialists developing the CPT protocol and testing the modifications that we propose, as national CPT consultants for thousands of clinicians training in CPT worldwide over the last decade, and by incorporating the insight and tips from our CPT colleagues and community.

Overview of the book

This book guides the clinician through the theory that informed the development of CPT with particular attention to how we, as clinicians, rely on theory in our case conceptualization and leverage the wisdom and guidance that theoretical underpinnings provide us at critical therapy decision points. We then trace the development of CPT in a brief review of the 20+ published randomized clinical trials to date with the goal of summarizing how well CPT fared in each study and, most importantly, what useful clinical information can be gleaned that directly informs our CPT delivery of care. We next translate the voluminous effectiveness research, uncontrolled trials, and studies to understand more precisely how to treat PTSD with CPT in the context of all different kinds of challenges to optimal therapy outcomes. We apply the same strategy to understanding how therapy might (or might not) be enhanced with modifications to better meet the needs of the full range of our diverse patients from all walks of life whom we may be treating in a variety of clinical settings and healthcare systems.

The following case vignettes provide examples of patients who might present in any type of clinical setting. We highlight both the clinical considerations that we would note at the outset of therapy that might provide us hints as to specific CPT directions we might want to pursue. We also note the potential challenges to optimal therapy outcomes that might emerge over the administration of the CPT protocol. Finally, we refer back to these cases throughout the remainder of the book to provide clinical examples of the strategies we suggest to achieve our therapy goals—recovery!

Case studies

The following case vignettes are constructed from a variety of patients' stories across therapists and intended to represent the unique nature of each patient's traumatic event, trauma history, social support system, psychiatric comorbidity, and clinical presentation. While there is no "typical" PTSD patient, the clinical cases we present here are representative of the types of complexities and challenges that we collectively, as CPT therapists, grapple with during the course of treatment for PTSD. We will return to these cases, and the clinical complexities that they pose, to use as examples throughout the book. Any similarities between these case vignettes and actual patients are entirely coincidental.

Case 1: Anna's story

Anna is a 32-year-old Veteran who had separated from the military after 8 years of service. She joined the armed forces at age of 17—her parents signed her papers for her since she was under 18 years of age. Anna was born and raised in a small town in rural Texas about 50 miles from the Mexican border. Anna was the youngest of six and the only girl. Her family lived on 4 acres of land and her parents consistently experienced significant difficulty finding work and making ends meet. She and her brothers were often left to fend for themselves and frequently found themselves in trouble at home, school, and with the local police. Punishments at home were particularly severe, especially when her parents were drinking. Anna recalls the day a recruiter for the United States Army came to her home to talk with two of her brothers about their interest in joining the armed forces. As Anna listened, she saw a way out of her small town and her parents signed the necessary papers without hesitation. Joining the Army seemed to be an escape from a fairly desperate situation for Anna. Girls rarely finished high school in her town and several of her classmates were pregnant or had already had children by age of 17. Anna had known that she was gay since she was 12 and she believed that her sexual orientation would not be readily accepted in her small town. Joining the Army and serving her country presented a lifeline to Anna in a very difficult and seemingly dead-end environment. She and two of her brothers enlisted and began basic training 6 months later.

For the first 4 years, Anna's experiences were everything she had anticipated and more. She thrived on the order and structure of the military and excelled in every aspect of her training and, eventually, in her service. Although she was one of the few women in her company, she considered her fellow soldiers to be her brothers. She often said that she would take a bullet for any of them and knew that they would do the same for her. Anna had never known such pride and solidarity before in her life and she thrived on the order and discipline and planned to forge her career in the military. With the attack on the United States on September 11, 2001, the United States armed forces galvanized and within 8 months, Anna was deployed to Afghanistan. Although at the time, the 1994 Direct Ground Combat Definition and Assignment Rule prohibited women from engaging in direct combat roles, the nature of the warfare in Afghanistan and Iraq blurred the definition of "direct combat" as the traditional front lines of battle were obscure, particularly in urban settings. Anna's first deployment lasted 7 months and she performed admirably with commendations from her command.

Within 12 months, Anna received orders for her second deployment, this time to Iraq. In an effort to be culturally sensitive to the customs and religious beliefs of the Iraqi women, Army women were attached to Marine units and accompanied the Marine squads when they went out on patrols, which often included house-to-house searches for weapons and insurgents. This second deployment was markedly different from the first. Anna was the only female embedded in the unit and was not a Marine—a branch of service that has historically been much more male-dominated. Anna's main function during patrols was to contain and calm the Iraqi women who, according to their religious beliefs, could not be alone in a room with male strangers such as the Marines and could not be searched for weapons by men. Anna's job was to sequester the women in a separate room and ascertain that they were not hiding weapons while the Marines searched the residence and conducted the necessary interrogations. Most of these missions were conducted in the dead of night to preserve the element of surprise. For the same purpose, the searches happened efficiently and quickly. Once a house was cleared, the Marines moved rapidly to the next residence. Anna's job was unique among the squad members as she was often alone in a fairly chaotic situation with multiple women and children—any of whom could have been armed and dangerous. She was not in immediate contact with the rest of the unit as she was sequestered with the women. On more than one occasion, she was accidentally left behind when the Marines moved on to the next residence. During her 8 months in Iraq, she went on countless raids and gained the respect of the Marines time and again. She and her unit came under fire many times, she fired her weapon on several occasions, and she witnessed multiple traumatic events.

With 6 weeks left in her deployment, Anna and her squad discovered a substantial cache of weapons that needed to be removed. The timing was bad because daylight was approaching and additional vehicles needed to be called in to help remove or destroy all the weapons. Word quickly spread throughout the neighborhood that the Marines were bunkered down in the home and they took heavy fire as they finally moved out. Anna was one of the last to board her vehicle and was shot in her upper arm. The medic saw her get hit and immediately raced toward her. A step before he reached her, a sniper fired from an unseen vantage point and the medic, a 21-yearold Iowa native, well-loved by all, pitched forward and died in Anna's arms. Anna remembers more Marines grabbing her and her fallen brother and being pulled into the nearest Humvee. She remembers screams of pain and despair and the jolting ride back to base. She recalls being bandaged and realizing that she had sustained "only a minor wound." She remembers the de-briefing and then falling asleep. When she woke up, it was dark again; she had slept through the remainder of that day. She wandered out and found her fellow soldiers who had started drinking and decompressing from the terrible day. She joined them and as the night progressed, so did the amount of alcohol consumed. Anna stumbled back to the barracks and was followed by two of the Marines. One Marine made suggestive comments to her soliciting sexual favors and the other laughed. Anna refused and tried to walk away. One of the men grabbed her and forcibly kissed her on the mouth and groped her under her shirt while the other laughed. Anna was eventually able to pull herself away and ran to her bunk, crying and shaking. The next morning she reported the whole assault to her command and measures were put in place to keep the Marines away from her (they were re-assigned to another barracks, were told to stay 100 feet from her, she was re-assigned to another squad). Over the next few weeks, Anna felt more and more like an outsider, needing to re-establish relationships and trust with a new squad and essentially starting all over again.

She remained isolated, did not sleep for fear of being attacked while she lay in bed, she was jumpy and easily startled, and her performance on missions slipped. She was diagnosed with PTSD and major depression and she returned to the states. Once she returned home, her distress increased and she began drinking heavily. Her interactions with friends and family deteriorated and she was overtly angry and even violent at times. She eventually left the military and had difficulty functioning—could not find gainful employment, maintain relationships, and could not tolerate driving. Her family tried to help her enroll in mental health services in the VA, but she dropped out of therapy several times after a session or two. At the age of 32, Anna had diagnoses of PTSD, major depression, and alcohol dependence.

Immediate clinical considerations

- *Multiple trauma history across lifespan*: It may be difficult to determine the index event from which to begin CPT.
- *Social supports*: While Anna is isolating, it does sound as though she has a family network engaged in helping her recover.
- *Comorbidity:* Anna currently has several diagnoses. Deciding if PTSD is the primary disorder will be important.
- *Previous therapy history*: Anna has already dropped out of therapy following several attempts to engage in the process. She is at risk for premature drop-out from CPT.
- *Cultural considerations*: Anna's own sexual orientation may be a factor in her stuck points about her sexual assault by a fellow Marine. The fact that the medic was shot by an Iraqi may also introduce cultural and potentially religious influences into the therapeutic process.

Potential challenges to optimal therapy outcomes

- Emotional regulation/anger: Careful assessment and consideration of Anna's anger and volatility is warranted. Both may increase as she engages with her trauma memory over the course of CPT. Will Anna's anger impede her recovery?
- *Sleep*: It is mentioned several times that Anna is not sleeping. Sleep impairment may influence her ability to engage in therapy and concentrate when in session and during out-of-session practice work. Has Anna's sleep impairment become a case of primary insomnia and how will her lack of sleep influence her engagement and success in treatment?
- *Comorbid mental health difficulties*: Understanding drinking patterns will be important in assessing and monitoring the influence of alcohol use on Anna's ability to engage in treatment. Can we treat alcohol dependence and PTSD concurrently?
- *Logistics*: Anna is not working and is having difficulty driving. Will there be any logistical difficulties in getting to therapy?

Case 2: Steve's story

Steve is a 46-year-old male who currently works as a forklift operator. He has been married for 20 years and has 3 children. Over the last 2 years Steve has grown increasingly withdrawn from family and friends ever since he was in a serious car accident and suffered severe injuries, which continue to cause him chronic back pain. Steve had worked with the same crew on his job for years and felt comfortable with his colleagues. He was switched over to another crew and lost the familiarity and ease of these longstanding relationships. He seems absent-minded at work and has neglected to engage in basic safety procedures and has received several written warnings. He is currently on probation at work and may be in danger of losing his job. He has also become increasingly isolated from family and friends. He and his wife have not been intimate in over a year and he resists attending any of his children's school functions and extracurricular events. He refuses to allow his kids to socialize in the majority of the activities that they are invited to participate by friends and neighbors. He becomes agitated and irate if any family members are late coming home or do not call when they said they would. His wife finally threatens that she will take the kids and leave him if he does not get help.

Steve begins therapy and is diagnosed with major depression. Steve recalls that this depression began after the motor vehicle accident. Upon further inquiry, Steve's therapist discovers that he becomes very distressed and experiences his heart racing and trouble breathing when he is reminded of the car accident. He avoids driving on highways and, in fact, avoids driving whenever possible. When he does have to drive, he is excessively alert and on guard. Sounds that remind him of the accident (such as glass breaking or squealing tires) are very upsetting. Steve's therapist diagnoses him with PTSD secondary to this motor vehicle accident and they begin CPT. Ten sessions of CPT go by and there is little improvement in Steve's symptoms and functioning.

One evening, Steve returns home unexpectedly early and his two sons are playing cops and robbers. Steve is confronted with his two screaming boys acting out a "bad guy" scene in their game. Steve has a full flashback, perceiving he is back in his own childhood being assaulted. Steve and his children are frightened by his reaction and Steve describes the flashback to his therapist at the next session. During this session, Steve discloses his childhood history to his therapist. He recounts that both of his parents were very violent with one another for the first 6 years of his childhood. He witnessed much of this violence and was also subjected to much physical abuse himself. As the oldest of three boys, he tried to take the brunt of his parents' assaults whenever possible and he particularly tried to protect his youngest brother, Jeffrey. Four years apart in age, Jeffrey idolized Steve and Steve tried everything he could to shield Jeffrey from the violence in the household. Around the time that Steve turned 6 years old, Steve's father left and never returned. Steve's mother named Steve as the head of the household and prostituted Steve for money and drugs. Steve's mother threatened that he and his brothers would be separated and placed in foster care if he told anyone, so he never did. At age of 12, Steve tried to run away but returned after living for some time on the streets because he could not leave his brothers to suffer this same fate. It is very difficult for Steve to share his memories with his therapist. He is sweating profusely and appears to dissociate during the session repeatedly. He tells his therapist that he has avoided thinking about these memories for years, that he has locked this part of his life away and never wants to revisit it again. As his sons become the ages that he and his brothers were when the sexual assaults began, the memories have flooded back. He says he cannot talk about them for fear that he will lose control. He does not elaborate, but says that there was a time in his life when he did lose control. He says he can never go down that road again. He leaves therapy extremely shaken and upset.

Immediate clinical considerations

- *Trauma history*: Steve reports a significant trauma history with multiple different types of events over a substantial period of time. The importance of a complete trauma history will be critical in identifying the index trauma as well as the cumulative effect of the entire trauma history and the contribution of the history to current views of self, world and others (over-accommodated stuck points).
- *Avoidance*: Steve has avoided telling anyone about these traumatic events for years. It may be quite difficult for him to engage with the trauma memory. That being said, he has not dropped out of therapy after 10 consecutive sessions and he has disclosed this trauma to his therapist, suggesting excellent trust and rapport.
- *Social support*: Steve clearly has a loving family who is willing to support him in getting the help he needs.
- *Poor response to therapy thus far*: After 10 sessions, Steve has not responded well to CPT. Treatment decisions will need to be made as to whether CPT is a good fit or not.

Potential challenges to optimal therapy outcomes

- *Current major stressors*: Steve's distress is clearly resulting in impairment in two major domains of functioning, occupational and relational. He is on probation at work and at risk for ultimately losing his job. His symptoms are also interfering with his relationships with his wife and sons and, while they are supportive, his wife has also given him an ultimatum that he needs to get help and change course.
- *Avoidance*: Steve's avoidance of thinking about his childhood trauma is quite high. He completed 10 sessions of therapy before he discloses his trauma history to the therapist and he reports that he has locked these memories away for years.

- *Engagement:* Steve's symptoms directly influence his ability to drive. He finds it difficult to get to sessions, particularly when he feels distressed during session and needs to get in the vehicle to head home.
- *Emotional regulation*: Steve's distress was quite high when he left therapy and he was dissociative in session. His therapist notes the level of emotionality and must consider whether this is a risk for dropout or a challenge to optimal recovery.
- *Concurrent mental and physical health difficulties*: Steve is also grappling with chronic pain from his accident and possibly medications. The pain is not only an additional stressor contributing to depressed mood but also can be a reminder of his traumatic event and trigger PTSD symptoms.

Case 3: Julie's story

Julie is a 28-year-old mother of a 4-year-old daughter. Julie was raised in a very conservative environment. Her parents are deeply religious and, as a single child, Julie's upbringing was their sole focus. Julie describes her relationship with her parents as supportive and respectful, but she never felt close to them. Julie's extracurricular activities included church services, singing in the church choir, and attending church philanthropic and social events. At the age of 12, she began piano lessons. Her piano teacher was member of the church and taught lessons out of his home. Over time and during these lessons, the teacher's frequent physical contact under the guise of piano instruction became more sexual in nature, then progressed in severity and he eventually raped Julie. The rapes continued for almost a year until another student reported similar assaults and the teacher was prosecuted and imprisoned.

Although there was a very public trial, Julie's parents never discussed any of this with Julie except in an ancillary fashion with comments such as "nice girls don't do things like that" and "God punishes girls who tempt men." The teacher's crimes against Julie were never reported and the teacher was never punished. During this time, Julie had grown more and more withdrawn and isolated. Her grades at school dropped and she barely passed the 8th grade. Her transition to high school was extremely difficult and she often missed school due to headaches and stomachaches. She went from a bright and cheerful child to a withdrawn and isolated teenager. Her grades continued to suffer and her dreams of attending college and becoming a veterinarian faded away. Her parents were not overly concerned with her school attendance and grades but did insist that she continue to attend church.

During her senior year, a new member of the church (Ted) introduced himself to her parents and began coming over to dinner. Ted was 12 years older than Julie and took a real interest in her and they began dating. Julie felt as if a new life had been offered to her. Ted was very attentive to detail and began choosing her outfits and would buy her clothes for her. He ordered for her when they went out to dinner and chose their activities. Julie felt treasured and protected.

He introduced her to his circle of friends, many of whom were also socially connected to her parents. Julie graduated from high school and the few friends she had slipped away. Julie took a job as an assistant in a local library and Ted would drive her and pick her up from work. He would often join Julie and her family for dinner and attend services with them. Their relationship was largely non-intimate with the exception of a good night kiss at the end of their dates. Within a year, they got engaged and, at the age of 20, Julie moved right from her parents' home to Ted's home and began her life as a married woman.

At first, Julie was delighted to have her own home and enjoyed keeping it clean, making meals for Ted and attending to his every need. She tolerated having sex with her husband which was mercifully brief and lacked intimacy or emotional connection. After a year went by and Julie had not gotten pregnant, Ted became more and more brusque and easily irritated, blaming her for their failure to conceive. Ted accused Julie of not attending to their marriage and family and forced to quit her job at the library to focus more on him and beginning a family. Julie became more and more isolated.

One day, Ted came home early from work and Julie was just returning from walking the dog. A man had stopped to ask her for directions and Ted saw them talking. He went into the house and when Julie joined him, he attacked her. This was the first of a cycle of physical assaults for any perceived infraction or inadequacy, followed by apologies and professions of love. In the midst of all of this, Julie became pregnant. The assaults stopped during her pregnancy and Julie became hopeful that her dreams of a loving family might still come true. After the baby was born, however, Ted grew more and more irritable and complained that Julie cared more for the baby than she did for him. Over time, the physical abuse increased steadily. Although Ted never hurt the baby, he constantly blamed Julie for his behaviors, citing her inadequacies as a wife as the cause of his violence. He threatened Julie that if she ever told anyone or left him, he would kill them. And Julie believed him. Besides, where would she go?

One day, after Julie's daughter had just turned 4 and had woken up the previous night hearing her father beating her mother, Julie spotted a flyer hanging in the laundromat while she was folding clothes. The flyer provided information for battered women to get help. Julie scooped up her daughter, gathered what clothes she had in the laundry pile and made the call. Julie was sheltered in a secure safe house and began the long process of separating from her husband. Within a year, she had secured a residence for herself and her daughter and a part-time job. Her daughter was enrolled in kindergarten and Julie secured a restraining order against Ted. Despite these remarkable strides, Julie was terrified all the time. Julie's fear was well founded. Ted would often appear in the few places that Julie frequented. He knew where they lived and where Julie's daughter went to school. She received calls from unknown numbers and worried it may be Ted. She was offered services in a local community mental health clinic and was diagnosed with PTSD. She began CPT.

Immediate clinical considerations

- *Trauma history*: Julie has experienced both childhood abuse and intimate partner violence. Both are significant and unique from one another. The clinician will have to determine which is the index trauma. Both are also chronic in nature and it will be important to identify a single incident from among the many assaults to start therapy.
- *Social support*: Julie is quite isolated. Her lack of supports will need to be considered in therapy.
- *Peritraumatic situation*: Beliefs around being unsafe or lack of trust may not be stuck points for Julie given that her husband continues to stalk her and has threatened her life and that of her daughter's.

Potential challenges to optimal therapy outcomes

- *Current major stressors*: Ongoing legal issues around custody and Julie's request for a divorce are major stressors for Julie. Relatedly, as Julie pursues custody and divorce, her safety risks significantly increase. The therapist will need to balance treatment priorities throughout the protocol.
- *Engagement*: Julie is a single mother living in supported care facility with a part-time and no financial or social resources. These barriers may decrease her ability to access care and attend therapy on a regular basis.
- *Concurrent mental and physical health difficulties*: Julie recently found out she is pregnant. Her therapist must consider her pregnancy timeline, the need for additional case management around this pregnancy (medical care, housing, etc.), and the added effects of stress on the mother and baby.

Setting the stage

Anna, Steve, and Julie are fairly representative of the types of patients that we treat across various clinical settings. Using these cases as examples, we hope to guide the reader through treating a broad array of patients suffering from PTSD while considering all of the challenges to optimal outcomes inherent in the disorder. We will provide clinical examples whenever possible and support our proposed treatment decisions and directions with evidence from published studies. By the end of this book, we hope you agree our premise that the question is not "is this patient a good candidate for CPT?" but instead, "How can I best make CPT work for this patient?"

References

American Psychiatric Association. (2013). *Diagnostic and statistical manual of mental disorders (DSM-5®)*. Washington, DC: American Psychiatric Pub.

American Psychological Association. (2017). Clinical practice guideline for the treatment of PTSD. Washington, DC: American Psychological Association. Available from: http://www.apa.org/ptsd-guideline/ptsd.pdf.

Australian Centre for Posttraumatic Mental Health (2013) Australian Guidelines for the Treatment of Acute Stress Disorder and Posttraumatic Stress Disorder. ACMPH: Melbourne.

Bisson, J. I., Berliner, L., Cloitre, M., Forbes, D., Jensen, T. K., Lewis, C., et al. (2019). The International Society for Traumatic Stress Studies New Guidelines for the Prevention and Treatment of PTSD: methodology and development process. Journal of Traumatic Stress, 32, 475–483.

Bradley, R., Greene, J., Russ, E., Dutra, L., & Westen, D. (2005). A multidimensional meta-analysis of psychotherapy for PTSD. *American Journal of Psychiatry*, *162*(2), 214–227.

Cusack, K., Jonas, D. E., Forneris, C. A., Wines, C., Sonis, J., & Middleton, J. C., et al. (2016). Psychological treatments for adults with posttraumatic stress disorder: a systematic review and meta-analysis. *Clinical Psychology Review*, *43*, 128–141.

Foa, E. B., Keane, T. M., Friedman, M. J., & Cohen, J. A. (Eds.). (2008). *Effective treatments for PTSD: practice guidelines from the International Society for Traumatic Stress Studies*. New York: Guilford Press.

Forbes, D., Creamer, M., Phelps, A., Bryant, R., McFarlane, A., & Devilly, G. J., et al. (2007). Australian guidelines for the treatment of adults with acute stress disorder and post-traumatic stress disorder. *Australian & New Zealand Journal of Psychiatry*, *41*(8), 637–648.

Galovski, T. E., Blain, L. M., Mott, J. M., Elwood, L., & Houle, T. (2012). Manualized therapy for PTSD: flexing the structure of cognitive processing therapy. *Journal of Consulting and Clinical Psychology*, *80*(6), 968.

Institute of Medicine. (2007). *Treatment of PTSD: An assessment of the evidence*. Washington, DC: National Academies Press.

Karlin, B. E., Ruzek, J. I., Chard, K. M., Eftekhari, A., Monson, C. M., & Hembree, E. A., et al. (2010). Dissemination of evidence-based psychological treatments for posttraumatic stress disorder in the Veterans Health Administration. *Journal of Traumatic Stress*, *23*(6), 663–673.

Monson, C. M., Shields, N., Suvak, M. K., et al. (2018). A randomized controlled effectiveness trial of training strategies in cognitive processing therapy: impact on patient outcomes. *Behaviour Research and Therapy*, *110*, 31–40.

National Institute for Clinical Excellence. (2005). *Post-traumatic stress disorder: The management of PTSD in adults and children in our primary and secondary care*. London: Royal College of Psychiatrists and The British Psychological Society.

Resick, P. A., Galovski, T. E., Uhlmansiek, M. O. B., Scher, C. D., Clum, G. A., & Young-Xu, Y. (2008). A randomized clinical trial to dismantle components of cognitive processing therapy for posttraumatic stress disorder in female victims of interpersonal violence. *Journal of Consulting and Clinical Psychology*, *76*(2), 243.

Resick, P. A., Monson, C. M., & Chard, K. M. (2017). *Cognitive processing therapy for PTSD: A comprehensive manual*. New York: Guilford Publications.

Schottenbauer, M. A., Glass, C. R., Arnkoff, D. B., Tendick, V., & Gray, S. H. (2008). Nonresponse and dropout rates in outcome studies on PTSD: review and methodological considerations. *Psychiatry: Interpersonal and Biological Processes*, *71*(2), 134–168.

Steenkamp, M. M., Litz, B. T., Hoge, C. W., & Marmar, C. R. (2015). Psychotherapy for military-related PTSD: a review of randomized clinical trials. *JAMA*, *314*(5), 489–500.

U.S. Department of Veteran Affairs and Department of Defense. (2017). VA/DOD clinical practice guidelines for the management of posttraumatic stress disorder and acute stress disorder. Available from: https://www.healthquality.va.gov/guidelines/MH/ptsd/VADoDPTSDCPGFinal012418.pdf.

Chapter 2

Ancestral roots: The origins of CPT

Chapter outline

Cognitive processing therapy (CPT) is interesting, and maybe a bit unique, in the number of theories that have informed its evolution over time. To trace the history and thought processes of the developer of CPT (Dr. Patricia Resick) over the last several decades, we suggest that clinicians read Chapter 1 of the most recently published manual (Resick, Monson, & Chard, 2017). It is quite fascinating to review the synthesis of different pieces of theory from a variety of schools of thought and understand how these pieces came together to build an intervention for posttraumatic stress disorder (PTSD), ultimately informing its development into what we know to be CPT today.

Sometimes, at face value, a review of theory can seem a bit dry. But, in reality, sound theory drives an intervention and, more importantly, serves to inform clinical decisions at various junctures throughout the course of therapy. In fact, having a firm understanding of the theory driving the intervention guides the clinician as to *why* he/she is asking the patient to do the types of things we ask patients do during therapy. For example, in the case of PTSD, why would we ever suggest that the patient think and talk about the worst thing that ever happened? On paper, it seems like a much better idea to NOT think about the event – to avoid. Engaging in the process of therapy and breaking through avoidance is expensive – emotionally, mentally, logistically, financially, and sometimes physically. We, as therapists, should have a very strong rationale for leading a patient down this road of engaging with the trauma memory.

The role of avoidance

Before we review the theory driving CPT, it might be helpful to think about the field of trauma recovery before CPT came into the picture. A complete historical review is beyond the scope of this book, but a few highlights might

Flexible Applications of Cognitive Processing Therapy. http://dx.doi.org/10.1016/B978-0-12-816715-1.00002-9

be helpful. Early learning theory sought to explain the development of PTSD through classical conditioning—essentially supporting the idea that learned associations can cause a continued fear response even after removal of the frightening stimuli. The Pavlov's dog experiments that readers may remember from Psychology 101 classes are a great example of classical conditioning. As you might recall, Pavlov presented dogs with food (unconditioned stimulus; UCS) and the dogs salivated (unconditioned response; UCR). Then, Pavlov paired a bell (conditioned stimulus; CS) with the food and, after several trials, removed the food. When the bell rang, the dogs still salivated (conditioned response; CR) without the food.

Case example: Putting classical conditioning into a PTSD context, let's take Steve's case as an example. Steve was sexually assaulted as boy in his mother's home. The sexual assault (UCS) was, of course, a horrific experience and he was very frightened (UCR) during and after these attacks, which occurred in this house (CS). Years later, seeing this house continue to elicit the same level of fear (CR; sweating, shaking, and thoughts that he will lose control). The house is not dangerous itself, but elicits a very strong fear reaction because of the learned association with danger. Classical conditioning is important in our understanding of PTSD because it explains, in part, the reasons that fear is experienced so strongly when the danger has passed.

Classical conditioning does not fully explain PTSD, however. According to classical conditioning, this learned fear response (CR) should extinguish over time. For example, if one continued to sound the bell and no food appeared, over time Pavlov's dogs would stop salivating. Similarly then, seeing his mother's house years later when Steve is completely out of danger should extinguish Steve's fear response. But we know in the case of PTSD, the fear response is often as strong (or almost as strong) as the response during the traumatic event. Mowrer's two-factor theory of fear adds the principles of instrumental learning to help explain why the fear response in PTSD does not extinguish over time. Essentially, instrumental learning suggests that behavior can be positively or negatively reinforced or punished. Positive reinforcement is much like reward and strengthens a response. Negative reinforcement (also called avoidance learning) is anything that results in the removal of a noxious event or state (including an undesirable emotion like fear) and strengthens behavior. A punishment, on the other hand, decreases the likelihood of a behavior occurring. Most germane to our understanding of PTSD is the idea of negative reinforcement.

Case example: Continuing with Steve's example, as soon as he is reminded of his assaults (by driving by the house or other reminders of the trauma), he goes to great lengths to put those memories and feelings away—essentially the avoidance symptoms of PTSD. In PTSD, people exert great effort to avoid anything that reminds them of their traumatic event. The substantial efforts required to be a successful avoider essentially prevents the process of extinction of the conditioned fear response. Steve needs to allow himself to engage with the trauma memory and feel his feelings in order to recover from PTSD—he needs to break through avoidance.

Avoidance seems to work in the short term, but, in reality, it keeps people trapped in PTSD in the long run. Mowrer's two-factor theory guided the development of PTSD interventions to prioritize breaking through avoidance in order to recover from PTSD. This point cannot be emphasized enough and PTSD therapists are constantly trying to understand the numerous ways that patients avoid thinking about their trauma, both in their daily lives and during session. In CPT, we observe avoidance in many forms (e.g., missing sessions, talking about topics not central to the trauma work, anger or dysregulated affect). We also certainly hear avoidance in all kinds of thoughts and beliefs (CPT stuck points: *I couldn't possibly do this therapy; The world is a dangerous place, so I can't go into public places; I can't trust men, so I could never date again.*)

A more recent theory explaining the development and maintenance of PTSD is called emotional processing theory (Foa & Rothbaum, 1998; Foa, Huppert, & Cahill, 2006). This theory argues that underlying PTSD exists a large and diffuse fear structure comprised of many relatively harmless stimulus representations that are all inaccurately linked to danger. Because this fear network is quite large and diffuse, any number of encounters with the stimuli contained in the fear structure can essentially light up the whole network and result in the types of fear responses seen in our PTSD patients. Because so many reminders (and reminders of reminders) can trigger the activation of this fear network, trauma survivors begin to perceive the whole world as dangerous and act accordingly (exaggerated startle, hypervigilance, etc.). Prolonged Exposure (PE) (Foa, Hembree, & Rothbaum, 2007) is guided by emotional processing theory. PE seeks to intentionally activate this fear network through imaginal and in vivo exposure. During this process, the patient has the opportunity to incorporate new information (e.g., experiencing the traumatic event is different in very important ways from being reminded of the traumatic event). Further, by confronting the memory, negative reinforcement (avoidance) is blocked, anxiety and fear is reduced through extinction, and patients gain mastery over the memory of their traumatic experience. Emotional processing theory is also clearly relevant to CPT. For example, CPT therapists understand the concept of natural feelings (those emotions not caused by our thoughts) and the need to let these natural feelings run their course. Providing the opportunity for patients to safely experience their natural affect (feel one's feelings) and encouraging patients to sit with their emotions is part of the recovery process inherent in CPT. For interested readers, we also recommend several writings by Dr. Michelle Craske (Craske, 2015; Craske, Treanor, Conway, Zbozinek, & Vervliet, 2014) on recent thinking of how new learning can be acquired during exposure-based therapy.

Cognitive theory

Perhaps most influential in the development of CPT is cognitive theory. Developed by Dr. Aaron T. Beck in the 1960s, cognitive theory led to the development of cognitive therapy for depression (Beck, Rush, Shaw, & Emery, 1979).

Cognitive theory suggests that people's interpretations of events cause their reactions to events (including emotional reactions). Erroneous or dysfunctional thoughts might be particularly implicated in causing intense emotions that disrupt functioning. The origins of Beckian cognitive theory are clearly apparent in CPT in it's emphasis on identifying erroneous and unhelpful thoughts, using Socratic questions to facilitate cognitive change, and the use of worksheets to help move the therapy into people's everyday lives. An important distinction between cognitive therapy for depression and CPT is that CPT is staged, with the initial primary focus on past-oriented cognitions specific to the trauma (e.g., *The trauma was my fault*). We move on to challenging more current and future-oriented cognitions (e.g., concerns about safety in the present) only after the trauma-related cognitions have largely resolved.

Our patients may ask us why they have developed PTSD when others have experienced the same (or similar) event and did not develop PTSD. Relying on cognitive theory to answer that question can be very helpful. According to cognitive theory, the way we think about or interpret an event causes our reactions to that event. In the case of PTSD, cognitive theory suggests that the interpretation of the traumatic event (e.g., the answer to the question, *why did this happen?*) cause one's reactions to the event. To illustrate this point, imagine that 10 people are on a train that derails in a terrible accident. They were all in the same car, they all experienced the same rescue and they all emerged relatively unhurt, but shaken up and bruised. When asked *why* they think this event happened, nine survivors talk about the equipment malfunction and terrible weather combination that caused the accident. The last survivor describes the fact that he never should have been on the train in the first place and that he always makes bad decisions. Given that the train accident was clearly caused by bad weather and equipment failure, we can imagine that the train accident was not caused by the passenger's bad decisions (an erroneous belief). This is a clear example of a faulty belief that may keep him stuck in PTSD.

Dr. Resick posits that PTSD is a disorder of non-recovery (Resick et al., 2017). Most people recover from exposure to traumatic events without being diagnosed with PTSD as indicated by the prevalence rates of PTSD (Kessler et al., 2017). This leads us to believe that someone who does go on to develop PTSD somehow got stuck along the path of natural recovery. Dr. Resick further suggests that it is precisely those erroneous thoughts such as "I should not have gotten on the train. I always mess up." that cause people to get stuck in PTSD. In CPT, we label those inaccurate cognitions that contribute to PTSD as "stuck points"!

Types of stuck points: One of the golden rules of CPT is to differentiate between types of stuck points for the express purpose of prioritizing assimilated stuck points over over-accommodated stuck points. The concept of assimilation, over-accommodation, and accommodation are informed by Hollon and Garber (1988). We all have an existing belief system (positive, negative, or neutral). Over the course of our lives, we organize the vast amounts of incoming information into various schemas to manage it all and to exert some level of prediction and control over our environment. For example, my schema about work is that if you show up to work and do a reasonable job then you will receive a paycheck. I use this schema to predict and control my environment to some extent (e.g., I make purchases based on this information. I set my alarm to get up on time based on this schema). Schemas organize information and lend some sense of order and predictability in our lives.

Order and predictability are important to us as human beings. If we thought there was a 50/50 chance we might not get paid, we likely wouldn't go to work any more. If we had no sense of the likelihood of our plane landing safely, we would likely never travel by air. If we had no anticipation that there was any sense of justice and societal order, we likely would never obey any traffic rules and commit all kinds of criminal acts. In the case of a traumatic event, our basic assumptions and schemas can be shattered. By definition, a traumatic event introduces information that is discrepant to one's schema. To recover from the trauma, survivors need to find a way to incorporate the very discrepant trauma information into existing schemas. It is not always a straightforward process. *Assimilation* is the process of altering the trauma information to fit the existing schema. In our example of the train derailment, the tenth survivor altered the trauma information by concluding the train derailment was caused by him (*I'm a mess, I'm the problem*). If he continues to hold onto this erroneous assimilated stuck point (and develop other stuck points), it is likely he will develop PTSD.

We must identify and challenge assimilated stuck points first during CPT (Galovski et al., 2016). Start at the beginning of the story (the trauma event) and understand your patient's thoughts processes about why each part of the trauma happened. It is critical to spend time here—get started right away in identifying the assimilated stuck points and prioritize them in challenging with Socratic Questions. Notice that this part of the process requires quite an extensive and detailed conversation about the trauma. Often, patients have numerous assimilated stuck points. Discovering them requires an in depth discussion during which you are also helping that patient break through avoidance and feel his/her feelings.

A second important concept incorporated into CPT is the concept of *over-accommodation*. While assimilation involves drastically altering trauma-related information in order to integrate this information into an existing belief system, over-accommodation involves drastically altering the entire existing belief system to integrate the trauma information.

Case example: Let's use Anna's story as an example. Anna had an existing belief system that centered around order and justice. She believed that if she gave 100% effort that she would be rewarded. Her experiences in the first 4 years of service in the Army provided much evidence in support of that belief system. She worked hard and excelled and was a highly regarded member of her unit. The sexual assault by a fellow solider shattered her beliefs about the world and others. Four years after separating from the army, Anna believed that the world is a dangerous place and that no one can be trusted. Both of these beliefs are over-accommodated stuck points and are great examples of drastic alterations to Anna's prior existing belief system that the world is generally a fair and just place—"*If I work hard, then I will come out on top.*"

Case example: Some people's life experiences have led them to develop fairly negative belief systems. In this case, trauma information can serve to cement or confirm these existing belief systems. Julie's story is a great illustration of a preexisting negative belief system. Prior to Julie's violent marriage, she had been raped by her music teacher and did not receive support or protection from her parents. She may have gone into her marriage with a belief system such as "I'm not worthy of love" or "Only bad things always happen to me." This belief system is consistent with her lifetime experiences. Julie then is abused in her marriage by her husband and this abuse confirmed her worldview and beliefs—these thoughts become stuck points keeping Julie mired in PTSD.

Clinical note: Julie's story is also a good example of the way different traumatic events across a person's life can really build on each other. We know we have to target the index event (the trauma that is the most severe) first in CPT. If we start with a "lesser" event then we may be colluding with avoidance and the patient will not get the full benefit of the therapy. However, it is not always clear which trauma is the index event. Searching for assimilated stuck points in the early sessions of CPT provides clues as to where the heart of PTSD is lying. Julie's assaults by her ex-husband may be the index event, but the related stuck points (e.g., *If I had been a better wife, he would not have beaten me*) might be supported by beliefs that were generated during her childhood assaults (e.g., *If I had been a better daughter, my parents would have cared enough to protect me from the music teacher*). In other words, stuck points and disrupted beliefs from the earlier trauma provide evidence for the stuck points associated with the adult trauma. Cognitive theory dictates that we sort out what the patient is telling herself and begin to dismantle one by one those erroneous thoughts that are keeping the patient stuck in non-recovery.

Prioritizing assimilation before over-accommodation: Tackling assimilated stuck points first in therapy cannot be stressed enough. We will spend time again on this concept later in Chapter 7 and we offer clinical examples and suggestions to guide the therapist in finding the elusive assimilated stuck points. They are always there! We address assimilated stuck points first because they lie at the heart of PTSD. They are the very beliefs about the trauma that halted the patient on his/her path of recovering naturally from the event. And the beliefs (usually self-blame) about why the event happened tend to provide evidence for more current and future-oriented beliefs (the over-accommodated stuck points). People's views of the world are colored by their beliefs about the trauma. Julie's assimilated stuck points about her childhood rape (e.g., *I am worthless and disgusting—that's why he treated me this way and my parents didn't stop him*) and her assaults by her husband (e.g., *If I had been a better wife, he wouldn't have attacked me*) may provide evidence for current, over-accommodated esteem-related stuck points (e.g., *I am unlovable*). Julie's beliefs that it was her fault that she was treated horribly by men (and not protected by her parents) provide evidence for the idea that she is undeserving of love today. By challenging Julie's erroneous beliefs about her role in her assaults, we remove the "evidence" shoring up her current beliefs about her self-worth. If these assimilated beliefs are not dealt with first, it is incredibly difficult to successfully address more current over-accommodated stuck points later, as patients will revert to this old way of thinking.

As CPT therapists become more and more experienced, we see the same patterns of stuck points emerge and they become a bit easier to identify. Over the years, we've noted some specific patterns that tend to emerge in survivors of different types of trauma. Table 2.1 provides an overview of some of the trauma-specific themes that CPT therapists might hear in both assimilated and over-accommodated stuck points. This list is not, by any means, exhaustive and the stuck point examples can certainly appear following different types of trauma other than where we've categorized them. Hopefully, these examples will be helpful in your own search for the often-elusive stuck points. Lastly, because cognitive theory dictates that we not only identify faulty beliefs, but also challenge and change them, we also inserted sample Socratic Questions to get you started in challenging these stuck points. Of course, these are all just examples and will be more or less relevant for each individual patient. Because we always prioritize assimilated stuck points before over-accommodated ones, the Socratic Questions included in the table are intended to challenge the assimilated stuck points.

Cognitive theory in clinical practice

No matter what therapy we deliver, no matter what our theoretical orientation is, and no matter how much CPT we administer, we will always find some cases clinically challenging. We will always find ourselves feeling lost somewhere along the way or feeling as if we've come to a dead end. As therapists, this can be disconcerting and leave us feeling very helpless. A natural reaction is to backpedal and come to the conclusion that this therapy (e.g., CPT) does not work for this patient. "My patient is not getting better, therefore CPT must not be working because he/she is too ____________ (fill in the blank)." Therapists might think their patients are too intellectual (or not intellectual enough), too emotionally dysregulated (or too numb), too old, too traumatized, have too many co-morbidities, too many psychosocial stressors. The main goal of this book is to provide practical clinical examples of how to overcome these very real therapy challenges and obstacles, and along the way, we summarize relevant CPT literature that dispels many of these concerns and provides empirical justification for our advice. As a very first step, try to distill the CPT process and rely on the simple underlying concepts when faced with clinical challenges.

TABLE 2.1 Common stuck points that can develop across different types of trauma.

Assimilated stuck points (This trauma happened to me because…)	**Over-accommodated stuck points** (This trauma has influenced my beliefs about the world, self, and others…)
Traumatic Event: Sexual assault and rape	
I didn't say no (or fight back) so I must have wanted it.	I'm damaged goods.
SQ: *Why didn't you fight back?* Usually trauma survivors actually did fight back and are minimizing, there was no choice, or there were very good reasons for not fighting back, such as they would have been hurt or killed.	
I was sexually aroused which means it wasn't a rape.	I'm disgusting/dirty and unworthy of love. Because of what happened no one will ever want me.
SQ: *Are there other reasons you might have been sexually aroused?* For example, because that's how bodies react when responding to stimulation.	
I made a bad choice (wore a short skirt, took a shortcut, was drinking) and that's why I was raped.	The world is a dangerous place.
SQ: *Were there any other times that you wore that skirt (took a shortcut, drank) and didn't get raped? Is there any other (better) reason that you were raped that night?* For example, the perpetrator's criminal behavior.	
I shouldn't have frozen. I allowed it to happen.	People cannot be trusted.
SQ: *I wonder why you "froze"? Is it possible that if you had responded differently, there would have been a different (worse) outcome*?	
Traumatic Event: Adult survivor of CSA/child maltreatment	
I didn't tell someone to make it stop.	If you stick up for yourself, you will get hurt.
SQ: *Why didn't you tell someone?* Usually trauma survivors have very good reasons or maybe they did try to tell and no one listened or they were punished.	
My siblings were abused because I didn't protect them.	My parents didn't protect me, so I must be worthless.
SQ: *What could you have done to protect them? Why did you choose not to do so? Were there any ways that you did protect or comfort them?*	
I deserved it. I accepted his presents, candy, drugs.	I'm worthless. I am a burden. I am too much for people. Everyone will leave me.
SQ: *How so? What was it that you did to deserve it?* Likely, these are also stuck points.	
Traumatic Event: Assault/home invasion	
It was my fault. I should have been more careful.	No place is safe.

TABLE 2.1 **Common stuck points that can develop across different types of trauma.** *(Cont.)*

Assimilated stuck points (This trauma happened to me because...)	**Over-accommodated stuck points (This trauma has influenced my beliefs about the world, self, and others...)**
SQ: *Walk me through it? How could you have been more careful and what information did you have at the time to guide your decisions?*	
Traumatic Event: Exposure to combat	
If I had done something differently, my buddy would be alive today.	I don't deserve happiness. PTSD is my punishment. I don't deserve to live when so many didn't come home.
SQ: *What could you have done differently and why didn't you?*	
I took a life. This is my fault.	I deserve to be punished. I am a murderer.
SQ: *What were the reasons behind taking a life? Are there any circumstances when it is necessary to take someone's life? Is "murderer" the right word?*	
I never should have enlisted.	The government failed me. Society failed me.
SQ: *What were the reasons you enlisted? What information did you have at the time? What information didn't you have at the time? Based on all of these facts and the same information, if you were to rewind history—would you enlist again? Would there be any reason not to?*	
I was supposed to keep my unit safe. I failed them.	The buck stops here. I would be a coward if I didn't accept responsibility.
SQ: *How did you try to keep them safe? Who taught you that it is your fault if your soldiers do not all come home?* (Usually the military). *Is the military aware that sometimes soldiers do not come home? How is it that they explain this? Is it possible that sometimes soldiers lose their life in the line of duty and it is nobody's fault?*	
If I had been a better leader, we'd all have come home safely.	Showing my feelings is weak.
SQ: *Can you be specific? In what ways were you not a good leader?* (The outcome does not mean the Veteran is at fault.)	
Traumatic Event: Intimate partner violence	
I went back (or didn't leave), so it is my fault that my kids and I are suffering.	I can't trust my own judgment.
SQ: *Why did you go back/stay?* Often battered women have nowhere else to go. Or, their perpetrators tell them they will kill them (or their children) if they leave. And the victims believe them. Sometimes the victims just want their lives back.	
If I hadn't mouthed off (been a better partner) he wouldn't have had to hit me.	(For a survivor who fought back). I am the same as him. (For a survivor who didn't fight back.) I am powerless. It is not safe to be assertive.

(Continued)

TABLE 2.1 Common stuck points that can develop across different types of trauma. (*Cont.*)

Assimilated stuck points (This trauma happened to me because…)	Over-accommodated stuck points (This trauma has influenced my beliefs about the world, self, and others…)
SQ: *Why did you mouth off? Does it make sense that you mouthed off? Does the punishment fit the crime?*	
I chose this partner so it must be my fault.	I'm not worthy of true love.
SQ: *Were there any other reasons that you chose this partner?* Usually people choose their partners for all the right reasons—love, belonging, comfort, and intimacy. Not because the partners hurts them. The violence tends to come later.	
Traumatic Event: War-related trauma (e.g., refugees)	
This happened because no one cared.	I'm alone in the world.
SQ: *Who is no one? Did anyone care?*	
This happened because people are animals.	There is no hope. This will never get better.
SQ: *Which people? Are there any examples of good people?* If someone is in therapy, there is hope.	
If I'd taken my family away sooner, [the bad event] wouldn't have happened	I can't protect anyone.
SQ: *Why didn't you take your family away? What information did you have at the time? Was it an option?*	
It was my fault because I let them go to the market (or crowded places)	There is no safety. There is no such thing as justice.
SQ: *Why did you let them go to the market? What information did you have at the time? Was there any way you could have known what would happen?*	
I should have fought harder.	I am useless because I let the soldiers take me.
SQ: *Why didn't you? What were your reasons? What were your options?*	
This must have been God's will.	God has forsaken me.
SQ: *If so, how might God want/expect you to go forward from this?* In these conversations it is helpful to understand the patient's religious beliefs first and then ask about opposite beliefs (punishment versus forgiveness; God's will versus human agency)	
Traumatic Event: Witnessing aftermath of trauma (e.g., first responders)	
This happened because the world is a terrible place.	The world is a terrible place.
SQ: *Are there ways that the world is not terrible? Is there a more specific reason why the event happened?* (Equipment malfunction, war, nature)	
I never should have pursued this profession. It's my fault for putting myself in this situation.	People are horrible. There is no compassion left in the world.

TABLE 2.1 Common stuck points that can develop across different types of trauma. (*Cont.*)

Assimilated stuck points (This trauma happened to me because…)	**Over-accommodated stuck points (This trauma has influenced my beliefs about the world, self, and others…)**
SQ: *Why did you choose this profession? At the time, were those good reasons?*	
I should have done more.	I'm incompetent.
SQ: What more could you have done? Why did you not do these things?	
Traumatic Event: Suicide	
If I had done more s/he would have lived.	The grief is never going to end.
SQ: *What more could you have done? Is it possible that no more could have been done? Is it possible that her choice was beyond your control? What does that mean to you?*	
If I had loved him/her more/been more present, s/he wouldn't have killed themselves.	If I stop feeling this way, it will be like forgetting them or letting myself off the hook.
SQ: *Could you have loved her more? If you had been able to prevent this, would you? Was this preventable?*	
I should have known.	I'm a failure.
SQ: *How could you have known? If you'd had any more information would you have done anything differently? Is it possible that her intent was not able to be known?*	
Traumatic Event: Homicide	
I should have known this was going to happen.	Danger is everywhere.
SQ: *Why should you have known? What did you miss? Were there other explanations for any clues or information at the time? Is it possible that there was no way you could have known?*	
I should have protected him/her more.	I can never let my guard down again.
SQ: *What could you have done differently? Why would you have changed your behavior that day? Is it possible that bad things happen even when we are doing our best?*	
It should have been me. I was the lesser person.	I'm unworthy of love and happiness.
SQ: *In what way? Is that how life works? Do we get to choose how these things happen and to whom?*	
If I had been on time, she wouldn't have been murdered.	If the perpetrator isn't convicted, I'll never have closure.
SQ: *What made you late? Had you ever been late before? Was there any information available at the time that would give you an indication that she was in danger?*	
His murder was payback for my past deeds. It's my fault.	Because I am a widow, I'm worthless

(*Continued*)

TABLE 2.1 Common stuck points that can develop across different types of trauma. (*Cont.*)

Assimilated stuck points (This trauma happened to me because...)	**Over-accommodated stuck points (This trauma has influenced my beliefs about the world, self, and others...)**
SQ: *Can you explain what you mean by that?* Really understanding the context around the situation can help pull this apart and see if there is any shared responsibility. Challenge the inaccurate parts.	
Traumatic Event: Motor vehicle accident	
If I'd been more careful, the accident wouldn't have happened.	If I drive again, the next accident will be worse. I can't trust myself behind the wheel.
SQ: *What did you do that was "not careful"? What was your intent? Did you have options? Why were you not more careful?*	
If I'd left earlier, the accident would not have happened.	The roads are not safe. The world is not safe.
SQ: *What information did you have at the time? Why did you not leave earlier?*	
Traumatic Event: Major medical event	
It's my body; it's my fault (the baby died).	Hospital are dangerous places, something bad will happen if I go to hospital.
SQ: *Tell me more about fault? Are there some things that are out of our control?*	
I should have had more control.	I have no control over my health.
SQ: *In what way? What was in your control? What parts were outside your control?*	
I should have told them I was in so much pain and gone to the hospital sooner.	You can't trust doctors to know what they're doing
SQ: *Why didn't you go to the hospital sooner?*	
Traumatic Event: Natural disaster	
God did this to punish me.	I deserve to be punished, have PTSD.
SQ: *Tell me more about that? Why was he punishing you? What did you do to deserve this? Was he also punishing all of the other people involved in this natural disaster? What about other natural disasters?*	
I shouldn't have lived there (e.g. in a place with earthquakes, tornados, wildfires).	I have no control.
SQ: *So why did you choose to live there? Is there anywhere that is completely free of risk?*	
I should have helped other people. I should have done more.	I don't deserve to be here.
SQ: *Were there any opportunities to help? Why didn't you? What did you do? Why did you make the choices you did?*	
People should have told us it was going to happen.	No one helped us. No one cared

TABLE 2.1 Common stuck points that can develop across different types of trauma. (*Cont.*)

Assimilated stuck points (This trauma happened to me because...)	Over-accommodated stuck points (This trauma has influenced my beliefs about the world, self, and others...)
SQ: *Why did no one warn you? Did anyone help? Why do you think no one helped? How did you get out of that situation? With or without help?*	

SQ, Socratic questions.

As we see it, the entire manual and process of CPT can be boiled down to the underlying premises of cognitive theory. Our job as therapists is to help improve mental health and well-being, so let's consider the issues and distress that bring our patients to therapy. No matter what the patient brings to the table, cognitive theory suggests that thoughts are contributing to the distress. If we can understand what the patient is telling him or herself, then we can begin to help him/her change his mind. After all, why would anyone keep considering a situation inaccurately if it is causing such distress? Fig. 2.1 might be helpful as a quick and dirty guide to relying on cognitive theory to guide therapists through the challenges of therapy in real time.

***Step 1*:** Cognitive therapists want to try to understand what it is that the patient is telling himself/herself. In CPT language, we want to identify the stuck

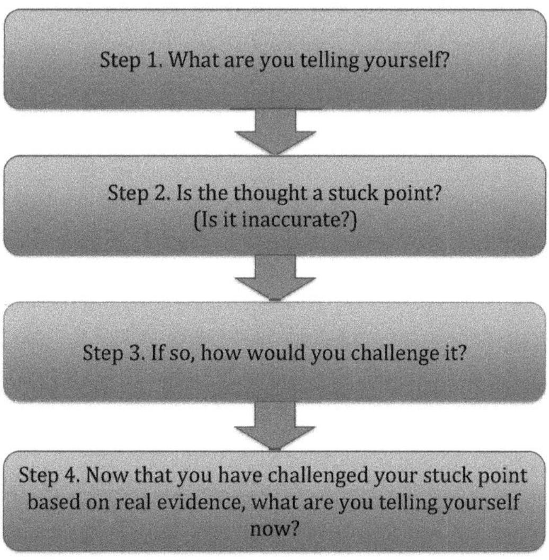

FIGURE 2.1 **CPT process of change in a nutshell.**

point. Really, the primary distinction between more general cognitive therapy and CPT in this regard is that we are focusing on the trauma and so are really exerting our efforts to identifying the stuck points that are relevant to PTSD. It is critical that we really drill down and find the thought that is driving the distress.

B = C Technique: One way to be sure that we are identifying the thought driving the distress is to imagine that an equal sign is required on your ABC sheet between columns B and C. In other words, the thought in column B must equal the emotion in column C. Let's use Steve's case example. Envision a situation in which Steve comes to session very agitated.

Steve: *I'm really having trouble calming down. I'm not sure I can focus on this today. I just came by to let you know that I am going to have to cancel today's appointment.*

Therapist: *What's going on?*

Steve: *I'm at work today operating the forklift and I see that this college kid who we just hired for the summer is not wearing his hard hat. Rule number 1—above all else, wear your hard hat. I just finished training with him the day before and his first day on the job, he pulls that stunt. I was crazy angry and went off on him. My boss told me I needed to leave for the day and cool down.*

Therapist (can apply the ABC model to this incident in her head or can pull out an ABC worksheet): *I can see you are still really angry about this. What is it about this situation that makes you so angry?*

Steve (stares at therapist as if this should be quite obvious): *He should have been wearing his hard hat*!

* In some cases, this thought might be a stuck point—we are always looking for "should statements." However, in this case, Steve has just stated a fact. Indeed, the new hire *should* have been wearing his hard hat. However, it is also likely that this type of mistake has happened before. It is doubtful that this thought alone is causing Steve's apparent rage—so angry that his boss asked him to leave the site and, several hours later, he is still quite angry. Recognizing that the thought in column B (*He should have been wearing his hard hat*) is **NOT** equal to the column C emotion (rage) will prompt the therapist to drill down a bit deeper to understand what thought is truly driving such a big emotional reaction.

Therapist: *You are absolutely right—no question about it. I've never been trained in any job that required a hard hat. Is it really dangerous to forget to wear your hat?*

Steve: *Yes—incredibly dangerous. Anything could go wrong at any minute and the only thing between you and a serious injury or worse is your hat.* (Therapist waits for him to continue.) *I can't protect people if they don't listen to me and follow the rules.*

Therapist: *Is it your job to protect him after you've trained him? Or does the responsibility shift to him?*

Steve: *I must protect him—he's just a dumb kid. If he gets hurt during a stupid summer job, it will be my fault. The worksite can be dangerous and his* *life is literally in my hands. When people don't follow the rules, there are really bad outcomes.*

Therapist: *OK—now I see why you are so upset about this. That's a lot of responsibility. I wonder if there is a stuck point in there?*

Step 2: Is the thought accurate? Staying with Steve's example, the therapist genuinely wants to know if there is a stuck point hidden in there. The therapist might query Steve's responsibility in the situation or the accuracy of his estimation of the amount of danger associated with not wearing a hard hat in that particular situation. In some cases, the thought might be quite accurate. The employee should indeed be wearing a hard hat at all times. However, the therapist still might sense that the level of emotion is not consistent with the infraction (after all, his boss needed him to leave the worksite, suggesting his anger was beyond the normal range for such an incident). If the thought is accurate, we would not challenge the thought. We would instead look for a different thought which might be contributing to Steve's anger and agitation. A likely candidate would be a trauma-related stuck point. Maybe something about this situation remined him of his own traumatic experiences? The trick is to figure out a way to broach this subject without putting words into the patient's mouth or drawing associations and conclusions that are artificial.

Therapist: *That amount of responsibility at work is daunting. It must be exhausting. I know you've mentioned that you have similar levels of responsibility at home with two growing and active kids. Do you ever find an opportunity to let your guard down? How do you manage all of this?*

Steve: *I can't let my guard down. I never have been able to.*

Therapist: *I remember our recent conversation about all of the efforts you made to protect your little brother from the men who were hurting you. It seems like a very long history of being the protector.*

Steve: *I can't fail to protect my kids, my wife and my crew the way I failed my brother.*

Therapist: *That's important what you just said—'I failed my brother'. I wonder if that might be really at the heart of this anger when you see a similar situation unfold – this college kid in danger. Can we work on that one a bit?*

Clinical note: Notice how the patient came in saying he was just there to essentially cancel his appointment. He said he was too irate to be present and attend session. However, he did show up; he could have called to cancel. The therapist takes this opportunity to meet him where he is at—talking about this stressful day and then found a gateway to understand the relationship between the significant distress he is experiencing and his trauma-related cognitions. This was accomplished by Socratic questions which allowed the patient to get to the true source of his distress.

Step 3: Once you have a stuck point, you can begin the work of cognitive restructuring. As CPT therapists know, we rely heavily on Socratic questions to challenge stuck points and essentially help patients to change their minds based on real evidence. This book includes lots of examples of Socratic questions which we hope you find helpful, especially when stuck points are elusive and difficult to identify.

Step 4: Through Socratic questions, the patient will begin to see that the stuck point is inaccurate (remember—we do not challenge accurate thoughts or facts, so theoretically the patient should be able to change his or her mind in the direction of accuracy). Step 4 involves the final step in changing one's mind. If the stuck point is no longer accurate, then what might be a new and more accurate conclusion? This is the alternative thought.

Clinical note: Sometimes the patient changes his/her mind as quickly and completely as turning on a lightbulb (lightbulb moment). Other times, the patient needs to really digest this way of thinking and it takes some time to sink in. Still other times, the patient really seems resistant to changing his/her mind despite all of the evidence against the stuck point. Throughout the book, we will discuss at length about what might be getting in the way of generating (and believing) the alternative thought.

The role of emotion

Of course the ultimate goal of therapy is for the patient to *feel* better. The emphasis on cognitive theory can seem to indicate that we are only interested in thoughts—and that might seem pretty dry and robotic. However, in the CPT dismantling study and subsequent trials (discussed in the next chapter), we learned that by focusing primarily on the cognitions (stuck points) and through Socratic questions, we provided the opportunity and space for our patients to lay down this trauma burden, to safely tell their stories, to feel their feelings along the way as they engaged with their trauma memories and genuinely thought through all the misconceptions and faulty beliefs that they had been holding as gospel truth, often for years. As CPT therapists, the success of the therapy does not lie in simply a changed stuck point—any good student can move from point A to Z on a worksheet. Real change is evident when a patient comes to the realization that he/she is not at fault for the worst thing that ever happened, starts living again, is able to cry, and then stop crying. CPT is a real conversation and we as CPT therapists have the privilege to walk this difficult journey with trauma survivors and assist them in finding the light at the end of their tunnels.

Should we combine elements of other therapies to strengthen our outcomes?

We are often asked by clinicians if we think it would be helpful to add additional techniques to CPT such as in vivo exposures, mindfulness, empty chair techniques, skills training, and affect regulation. These are always great questions! Seemingly, it makes logical sense to add elements of other effective therapies to CPT to increase the overall outcomes. In fact, in the old days general cognitive-behavioral therapies (CBTs) often included everything and the kitchen sink!

However, combining other therapies and techniques can also have the effect of diluting the intervention that you are trying to strengthen. This dilution can happen because different techniques are not always theoretically consistent and, as such, the inconsistencies can result in conflicting messages to the patient. For example, as described earlier, cognitive theory dictates that the mechanism of action in the therapy is identifying beliefs and thoughts that are causing the distress. So, the consistent message to the patient is to exert effort in really thinking about what it is that you are telling yourself.

Introducing other interventions can be contraindicated for several reasons. First, we really consider the minutes that patients spend in therapy to be like liquid gold—very valuable. As such, we need to be spending time on the techniques at hand or else we've diluted the therapy simply by not providing the proper dose. Second, introducing other techniques that are theoretically inconsistent can actually be confusing to the patient as they suggest mixed messages. For example, many of our patients have substantial difficulty managing and regulating emotion. Significant emotional regulation deficits are not uncommon at all in PTSD. In CPT, we would help the patient to identify the thought that is driving the emotion. We provide lots of examples of this application in later chapters. Suffice it to say that putting trauma-focused therapy on hold to work on skills and affect regulation strategies may be giving the patient the message that he or she is too fragile to begin trauma-focused work. This becomes evidence for our patients that they can't tolerate their emotions. Hmmmm, sounds like a stuck point to us! We certainly recognize that there are times when it makes good clinical sense to diverge from the protocol and add a different intervention. Chapter 5 describes this process in detail. But these divergences really are few and far between and every time therapists diverge from the theoretical premises of the treatment model, we really risk colluding with avoidance and not providing the treatment that will best alleviate the symptoms at hand—the PTSD. Finally, when we add other techniques to CPT, we risk the generalizability of the cognitive strategies to larger life issues and to the sequelae of other traumatic events. The sheer continuity of guiding the patient in approaching whatever is on the table from a cognitive lens helps bring this new way of thinking into everyday lives where the patients need it the most.

To demonstrate this point, when I (TG) first began practicing CPT, I was approached by a professional truck driver to treat PTSD secondary to a horrible accident that had occurred some years ago. I had actually just completed a trial with my mentor, Dr. Ed Blanchard, in which we had successfully tested a CBT protocol to treat survivors of motor vehicle accidents (MVAs) with PTSD (Blanchard et al., 2003). On one hand, it would have been logical to apply this protocol to my MVA patient. However, I was really interested in understanding the influence of cognitive change on PTSD. Rather than establishing a hierarchy list and in vivo exposures as suggested in the CBT manual (imagine being behind the wheel of the truck, go to the truck yard, sit behind the wheel of a truck, drive in the parking, drive on a side street, etc.), we began CPT. As per the protocol, we moved through the assimilated stuck points in the early phase of therapy. During these sessions, the patient described all kinds of activities he was avoiding due to PTSD. His wife drove him to every session, he could not talk (even by phone) to any of his fellow truckers, could not drive by several specific areas, and had not been to the truckyard since the accident. He had been quite close to retirement and was not able to finish his years of service because he was not able to sit behind the wheel of a truck. Prior to the accident (which was not his fault), he had had a pristine driving record.

As these avoidance behaviors were mentioned throughout therapy, we would spend some time identifying the stuck point behind the scenarios. *Why* couldn't he go to the truckyard? *Why* couldn't he talk on the phone with his old buddies? *What* was preventing him from living the life he wanted to live? Quite independently, the patient started to apply the therapy (this process of examining *what* he was telling himself that was preventing him from doing the things he wanted to do) to each of the challenging situations in his life. In the second half of the therapy, he surprised me more and more – he drove himself to therapy (he came from quite a distance), he then drove his family to a wedding in Chicago (including through city traffic), he went back to the truckyard, and eventually, he headed back to work. From the therapist perspective, this was a most memorable case and a powerful lesson. The cognitive process of changing your own mind is very empowering. I never once told him what to do. I never even suggested that he change any of these avoidance behaviors. I just basically asked the question, if this behavior is limiting your life, why are you doing it? And if the reason isn't sound, then why not change your mind? This was one of my first CPT cases and it is available as a case report (Galovski & Resick, 2008).

Summary

There are several excellent and evidence-based treatments for PTSD. We highly recommend that you choose an evidence-based therapy to treat PTSD, avoid adapting the models, and stay theoretically consistent with the therapy you choose. The science supporting these evidence-based interventions suggest that this plan of action gives our patients suffering from PTSD the best chance for recovery.

References

Beck, A. T., Rush, A. J., Shaw, B. F., & Emery, G. (1979). *Cognitive therapy of depression*. New York: Guildford Press.

Blanchard, E. B., Hickling, E. J., Devineni, T., Veazey, C. H., Galovski, T. E., Mundy, E., Malta, L. S., & Buckley, T. C. (2003). A controlled evaluation of cognitive-behavioral therapy for posttraumatic stress in motor vehicle accident survivors. *Behaviour Research and Therapy*, *41*, 79–96. doi: 10.1016/S0005-7967(01)00131-0.

Craske, M. (2015). Optimizing exposure therapy for anxiety disorders: an inhibitory learning and inhibitory regulation approach. *Verhaltenstherapie*, *25*(2), 134–143. doi: 10.1159/000381574.

Craske, M. G., Treanor, M., Conway, C. C., Zbozinek, T., & Vervliet, B. (2014). Maximizing exposure therapy: an inhibitory learning approach. *Behaviour Research and Therapy*, *58*, 10–23. doi: 10.1016/j.brat.2014.04.006.

Foa, E. B., Hembree, E. A., & Rothbaum, B. O. (2007). Prolonged Exposure Therapy for PTSD: Emotional processing of traumatic experiences–Therapist Guide, pp. 37–44. New York: NY: Oxford University Press. doi: 10.1093/med:psych/9780195308501.003.0003.

Foa, E. B., Huppert, J. D., & Cahill, S. P. (2006). Emotional processing theory: an update. In B. O. Rothbaum (Ed.), *Pathological anxiety: emotional processing in etiology and treatment* (pp. 3–24). New York: Guilford Press.

Foa, E. B., & Rothbaum, B. O. (1998). *Treating the trauma of rape*. New York, NY: Guilford Press.

Galovski, T. E., & Resick, P. A. (2008). Cognitive processing therapy for posttraumatic stress disorder secondary to a motor vehicle accident: a single-subject report. *Cognitive and Behavioral Practice*, *15*(3), 287–295. doi: 10.1016/j.cbpra.2007.11.005.

Galovski, T. E., Harik, J. M., Blain, L. M., Farmer, C., Turner, D., & Houle, T. (2016). Identifying patterns and predictors of PTSD and depressive symptom change during cognitive processing therapy. *Cognitive Therapy and Research*, *40*(5), 617–626. doi: 10.1007/s10608-016-9770-4.

Hollon, S. D., & Garber, J. (1988). Cognitive Therapy. In L. Y. Abramson (Ed.), *Social cognition and clinical psychology: a synthesis* (pp. 204–253). New York: Guilford Press.

Kessler, R. C., Aguilar-Gaxiola, S., Alonso, J., Benjet, C., Bromet, E. J., Cardoso, G., Degenhardt, L., de Girolamo, G., Dinolova, R. V., Ferry, F., & Florescu, S. (2017). Trauma and PTSD in the WHO world mental health surveys. *European Journal of Psychotraumatology*, *8*(Suppl. 5), 1353383.

Resick, P. A., Monson, C. M., & Chard, K. M. (2017). *Cognitive processing therapy for PTSD: a comprehensive manual*. New York: Guilford Publications.

Chapter 3

Treatment development: The early years

Chapter outline

Research in the development and establishment of psychotherapy has proliferated over the last 4 decades. Cognitive-behavioral interventions, in particular, have demonstrated substantial empirical support in the remediation of post-traumatic stress disorder (PTSD). Since the beginning of this accumulation of evidence, the scientific community's endorsement of specific therapies as "empirically supported" and "evidence-based" has resulted in the development of best practice guidelines by numerous national organizations (e.g., American Psychological Association, 2017; US Department of Veteran Affairs, 2017). Related to the establishment of clear treatment guidelines, efforts toward dissemination of these interventions to community care have significantly increased (Karlin et al., 2010). Despite this exponential growth in treatment outcome research and these historically herculean efforts to disseminate interventions developed in academic settings and tested in randomized controlled trials (RCTs), barriers to implementing evidence-based practices (EBP) into clinical care remain.

Why is there such a wide gap between research and practice? The extant literature is replete with numerous explanations for the historical difficulties in the successful dissemination and implementation of EBPs (Freiheit, Vye, Swan, Cady, 2004; Kazdin, 2008). Objections to the integration of EBPs into clinical practice may stem from general dissonance around the application of the seemingly rigid "cookbook approach" of manualized therapies to the perceived complexity of distress observed in many clients seeking services in community care settings. The idea that the "therapy developed in an academic ivory tower somewhere couldn't possibly be a good fit for the complicated patient sitting

Flexible Applications of Cognitive Processing Therapy. http://dx.doi.org/10.1016/B978-0-12-816715-1.00003-0

across from me" is a very real concern for many clinicians across a host of clinical care settings. In fact, that concern is what drove these authors to construct our clinical trials and indeed to write this book!

The debate over the inception of EBP guidelines began almost immediately following the APA Task Force on Promotion and Dissemination of Psychological Procedures' (1995) recommendations. A host of criticism for the implausibility of the APA's recommended use of empirically supported treatments (ESTs) in clinical practice resounded through both clinical and academic circles resulting in a special issue of JCCP (1998). Some of the strongest criticism against the proclaimed empirical support of the cited interventions included the lack of flexibility of treatment manuals in RCTs (Beutler & Howard, 1998; Shadish, Matt, Navarro, Siegle, et al., 1997), the focus on outcome rather than process of therapy (Barlow, 1996), the fixed number of sessions contained in protocols (Goldfried & Wolfe, 1998), the use of highly trained, expert clinicians to administer the intervention (Chambless & Hollon, 1998), the focus on diagnostic outcome rather than client level of functioning and lack of overall ecological validity (Persons & Silberschatz, 1998; Beutler, 1998). More recently, patient attrition and non-response rates reported in RCTs have also been noted as evidence against the notion that a given psychotherapy has enough empirical support to be labeled as a best practice. RCTs for manualized PTSD treatments alone indicate that approximately one-third of the participants remain refractory to treatment and approximately one-quarter of the samples drop out prematurely (Bradley et al. 2005; Schottenbauer et al., 2008). Although continued empirical support and significant advances have been realized since the beginning of this debate in the 1990s, efforts toward the integration of EBPs into community care remain challenging at best (Kazdin, 2008).

Over time, and with the continued advancement of research and training in EBPs, the controversy of the mid-1990s around identifying some therapies as evidence-based has perhaps died down a bit. RCTs have continued to refine methodology such as much broader inclusion criteria, less expert clinicians on research trials, and more sophisticated analyses and reporting guidelines that consider treatment drop-outs, missing data, and the inclusion of effect sizes. However, the uptake of EBPs into clinical care has continued to be poor. Some of the lack of translation of EBPs into clinical care may be due to therapist's own stuck points. Over the years, we've heard quite a few. Table 3.1 provides some examples of common therapist stuck points as they relate to challenges that we face in treating patients with PTSD. It is important to note that therapists come by these stuck points honestly. We all want to do our best for our patients and it is not always readily apparent that manualized therapies can best meet our patient's complex and varied needs. Further, there is no way that anybody (therapist, professor, researcher) can stay on top of the copious amounts of research and literature in the field—making it difficult as a therapist to stay informed as to the latest modifications of CPT (or any other therapy for that matter). This book seeks to

TABLE 3.1 Therapist stuck points.

Clinical challenge	Stuck point
Aging adult	CPT won't work with patients with cognitive decline or memory impairment.
Chronic PTSD	My patient has had PTSD for far too long to really change.
Complex trauma history	My patient could never focus on just one event.
Comorbid mental health disorders or physical health complications	My patient will get worse if we talk about her trauma. CPT won't be as effective with ____ (Borderline PD, substance use, TBI, etc.).
Affect dysregulation, dissociation	My patient is too fragile to think about her trauma. She will worsen.

provide a summary of all of the advances in CPT to help all of us challenge our own therapist stuck points.

CPT randomized clinical trials

We thought it would be helpful to provide a review of the published CPT randomized clinical trials to date. Our goals are to provide an accessible reference (Table 3.2) that provides information on the types of trauma patients recruited for CPT studies, descriptions of the patient populations including the extent of the participants' prior trauma history, comorbid mental illnesses, and demographics, and the relative success of the therapy in treating PTSD and depression. While PTSD is always the primary target of CPT, we closely watch improvement in depressive symptoms as well given that the two tend to occur hand in hand. Table 3.2 also documents improvement in depression over the CPT trials.

Random assignment

In order to provide the most accessible references in Table 3.1, we are including only studies that randomized participants to two or more treatment conditions. This is important because randomized trials help us to determine if the improvement is due to the therapy itself. For example, if participants are randomly assigned to CPT or to a waitlist or symptoms monitoring control condition, we know that any improvement in PTSD for those participants receiving CPT over and above improvement in the control condition is due to CPT, not something else like the passage of time. Some studies randomized participants to CPT or another gold standard treatment (e.g., Prolonged Exposure (PE); Foa, Hembree, & Rothbaum, 2007). In these studies, we are interested to see if the

TABLE 3.2 Review of the published CPT clinical trials for guidance in clinical care.

Study and location	ITT sample descriptives	Type of index trauma and primary outcomes (measures)	Comorbid diagnoses and prior trauma history	Comparison conditions	Percent change in PTSD from pre- to posttreatment for ITT samples (based on CAPS unless otherwise noted)	Effect sizes for ITT samples (based on CAPS unless otherwise noted)
Resick et al. (2002) USA	*N*= 171 100% Female *M*= 32 years Civilians	Sexual assault PTSD (CAPS, PSS) Depression (BDI) Guilt (TRGI)	44% MDD (CPT group) 48% MDD (PE group) 41% sexually abused as children 86% experienced other crimes	12 sessions CPT (*n*= 62) vs. 9 sessions prolonged exposure (*n*= 62) vs. 6-week minimal attention wait list (*n*= 47)	CPT: 48% (27% dropped out) PE: 41% (27% dropped out) MA: 0.8% (15% dropped out)	CPT was more effective than MA at Post-tx Hedge's *g* = .97 CPT was more effective than PE at Post-tx Hedge's *g* = .14
CPT and PE were both effective at decreasing PTSD and depression, and both were superior to MA. CPT participants showed more improvement on measures of guilt as compared to PE. This study demonstrated that CPT was as effective as the gold standard therapy, PE.						
Ahrens & Rexford (2002) USA	*N*= 38 100% Male *M*= 16 years Civilians (incarcerated adolescents)	Mixed trauma prior to adolescent incarceration PTSD (PSS-SR) Depression (BDI) Overall Function: (IES)	40% ADD/ADHD 68% Prior trauma, 29% w/multiple trauma 32% Witnessed death of known individual 52% Prior head injury leading to loss of consciousness	8 sessions Cognitive Processing Therapy (*n*= 19) vs. Wait-list Control (*n*= 19)	Note: PTSD symptoms measured by PSS-SR CPT: 54% WL: –5%	Unavailable
CPT was effective at decreasing PTSD, depression, and overall functioning, while the control was not. Further, this study demonstrated effectiveness of CPT in an adolescent sample.						

Chard (2005) USA	N= 71 100% Female M = 33 years Civilians	Childhood sexual assault (CSA) PTSD (CAPS-SX, MPSS) Depression (BDI-II) Dissociation (DES-II)	40% MDD 57% Recall >100 incidents of childhood sexual assault (CSA)	17 weeks of group and individual CPT for Sexual Abuse Survivors (n= 36) vs. 17 week wait-list Minimal Attention (n= 35)	CPT-SA: 86% (18% dropped out) MA: 8% (21% dropped out)	CPT-SA was more effective than MA at Post-tx Cohen's d = 1.52
CPT-SA was significantly better at decreasing PTSD, depression, and dissociation than MA. Results were maintained for 1-year post-tx. This study demonstrated that CPT is quite effective in treating PTSD even in the context of complex trauma histories such as chronic childhood sexual abuse.						
Monson et al. (2006) USA	N= 60 90% Male M = 55 years Veterans (80% Vietnam Era)	Chronic military-related PTSD (e.g., combat, sexual, noncombat physical assault) PTSD (CAPS, PCL) Depression (BDI) Anxiety (STAI)	Mood Disorder: 55% current, 88% lifetime Other anxiety measures: 48% current, 60% lifetime SAD: 2% current, 80% lifetime	12 sessions CPT (n= 30) vs. 10-week wait list (n= 30)	CPT: 32% (20% dropped out) WL: 4% (13% dropped out)	CPT was more effective than WL at Post-tx Hedge's g = 1.12
CPT was effective at significantly reducing PTSD and related symptoms compared to the WL control. There were decreases in depression scores in the CPT condition but not WL. This was the first study to test CPT in a Veteran population presenting with chronic PTSD.						

(Continued)

TABLE 3.2 Review of the published CPT clinical trials for guidance in clinical care. (*Cont.*)

Study and location	ITT sample descriptives	Type of index trauma and primary outcomes (measures)	Comorbid diagnoses and prior trauma history	Comparison conditions	Percent change in PTSD from pre- to posttreatment for ITT samples (based on CAPS unless otherwise noted)	Effect sizes for ITT samples (based on CAPS unless otherwise noted)
Resick et al. (2008) USA	*N*= 150 100% Female *M* = 35 years Civilians	Interpersonal violence PTSD (CAPS, PDS) Depression (BDI-II)	50% MDD 20% Panic Disorder 47% reported >10 childhood victimization events, 47% >10 adult victimization events	12 sessions (standard) CPT (*n*= 53) vs. 7 sessions CPT Written Accounts only (*n*= 50) vs. 12 sessions CPT-C (Cognitive therapy only) (*n*= 47)	Note: PTSD symptoms measured by PDS CPT: 51% (34% dropped out) CPT WA: 36% (26% dropped out) CPT-C: 58% (22% dropped out)	Note: Effect sizes for slopes over time calculated by PDS for: CPT: Cohen's *d* = 1.68 WA: Cohen's *d* = 1.54 CPT-C: Cohen's *d* = 1.82
Patients in all three groups showed significant decreases in PTSD and depression. Over time, patients in the CPT-C group showed greater improvements in PTSD symptoms than the WA group. This dismantling study demonstrated that the trauma narrative was not a necessary treatment element. Currently, writing the trauma narrative is optional and we leave the choice up to the patient to decide.						
Forbes et al. (2012) Australia	*N*= 59 97% Male CPT: *M*= 53 years TAU *M*= 54 years Veterans (>50% Vietnam era)	Military trauma PTSD (CAPS, PCL) Depression (BDI-II)	80% Current mood disorder 73% Current other anxiety diagnosis 44% Current substance abuse or dependence (SAD)	12 sessions CPT (*n*= 30) vs. Treatment as Usual (*n*= 29)	CPT: 36% (30% dropped out) TAU: 11% (31% dropped out)	CPT was more effective than TAU from Pre-to Post-tx Hedge's *g* = .97
CPT was effective at reducing PTSD and depression while treatment as usual was largely ineffective. This study offered an important replication of the effectiveness of CPT in a non-US Veteran population.						

Galovski et al. (2012) USA	N= 100 69% Female M= 40 years Civilians	Adult interpersonal violence PTSD (CAPS, PDS) Depression (BDI-II)	648% Current MDD 25% Current Panic Disorder 34% Lifetime Substance Dependence 8% reported CSA, 59% child physical abuse, 52% adult sexual assault, 67% adult physical assault, 54% domestic violence	4-18 weeks modified CPT (n= 53) vs. 10 weeks Symptom-Monitoring Delayed Treatment (n= 47)	MCPT: 64% SMDT: 21% *Following completion of SMDT, 25 participants crossed over to MCPT. Thus the total ITT MCPT sample = 69. Drop-out rate was 28%.	MCPT was more effective than SMDT: Hedge's g = 1.35
MCPT led to greater improvement in PTSD and depression than did SMDT. Gains were maintained at 3-month f/u. This study demonstrated that therapists can tailor treatment length to meet patient needs. Some patients recover sooner than 12 sessions and are "done" early while others require more time. Further, we learned from this study that allowing emergency sessions (and then returning to CPT after the crisis is stabilized) does not compromise the effectiveness of the CPT.						
Nixon (2012) Australia	N= 30 53% Male M= 41 years Civilians	Assault survivors with Acute Stress Disorder (ASD) PTSD (CAPS, PDS, PTCI) Depression (BDI-II)	63% Mood disorder 27% Anxiety disorder Trauma hx not reported	6 sessions CPT (n= 17) vs. Supportive Counseling (n= 13)	Note: PTSD measure by PDS CPT: 66% (24% dropped out) SC: 43% (38% dropped out)	CPT was more effective than SC at Post-tx Cohen's d= .82
This study demonstrated the feasibility and success of CPT in treating individuals soon after exposure to trauma and suffering from acute stress disorder.						

(Continued)

TABLE 3.2 Review of the published CPT clinical trials for guidance in clinical care. (*Cont.*)

Study and location	ITT sample descriptives	Type of index trauma and primary outcomes (measures)	Comorbid diagnoses and prior trauma history	Comparison conditions	Percent change in PTSD from pre- to posttreatment for ITT samples (based on CAPS unless otherwise noted)	Effect sizes for ITT samples (based on CAPS unless otherwise noted)
Bass et al. (2013) Demo-cratic Republic of Congo[a]	N= 405 100% Female CPT-C: M = 37 years Individual Sup-port: M= 34 years Civilians	Sexual violence PTSD (HTQ) Depression/Anxi-ety (HSCL-25) Overall Function: Functional Impairment Score	74% Probable PTSD 70% Probable De-pression/ Anxiety Trauma hx not reported	12 sessions group CPT-C (n= 157) vs. Individual Sup-port Group (n= 248)	Note: PTSD symp-toms measured by HTQ CPT-C: 58% (10% dropped out) IS: 23% (27% dropped out)	Note: Effect sizes calculated using HTQ from Pre-tx to Post-tx CPT-C was more effective than IS: Between groups effect size Co-hen's d= 1.4
This study demonstrated the ability to translate CPT into a different language, implement CPT in a different culture with few resources, and the feasibility of teaching CPT to therapists with relatively little formal education. Further, this study taught us that we can implement CPT even when patients are exposed to ongoing traumatic events.						
Suris et al. (2013) USA	N= 86 85% Female M = 46 years Veterans	Military Sexual Trauma PTSD (CAPS, PCL) Depression (QIDS)	Not reported	12 sessions CPT (n= 52) vs. 12 sessions Present Centered Therapy (n= 34)	CPT: 24% (38% dropped out) PCT: 18% (18% dropped out)	Pre to post-tx effect sizes: CPT: Cohen's d = 1.02 PCT: Cohen's d = .80 Between-group: CPT was more ef-fective than PCT: Cohen's d = .49
PTSD and depression improved significantly in both treatment groups. Effect sizes were larger in the CPT group. This study offered another impor-tant replication of the effectiveness of CPT in an independent site and speaks to the importance of fidelity to the protocol in achieving outcomes.						

Bolton et al., (2014) Northern Iraq[b]>	N= 281 58% Female M= 40 years Civilian and Veteran 50% with no education	Systematic violence PTSD (HSQ) Depression (HSCL-25) Guilt (TRGI) Overall Function: Functional Impairment Score	41% physically tortured 55% imprisoned 14% exposed to gas attacks	12 sessions CPT (n= 101) vs. 12 sessions Behavioral Activation (n= 114) vs. 12-week wait list (n= 66)	Note: PTSD symptoms measured by HTQ from Baseline to follow-up (Pre-tx to Post-tx) CPT: 45% (21% dropped out) BA: 38% (28% dropped out) WL: 23% (15% dropped out)	CPT was more effective than all WL controls at Post-tx: Between groups effect size Cohen's d= .71. BA Cohen's d= .47
This study demonstrated the effectiveness of CPT and BA (the two were not directly compared) in a low-resource country. Individuals were included in the study based on elevated depression rather than PTSD. CPT had significant effects on improving functioning, traumatic grief, and anxiety. This study is another example of adapting CPT for a low-literacy context and translating the treatment protocol into a new language and culture. Non-specialized health care workers provided the interventions suggesting that these therapies can be delivered for survivors of systematic violence even by workers with limited prior mental health experience.						
Morland et al. (2014) USA	N= 125 100% Male M = 55 years Veterans (83% Vietnam era)	PTSD (CAPS)	MDD: 29% current, 64% lifetime Anxiety Disorder: 19% current, 22% lifetime Substance Use Disorder: 18% current, 77% lifetime	12 sessions Group CPT-C In Person (n= 64) vs. 12 sessions Group CPT-C Video teleconferencing (n= 61)	CPT-C "IP": 15% (14% dropped out) CPT-C VTC: 23% (18% dropped out)	CPT-C VTC was more effective than CPT-IP at post-tx Cohen's d = .27
CPTC-VTC was as effective at reducing PTSD symptoms as was CPTC NP and gains were maintained through 6-mo f/u. This was the first study to demonstrate that CPT could effectively be administered distally via tele-conferencing to male Veterans.						

(*Continued*)

TABLE 3.2 Review of the published CPT clinical trials for guidance in clinical care. (*Cont.*)

Study and location	ITT sample descriptives	Type of index trauma and primary outcomes (measures)	Comorbid diagnoses and prior trauma history	Comparison conditions	Percent change in PTSD from pre- to posttreatment for ITT samples (based on CAPS unless otherwise noted)	Effect sizes for ITT samples (based on CAPS unless otherwise noted)
Morland et al. (2015) USA	*N*= 126 100% Female *M* = 46 years Veterans, reserves/guard, civilians (67% OIF/OEF)	PTSD (CAPS)	MDD: 30% current, 76% lifetime Anxiety disorder: 27% current, 34% lifetime Substance Use Disorder: 3% current, 53% lifetime	12 sessions Group CPT-C In Person (*n*= 63) vs. 12 sessions Group CPT-C VTC (*n*= 63)	CPT-C NP: 20% (21% dropped out) CPT-C VTC: 25% (24% dropped out)	CPT-C VTC was equally as effective as CPT-C NP at Post-tx Cohen's *d* = .06
This study demonstrated that administering CPT via telemental health was equally effective as in-person sessions. This study extended previous findings to female (primarily post-9/11) Veterans.						
Resick et al. (2015) USA	*N*= 108 93% Male *M* = 32 years Active Duty Military	Combat-related PTSD (PCL-S, PSS-I) Depression (BDI-II)	Not reported	12 sessions CPT-C (*n*= 56) vs. 12 sessions Present-Centered Therapy (*n*= 52)	Note: PTSD measured in terms of a clinically significant drop on PCL-S (at least 10 points from pre to post-tx) CPT-C: 49% (9% completed all 12 sessions) PCT: 34% (19% completed all 12 sessions)	Note: Effect sizes calculated using PSS-I from baseline to 1-year follow-up Effect sizes for slopes over time: CPT-C Cohen's *d* = 1.21 PCT Cohen's *d* = 1.01
This study was the first to test CPT in an active duty population. The results demonstrate that the therapy translates well to service members suffering from PTSD. Importantly in this study, gains continued beyond the end of therapy for both CPT-C and PCT. This study also showed that a non-trauma-focused therapy such as PCT is effective in treating PTSD.						

Weiss et al. (2015) Southern Iraq[b]	N= 342	Systematic violence PTSD (HTQ) Depression (HSCL-25)	Not reported	8–12 sessions Common Elements Treatment Approach (CETA) (n= 99) vs. CETA wait list (n= 50) -- 12 sessions CPT (n= 129) vs. CPT wait list (n= 64)	Note: PTSD symptoms measured by HTQ from Baseline to follow-up (Pre-tx to Post-tx) CETA: 70% (2% dropped out) CETA WL: 25% (no one dropped out) CPT: 71% (17% dropped out) CPT WL: 59% (no one dropped out)	Note: Effect sizes calculated using HTQ at follow-up CETA was more effective than WL= Cohen's d = 2.40 CPT was more effective than WL Cohen's d = .41
This study demonstrated the effectiveness of CPT and CETA (the two were not directly compared) in a low-resource country and in the context of ongoing exposures to war. The controls in the CPT arm improved significantly (large effects; d = 1.54) while the controls in the CETA arm did not. These differences across the arms of the studies makes it difficult to compare the between group effects. This study is also another example of translating the treatment protocol into a new language and culture. It should be noted that non-specialized health care workers provided the interventions suggesting that these therapies can be disseminated effectively across settings and populations.						
Butollo et al. (2016) Germany	N= 141 67% Female CPT group M= 34 years Dialectical Exposure Therapy group M= 38 years Civilians	Mixed trauma PTSD (IES-R; PDS) Overall Function: (BSI)	47% Affective Disorders 46% Anxiety Disorders	15–24 sessions CPT (n= 67) vs. 4–24 sessions Dialogical Exposure Therapy (n= 74)	Note: PTSD measured using IES-R CPT: 58% (15% dropout rate) DET: 42% (12% dropout rate)	Note: Effect sizes calculated using IES-R CPT Hedge's g = 1.57 DET Hedge's g= 1.14 Between group effect sizes favored CPT: Hedge's g = .25
This study offers another replication of CPT in an independent, non-US clinical setting. Prior to this study, CPT had not been directly compared with DET (an integrated gestalt-derived, non-cognitive -behavioral intervention). Interestingly, this study reported that younger patients benefited more from CPT than older patients. There was no difference by age for DET.						

(Continued)

TABLE 3.2 Review of the published CPT clinical trials for guidance in clinical care. (*Cont.*)

Study and location	ITT sample descriptives	Type of index trauma and primary outcomes (measures)	Comorbid diagnoses and prior trauma history	Comparison conditions	Percent change in PTSD from pre- to posttreatment for ITT samples (based on CAPS unless otherwise noted)	Effect sizes for ITT samples (based on CAPS unless otherwise noted)
Galovski et al. (2016) USA	*N*= 108 100% Female *M*= 37 years Civilians	Adult interpersonal violence survivors with sleep problems PTSD (CAPS) Depression (BDI-II) Sleep (PSQI, ISI)	Index trauma: Interpersonal violence In addition: 71% reported CSA 59% child physical abuse 58% adult sexual assault 63% adult physical assault, 32% adult criminal victimization, 56% domestic violence	Sleep and symptom monitoring plus CPT: 3 weeks symptom monitoring then 12 sessions CPT (*n*= 56) vs. Hypnosis plus CPT: 3 weeks hypnosis then 12 sessions of CPT (*n*= 52)	ssmCPT: 66% (48% dropped out) hypCPT: 69% (41% dropped out)	Between group effect sizes per treatment phase: From pre to post hypnosis/ssm phase: hypCPT improved more than ssmCPT ES = .45 From pre CPT to post: ssmCPT favored hypCPT ES = .72

This study sought to treat clinically significant sleep impairment prior to CPT with the hypothesis that improving sleep would augment recovery form PTSD and depression. While sleep-directed hypnosis was indeed found to be effective in improving PTSD-related sleep impairment, the improvements did not augment recovery from PTSD (both groups recovered equally well from PTSD). Improvement in sleep impairment did, however, hasten recovery from depression.

Maieritsch et al. (2016) USA	$N = 90$ 93% Male $M = 31$ years OIF/OEF Veterans	Military-related (i.e., combat, sexual, noncombat physical assault) PTSD (CAPS, PCL) Depression (BDI-II)	Not reported	12 sessions In-Person CPT-C ($n = 45$) vs. 12 sessions CPT-C video teleconferencing (TMH) ($n = 45$)	CPT-C IP: 34% (44% dropped out) CPT-C TMH: 37% (42% dropped out)	CPT IP at Post-tx Cohen's $d = 0.9$ CPT TMH at Post-tx Cohen's $d = 1.4$
This study extended the literature on the effectiveness of CPT in treating PTSD via video teleconferencing to post-9/11 male Veterans.						
Maxwell et al. (2016) USA	$N = 16$ 81% Female $M = 22$ years Civilians	Adults with PTSD from mixed traumas PTSD (MPSS-SR) Depression (BDI-II) Memory (AMT, AMT–LAT) Global Functioning (GAF)	94% Prior tx or counseling 38% Prior psychiatric hospitalization	12 sessions individual CPT ($n = 8$) vs. 6 sessions Memory Specificity Training ($n = 8$)	*Note: PTSD measured by MPSS-SR from pre-tx to 3-mo follow-up CPT: 30% MeST: 23% (no one dropped out)	*Note: PTSD effect sizes calculated using MPSS-SR CPT was more effective than MeST across time (baseline to post-tx to 3-mo f/u): Cohen's $d = .50$
This was a small study rendering it difficult to generalize findings to the larger population. Results showed that patients benefited more form CPT with a moderate effect size. The authors speculated that the MeST therapy would effectively target the reconsolidation of memory and understood this to be important in recovery from PTSD. However, results showed that both groups performed equally well on increasing their ability to retrieve specific memories.						

(Continued)

TABLE 3.2 Review of the published CPT clinical trials for guidance in clinical care. (*Cont.*)

Study and location	ITT sample descriptives	Type of index trauma and primary outcomes (measures)	Comorbid diagnoses and prior trauma history	Comparison conditions	Percent change in PTSD from pre- to posttreatment for ITT samples (based on CAPS unless otherwise noted)	Effect sizes for ITT samples (based on CAPS unless otherwise noted)
Resick et al. (2017) USA	*N*= 268 91% Male *M* = 32 years Active Duty Military	Combat-related PTSD (PSS-I, PCL-S) Depression (BDI-II)	64% Current post-concussive symptoms 17% Hazardous Drinkers	12 sessions individual CPT (*n*= 135) vs. 12 sessions group CPT (*n*= 133)	Reliable change index was reported: For individual CPT: reliable change occurred in 43% (24% dropped out of individual CPT and 13% were pulled out for military reasons) For Group CPT: Reliable change occurred in 17% (32% dropped out of group CPT and 11% were pulled out for military reasons)	Note: Effect sizes calculated using PSS-I at Post-tx Indiv. CPT Cohen's *d*= 1.3 Group CPT Cohen's *d*= .7 Between-condition differences favored individual CPT: Cohen's *d*= .6

This study directly compared group to individual delivery of CPT in an active duty military sample. The results favored individual administration of therapy over group, with patients receiving individual therapy benefiting almost twice as much. Reliable change index can be interpreted as the extent to which we can assume that change is "real" and not just due to measurement error. Thus this study showed that almost half of those receiving individual therapy evidenced "real" change while less than 20% in the group condition realized reliable improvement in PTSD symptoms.

Jak et al. (2019) USA	*N*= 101 89% Male *M* = 34 years OEF/OIF/ OND-era Veterans	Military-related PTSD (PCL-S) Traumatic Brain Injury (TBI): (Warrior Administered Retrospective Casualty Assessment Tool)	PTSD plus mild to moderate suspected TBI (*M* = 2.8 TBI events) 57% prior PTSD tx	12 sessions (standard) CPT sessions (*n*= 50) vs. 12 sessions of SMART CPT intervention (*n*= 51)	Note: PTSD symptoms measured by PCL-S CPT: 33% (51% dropped out) SMART CPT: 30% (43% dropped out)	Unavailable
This study suggests that adding components of a compensatory cognitive training (designed to target neuropsychological symptoms associated with traumatic brain injury) to CPT resulted in improvements in these domains above and beyond neuropsychological improvements observed in CPT (and improvement in PTSD) alone.						
Kozel et al. (2018) USA	*N*= 103 OEF/OIF Adult Male and Female Veterans Ages 18 – 60	Combat-related PTSD (CAPS, PCL, M-PTSD) Depression (QIDS) Overall Function: IPF	Not reported	Sham repetitive Transcranial Magnetic Stimulation prior to 12 sessions CPT vs. (*n*= 49) Active repetitive Transcranial Magnetic Stimulation prior to 12 sessions of CPT (*n*= 54)	Sham + CPT: 45% (39% dropped out) rTMS + CPT: 59% (41% dropped out)	rTMS + CPT was more effective than Sham + CPT from pre-tx to 1 month f/u: Cohen's *d*= .61
This study showed that the addition of TMS to CPT improved overall outcome with moderate effects. It should be noted that results are difficult to generalize to the larger PTSD population as there were a significant number of exclusionary criteria – many of which are conditions that would be contraindicated with TMS.						

(*Continued*)

TABLE 3.2 Review of the published CPT clinical trials for guidance in clinical care. (*Cont.*)

Study and location	ITT sample descriptives	Type of index trauma and primary outcomes (measures)	Comorbid diagnoses and prior trauma history	Comparison conditions	Percent change in PTSD from pre- to posttreatment for ITT samples (based on CAPS unless otherwise noted)	Effect sizes for ITT samples (based on CAPS unless otherwise noted)
Sloan et al. (2018) USA	N= 126 52% Male M = 44 years Civilians + Veterans	Mixed traumas, for example, combat-related, sexual, non-sexual, motor vehicle crash, injury from other accidental causes PTSD (CAPS-5)	Not reported	12 sessions CPT (n= 63) vs. 5 sessions Written Exposure Therapy (n= 63)	CPT: 33% (40% dropped out) WET: 26% (6% dropped out)	CPT from Baseline to 6-weeks Cohen's d= 1.13 WET from Baseline to 12-weeks Cohen's d= .82 Between groups: baseline to post-treatment effects favored CPT: Cohen's d= .29

The results showed that WET and CPT were largely equivalent with the exception of one time point (after both treatments had concluded) in which CPT participants improved more than those in WET. These differences were not apparent 12 weeks later at the follow-up assessment interval.

Pearson et al. (2019) USA	*N* = 73 100% Female Native American (AIAN: American Indian and Alaska Native) Ages 18–60 Civilians	Mixed trauma often related to substance abuse and high-risk sexual behavior PTSD (PSS-SR) Substance Abuse/High Risk Behavior: (Alcohol Short Inventory of Problems, Drug Use Frequency, High-Risk Sexual Behavior)	70% Substance Abuse Disorder 68% Prior PTSD	6 weeks culturally adapted CPT-C (w/out trauma narrative) (*n* = 37) vs. 6-week wait list (*n* = 36)	Note: PTSD symptoms measured by PSS-SR Culturally-adapted CPT-C: 46% (70% dropped out) WL: 25%	Note: PTSD effect size calculated from PSS-SR through follow-up Culturally adapted CPT-C was more effective than WL over time: Cohen's *d* = 1.03
CPT was very effective in treating PTSD within the AIAN community—an under-researched population with high trauma exposure and significant PTSD, substance use, and high-risk sexual behavior. Promising results emerged with respect to reductions of substance use and high-risk sexual behaviors. The dropout rates in this study were very high. These results suggest that if we are able to keep people in trauma-focused therapy, such as CPT, they can get better. However, it is difficult to retain people in these treatments, particularly with substance use disorder comorbidity.						

Note. ADD/ADHD, Attention-Deficit Disorder/Attention-Deficit Hyperactivity Disorder; AMT, Autobiographical Memory Test; AMT LAT, Autobiographical Memory Test total latency time; BA, Behavioral Activation; BDI, Beck Depression Inventory; BDI-II, Beck Depression Inventory-II; CAPS, Clinician-Administered PTSD Scale; CAPS-SX, Clinician-Administered PTSD Scale, 1-Week Symptom Status Version; CPT, Cognitive Processing Therapy; DES-II, Dissociative Experiences Scale-II; GAF, Global Assessment of Functioning; HSCL-25, Hopkins Symptom Checklist; HTQ, Harvard Trauma Questionnaire; IES, Impact of Events Scale; IES-R, Impact of Events Scale-Revised; IPF, Inventory of Psychosocial Functioning; ISI, Insomnia Severity Index; LEC, Life Events Checklist; MDD, Major Depressive Disorder; MEST, Memory-Specific Training; MPSS, Modified PTSD Symptom Scale; MPSS-SR, Modified PTSD Symptom Inventory – Self-Report; M-PTSD, Mississippi Scale for Combat Related PTSD; PCL, Posttraumatic Stress Disorder Checklist; PCL-S, PTSD Checklist Stressor Specific Version; PCT, Present-Centered Therapy; PDS, Posttraumatic Diagnostic Scale; PSS, PTSD Symptom Scale; PSS-I, PTSD Symptom Scale-Interview; PSS-SR, PTSD Symptom Scale Self-Report; PSQI, The Pittsburgh Sleep Quality Index; PTCI, Posttraumatic Cognitions Inventory; PTSD, Posttraumatic Stress Disorder; SAD, Substance Abuse Disorder; SmartCPT, Integration of compensatory cognitive training components from CogSMART (Cognitive Symptom Management and Rehabilitation Therapy) with CPT; STAI, State-Trait Anxiety Disorder; TRGI, Trauma-Related Guilt Interview; QIDS, Quick Inventory of Depressive Symptomology

[a] *Study measures were translated into 5 local languages: Kibembe, Kifuliro, Kihavu, Mashi, and Swahili.*

[b] *CPT intervention was administered by local Community Mental Health Workers fluent in the local language while supervised using an apprenticeship model (Murray et al., 2011) via phone or in-person meetings and supported by US experts.*

therapies are superior to one another in some way or if they are essentially equivalent. To accomplish this, we calculated the percent change on PTSD symptoms. It should be noted that the gold standard for assessing PTSD is the Clinician Administered PTSD Scale (CAPS). Most RCTs use the CAPS to diagnose PTSD and assess change and we note in our table when other instruments were used.

Effect sizes

We also note the effect sizes reported in the studies. Effect sizes are helpful in providing an estimate of the magnitude of change. Statistical significance reflects the probability that any between group differences are not just due to chance, while the effect size indicates the size of the difference. As a rule of thumb, anything less than .02 can be translated to a small difference (not really clinically meaningful), .2–.5 is a medium effect, and a large difference is indicated by an effect size greater than .5. On average, recent meta-analytic studies have shown that CPT has the largest effect sizes of all the existing evidence-based treatments in studies with soldiers and Veterans (Haagen, Smid, Knipscheer, et al., 2015) and across all trauma populations, the average effect size is 1.69 (Watts, Schnurr, Mayo, Young-Xu, Weeks, & Friedman, 2013). This means that, on average, people who receive CPT across all studies included in the meta-analysis showed large improvements in PTSD symptoms over treatment.

Attrition

As discussed throughout the book, breaking through avoidance is critical in recovering from PTSD. Missing sessions and premature termination of therapy is one way that our patients avoid. As therapists, we understand that therapy is expensive—financially, mentally, and emotionally. We have all had our share of dropouts. The clinical trials are no different. Dropout rates in PTSD can be quite high—even up to 70% in one study. They most typically range between 20% and 30%. In Table 3.2, we report the clinical trial outcomes from our intent to treat (ITT) analyses. These offer a conservative view of the treatment effectiveness. Essentially, we are estimating improvements in PTSD including every participant's data, even the people who never attended one session. We do not report the completer analyses (those who actually received the full dose of treatment), but obviously the effects are typically much stronger in the completer group. This makes sense—and our take home message is that those who get the full dose of therapy have a high likelihood of recovery from PTSD. The trick is to help our patients break through avoidance and stick with the process of change. We provide lots of clinical dialogue and examples throughout the next section of the book to help guide therapists in challenging stuck points related to therapy dropout (e.g., "I can't tolerate thinking about my trauma.").

Clinical relevance

Finally, we added a summary statement for each of the RCTs that we reviewed. Hopefully this information will help therapists and patients to make informed choices about how and when to modify CPT and for whom CPT works. Finally, we end the chapter with a brief summary of the take-home messages from the published CPT RCTs to date. While the information in the table focuses primarily on PTSD recovery, the summary statements include information about outcomes beyond PTSD (e.g., depression, guilt, etc.). Chapter 4 goes into more detail about improvements in secondary outcomes that have been observed in CPT studies.

Long-term follow-ups

While we did not list each studies' long-term follow-up individually, it should be noted that RCTs typically include a re-assessment of treatment gains and symptoms status at some point after the end of therapy. In the CPT trials, this timeframe ranged from 3 months to 5+ years. Overall, studies show that gains made in treatment are very well-maintained. This makes sense—if a patient is telling herself that the trauma "is all my fault," then changes her mind based on real evidence, she will feel better. There is no reason for her to suddenly start thinking that it is all her fault again and the gains made in treatment will be maintained. In perhaps the longest follow-up period ever assessed in PTSD treatment outcome studies, Resick et al. (2012) re-evaluated research participants who had been randomized to either CPT or PE in the first large scale trial of CPT ever conducted (Resick et al., 2002). Almost all participants were located (88%) and PTSD was re-assessed in 74% of the original sample. On average, these re-assessments took place about 6 years after the conclusion of treatment. Results showed that treatment gains in PTSD and depression were very well-maintained for both CPT and PE participants. These gains were not due to further psychotherapy or medications. It can be concluded from this study (and supported by follow-up analyses form other RCTs) that treatment gains in CPT are long-lasting and there is very little relapse.

Summary

This sentence should read: CPT has been developed, tested, and found to be effective in a number of populations including civilian adolescents and adults, military, and Veterans as well as across different types of trauma exposures including sexual assault, intimate partner violence, war exposures, accidents, and combat. CPT has been rigorously tested in a number of different countries including the United States, Canada, Germany, Iraq, the Democratic Republic of Congo, and Australia, and demonstrates strong effects in each culture. CPT has been administered in group and individual format and there is evidence to suggest that while both are effective, individual treatment may be more successful in treating PTSD symptoms. Chapter 4 will describe treatment gains and outcomes that extend beyond PTSD and depression.

References

Ahrens, J., & Rexford, L. (2002). Cognitive processing therapy for incarcerated adolescents with PTSD. *Journal of Aggression, Maltreatment, and Trauma, 6*, 201–216.

American Psychological Association. (2017). *Clinical practice guideline for the treatment of PTSD*. Available from: http://www.apa.org/ptsd-guideline/ptsd.pdf.

Barlow, D. H. (1996). Health care policy, psychotherapy research, and the future of psychotherapy. *American Psychologist, 51*(10), 1050–1058 Available from: http://dx.doi.org/10.1037/0003-066X.51.10.1050.

Bass, J. K., Annan, J., McIvor Murray, S., Kaysen, D., Griffiths, S., Cetinoglu, T., Wachter, K., Murray, L. K., & Bolton, P. A. (2013). Controlled trial of psychotherapy for Congolese survivors of sexual violence. *New England Journal of Medicine, 368*(23), 2182–2191.

Beutler, L. E. (1998). Identifying empirically supported treatments: what if we didn't? *Journal of Consulting and Clinical Psychology, 66*, 113–120.

Beutler, L. E., & Howard, K. I. (1998). Clinical utility research: an introduction. *Journal of Clinical Psychology, 54*, 297–301.

Bolton, P., Bass, J. K., Zangana, G. A. S., Kamal, T., Murray, S. M., Kaysen, D., Lejuez, C. W., Lindgren, K., Pagoto, S., Murray, L. K., & Van Wyk, S. S. (2014). A randomized controlled trial of mental health interventions for survivors of systematic violence in Kurdistan, Northern Iraq. *BMC Psychiatry, 14*(1), 360.

Bradley, R. B., Greene, J. M. A., Russ, E. B. A., & Dutra, W. D. (2005). A multi-dimensional meta-analysis of psychotherapy for PTSD. *American Journal of Psychiatry, 162*, 214–227.

Butollo, W., Karl, R., Konig, J., & Rosner, R. (2016). A randomized controlled clinical trial of dialogical exposure therapy versus cognitive processing therapy for adult outpatients suffering from PTSD after type I trauma in adulthood. *Psychother Psychosom, 85*, 16–26. doi: 10.1159/000440726.

Chambless, D. L., & Hollon, S. D. (1998). Defining empirically supported therapies. *Journal of Consulting and Clinical Psychology, 66*, 7–18.

Chard, K. M. (2005). An evaluation of cognitive processing therapy for the treatment of posttraumatic stress disorder related to childhood sexual abuse. *Journal of Consulting and Clinical Psychology, 73*(5), 965–971.

Foa, E. B., Hembree, E. A., & Rothbaum, B. O. (2007). Prolonged exposure therapy for PTSD: Emotional Processing of Traumatic Experiences: Therapist guide Oxford University Press. doi:10.1093/med:psych/9780195308501.003.0003.

Forbes, D., Lloyd, D., Nixon, R. D., Elliott, P., Varker, T., Perry, D., …, & Creamer, M. (2012). A multisite randomized controlled effectiveness trial of cognitive processing therapy for military-related posttraumatic stress disorder. *Journal of Anxiety Disorders, 26*(3), 442–452.

Freiheit, S. R., Vye, C., Swan, R., & Cady, M. (2004). Cognitive-behavioral therapy for anxiety: is dissemination working? *The Behavior Therapist, 27*(2), 25–32.

Galovski, T. E., Blain, L. M., Mott, J. M., Elwood, L., & Houle, T. (2012). Manualized therapy for PTSD: Flexing the structure of cognitive processing therapy. *Journal of Consulting and Clinical Psychology, 80*, 968–981.

Galovski, T. E., Harik, J. M., Blain, L. M., Elwood, L., Gloth, C., & Fletcher, T. D. (2016). Augmenting cognitive processing therapy to improve sleep impairment in PTSD: a randomized controlled trial. *Journal of Consulting and Clinical Psychology, 84*, 167–177.

Goldfried, M. R., & Wolfe, B. E. (1998). Toward a more clinically valid approach to therapy research. *Journal of Consulting and Clinical Psychology, 66*, 143–150.

Haagen, J., Smid, G., Knipscheer, J., et al. (2015). The efficacy of recommended treatments for veterans with PTSD: a metaregression analysis. *Clinical Psychology Review, 40*, 184–194.

Jak, A. J., Jurick, S., Crocker, L. D., Sanderson-Cimino, M., Aupperle, R., Rodgers, C. S., …, & Keller, A. V. (2019). SMART-CPT for veterans with comorbid post-traumatic stress disorder and history of traumatic brain injury: a randomised controlled trial. *Journal of Neurology, Neurosurgery, and Psychiatry*, *90*(3), 333–341.

Karlin, B. E., Ruzek, J. I., Chard, K. M., et al. (2010). Dissemination of evidence-based psychological treatments for posttraumatic stress disorder in the Veterans Health Administration. *Journal of Traumatic Stress*, *23*, 663–673.

Kazdin, A. E. (2008). Evidence-based treatment and practice: new opportunities to bridge clinical research and practice, enhance the knowledge base, and improve patient care. *American Psychologist*, *63*(3), 146–159.

Kozel, et al. (2018). Repetitive TMS to augment cognitive processing therapy in combat veterans of recent conflicts with PTSD: a randomized clinical trial. *Journal of Affective Disorders*, *229*, 506–514 Available from: http://dx.doi.org/10.1016/j.jad.2017.12.046.

Maieritsch, K. P., Smith, T. L., Hessinger, J. D., Ahearn, E. P., Eickhoff, J. C., & Zhao, Q. (2016). Randomized controlled equivalence trial comparing videoconference and in person delivery of cognitive processing therapy for PTSD. *Journal of Telemedicine and Telecare*, *22*, 238–243.

Maxwell, K., Callahan, J. L., Holtz, P., Janis, B. M., Gerber, M. M., & Connor, D. R. (2016). Comparative study of group treatments for posttraumatic stress disorder. *Psychotherapy*, *53*(4), 433.

Monson, C. M., Schnurr, P. P., Resick, P. A., Friedman, M. J., Young-Xu, Y., & Stevens, S. P. (2006). Cognitive processing therapy for veterans with military-related posttraumatic stress disorder. *Journal of Consulting and Clinical Psychology*, *74*(5), 898–907.

Morland, L. A., Mackintosh, M. A., Greene, C. J., Rosen, C., Chard, K., Resick, P., …, & Frueh, B. C. (2014). Cognitive processing therapy for posttraumatic stress disorder delivered to rural veterans via telemental health: a randomized noninferiority clinical trial. *Journal of Clinical Psychiatry*, *75*(5), 470–476. doi: 10.4088/JCP.13m08842.

Morland, L. A., Mackintosh, M., Rosen, C. S., Willis, E., Resick, P., Chard, K., …, & Frueh, B. C. (2015). Telemedicine vs. in-person delivery of cognitive processing therapy for women with posttraumatic stress disorder: a randomized non-inferiority trial. *Depression and Anxiety*, *32*, 811–820. doi: 10.1002/da.22397.

Murray, L. K., Dorsey, S., Bolton, P., Jordans, M. J., Rahman, A., Bass, J., & Verdeli, H. (2011). Building capacity in mental health interventions in low resource countries: an apprenticeship model for training local providers. *International Journal of Mental Health Systems*, *5*(1), 5–30.

Nixon, R. D. (2012). Cognitive processing therapy versus supportive counseling for acute stress disorder following assault: a randomized pilot trial. *Behavior Therapy*, *43*(4), 825–836.

Pearson, C. R., Smartlowit-Briggs, L., Belcourt, A., Bedard-Gilligan, M., & Kaysen, D. (2019). Building a tribal–academic partnership to address PTSD, substance misuse, and HIV among American Indian women. *Health Promotion Practice*, *20*(1), 48–56.

Persons, J. P., & Silberschatz, G. (1998). Are results of randomized controlled clinical trials useful to clinicians? *Journal of Consulting and Clinical Psychology*, *66*, 126–135.

Resick, P. A., Nishith, P., Weaver, T. L., Astin, M. C., & Feuer, C. A. (2002). A comparison of cognitive processing therapy, prolonged exposure and a waiting condition for the treatment of posttraumatic stress disorder in female rape victims. *Journal of Consulting and Clinical Psychology*, *70*, 867–879.

Resick, P. A., Galovski, T. E., Uhlmansiek, M. O., Scher, C. D., Clum, G. A., & Young-Xu, Y. (2008). A randomized clinical trial to dismantle components of cognitive processing therapy for posttraumatic stress disorder in female victims of interpersonal violence. *Journal of Consulting and Clinical Psychology*, *76*, 243–258.

Resick, P. A., Williams, L. F., Suvak, M. K., Monson, C. M., & Gradus, J. L. (2012). Long-term outcomes of cognitive–behavioral treatments for posttraumatic stress disorder among female rape survivors. *Journal of Consulting and Clinical Psychology, 80*(2), 201–210. doi: 10.1037/a0026602.

Resick, P. A., Wachen, J. S., Mintz, J., Young-McCaughan, S., Roache, J. D., Borah, A. M., …, Borah, E. V., Dondanville, K. A., Hembree, E. A., Litz, B. T., Peterson, A. L., & On behalf of the STRONG STAR Consortium (2015). A randomized clinical trial of group cognitive processing therapy compared with group present-centered therapy for PTSD among active duty military personnel. *Journal of Consulting and Clinical Psychology, 83*, 1058–1068 Available from: http://dx.doi.org/10.1037/ccp0000016.

Resick, P. A., Wachen, J. S., Dondanville, K. A., Pruiksma, K. E., Yarvis, J. S., Mintz, J., …, Peterson, A. L., & the STRONG STAR Consortium (2017). Effect of group vs. individual Cognitive Processing Therapy in active-duty military seeking treatment for posttraumatic stress disorder: A randomized clinical trial. *JAMA Psychiatry, 74*(1), 28–36 Available from: http://dx.doi.org/10.1001/jamapsychiatry.2016.2729.

Schottenbauer, M. A., Glass, C. R., Arnkoff, D., Tendick, V., & Hafter Gray, S. (2008). Nonresponse and dropout rates in outcome studies on PTSD: review and methodological considerations. *Psychiatry: Interpersonal and Biological Processes, 71*, 134–168 Available from: https://doi.org/10.1521/psyc.2008.71.2.134.

Shadish, W. R., Matt, G. E., Navarro, A. M., Siegle, G., Crits-Christoph, P., Hazelrigg, M. D., …, & Weiss, B. (1997). Evidence that therapy works in clinically representative conditions. *Journal of Consulting and Clinical Psychology, 65*(3), 355–365 Available from: http://dx.doi.org/10.1037/0022-006X.65.3.355.

Sloan, D. M., Marx, B. P., Lee, D. J., & Resick, P. A. (2018). A brief exposure-based treatment vs cognitive processing therapy for posttraumatic stress disorder: a randomized noninferiority clinical trial. *JAMA Psychiatry, 75*(3), 233–239. doi: 10.1001/jamapsychiatry.2017.4249.

Suris, A., Link-Malcolm, J., Chard, K., Ahn, C., & North, C. (2013). A randomized clinical trial of cognitive processing therapy for veterans with ptsd related to military sexual trauma. *Journal of Traumatic Stress, 26*(1), 28–37.

U.S. Department of Veteran Affairs and Department of Defense. (2017). *VA/DOD clinical practice guidelines for the management of posttraumatic stress disorder and acute stress disorder.* Available from: https://www.healthquality.va.gov/guidelines/MH/ptsd/VADoDPTSDCPGFinal012418.pdf.

Watts, B. V., Schnurr, P. P., Mayo, L., Young-Xu, Y., Weeks, W. B., & Friedman, M. J. (2013). Meta-analysis of the efficacy of treatments for posttraumatic stress disorder. *Journal of Clinical Psychiatry, 74*, 541–550.

Weiss, W. M., Murray, L. K., Zangana, G. A. S., Mahmooth, Z., Kaysen, D., Dorsey, S., …, & Bolton, P. (2015). Community-based mental health treatments for survivors of torture and militant attacks in Southern Iraq: a randomized control trial. *BMC Psychiatry, 15*(1), 249.

Chapter 4

Emerging as an effective therapy: CPT is put to the test

Chapter outline

In the previous chapter, we reviewed the evidence-base for CPT derived from randomized clinical trials (RCTs). Clearly these types of studies are important to establish the efficacy of a treatment, that is, does this therapy work? In this chapter, we discuss findings from non-controlled trials and related studies that speak more to the *effectiveness* of CPT, that is, how does CPT perform in the "real world"? It is important to note that efficacy/effectiveness is not a dichotomy. We can have high quality randomized studies that examine how well a treatment performs in front-line mental health settings when delivered by the service's clinicians. A multitude of CPT studies have done that, albeit with varying levels of supervisory support (LoSavio, Dillon, et al., 2019; Monson et al., 2018; Nixon et al., 2016). We particularly focus on studies that might have had less methodological rigor in terms of whether diagnostic outcomes were independently verified or treatment quality checked, and in the degree of supervisory support provided. These types of effectiveness (or "real world") studies can be particularly informative for clinicians because the CPT was delivered as part of routine care with patients who are representative of a clinician's typical caseload. This chapter also focuses on outcomes beyond PTSD and depression, as this also reflects the reality of many "real world" clinical settings. For example, effectiveness studies typically have patients with multiple comorbidities, chaotic lives, and ongoing stressors, who may struggle with

Flexible Applications of Cognitive Processing Therapy. http://dx.doi.org/10.1016/B978-0-12-816715-1.00004-2

medication changes, and show varying levels of motivation to seek help. An additional and important component of effectiveness studies is that they tell us useful information about the more diffuse effects of CPT on important clinical issues that accompany PTSD which are not always measured or initially reported in RCTs. These studies are important in demonstrating that receiving CPT improves patient's health outcomes, reduces their use of physical and mental health services, can lead to positive changes in sexual behavior, and even reduce the risk of later interpersonal violence. Although covered in more detail in later chapters, we will also see the wide range of patient types and settings in which CPT has been used successfully.

CPT is effective across a myriad of settings and diverse patient groups

The broad reach of CPT will be apparent throughout the various chapters and it is not our intention here to review every study or project that has been conducted; rather, we aim to give a snapshot of the clinical utility of CPT. As discussed in the previous chapter, the first randomized trials of CPT were conducted with women from the community who had experienced interpersonal assault. Similarly, CPT has continued to show positive effects in community samples including those with serious mental illness as part of jail diversion programs (Feingold, Fox, & Galovski, 2018), and those seeking help through public and private mental health services (LoSavio, Dillon, et al., 2019; Pearson, Kaysen, Huh, & Bedard-Gilligan, 2019) and delivered via telehealth in primary care settings (Fortney et al., 2015). Although CPT was created for use with adults, it has been used in group format for adolescents incarcerated in a correctional youth facility who had experienced a range of traumas (Ahrens & Rexford, 2002) and a modified version which included emotional regulation skills (among others) has been successfully delivered to youth with PTSD secondary to physical or sexual abuse in Germany (Matulis, Resick, Rosner, & Steil, 2014; Rosner et al., 2019). More recently, CPT has been used for youth in community mental health settings in the United States (Losavio, Murphy, & Resick, 2019), with a similar rollout about to start in Australia by one of the authors (RN).

There has been an explosion in the delivery of CPT to Veteran and active duty military populations in recent years, primarily in the United States. CPT has been seen to be effective in outpatient settings for both active duty (Aronson et al., 2018) and Veteran patients (Dickstein, Walter, Schumm, & Chard, 2013) or mixtures of both (Monson et al., 2018). Improvements are also seen in those being treated in inpatient or residential settings, typically in group or combined group/individual formats (Alvarez et al., 2011 Hale, Rodriguez, Wright, Driesenga, & Spates, 2018; Graca, Palmer, & Occhietti, 2014; Walter, Dickstein, Barnes, & Chard, 2014).

In the above studies, it is important to remember that clinical gains in PTSD are being achieved in the context of multiple comorbidities and other challenges. For example, therapists in Feingold et al. had to navigate issues such as homelessness in their patients, and over 20% of the patients seen in Monson et al. had comorbid personality disorder. Physical and psychological comorbidities are the norm in most samples, especially Veteran patients in these studies.

Why do patients get better?

When people show up for treatment, sometimes their goal is to treat their primary PTSD symptoms such as nightmares and hyperarousal, but just as often it is for broader change in their lives—"I want my relationship with my wife to be better." "I'm scared I'm going to lose my job." "I'm in so much pain." Although treating the PTSD helps someone reach those goals, it is helpful to see how CPT performs in addressing these broader concerns. A goal of this chapter is to present an overview of the broad impacts CPT can result in, beyond the reduction of primary PTSD symptoms. Before discussing the impact of CPT on major domains of functioning, it is worth talking about one of the chief mechanisms that is hypothesized to underlie PTSD recovery. As discussed in earlier chapters, at its heart, CPT is founded on the proposal that unhelpful beliefs and interpretations of one's trauma, self and the world maintains PTSD, hence the strong focus on patient's stuck points during therapy. Does CPT actually change these? We certainly know that CPT results in PTSD symptom reduction (and often remission of PTSD altogether), but it would be useful to know that one of the key mechanisms of the problem also changes; otherwise, we should be worried about the potential of relapse. In other words, if beliefs that are keeping people stuck in PTSD (stuck points) are not identified and altered, then symptoms might temporarily reduce, but the underlying cognitions simmer away and PTSD does not remit.

We have substantial evidence that the efforts of our patients in completing worksheets (and the time we spend as therapists in Socratic dialogue) pay off. We see this when we use self-report questionnaires measuring unhelpful traumatic beliefs that show significant reductions following treatment (Holliday et al., 2014; Owens, Pike, & Chard, 2001) as well as when patients' Impact Statements at the beginning and end of therapy have been coded independently (Price, MacDonald, Adair, Koerner, & Monson, 2016; Sobel, Resick, & Rabalais, 2009). CPT also results in changes in beliefs about the dangerousness of experiencing anxiety (i.e., anxiety sensitivity; Gutner, Nillni, Suvak, Wiltsey-Stirman, & Resick, 2013). Importantly, changes in beliefs predict later outcome (Gobin et al., 2018), and when the time course of changes in beliefs and symptoms has been examined during therapy, we see that reductions in self-blame and negative self-beliefs precede improvements in PTSD symptoms (Schumm, Dickstein, Walter, Owens, & Chard, 2015; Zalta et al., 2018). The importance of cognitive change for long-term recovery has also been demonstrated. Although these data are derived from a well-controlled RCT study and have yet to be studied in routine treatment settings, data from self-reports

(Scher, Suvak, & Resick, 2017) and coded impact statements (Iverson, King, Cunningham, & Resick, 2015) showed that adaptive and maladaptive changes were respectively associated with PTSD severity 5–10 years after therapy completion. For example, those patients who continued to improve accommodated thinking showed lower PTSD and depression at follow-up, whereas the opposite was seen if patients regressed in over-accommodated thinking. Better outcomes at follow-up were associated with further reductions of negative trauma-related beliefs.

Although it should be obvious, the findings above really show the importance of identifying, unpacking, and ultimately resolving patients' stuck points. Patients also tell us how critical this is, whether it be through changes we see in Impact Statements, or in qualitative interviews when we ask them what *they* think are the contributors to their recovery (Hundt, Barrera, Arney, & Stanley, 2017).

Case example: Let's think about Anna, who has dropped out of therapy previously. The short case history highlights several possible stuck points that might contribute to her current PTSD (e.g., self-blame around her fellow soldier's death, beliefs about not being able to cope with trauma memories, leading to self-medication with alcohol). It is likely that exploring reasons for her difficulty in engaging in therapy will be equally important. For example, negative expectancies of treatment success (*I'm too damaged to get better*) could be getting in the way. Shifts in these and related beliefs are the engine for driving symptom changes in CPT.

PTSD is not the only domain that improves after CPT

Although reducing the severity of PTSD symptoms is certainly an important goal of CPT therapists and something that patients are seeking when they come to us, PTSD seeps into many areas of our patients' lives, impacting their day-to-day functioning and relationships. When we treat PTSD, we also have an opportunity to positively impact these domains. We now briefly report on the wide range of other important areas that seem to benefit from CPT, and in later chapters, talk about strategies that could be used when impairment in these other domains seem to interfere with a patient's recovery or delivery of CPT.

Improvements on general well-being and interpersonal relationships

Those with PTSD frequently report lower quality of life relative to those without PTSD, and this impacts a range of domains including work and family contexts (Galovski, Sobel, Phipps, & Resnick, 2005; Vogt et al., 2017). Addressing PTSD symptoms typically has the effect of improving our patients lives in general, and this is certainly demonstrated by a number of findings from effectiveness studies. Accordingly, patients who have undertaken CPT report significant improvements in social functioning whether this is improved quality of relationships or increased participation in community activities (Forbes et al., 2012; Hall et al., 2014; Holliday, Williams, Bird, Mullen, & Surís, 2015; Schumm, Gore, Chard, & Meyer, 2017). We would also highlight what is likely an important bi-directional relationship in terms of social support, especially support derived from significant others. Good support on this front is also associated with patients being more likely to complete CPT (Meis et al., 2019) and has been associated with greater reduction of PTSD severity in trauma-focused treatments (Shnaider, Sijercic, Wanklyn, Suvak, & Monson, 2017). We'll return to this issue later when discussing the cases of Anna, Steve, and Julie, given they have different levels of support, which could impact their progression throughout the treatment. Finally, we would note that we need more research on the functional impacts of CPT in routine settings. To date, most of the positive outcomes of CPT on these domains still come from randomized trials outside of routine care practices (Bass et al., 2013; Bosch et al., 2019; Galovski et al., 2005; Galovski, Blain, Mott, Elwood, & Houle, 2012; Monson et al., 2012; Shnaider et al., 2014; Wachen, Jimenez, Smith, & Resick, 2014). Despite this, the findings above are relevant when we consider the case of Julie, who is particularly isolated socially. On the positive side, we can be optimistic that successfully treating her PTSD may very well help her increase her social networks and/or improve relationships with others. However, we need to be mindful that her low level of support presently places her at risk for poor engagement in the therapeutic process. We will discuss how we might address this in subsequent chapters.

Dissociation

We sometimes find that therapists are concerned that due to a patient's dissociative tendencies they are not ready or will not benefit from CPT, although therapists trained in therapies such as CPT tend not to endorse this concern (Raza & Holohan, 2015). We address how to manage this clinically in later chapters, but we do know that CPT can reduce dissociative experiences in patients. This has been observed in adolescents who had experienced childhood abuse where reductions in dissociative severity following therapy were substantial (Matulis et al., 2014). Indeed, for those interested in quantifying such changes, the effect size of this reduction was $d = 0.74$ (pre-post). We see significant reductions in dissociation in adult patients who have participated in clinical trials (Chard, 2005; Galovski, Blain, Chappuis & Fletcher, 2013), and one study found that patients who were considered "high dissociators" appeared to benefit most from CPT when they wrote a trauma account as part of therapy relative to those who only received the cognitive therapy component of CPT (Resick et al., 2012). We see dissociation can improve in those who have had non-interpersonal trauma. For example, one of us (TG) treated a professional truck driver who experienced significant dissociation following a severe MVA, which resolved as his PTSD was addressed (Galovski & Resick, 2008). Although based on one study, more rapid improvements in dissociation were observed in women relative to men, although this difference decreased if successful treatment completers were examined (Galovski et al., 2013).

Health and somatic complaints

Those with PTSD tend to have more health concerns than non-PTSD or trauma-exposed individuals (King, 2019). Although largely based on self-report, we see in both civilian and Veteran samples that CPT results in significant improvements in patients' physical health and reduced interference from health issues on day to day functioning (Holliday et al., 2015). These changes are also observed when measures of disability have been used (Schumm et al., 2017). Although limited data exists on other health outcomes, modified CPT with smoking cessation strategies has also been observed to assist smokers with comorbid PTSD to reduce or quit smoking (Dedert et al., 2016). These health findings are consistent with more tightly controlled studies (Galovski, Monson, Bruce, & Resick 2009; Galovski et al., 2012). It is worth noting that physical wellness does not always improve after therapy, including CPT (Forbes et al., 2012) although on some occasions this might be specific to the population under study (e.g., aging Veterans where some physical decline is not unexpected). As discussed in later chapters, attention to health issues, especially chronic pain, is important in PTSD treatment given somatic complaints can attenuate therapy outcomes (Hale et al., 2018). We'll see how pain can be tackled within CPT when we discuss how comorbid conditions can be addressed in the context of treating PTSD.

Sexual functioning

Many of our patients have difficulties with respect to intimacy, especially those who have experienced sexual trauma, and they can be at risk of further revictimization, especially if engaged in risky sexual behaviors. Reductions in sexual risk behaviors following CPT have been observed in Native American women already showing high-risk activity (Pearson et al., 2019), and improved sexual functioning has been seen in women who received CPT following sexual assault (Galovski et al., 2005). Although a number of our patients avoid physical intimacy, sometimes patients might describe the opposite. It is important for the therapist to tease apart whether apparent "hypersexuality" or "promiscuity" is an accurate label or reflects an underlying stuck point in how a patient may label behavior that sits on the normal continuum. There is little published literature on this domain with respect to PTSD but Larsen (2019) reported a case study where hypersexuality was conceptualized as a component of the patient's PTSD, serving as a form of avoidance that enabled him to distract himself from distressing thoughts and emotions. Successful treatment of his main trauma (MST) resulted in reduced PTSD, improved intimacy with his partner, and ceasing extensive use of pornography. Although this domain of functioning requires more research, we have numerous examples of how CPT results in wider functional improvement in terms of relationships, social support, and general quality of life, as summarized throughout this book.

Reducing PTSD reduces suicidal ideation

Ensuring our patients are likely to benefit from therapy and to remain safe while completing therapy is, of course, our greatest priority. Concerns that trauma focused therapies may exacerbate problems like suicidality or self-injurious behaviors are not new (Becker, Zayfert, & Anderson, 2004), and they still give many therapists pause when considering whether to offer PTSD treatments (Cook, Dinnen, Thompson, Simiola, & Schnurr, 2014). Fortunately, more and more research indicates that suicidal ideation (SI) *reduces* as a function of CPT. Most of the data come from military and Veteran samples, a population at elevated risk of suicide (Black, Gallaway, Bell, & Ritchie, 2011).

In active duty military, Bryan and colleagues (2016) reported that for those who had SI at the beginning of treatment, this significantly decreased after treatment and remained improved at 12-month follow-up. Exacerbation of SI during treatment occurred for 1 of the 11 members with pre-existing SI, and none over the follow up period, in contrast to 3 of 8 members in a nontrauma focused therapy who showed exacerbation. The study also found relatively low levels of new onset SI, which did not differ between CPT and the nontrauma-focused therapy, and importantly no patients attempted suicide throughout the study period. In a small study, reductions in SI severity were observed when Veterans were treated with intensive CPT (delivered over 2 weeks) (Bryan et al., 2018). This is a promising finding given potential concerns that intensive treatments might not be well tolerated, concerns not supported by this study nor other studies on intensive cognitive therapy approaches for PTSD (Ehlers et al., 2014). It is worth noting the Bryan study was conducted outside of a traditional inpatient setting. In a civilian sample of female sexual assault survivors, there were significant reductions in SI that were associated with reductions in PTSD, and these improvements were maintained when women were followed-up 5–10 years later (Gradus, Suvak, Wisco, Marx, & Resick, 2013). These improvements were slightly larger for CPT than the comparison therapy (PE in this case), which the authors postulated may have been due to the strong cognitive focus of CPT that addresses cognitions likely to contribute to hopelessness and suicidality (e.g., self-blame).

Relevant to our clinical work, this does raise the issue as to what aspects of therapy might be the important ingredient for reducing such ideation. Some of the findings suggest there may be sample-specific elements; for example, reduction in SI in an active duty military sample was driven more by reductions in depression symptoms than PTSD (Bryan et al., 2016) whereas reductions in PTSD seemed to drive this change in civilian sexual assault and Veteran samples, respectively (Gradus et al., 2013; Horwitz, Miron, & Maieritsch, 2019). Although they did not have the sample size to examine these variables as a possible mechanism of action, Holliday and colleagues observed that suicide-specific beliefs that might increase an individual's vulnerability to suicide (e.g., the belief that suicide is the only way to solve one's problems) significantly decreased following CPT in survivors of MST (Holliday, Holder, Monteith, & Surís, 2018). Another clinically relevant point was that in the only CPT study to date to examine symptom cluster changes and associated impacts on SI, Horwitz et al. (2019) found that while the symptom of self-blame was more strongly correlated with SI prior to treatment in Veterans, it was the detachment symptom that was most related to SI at posttreatment. Coupled with the finding of Bryan et al. who saw depression symptoms as a driver of SI in their military sample, this suggests that, as clinicians, we should be mindful of unresolved depression at the end of treatment, especially in the context of active SI. Although in general these studies show CPT can be safely used with many of our patients, we acknowledge that these findings are predominately focused on SI and not actual attempts or severe nonsuicidal self-injury. This makes clinical sense, given current clinical guidelines indicate treatments such as CPT are for those who do not have *active* suicidal *intent*. That said, the studies show that CPT is not associated with increased adverse events such as self-harm or suicide attempts, despite many of the patients in these studies having such histories.

CPT in the context of violence

Clinicians frequently ask about whether one can provide CPT in a context where there is ongoing violence, or a lack of safety. Although we do not have studies yet looking at the safety and effectiveness of providing CPT while individuals are in relationships with ongoing familial violence and whether those patients' outcomes differ from those in safer environments, we do have some studies that may help guide us. A small pilot feasibility study was conducted looking at a modified CPT treatment delivered to Congolese women exposed to ongoing intimate partner violence while in a refugee camp in Tanzania (Greene et al., 2019). The project did not report on clinical outcomes but found that CPT was well tolerated and that there were no adverse events associated with participating. Generally, the participants reported feeling safe receiving CPT, with only 1 reporting concerns that if her husband knew of her participation it would be a problem for her. CPT may also reduce the risk of re-victimization. Pooling the results of women who had received variants of CPT, Iverson et al. (2011) found that the greater the reduction in PTSD and depression during treatment, the less likely patients were to experience physical violence from partners in the subsequent 6-months following therapy. We have further insights when we look at the studies providing CPT in conflict settings. In a reanalysis of CPT provided to sexual assault survivors in the Democratic Republic of Congo (Kaysen et al., 2019), the communities were divided into groups based on the level of active violence in the immediate vicinity to look at whether CPT could be provided in a setting where there is active conflict. The access that armed groups had to these communities caused frequent displacement of community members. All sites reported at least one incident of violence during the intervention period, ranging from site-wide attacks and looting to kidnapping and attacks by armed groups on specific individuals leading to injury or death. Residing in a site with greater conflict was associated with higher symptoms but women had similar improvement over time as those living in sites that were more stable.

Anger, a symptom of PTSD, can present a clinical challenge. Dealing with patients' anger can be challenging for clinicians, although it is important to note that not all anger is dysregulated and that anger is different from aggression. We do have studies demonstrating that anger can improve as a result of CPT; however, we do not have data yet on reductions in aggressive behavior. Data from the Iverson study mentioned above showed that anger also significantly reduced following treatment (Resick et al., 2008), although this was restricted to a subscale that indexed suppressed anger, not outwardly expressed anger. As noted by the authors, outward anger was not particularly high at baseline. In contrast, significant reductions in outward anger have been reported following CPT in Veterans (Forbes et al., 2012) and civilians (Galovski et al., 2013) although the latter found women showed greater reductions than men. Clinically it is useful to note that higher pretreatment anger attenuated CPT outcomes in the Forbes sample (Lloyd et al., 2014), a finding seen in an earlier study of Veterans receiving CPT in a residential setting (Owens, Chard, & Cox, 2008). Although the mechanisms underlying this finding were not tested, an interesting finding, also with a Veteran sample, is that of Miles and colleagues. They found that pretreatment *fear* of the experience of anger was associated with *less* severe PTSD following CPT (Miles, Smith, Maieritsch, & Aheran, 2015). Although not tested directly, we would postulate that addressing stuck points about losing control and fear of emotions, typically elements of therapeutic discussions within CPT, might have contributed to this finding. In contrast to Lloyd et al. is the observation that higher levels of antisocial personality traits as measured with a personality measure were associated with greater reductions in PTSD symptoms in a Veteran sample (Hale et al., 2018). Whether the different treatment contexts (outpatient versus residential) or measures (an explicit anger measure versus a personality measure) or other variables account for this discrepancy is unclear. In sum, findings are accumulating that diverse aspects of safety can be improved as a result of CPT.

Case example: A feature of Steve's presentation is anger and associated outbursts. A reasonable concern is that this could escalate, leading to further impairment in his work setting and relationships. Coupled with challenges in emotional regulation (e.g., his dissociation in session) and ongoing pain, there is a significant risk of poor treatment response and dropout. However, the findings discussed above indicate that all of these domains (anger, emotional regulation, health) can improve substantially with CPT. The therapeutic challenge is knowing how to navigate this during therapy and knowing when (and when not!) to deviate from CPT. We begin to unpack this tricky path in the following chapter.

Summary

The benefits of CPT on improving PTSD outcomes is well established across different samples, delivery methods, and settings. This chapter has expanded on earlier chapters to illustrate that these findings are replicated beyond more tightly controlled randomized studies to studies conducted in a range of contexts that we believe captures the experience of most therapists who work with PTSD. That is, whether this be in sole private practice, general community mental health, or specialized settings where patients with PTSD patients are the norm. More importantly, we have shown that CPT, a treatment originally designed to specifically treat PTSD, can have wide ranging impacts on functioning beyond PTSD. Many of our patients will notice significantly improved functioning in their interpersonal relationships and broader social network. Patients' health concerns can significantly decrease. Aspects of problematic emotional regulation and distress including dissociation, suicidal ideation and anger can also show meaningful change. Although not the panacea for PTSD, for a protocol not designed to directly address comorbid issues such as these, CPT strikes us as having a great deal of versatility for the many associated problems that accompany PTSD. In the next chapter, we take off the rose-tinted glasses, and begin to outline some of the strategies we suggest when CPT is not going as planned.

References

Ahrens, J., & Rexford, L. (2002). Cognitive processing therapy for incarcerated adolescents with PTSD. *Journal of Aggression, Maltreatment & Trauma*, *6*, 201–216. doi: 10.1300/J146v06n01_10.

Alvarez, J., McLean, C., Harris, A. H., Rosen, C. S., Ruzek, J. I., & Kimerling, R. (2011). The comparative effectiveness of cognitive processing therapy for male veterans treated in a VHA posttraumatic stress disorder residential rehabilitation program. *Journal of Consulting and Clinical Psychology*, *79*, 590–599. doi: 10.1037/a0024466.

Aronson, K. R., Welsh, J. A., Fedotova, A., Morgan, N. R., Perkins, D. F., & Travis, W. (2018). Treating PTSD in active duty service members using cognitive processing therapy or prolonged exposure therapy: examining everyday practice at a military outpatient clinic. *Military Psychology*, *30*, 465–475. doi: 10.1080/08995605.2018.1478550.

Bass, J. K., Annan, J., McIvor Murray, S., Kaysen, D., Griffiths, S., Cetinoglu, T., …, & Bolton, P. A. (2013). Controlled trial of psychotherapy for Congolese survivors of sexual violence. *New England Journal of Medicine*, *368*, 2182–2191. doi: 10.1056/NEJMoa1211853.

Becker, C. B., Zayfert, C., & Anderson, E. (2004). A survey of psychologists' attitudes towards and utilization of exposure therapy for PTSD. *Behaviour Research and Therapy*, *42*, 277–292. doi: 10.1016/S0005-7967(03)00138-4.

Black, S. A., Gallaway, M. S., Bell, R., & Ritchie, E. C. (2011). Prevalence and risk factors associated with suicides of army soldiers 2001-2009. *Military Psychology*, *23*, 433–451, 10.1.

Bosch, J., Mackintosh, M. -A., Wells, S. Y., Wickramasinghe, I., Glassman, L. H., & Morland, L. A. (2019). PTSD treatment response and quality of life in women with childhood trauma histories. Psychological Trauma: Theory, Research, Practice, and Policy. Advance online publication. doi: 10.1037/tra0000468.

Bryan, C. J., Clemans, T. A., Hernandez, A. M., Mintz, J., Peterson, A. L., Yarvis, J. S., & … STRONG STAR Consortium. (2016). Evaluating potential iatrogenic suicide risk in trauma-focused group cognitive behavioral therapy for the treatment of PTSD in active duty military personnel. *Depression and Anxiety*, *33*, 549–557. doi: 10.1002/da.22456.

Chard, K. M. (2005). An evaluation of cognitive processing therapy for the treatment of posttraumatic stress disorder related to childhood sexual abuse. *Journal of Consulting and Clinical Psychology*, *73*, 965–971. doi: 10.1037/0022-006X/73.5.965.

Cook, J. M., Dinnen, S., Simiola, V., Thompson, R., & Schnurr, P. P. (2014). VA residential provider perceptions of dissuading factors to the use of two evidence-based PTSD treatments. *Professional Psychology: Research and Practice*, *45*, 136–142. doi: 10.1037/a0036183136.

Dedert, E. A., Resick, P. A., McFall, M. E., Dennis, P. A., Olsen, M., & Beckham, J. C. (2016). Pilot cases of combined cognitive processing therapy and smoking cessation for smokers with posttraumatic stress disorder. *Behavior Therapy*, *47*, 54–65. doi: 10.1016/j.beth.2015.09.002.

Dickstein, B. D., Walter, K. H., Schumm, J. A., & Chard, K. M. (2013). Comparing response to cognitive processing therapy in military veterans with subthreshold and threshold posttraumatic stress disorder. *Journal of Traumatic Stress*, *26*, 703–709, 0.1002/jts.21869.

Ehlers, A., Hackmann, A., Grey, N., Wild, J., Liness, S., Albert, I., …, & Clark, D. M. (2014). A randomized controlled trial of 7-day intensive and standard weekly cognitive therapy for PTSD and emotion-focused supportive therapy. *American Journal of Psychiatry*, *171*, 294–304. doi: 10.1176/appi.ajp.2013.13040552.

Feingold, Z. R., Fox, A. B., & Galovski, T. E. (2018). Effectiveness of evidence-based psychotherapy for posttraumatic distress within a jail diversion program. *Psychological Services*, *15*, 409–418. doi: 10.1037/ser0000194.

Forbes, D., Lloyd, D., Nixon, R. D. V., Elliott, P., Varker, T., Perry, D., ..., & Creamer, M. (2012). A multisite randomized controlled effectiveness trial of cognitive processing therapy for military-related posttraumatic stress disorder. *Journal of Anxiety Disorders*, *26*, 442–452. doi: 10.1016/j.janxdis.2012.01.006.

Fortney, J. C., Pyne, J. M., Kimbrell, T. A., Hudson, T. J., Robinson, D. E., Schneider, R., …, & Schnurr, P. P. (2015). Telemedicine-based collaborative care for posttraumatic stress disorder: a randomized clinical trial. *JAMA Psychiatry*, *72*, 58–67. doi: 10.1001/jamapsychiatry.2014.1575.

Galovski, T. E., & Resick, P. A. (2008). Cognitive processing therapy for posttraumatic stress disorder secondary to a motor vehicle accident: a single-subject report. *Cognitive and Behavioral Practice*, *15*, 287–295, 1077-7229/08/287-295$1.00/0.

Galovski, T. E., Blain, L. M., Chappuis, C., & Fletcher, T. (2013). Sex differences in recovery from PTSD in male and female interpersonal assault survivors. *Behaviour research and therapy*, *51*, 247–255. doi: 10.1016/j.brat.2013.02.002.

Galovski, T. E., Blain, L. M., Mott, J. M., Elwood, L., & Houle, T. (2012). Manualized therapy for PTSD: Flexing the structure of cognitive processing therapy. *Journal of Consulting and Clinical Psychology*, *80*, 968–981. doi: 10.1037/a0030600968.

Galovski, T. E., Monson, C., Bruce, S. E., & Resick, P. A. (2009). Does cognitive–behavioral therapy for PTSD improve perceived health and sleep impairment? *Journal of Traumatic Stress: Official Publication of The International Society for Traumatic Stress Studies*, *22*, 197–204. doi: 10.1002/jts.20418.

Galovski, T. E., Sobel, A. A., Phipps, K. A., & Resick, P. A. (2005). Trauma recovery: beyond posttraumatic stress disorder and other axis I symptom severity. In T. A. Corales (Ed.), *Trends in posttraumatic stress disorder research* (pp. 207–227). Hauppauge, NY, US: Nova Science Publishers.

Gobin, R. L., Mackintosh, M. A., Willis, E., Allard, C. B., Kloezeman, K., & Morland, L. A. (2018). Predictors of differential PTSD treatment outcomes between veteran and civilian women after cognitive processing therapy. *Psychological Trauma: Theory, Research, Practice, and Policy, 10*, 173–182. doi: 10.1037/tra0000266173.

Graca, J. J., Palmer, G. A., & Occhietti, K. E. (2014). Psychotherapeutic interventions for symptom reduction in veterans with PTSD: An observational study in a residential clinical setting. *Journal of Loss and Trauma, 19*, 558–567. doi: 10.1080/15325024.2013.810441.

Gradus, J. L., Suvak, M. K., Wisco, B. E., Marx, B. P., & Resick, P. A. (2013). Treatment of posttraumatic stress disorder reduces suicidal ideation. *Depression and Anxiety, 30*, 1046–1053. doi: 10.1002/da.22117.

Greene, M.C., Rees, S., Likindikoki, S., Bonz, A.G., Joscelyne, A., Kaysen, D., ..., & Tol, W.A. (2019). Developing an integrated intervention to address intimate partner violence and psychological distress in Congolese refugee women in Tanzania. Conflict and Health, 13(1), 38. doi: 10.1186/s13031-019-0222-0

Gutner, C. A., Nillni, Y. I., Suvak, M., Wiltsey-Stirman, S., & Resick, P. A. (2013). Longitudinal course of anxiety sensitivity and PTSD symptoms in cognitive-behavioral therapies for PTSD. *Journal of Anxiety Disorders, 27*, 728–734. doi: 10.1016/j.janxdis.2013.09.010.

Hale, A. C., Rodriguez, J. L., Wright, T. P., Driesenga, S. A., & Spates, C. R. (2018). Predictors of change in cognitive processing therapy for veterans in a residential PTSD treatment program. *Journal of Clinical Psychology, 75*, 364–379. doi.org/10.1002/jclp.22711.

Hall, B. J., Bolton, P. A., Annan, J., Kaysen, D., Robinette, K., Cetinoglu, T., ..., & Bass, J. K. (2014). The effect of cognitive therapy on structural social capital: results from a randomized controlled trial among sexual violence survivors in the Democratic Republic of the Congo. *American Journal of Public Health, 104*, 1680–1686. doi: 10.2105/AJPH.2014.301981.

Holliday, R., Holder, N., Monteith, L. L., & Surís, A. (2018). Decreases in suicide cognitions after cognitive processing therapy among veterans with posttraumatic stress disorder due to military sexual trauma: a preliminary examination. *The Journal of Nervous and Mental Disease, 206*, 575–578. doi: 10.1097/NMD.0000000000000840.

Holliday, R., Link-Malcolm, J., Morris, E. E., & Surís, A. (2014). Effects of cognitive processing therapy on PTSD-related negative cognitions in veterans with military sexual trauma. *Military Medicine, 179*, 1077–1082. doi: 10.7205/MILMED-D-13-00309.

Holliday, R., Williams, R., Bird, J., Mullen, K., & Surís, A. (2015). The role of cognitive processing therapy in improving psychosocial functioning, health, and quality of life in veterans with military sexual trauma-related posttraumatic stress disorder. *Psychological Services, 12*, 428–434. doi: 10.1037/ser0000058428.

Horwitz, A. G., Miron, L., & Maieritsch, K. P. (2019). Prospective associations between DSM–5 PTSD symptom clusters and suicidal ideation in treatment-seeking veterans. *Psychological Services, 16*, 321–328. doi: 10.1037/ser0000215321.

Hundt, N. E., Barrera, T. L., Arney, J., & Stanley, M. A. (2017). It's worth it in the end": veterans' experiences in prolonged exposure and cognitive processing therapy. *Cognitive and Behavioral Practice, 24*, 50–57. doi: 10.1016/j.cbpra.2016.02.003.

Iverson, K. M., Gradus, J. L., Resick, P. A., Suvak, M. K., Smith, K. F., & Monson, C. M. (2011). Cognitive–behavioral therapy for PTSD and depression symptoms reduces risk for future intimate partner violence among interpersonal trauma survivors. *Journal of Consulting and Clinical Psychology, 79*, 193–202. doi: 10.1037/a002251.

Iverson, K. M., King, M. W., Cunningham, K. C., & Resick, P. A. (2015). Rape survivors' trauma-related beliefs before and after cognitive processing therapy: associations with PTSD and depression symptoms. *Behaviour Research and Therapy, 66*, 49–55. doi: 10.1016/j.brat.2015.01.002.

Kaysen, D., Stappenbeck, C.A., Carroll, H., Fukunaga, R., Robinette, K., Dworkin, E.R., ..., & Bass, J. (in press). Impact of setting insecurity on cognitive processing therapy implementation and outcomes in Eastern Democratic Republic of the Congo. European Journal of Psychotraumatology.

King, A. P. (2019). Somatic health issues in trauma-related disorders: effects on psychobiological axes affecting mental and physical health. In *Person Centered Approach to Recovery in Medicine*. Cham: Springer, pp. 177–216.

Larsen, S. E. (2019). Hypersexual behavior as a symptom of PTSD: using cognitive processing therapy in a veteran with military sexual trauma-related PTSD. *Archives of Sexual Behavior, 48*, 987–993. 0.1007/s10508-018-1378-1.

Lloyd, D., Nixon, R. D. V., Varker, T., Elliott, P., Perry, D., Bryant, R. A., …, & Forbes, D. (2014). Comorbidity in the prediction of cognitive processing therapy treatment outcomes for combat-related posttraumatic stress disorder. *Journal of Anxiety Disorders, 28*, 237–240. doi: 10.1016/j.janxdis.2013.12.002.

LoSavio, S. T., Dillon, K. H., Murphy, R. A., Goetz, K., Houston, F., & Resick, P. A. (2019). Using a Learning Collaborative Model to Disseminate Cognitive Processing Therapy to Community-Based Agencies. *Behavior Therapy, 50*, 36–49. doi: 10.1016/j.beth.2018.03.007.

LoSavio, S. T., Murphy, R. A., Patricia A., & Resick, P. A. (2019). Treatment outcomes of adolescents versus adults receiving cognitive processing therapy for posttraumatic stress disorder in the community. Manuscript in preparation.

Matulis, S., Resick, P. A., Rosner, R., & Steil, R. (2014). Developmentally adapted cognitive processing therapy for adolescents suffering from posttraumatic stress disorder after childhood sexual or physical abuse: a pilot study. *Clinical Child and Family Psychology Review, 17*, 173–190. doi: 10.1007/s10567-013-0156-9.

Meis, L. A., Noorbaloochi, S., Hagel Campbell, E. M., Erbes, C. R., Polusny, M. A., Velasquez, T. L., …, & Tuerk, P. W. (2019). Sticking it out in trauma-focused treatment for PTSD: it takes a village. *Journal of Consulting and Clinical Psychology, 87*, 246–256. doi: 10.1037/ccp0000386.

Miles, S. R., Smith, T. L., Maieritsch, K. P., & Ahearn, E. P. (2015). Fear of losing emotional control is associated with cognitive processing therapy outcomes in US veterans of Afghanistan and Iraq. *Journal of Traumatic Stress, 28*, 475–479. doi: 10.1002/jts.22036.

Monson, C. M., Macdonald, A., Vorstenbosch, V., Shnaider, P., Goldstein, E. S., Ferrier-Auerbach, A. G., & Mocciola, K. E. (2012). Changes in social adjustment with cognitive processing therapy: effects of treatment and association with PTSD symptom change. *Journal of Traumatic Stress, 25*, 519–526. doi: 10.1002/jts.2173.

Monson, C. M., Shields, N., Suvak, M. K., Lane, J. E., Shnaider, P., Landy, M. S., …, & Stirman, S. W. (2018). A randomized controlled effectiveness trial of training strategies in cognitive processing therapy for posttraumatic stress disorder: impact on patient outcomes. *Behaviour Research and Therapy, 110*, 31–40. doi: 10.1016/j.brat.2018.08.007.

Nixon, R. D., Best, T., Wilksch, S. R., Angelakis, S., Beatty, L. J., & Weber, N. (2016). Cognitive processing therapy for the treatment of acute stress disorder following sexual assault: a randomised effectiveness study. *Behaviour Change, 33*, 232–250. doi: 10.1017/bec.2017.2.

Owens, G. P., Chard, K. M., & Ann Cox, T. (2008). The relationship between maladaptive cognitions, anger expression, and posttraumatic stress disorder among veterans in residential treatment. *Journal of Aggression, Maltreatment & Trauma, 17*, 439–452. doi: 10.1080/10926770802473908.

Owens, G. P., Pike, J. L., & Chard, K. M. (2001). Treatment effects of cognitive processing therapy on cognitive distortions of female child sexual abuse survivors. *Behavior Therapy, 32*, 413–424. doi: 10.1016/S0005-7894(01)80028-9.

Pearson, C. R., Kaysen, D., Huh, D., & Bedard-Gilligan, M. (2019). Randomized control trial of culturally adapted cognitive processing therapy for PTSD substance misuse and HIV sexual risk behavior for Native American women. *AIDS and Behavior, 23*, 695–706. doi: 10.1007/s10461-018-02382-8.

Price, J. L., MacDonald, H. Z., Adair, K. C., Koerner, N., & Monson, C. M. (2016). Changing beliefs about trauma: a qualitative study of cognitive processing therapy. *Behavioural and Cognitive Psychotherapy, 44*, 156–167. doi: 10.1017/S1352465814000526.

Raza, G. T., & Holohan, D. R. (2015). Clinical treatment selection for posttraumatic stress disorder: suggestions for researchers and clinical trainers. *Psychological Trauma: Theory, Research, Practice, and Policy, 7*, 547–554. doi: 10.1037/tra0000059.

Resick, P. A., Williams, L. F., Suvak, M. K., Monson, C. M., & Gradus, J. L. (2012). Long-term outcomes of cognitive–behavioral treatments for posttraumatic stress disorder among female rape survivors. *Journal of Consulting and Clinical Psychology, 80*, 201–210. doi: 10.1037/a0026602.

Resick, P. A., Galovski, T. E., Uhlmansiek, M. O., Scher, C. D., Clum, G. A., & Young-Xu, Y. (2008). A randomized clinical trial to dismantle components of cognitive processing therapy for posttraumatic stress disorder in female victims of interpersonal violence. *Journal of Consulting and Clinical Psychology, 76*, 243–258. doi: 10.1037/0022-006X.76.2.243.

Rosner, R., Rimane, E., Frick, U., Gutermann, J., Hagl, M., Renneberg, B., …, & Steil, R. (2019). Effect of developmentally adapted cognitive processing therapy for youth with symptoms of posttraumatic stress disorder after childhood sexual and physical abuse: a randomized clinical trial. *JAMA Psychiatry, 76*, 484–491. doi: 10.1001/jamapsychiatry.2018.4349.

Scher, C. D., Suvak, M. K., & Resick, P. A. (2017). Trauma cognitions are related to symptoms up to 10 years after cognitive behavioral treatment for posttraumatic stress disorder. *Psychological Trauma: Theory, Research, Practice, and Policy, 9*, 750–757. doi: 10.1037/tra0000258.

Schumm, J. A., Dickstein, B. D., Walter, K. H., Owens, G. P., & Chard, K. M. (2015). Changes in posttraumatic cognitions predict changes in posttraumatic stress disorder symptoms during cognitive processing therapy. *Journal of Consulting and Clinical Psychology, 83*, 1161–1166. doi: 10.1037/ccp0000040.

Schumm, J. A., Gore, W. L., Chard, K. M., & Meyer, E. C. (2017). Examination of the World Health Organization disability assessment system as a measure of disability severity among veterans receiving cognitive processing therapy. *Journal of Traumatic Stress, 30*, 704–709. doi: 10.1002/jts.22243.

Shnaider, P., Sijercic, I., Wanklyn, S. G., Suvak, M. K., & Monson, C. M. (2017). The role of social support in cognitive-behavioral conjoint therapy for posttraumatic stress disorder. *Behavior Therapy, 48*, 285–294. doi: 10.1016/j.beth.2016.05.003.

Shnaider, P., Vorstenbosch, V., Macdonald, A., Wells, S. Y., Monson, C. M., & Resick, P. A. (2014). Associations between functioning and PTSD symptom clusters in a dismantling trial of cognitive processing therapy in female interpersonal violence survivors. *Journal of Traumatic Stress, 27*, 526–534. doi: 10.1002/jts.21954.

Sobel, A. A., Resick, P. A., & Rabalais, A. E. (2009). The effect of cognitive processing therapy on cognitions: impact statement coding. *Journal of Traumatic Stress, 22*, 205–211. doi: 10.1002/jts.20408.

Vogt, D., Smith, B. N., Fox, A. B., Amoroso, T., Taverna, E., & Schnurr, P. P. (2017). Consequences of PTSD for the work and family quality of life of female and male US Afghanistan and Iraq War veterans. *Social Psychiatry and Psychiatric Epidemiology*, *52*, 341–352. doi: 10.1007/s00127-016-1321-5.

Wachen, J. S., Jimenez, S., Smith, K., & Resick, P. A. (2014). Long-term functional outcomes of women receiving cognitive processing therapy and prolonged exposure. *Psychological Trauma: Theory, Research, Practice, and Policy*, *6*, S58–S65. doi: 10.1037/a0035741.

Walter, K. H., Dickstein, B. D., Barnes, S. M., & Chard, K. M. (2014). Comparing effectiveness of CPT to CPT-C among US veterans in an interdisciplinary residential PTSD/TBI treatment program. *Journal of Traumatic Stress*, *27*, 438–445. doi: 10.1002/jts.21934.

Zalta, A. K., Held, P., Smith, D. L., Klassen, B. J., Lofgreen, A. M., Normand, P. S., …, & Karnik, N. S. (2018). Evaluating patterns and predictors of symptom change during a three-week intensive outpatient treatment for veterans with PTSD. *BMC Psychiatry*, *18*, 242. doi: 10.1186/s12888-018-1816-6.

Part II

Flexible Administrations of the CPT Manual

Chapter 5

Challenges to optimal therapy outcomes

Chapter outline

As discussed in Chapter 2, there are barriers to the integration of evidence-based practices like cognitive processing therapy (CPT) into clinical care. Perhaps one of the most significant barriers is the perception of the rigidity of the therapeutic approach to treating a single disorder. Treatment protocols can be written (and read) as if the intent is to utilize the manual as one would utilize a cookbook. However, there is a lack of precision in psychotherapy that renders a cookbook approach to psychotherapy ineffective. A cookbook, by definition, must be precise. If a recipe calls for two cups of flour and you use only one cup, the end result will be a culinary disaster!

But, that level of precision is not warranted when administering a manualized protocol like CPT. Take, for example, the practice assignments in CPT.

Flexible Applications of Cognitive Processing Therapy. http://dx.doi.org/10.1016/B978-0-12-816715-1.00005-4

The CPT "recipe" calls for a worksheet a day between sessions 9 and 10. Is it a therapeutic disaster if the patient completes six CBWs? One CBW? None? Of course not—the therapy is much more flexible than the concern of a "cookbook approach" to clinical care suggests. In this chapter, we will discuss the typical challenges that arise during the administration of the protocol and provide guidance around the necessary therapist flexibility and creativity that can help navigate these challenges while maintaining fidelity to the protocol and not compromising care.

Walking the fine line between fidelity and flexibility

Despite the substantial accumulation of empirical support for the efficacy of evidence-based interventions designed to treat diagnostically defined clinical needs such as posttraumatic stress disorder (PTSD), single disorder protocols have not been widely adopted by providers in routine clinical care (Rosen et al., 2016). The transportability of these protocols from academic to clinical settings has been challenging for a number of reasons. There are a number of answers to the burning question: *why is the implementation of evidence-based protocols sometimes difficult during the course of clinical care?*

Therapists have historically reacted strongly to the idea that therapy can be manualized, resisting the idea that therapy resembles a cookbook or results in a one-size-fits-all approach to care (see the special issue of the *Journal of Consulting and Clinical Psychology*, 1998, for a review.) No two people are exactly alike and certainly no two patients' experiences and stories are alike. It follows then that psychotherapy must be *personalized* to meet the individual patient's needs. That being said, the format of therapy and the structure of the protocol can certainly be standardized, and, as such, can be evaluated for its effectiveness in treating any given disorder. Chapter 3 provides an excellent overview of the methodologically rigorous studies that have tested and, indeed, improved the CPT protocol over the course of the last 2 decades.

When administering CPT, the therapist must appreciate and consider the entirety of the patient's story and experiences, prioritize targets for intervention that will bring the patient the most relief, and persevere in guiding the therapy to optimal outcomes even when faced with the barriers and obstacles that will inevitably arise. The challenge is accomplishing this feat while maintaining fidelity to the manual, lest one risk compromising the therapy's effectiveness.

The flexibility and fidelity balancing act

Flexibility: Personalizing one's approach to clinical care while maintaining fidelity to the manual is challenging! The reward can be great, but the risks are high. On the one hand, engagement in therapy might increase and the patient might stay in treatment longer if his/her needs are being better met with a more flexible approach (Kehle-Forbes, Meis, Spoont, & Polusny, 2016; Niles et al., 2018). Staying in treatment longer obviously increases the likelihood that the patient will receive an optimal dose of therapy, which, in turn, increases the likelihood that the patient will improve! Likewise, a more flexible approach might intentionally and specifically target a wider breadth and scope of trauma-related outcomes (beyond the 20 core symptoms of PTSD). Thus, a more personalized approach to care that considers the patient's full clinical presentation would theoretically result in more holistic outcomes.

Fidelity: On the other hand, the therapist can overextend the therapeutic goals and essentially take on more than any one intervention can feasibly manage. Broadening the scope of therapy runs the risk of watering down a protocol until it is almost unrecognizable. The trick to maintaining this balance—modifications with the manual—cannot conflict with the core goals of the intervention and the tenets of the theory driving the protocol (Chapter 2) or with the evidence-based cornerstones of the therapy (Chapter 6). The challenge is to administer a protocol that maintains fidelity to the underlying theory and evidence-based cornerstones of the therapy while being flexible enough to accommodate the variety of clinical presentations *and* navigate the universe of possible challenges that will inevitably arise through the course of trauma-focused work. The first step in learning to balance this fine line is to appreciate the therapeutic benefits of continuous assessment.

The clinical value of continuous assessment

The CPT manual stresses the importance of continuous assessment of PTSD (and often depression) symptoms throughout the protocol. How do you, the therapist, know that the patient is improving (or not) if you are not specifically asking the question? One of the best ways to assess progress is through the use of standardized measures. The importance of using standardized instruments coupled with clinical judgment to evaluate patient progress is echoed across the cognitive-behavioral treatment outcome literature, irrespective of what disorder one is treating. We recognize that there are multiple ways to assess progress and that our self-report measures are not infallible, in fact far from it. But measures like the PTSD Checklist (PCL; Weathers et al., 2013) are quite important for keeping tabs on PTSD symptoms, measuring success, as well as providing warning that the therapy is not progressing in the way that we, the therapists, had anticipated.

Utilizing the PCL as a clinical tool

We think about using the PCLs like we would use a thermometer. PCLs help keep tabs on the "temperature of PTSD" as we try to head toward "normal"—or recovery from PTSD. PCLs can also be quite helpful as a clinical tool because they can provide important information about directions to take in therapy. For example, it is important for therapists to know when symptoms are decreasing over the course of therapy. It is critical to know when symptoms are not improving and the PCL provides us that information. Perhaps even more importantly, the PCL can give us clues as to *why* PTSD symptoms are not resolving. Several papers have traced the typical trajectory of PTSD symptom improvement during CPT over time. Some studies have shown that scores have generally trended downward over the course of the CPT protocol in a linear fashion and other studies have shown that scores have hovered for a bit (usually sessions 1–4) before trending down (Galovski et al., 2016; Nishith, Resick, & Griffin, 2002). Taken together, these studies give therapists guidance that (1) we should expect scores to decrease over CPT, and (2) that people differ in terms of their rates and slopes (trajectories) of change.

If scores are not going down or if symptoms appear to be getting worse, the clinician should be asking *WHY?* As discussed in Chapter 2, basic cognitive theory dictates that people can change their minds, particularly about erroneous beliefs that are causing them pain. So, if I am telling myself that the worst thing that ever happened to me is my fault (and this belief is causing me real distress), BUT upon further inspection, it turns out that it is entirely not my fault, logically I should change my mind and feel better. On paper, this seems very straightforward and is theoretically sound. So if this process is not unfolding in this way over the course of CPT for any given patient, we should be asking why. *Why* is it hard for this person sitting across from me to change his/her mind? *What* is getting in the way? The answer will likely be quite different for different patients.

Are the stars aligned?

First, consider if all the stars are aligned. If PCL scores are not going down, but all other data are consistent with a patient moving toward full recovery, then the problem may be the PCL (or whatever assessment you are using). For example, if Steve comes to session 10 and is describing vastly improved work relations (e.g., a promotion) and going on date nights with his wife for the first time in years, and Socratic questions demonstrates how his stuck points are largely resolved—these are signs of improvement! However, if his PCL scores are still high, then the relevant "stars" are not aligned. For example, maybe he is answering these questions habitually, in the way he has "always" felt, versus reflecting on his symptoms over the last week. Providing some additional assessment will help to accurately estimate Steve's progress. Table 5.1 describes some likely culprits for elevated PTSD scores and some suggestions for intervening.

Leveraging the PCL to find stuck points and inform Socratic questions

PTSD and other trauma-related disorders are unique among mental disorders in that they are caused by an external event. PTSD is also unusual as compared to most other psychiatric disorders in the heterogeneity of its symptom

TABLE 5.1 Potential reasons for elevated PTSD scores over therapy and suggestions for interventions.

High PCL scores: likely culprits	Interventions
Scores reflect how the patient has always felt	Ask for examples of the clinically significant changes over the course of the past week. If there are no current examples, highlight the instruments' directions: *scores are supposed to reflect symptoms experienced in the past week only*.
Scores reflect psychosocial distress	Partial out normal human reactions and PTSD symptoms. For example, Julia's fear of her ex-husband's stalking is not hypervigilance because her estimation of danger is accurate. Separating out emotions that are normal and not psychopathology is important in the patient's long-term recovery.
Difficulty in understanding the CPT material	Break down the process of identifying and challenging a stuck point. If the material is confusing to the patient, the manual has many alternative worksheets, etc. Symptoms may not be decreasing because the patient is experiencing difficulty with the worksheets (misinterpreting questions, etc.).
Assimilation not yet resolved	Scores may be staying high because the core assimilated stuck points have not yet been identified or resolved. See Chapter 6 for clinical hints and strategies to find the lynchpin stuck point and hone your Socratic questions.
Multiple traumas	It is possible that scores remain high because the patient needs to address a second trauma. We expect the skills to generalize from one trauma to the next, but sometimes a little additional time spent on a second (or third, etc.) trauma in session is helpful. The therapist DOES NOT need to start over with the protocol. Simply identify the stuck points that are associated with the new trauma and challenge them using the relevant worksheets. This situation may emerge when the second trauma is significantly different from the first (completely different set of stuck points) or when the second trauma likely should have been the index trauma in the first place.
Unknown index trauma	Similar to the intervention earlier—sometimes the therapist does not know about the true index trauma—because the patient has been avoiding talking about it. This is difficult to elicit because the therapist knowing about the true index trauma depends on the patient disclosing this information. However, often there are clinical hints—the patient refuses to talk about a period of his/her life, alludes to something that cannot be discussed, etc. When the new trauma comes to light, the therapist should allow plenty of time and space for the patient to lay down this burden and stay focused on related assimilated stuck points.
Uncovered stuck points	Scores may be high because the patient has not clearly articulated the stuck point driving the distress yet (and so has not had the opportunity for resolution). There are multiple hints in Chapter 6 for helping the patient to hone the stuck point and for improving therapist's ability to pose Socratic questions.

constellation. The Diagnostic Statistical Manual-Version 5 (DSM-5; American Psychological Association, 2013) definition of PTSD includes 20 symptoms across 4 different clusters. As a result, patients with PTSD may present in very different ways depending on which symptoms are endorsed. This also contributes to complexity in intervening when individual symptoms can remit at varying rates. Tracking PTSD symptoms with a validated measure such as the PCL helps the therapist view which of the PTSD symptoms are not improving. This information is critical in discovering stuck points and prioritizing which ones to challenge on worksheets and with Socratic questions.

Case example

Imagine that Anna is on session 10 of CPT. Her assimilated stuck points are largely resolved. She does not believe that the medic's death was her fault. But her PCL scores are still hovering over the clinical cutoffs. Closer examination reveals that she is not experiencing nightmares and other Cluster B symptoms any longer and her cognitions and mood have vastly improved (Cluster D), but her hyperarousal and avoidance symptoms are really driving her elevated scores.

Therapist: *I can see that you are still feeling easily startled and describing some hypervigilance. Can you give me an example of when these symptoms occurred over the last week?* [Getting concrete examples of symptoms can really help challenge-related stuck points—particularly when you have moved on to over-accommodated stuck points. Challenging concepts globally can be much more difficult. If you challenge a specific example successfully, then you can encourage the patient to repeat that process when similar situations arise in the future.]

Anna: *Honestly, a great example is when I drive here. In fact, driving here is pretty much the only time during the week that I will get behind the wheel of the car.*

Therapist: *OK, I see that you also are experiencing some avoidance symptoms over the past week. Are there other situations that you might be avoiding besides driving?*

Anna: *Driving is a big one—I am finding that I am more interested in going out with my friend than I have been in the past, but I still say no to social events if they require driving. I'm lucky I can walk to work, but I can't walk here and no one can drive me. I find myself getting pretty stressed as I anticipate having to drive over here. In fact, I think this is getting worse for me.*

Therapist: *Ok—this is really good information. Let's back up for a second. Let's take the example of driving to therapy—think about that as the "A" column of a CBW.* [Therapist can even pull out a CBW if helpful.] *The hypervigilance, fear, and anxiety that you describe would be the feelings attached to the situation (column C). What would be the stuck point?*

The therapist then would pass the reins of the therapy over to Anna to identify what it is she is telling herself that is getting in the way of her reengagement into the life she wants to lead (stuck point). The therapist would then ask her how she would challenge this identified stuck point. In summary, the therapist "heard" what Anna was telling her via the PCL (I am hurting in this way …). The therapist then helped Anna to link her CPT skills to her distress (identifying the stuck point driving her distress—maybe something like, "I am in great danger on the roads"). Then the therapist gently guides the patient toward intervening in her own distress with the skills she has acquired throughout therapy (challenging her stuck point) and ultimately coming to a more accurate estimation of her safety on the roadways (the level of danger here in the United States is much different than in Iraq where enemy combatants were intentionally trying to harm her). This is a good example of how intervening in the core symptoms of PTSD (avoidance and hyperarousal) can positively impact functioning—Anna may be able to drive more often and socialize a bit more as her concerns about her safety lessen.

Recovery beyond the core symptoms of PTSD

Prioritizing patient needs is clinically complex. Single disorder protocols cannot provide specific guidance in *intervening* with the universe of symptoms, conditions, and stressors that can occur during the administration of a protocol (e.g., amplified eating disordered behavior or substance misuse, health-related complications, major life events) nor those that may emerge or flare while treating the primary disorder (e.g., PTSD). We build on this in the following sections.

Functioning

The impact of living with PTSD on psychosocial functioning is often high, with substantial impairment across major domains such as employment and educational pursuits, relationships, recreation, and sexual functioning. We saw the impact of Steve's anger on occupational and marital functioning in our case example. As described earlier, keeping our eye on the core symptoms of PTSD with repeated, standardized measures such as the PCL is critical in taking the "temperature" of PTSD and gauging improvement and recovery. However, PTSD is much larger than those 20 core symptoms. In fact, patients commonly seek treatment due to impairment in functioning (poor relationships, employment difficulties, etc.), perhaps even more so than they seek treatment for core symptoms of PTSD (Falsetti, Erwin, Resnick, Davis, & Combs-Lane, 2003; Galovski, Sobel, Phipps, & Resick, 2005; Shalev, 2000). Evidence-based psychotherapies (EBPs) like CPT directly target core symptoms of the disorder. Theoretically, it is expected that impairment in functioning (Criterion G of PTSD) will improve as the core symptoms of the disorder improve. As noted, our studies of CPT track PTSD and depression core symptoms as primary outcomes. The CPT manual specifically instructs therapists to track the core symptoms of PTSD over the course of CPT and to use reductions in these symptoms to determine patient progress and, ultimately, as indicators of recovery. While targeting the core symptoms of PTSD in a primary fashion is both practical and moderately successful in generalizing to improvement in other areas of mental and physical health, targeting improvement in functioning in only an indirect manner (via improvement in core symptoms) can result in less than optimal recovery in the very domains that are most important to patients.

Case example

Let's use our example of Steve. Steve's core symptoms of PTSD are increasing in severity and manifesting in irritability and angry outbursts, which, in turn, are resulting in increases in impairment in functioning (occupational and marital). Both his marriage and his job are at risk and he is at session 4. The therapist has a number of choices.

- First, the therapist can *continue exactly on protocol*, which may mean focusing on assimilated stuck points and remaining trauma-focused. The rationale for this choice is that his assimilated stuck points are contributing to his PTSD symptoms (anger) and leading to the angry outbursts at work and home. Resolving PTSD symptoms will have a palliative effect on anger with corresponding improvement in his workplace behaviors. The *risk* is that the anger behaviors might escalate in the meantime and the patient might lose his job.
- Second, the therapist can decide that the timing is not right for trauma-focused therapy and that the patient needs some affect regulation or other strategy prior to CPT to better prepare him for the trauma work. The risk in this decision to *abandon CPT* is that the patient might get the message that he is too fragile for trauma-focused work and might not return to the therapy at a later time. It is highly likely that the impairment in marital and occupational functioning is related to the PTSD. As such, any other intervention is just a band-aid—desisting care for PTSD when PTSD is the core problem is akin to putting a band-aid on an infection rather than treating the underlying cause—it will be ineffective.
- Finally, a third option is to *modify the protocol* and intervene with the challenges that are presenting barriers to a smooth course of therapy, within the context of the CPT protocol. The case formulation approach to care described in this chapter outlines this third option.

Comorbidity

Adding to the clinical complexity, PTSD rarely occurs in isolation, and can be accompanied by substantial comorbidity, particularly depression, substance use disorders, and disorders across the anxiety spectrum. Single disorder protocols are specifically designed to treat one psychiatric disorder. Given the high rates of comorbidity, the number of empirically supported protocols in which a clinician theoretically must be trained to effectively treat PTSD and each possible comorbid disorder may be unrealistic (Powell, Proctor, & Glass, 2014). Anna is a good example of a patient who struggles with one or more comorbid disorders in addition to PTSD. In her case, increases in drinking and compromising her recovery from alcohol misuse are of concern to Anna. It may be impossible (and even unnecessary) for one therapist to treat both disorders simultaneously, but by monitoring drinking patterns over the course of CPT, the therapist and patient can make clinically wise choices and incorporate Anna's concerns for her continued sobriety in her CPT care. Depending on what emerges over the course of CPT, this care may range from merely formally monitoring drinking behaviors via daily dairies to relying on resources (AA sponsor), concurrent care, or additional referrals if necessary. Chapter 10 describes the rich literature on treating PTSD and a host of common comorbid disorders with CPT. However, generally speaking, in clinical cases in which comorbid symptoms do not remit with the PTSD protocol, little guidance is currently offered to the clinician whether they should continue treatment, begin a second (or different) protocol or refer out for specialized care elsewhere. We touch on these issues here and in later chapters.

Physical health complications

Clinical presentations also can be complicated by enduring physical injuries and conditions sustained during the traumatic event (e.g., traumatic brain injury, memory loss, chronic pain in soft tissue injuries). It is also likely that the psychological distress inherent in PTSD and depression also influences health and health-related concerns. We have some studies suggesting that as PTSD symptoms improve with CPT, health-related concerns improve as well (Galovski, Monson, Bruce, & Resick, 2009). However, the influence of health-related complications on recovery from PTSD (and vice versa) is likely variable across different types of disorders and symptoms.

Challenges to optimal treatment outcomes (COTOs)

All the possible barriers to optimal outcomes are impossible to quantify. However, decades of clinical research yields clear domains composed of specific barriers to optimal outcomes. Broadly defined, these domains of barriers include emotional dysregulation, avoidance, ambivalence, comorbidity, and situational factors. Assessment across these domains can yield important clinical information, alerting both the patient and therapist about potential *challenges to optimal treatment outcomes (COTOs)*.

COTOs are any and all potential challenges or clinical issues that might arise during therapy and present obstacles for staying on course with a therapy protocol. COTOs are not specific to PTSD and can arise in any clinical situation from the treatment of a medical condition to the treatment of the full range of psychiatric disorders. Although they can vary in terms of severity and the amount of clinical attention that they warrant, for our purposes we will consider COTOs to be fairly major events that warrant serious consideration and decision-making around diverging from the CPT protocol. Broadly defined, COTOs can fall into one of five categories. Clinical assessment of the presence or absence of COTOs in each category is important.

Domains of challenges to optimal therapy outcomes

1. **Avoidance**: Avoidance is a hallmark of PTSD. Avoidance strategies can be fairly entrenched and difficult to dislodge. The vast majority of avoidance behaviors can be addressed within the CPT protocol. However, at times, the strategies that are conceptualized as avoidance may reach severity levels that warrant specific clinical attention. Questions that typically arise:
   a. My patient is not doing any practice work at all—is CPT the right therapy?
   b. My patient's gambling/drinking/binge eating/gaming has increased in severity—should I switch to a different therapy?
   c. My patient's agoraphobic or hypervigilant behaviors are keeping him/her from attending therapy—is this working?
2. **Engagement**: Motivation to change and engagement in therapeutic process is clearly related to successful outcomes in therapy. When therapy engagement is low, it can be difficult to know if we are on the right track as therapists and whether the therapy we are administering best meets the individual patient's needs. Questions that may arise:
   a. Does my patient understand/accept the rationale for this? Or are we just going through the motions?
   b. I am not seeing a lot of effort (or emotion) in session and not a lot of work between sessions—is this the right therapy?
3. **Emotional regulation**: Weighing the severity of emotional affect, the patient's ability to tolerate engagement with the memory, and sometimes related patient risk (suicidality, self-harm, homicidality), is perhaps one of the biggest challenges for therapists in implementing trauma-focused therapies. Relevant questions that might arise include:
   a. My patient is telling me that she/he cannot tolerate thinking about her/his trauma. Is this too much for him/her?
   b. My patient is showing no emotion at all—should I continue?
   c. My patient is reporting increasing anger between sessions—is this therapy making his/her life or situation or mental health worse?
   d. I am worried that my patient cannot tolerate this yet and needs time to learn affect regulation strategies first—should I hold off on trauma-focused therapy?
4. **Concurrent and comorbid mental and physical health difficulties:** We know that PTSD rarely occurs in isolation and that the abundance of concurrent disorders and conditions complicate the administration of trauma-focused protocols. It is less clear how to prioritize clinical issues that are ongoing or may emerge during CPT. Questions that may arise:
   a. My patient has a TBI, learning disability, below average intelligence, cognitive impairment, etc. Is CPT work too complex for this person? He/she does not seem to be understanding the worksheets.
   b. My patient is drinking and/or using substances (see Anna's example). Should I stop therapy?

c. My patient cannot concentrate, seems to be dozing off in therapy, reports significant sleep difficulties, and says it is getting worse. Is this working or making symptoms worse?

5. **Current major stressors:** Beyond PTSD-related stressors, life happens while people are in therapy, and emergencies, crises and major psychosocial stressors can emerge during CPT, a therapy that targets PTSD specifically. Therapists have to weigh up whether to stay trauma-focused (and not collude with avoidance) versus taking a patient-centered approach and meeting the patient's most pressing needs. Prioritizing and balancing these major life events and the trauma focus of therapy is an individualized process that often needs to happen within session, in real time. Relevant questions:
   a. My patient has a significant, ongoing life event (trouble at work, pending divorce, disabled dependent) that seems to pull time away from the protocol. Maybe the time is not right for trauma-focused work?
   b. My patient just received some very bad news (medical diagnosis, death in family, etc.). Should I stop therapy for PTSD to focus on this life stressor?

Case example

Julie's situation provides us with an example of the influence of ongoing major, independent psychosocial stressors on engagement in therapy for PTSD. Her abusive ex-husband is making specific threats to her and engaging in stalking behaviors. Julie's concerns are not stuck points ("I cannot trust him" and "I am in danger"), because they are accurate estimations of the danger that she faces. The severity of the threat may change in real time. A flexible approach to care provides space in the CPT therapy to manage this trauma-related stressor.

Case formulation approach and cognitive therapy

A case formulation approach to therapy has been used for decades with documented success in cognitive therapies specifically. For example, Person's case formulation (Persons, Roberts, Zalecki, & Brechwald, 2006) approach to cognitive therapy across multiple disorders considers a two-level model of psychological problems. Level 1, overt difficulties, consists of the explicit problems that our patients report and that we observe (social isolation, angry encounters, excessive drinking). Level 2, the underlying psychological mechanism, is the root or cause of the overt difficulties. From a cognitive perspective a core belief about oneself, the world, or others is often the underlying psychological mechanism causing the overt difficulties. An example of a core belief may be "I am not worthy of love." If one truly considers oneself to be worthless, it is easy to see that this would lead to social isolation, anger at the world, and alcohol misuse. Underlying psychological mechanisms influences the mood, behavior, and thoughts of the patient. Much of what we observe in our patients' clinical presentations may emerge from their worldviews that were presumably shaped or affected by their traumatic event.

More recently, transdiagnostic conceptualizations of psychological distress and mental illness have proliferated and continue to expand the concept of underlying or core mechanisms that contribute to the thoughts, feelings, and behaviors that patients describe as troublesome in therapy (Gutner, Galovski, Bovin, & Schnurr, 2016). This shift has largely been guided by basic research highlighting core, common mechanisms responsible for both the development and maintenance of emotional disorders. Identifying and understanding the role that core mechanisms may play in clinical presentations can aid therapists in addressing more complex clinical presentations without having to administer multiple concurrent or consecutive therapies.

Integrating case formulation into cognitive processing therapy

Numerous papers have been published suggesting the effectiveness of CPT across trauma populations including sexual trauma, domestic violence, interpersonal and community violence, war trauma, combat-related exposures, motor vehicle accidents, natural disasters, and hate crime violence (Chapters 3, 4, 11, 12). The therapy has been modified and expanded and tested cross-culturally with great success nationally and internationally (Kurdistan, Democratic Republic of Congo, Australia, Israel, and Europe, to name a few—Chapter 11). The materials have been translated into 11 different languages. The effectiveness of the intervention has also been demonstrated when PTSD co-occurs with a host of disorders including depression, panic, eating disorders, and severe mental illness (Chapter 10). Patients with comorbid personality disorders and extensive and complex trauma histories recover equally well (Chapters 8, 11).

BUT, we also know that approximately one-third of those who complete a course of PTSD do not realize as positive outcomes and still have PTSD at the end of therapy (Bradley et al., 2005; Cusack et al., 2016). We know that roughly one-third of patients dropout early (Swift & Grennberg, 2014). Because often patients drop out of treatment prematurely because of life stressors interfering with therapy, addressing these situations within the context of a modified treatment model may help to keep patients engaged in treatment and reduce premature dropout.

Applying a case formulation approach to CPT expands the clinician's ability to address the complexity of our patients suffering from PTSD, the full range of comorbid mental and physical health conditions, and the substantial psychosocial stressors and challenges that are often readily apparent.

Fitting a square peg in a round hole

As therapists trying to faithfully implement a structured, evidence-based intervention in a clinical setting, we can find ourselves feeling as if we are attempting to fit a square peg into a round hole. We may struggle with staying on target with the written word and structure of the manual while maintaining a person-centered approach to care and ensuring that the patient's needs are met. Our goals often seem aligned, but there are clinical cases and situations where the goals appear to be divergent. We may be left to wonder: "Is this therapy the right fit for my patient?"

Further, there are multiple situations in which impairment in functioning is gripping the patient's attention and deemed (by the patient) as a priority. This patient priority can stand in contrast to the CPT manual's clear instruction around remaining trauma focused and prioritizing assimilated stuck points before over-accommodated stuck points. This natural tension between meeting a patient's stated needs and adhering to the clear instructions in the treatment manual can present significant difficulty for the treating therapist. Navigating these therapeutic choices in real time can be challenging.

Integrating a case formulation approach to CPT for PTSD: Overarching goal

Integrating a case formulation approach into the CPT protocol allows the therapist to tailor the therapy to best meet the patient's needs without compromising the efficacy of CPT. Fig. 5.1 provides a model of continuous assessment of COTOs over therapy to inform treatment decisions and return to CPT.

1. *Assess*: To identify a given patient's likely barriers to care and recognize potential treatment-interfering symptoms and behaviors BEFORE they rupture therapy.

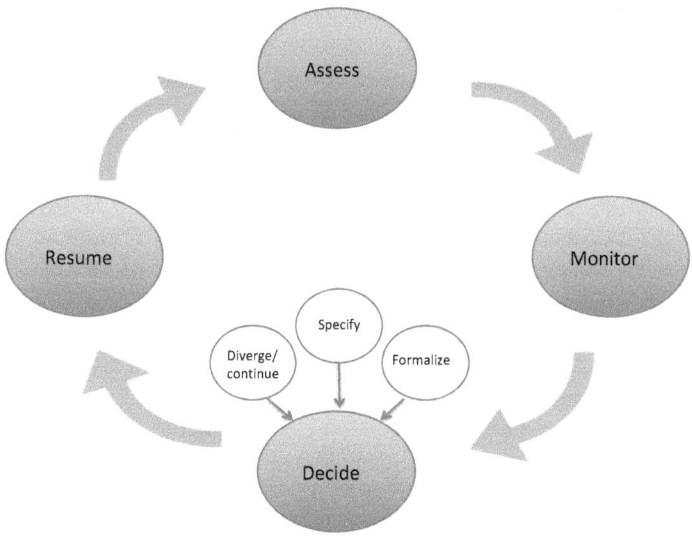

FIGURE 5.1 **Continuous assessment to inform decisions.**

2. *Monitor*: Monitor the severity of these barriers to optimal outcome throughout therapy to detect worsening.
3. *Decide*: Intervene if necessary or stay the course.
4. *Resume*: Return to therapy as soon as possible or continue therapy on protocol.

Case formulation approach to CPT: The assessment

While case formulation is an ongoing process throughout therapy, the assessment of potential challenges to optimal treatment outcomes begins at the very beginning of therapy. The initial assessment of PTSD is identical to routine clinical care. The patient is first diagnosed with PTSD, the recommendation of a trauma-focused, evidence-based therapy (CPT) is made, and the patient and therapist agree on a course of CPT. It is at this point that the case formulation approach is added to the CPT protocol.

Case formulation assessment

Session 1 of CPT provides much psychoeducation about what PTSD is and how it may have developed. This information provides the rationale for what the therapist is proposing a patient do in therapy. Adding the case formulation session just prior to beginning CPT provides the opportunity for the patient to become actively involved in his/her therapy and for the therapist and patient to really understand how the posttraumatic distress has influenced the trajectory of the patient's life and current functioning. Thus, the case formulation provides the opportunity for the patient and the therapist to develop a collaborative and cohesive plan that considers the rationale for staying trauma-focused while leaving room in the therapy to meet the patient's most pressing needs.

When: Conduct a case formulation session (often as part of an intake process) prior to CPT 1 to provide time to assess potential COTOs. If necessary, the patient and therapist can take two sessions to accomplish this part of the therapy—this is likely a rarity.

Rationale: Case formulation provides an opportunity to identify potential COTOs prior to therapy and a framework to manage COTOs on an ongoing basis throughout therapy as they emerge. By developing this early alert system and a framework for managing COTOs prior to therapy, therapists can minimize the impact of the COTO on recovery from PTSD. The case formulation puts the therapist and patient on the same page and helps to foster open, collaborative communication.

Goal: To better meet the patient's needs through an increased focus on a person-centered approach while maintaining fidelity to the protocol and the trauma-focus that is critical in treating PTSD.

Technique: Using the one-page clinical handout (Fig. 5.2) probe both patient strengths and COTO domains to assess the presence of any thoughts or

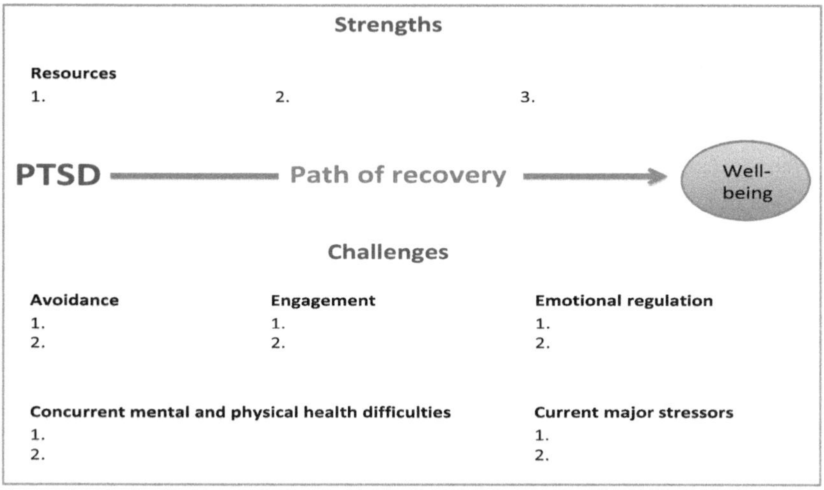

FIGURE 5.2 **Case formulation assessment of strengths and challenges.**

behaviors that may become a potential COTO during therapy. Add potential COTOs to the daily symptom diary to monitor throughout therapy.

The majority of cases will not require much modification at all. We know that over half of people who participate in PTSD lose their PTSD diagnosis (Steenkamp, Litz, Hoge, & Marmar, 2015). But we also know that about a third of patients drop out of treatment prematurely (see Chapter 3 for a review of CPT clinical trials; Chard, Kaysen, Galovski, Nixon, & Monson, in press). A subset of those who drop out never receive an adequate dose of treatment and do not recover from PTSD. We know that the reasons for dropout are often consistent with COTOs (avoidance, logistical barriers, etc.; Galovski, Blain, Mott, Elwood, & Houle, 2012). We also know that persistent PTSD even after a full course of therapy is also largely related to COTOs (emotional dysregulation, comorbidity, avoidance, etc.). So for those patients who are not as straightforward, weaving in a case formulation approach to care might truly push the needle further toward recovery. This concept is consistent with emerging models of care emphasizing personalized approaches to care delivery and the concept of continuum of care. Table 5.2 provides a session-by-session overview of CPT modified by a case formulation approach.

Case example

Julie's therapist diagnoses her with PTSD secondary to her assaults by her ex-husband. She next conducts a case formulation with Julie to get a sense of all the potential COTOs that might influence her recovery from PTSD. Julie has a number of strengths. Her love for her daughter is a great motivator to fully engage in treatment and get better. Her faith has been a real source of strength for her as well. In assessing domains of possible COTOs, three emerge as relevant

TABLE 5.2 Weaving a case formulation approach into CPT—session-by-session modifications.

Traditional CPT	Case formulation + CPT: session by session modifications
Session 0 or intake session.	Case formulation session assessing the patient's strengths and resources as well as each domain of possible COTOs.
Session 1: Psycho-education and identification of index trauma. Assign impact statement.	Provide feedback summarizing case formulation and begin process of tracking any identified COTOs on daily diaries. Assign Impact Statement and expand to query the relationship between the traumatic event and PTSD symptoms and the COTO.
Session 2: Understanding the impact of the traumatic event. Identifying stuck points. Introducing the ABC worksheets.	Query and include stuck points relevant to COTOs on stuck point log. Expand practice assignment to include doing at least 1 ABC sheet on any identified COTO.
Session 3: Understanding the relationship between thoughts and feelings.	Prioritize assimilated stuck points in Socratic questions. Expand practice assignment to include doing at least 1 ABC sheet related to any identified COTO.
Session 4: Prioritize challenging assimilation with gentle Socratic questions. Introduce challenging questions	Expand practice assignment to include doing at least 1 Challenging Question worksheet related to any identified COTO—particularly any that are elevated.
Session 5: Continue to prioritize challenging assimilation with gentle Socratic questions. Review challenging questions worksheets. Introduce problematic patterns of thought (PPT) worksheets.	Content is the same. Review Challenging Questions worksheets. Time is spent on worksheets related to COTO only if COTO is elevated. Prioritizing assimilation is the goal. Introduce Problematic Patterns of Thought worksheets—expand the assignment to include at least 1 sheet on patterns associated with COTOs.
Session 6: Review PPTs and introduce challenging beliefs worksheets. May be shifting to more over-accommodated stuck points.	Trauma-related (likely more over-accommodated stuck points) should continue to take priority. However, there may be time for pressing COTO-related stuck points that warrant clinical attention. This will vary from patient to patient.
Session 7: Continue to review CBWs. The patient is likely working on over-accommodated stuck points now, but continues to prioritize assimilated if present. Introduce modules and continue with CBWs.	In the absence of significant elevations in COTOs during the protocol AND if there is little evidence of remaining assimilated stuck points, this may be the point in therapy in which the therapist can more intentionally help the patient identify and challenge COTO-related stuck points.

TABLE 5.2 Weaving a case formulation approach into CPT—session-by-session modifications. (*Cont.*)

Traditional CPT	Case formulation + CPT: session by session modifications
Sessions 8–11: Introducing themes and challenging any relevant stuck points. Introduce the final Impact Statement assignment. Session 12: Complete therapy by reading final impact statement and evaluating change and future directions.	Continue to expand practice assignments to include at least 1 CBW on stuck points that are associated with COTOs and contribute to functioning and well-being. If needed, continue CPT beyond session 12 and leverage CPT skills to challenge stuck points contributing to impairment in domains of functioning. Expand Impact Statement to query beliefs related to any COTOs that were identified during the case formulation.

for Julie. Engagement might be problematic as Julie is a single mother and has very few supports and financial resources. Being the sole caregiver of her child might cause her to miss sessions if her child becomes ill, etc. "Physical health complications" are also COTOs for Julie as she has just found out that she is pregnant. Her pregnancy is particularly stressful because the father is her perpetrator and he does not know about the child. Finally, "major life stressors" is also a COTO because her husband is actively stalking her and she is involved in legal processes to try to protect herself and her daughter from him. Any of these COTOs has the potential to disrupt therapy or even become priorities over CPT sessions.

Monitor identified COTOs

In order to monitor and navigate these COTOs, the therapist and Julie customize a daily diary (see diary example, Fig. 5.3). Together they decide that monitoring her stress levels around childcare, her pregnancy, and her fears of her husband will be added to the diary. For each of these COTOs, Julie and her therapist establish anchors on a continuum of stress. For example, with respect to her pregnancy, "Best case" = feeling excited and happy about the idea of having another child. "Worst case" is when she feels terrified about having another of her ex-husband's children and very worried about if he will find out and how she will manage two kids. On her worst-case scenario days, when she is feeling very overwhelmed, Julie will self-harm by cutting. Her "current status" is feeling more concerned about getting started with therapy and her pregnancy concerns are being put on the back burner for the moment. Julie agrees to monitor her stress levels on these continuums on a daily basis.

Subject number: ____________________ **Date:** ____________________

Frequency per day:

0...Not at all
1...Slightly bothersome/1–2 times
2...Moderate or persistent/3–4 times
3...Severe, very strong, or upsetting/5–8 times
4...Extremely upsetting, impacts functioning/8–12 times
5...Debilitating, unable to function/continuous

Challenges to PTSD recovery

Date:							
Binge eating							
Best case			*Current status*				*Worst case*
Fighting at work							
Best case			*Current status*				*Worst case*
Homework/attendance							
Best case			*Current status*				*Worst case*
Insomnia							
Best case			*Current status*				*Worst case*
Drinking							
Best case			*Current status*				*Worst case*
Wanting to drink (urges)							
Best case			*Current status*				*Worst case*

FIGURE 5.3 Daily symptom monitoring diary.

Expand CPT to specifically target COTO-related stuck points

Note that the *daily diary* (Fig. 5.3) asks the patient to consider any *stuck points* that might be driving distress related to the COTO. There might not be! In the majority of situations, there will be a stuck point that is significantly contributing to the amount of distress around any given situation. Directing the patient to leverage the clinical skills that he/she is using to challenge trauma-related material will help generalize these skills to other areas of life as well as cement the learning involved in incorporating cognitive skills into one's daily repertoire. Is there a stuck point associated with an increase in symptoms? If so, it might be helpful to use your CPT worksheets to challenge the stuck point. Bring the diaries and completed worksheet back with you to the next session!

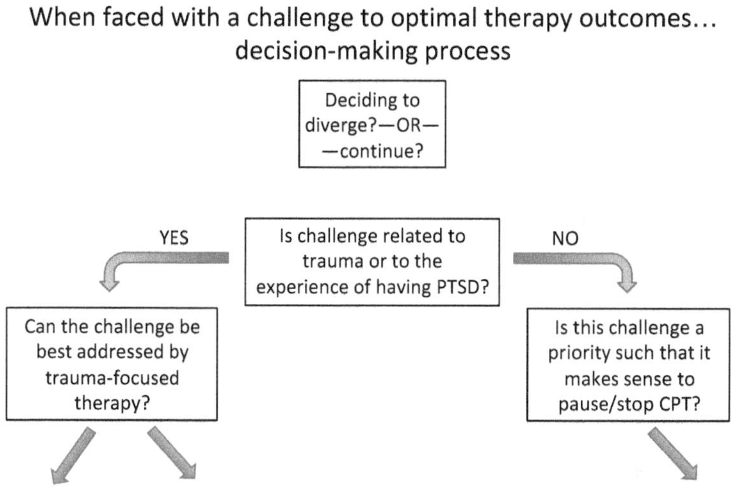

FIGURE 5.4 Process to decide to diverge from trauma-focused therapy or continue CPT.

Based on clinical information at hand including clinical judgment, data on trends and severity of COTOs via the diary, PCL scores, and anything else that is commonly used in clinical practice, the monitoring of all measurement should lead to the clinical decision as to whether or not to diverge from therapy or stay the course. As Julie moves through the therapy, the therapist will keep an eye on her daily diaries in the beginning of each session. If any of the stress levels move into a danger zone (e.g., Julie begins cutting), then this COTO may warrant more primary attention. See Fig. 5.4 as a guide and decision-making tool for the therapist to make these clinical decisions. The therapist might have to diverge from the protocol and intervene with the behavior. Fig. 5.4 provides some guidance on those types of decisions. Sessions 8–12 of CPT (sessions that focus on themes and tend to target more over-accommodated stuck points) can be intentionally expanded to specifically include directions for the patient to identify and challenge (on the CBWs) COTO-related stuck points and any related stuck points that are specifically getting in the way of return to *functioning, well-being, and reengagement in society.*

Diverging from the protocol

Rationale: The rationale for these decision-making processes is always consistent with the CPT manual (stay trauma-focused and prioritize assimilated stuck points) but provides (1) more guidance to manage COTOs that emerge, and (2) intentionally targets COTOs throughout with the goal of arriving at more holistic outcomes. The decision to diverge or stay trauma-focused should also be collaborative in nature. However, in order to offer the best care possible, the therapist should be weighing in with professional opinion and clinical judgment. Fig. 5.4 represents a decision tree to help guide the therapist in this process.

Stay the course: If the patient and therapist decide to continue with CPT, treatment clearly progresses as usual. Relying on CPT-consistent interventions such as identifying underlying stuck points and then using the skills and worksheets to challenge the stuck point will have palliative effects on the COTO and help the patient to understand the generalizability of the cognitive processing to every day life. The process of identifying the influence of the COTO in real time during the course of therapy, and then agreeing to move forward with CPT, often has the effect of diminishing the interference of the COTO on the therapeutic process while ensuring that the patient is both being heard and getting his/her needs met. Using Julie's example, imagine that her distress around her pregnancy increases and her therapist asks her to complete an ABC sheet. The belief that is identified is "I will hate my child and not be a good mother." This is clearly a stuck point and can be effectively challenged in the context of CPT—no divergence necessary.

Diverge: In the event that the COTO is deemed to be a priority, a number of steps and considerations are important.

1. Be sure to clearly identify that this is a time-limited divergence, stressing the importance of returning to the protocol.
2. Be sure to be clear that a divergence does not mean that the patient has been unsuccessful in therapy or that the therapy "does not work" for this patient. We do not want patients feeling as if they "failed" at trauma-focused therapy or that their PTSD is refractory.
3. Formalize the plan for the interim intervention with clear goals and parameters.
4. Specify the time frame anticipated before returning to CPT. If possible, set a next session date and time to resume CPT.

Continuing with Julie's case example, imagine that her distress increases and she starts missing a couple of sessions. Again, the therapist probes a bit further and discovers that Julie's husband has found out about the pregnancy and threatened her again, saying that he will kill her rather than let her raise their children. The fact that he knows about the pregnancy suggests that he knows where she lives and has eyes on her. This is a very viable threat given his past behaviors. There is no stuck point because her beliefs about safety are accurate and it may make sense to diverge from the CPT protocol to spend some time working on a safety plan.

In order to collaboratively formalize and specify the divergence from PTSD, therapists have found the following framework to be helpful (Fig. 5.5).

Content of the divergence

It would be impossible and unnecessary to provide clinical guidance on every COTO and every possible intervention that might occur during the course of CPT. Several chapters in this book review the literature on the effectiveness of CPT on a number of different secondary outcomes. Our basic premises have been to remain focused on the principles that guide CPT and use those

Patient's challenge: ______________________________

Decision to diverge

Rationale for divergence: ______________________________

Desired outcome or goal: ______________________________

Intervention designed to achieve goal: ______________

____

____

Plan to resume trauma-focused therapy

Plan for continued assessment of challenge:

Plan for return to trauma-focused therapy:

Anticipated date of next trauma-focused session:

Potential barriers to resuming therapy:

FIGURE 5.5 Framework to develop a plan to diverge from (and return to) the CPT protocol.

principles and CPT-consistent techniques whenever possible in order to continue to solidify learning and foster the generalizability of clinical skills for problems beyond PTSD.

We recognize that there may be cases that require a separate and unique intervention (Julie's case is a good example). Other examples may include instances in which patients may need a medical procedure, may need to be hospitalized for suicidality, may need to detox or enter rehab, etc. However, much of what constitutes COTOs can be managed within the course of CPT (first choice) or with CPT-consistent techniques. Fig. 5.6 provides general guidance on decision-making processes and the development of potential modifications to the CPT protocol.

Resuming CPT

There is little existing guidance on how much of a modification is too much. When has therapy truly become something besides CPT and what are the parameters around returning to trauma-focused work? The case formulation approach

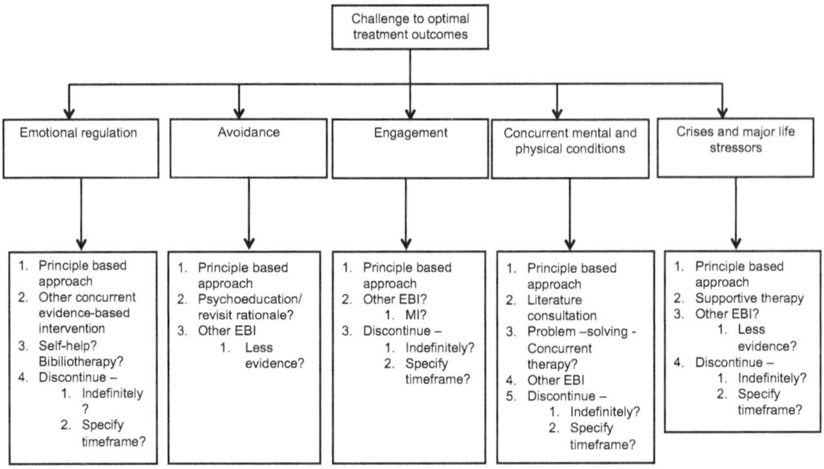

FIGURE 5.6 Framework to develop a plan to diverge from (and return to) the CPT protocol.

to CPT helps guide the clinician in returning to therapy after a necessary modification as efficiently and expediently as possible. By early identification of potential challenges to optimal outcomes, careful measurement and monitoring of those challenges, and a thoughtful and thorough plan of modifying CPT and then returning to the focus on trauma recovery, both therapists and patients should be well-positioned to resume therapy seamlessly.

We anticipate that CPT can resume after a modification with the very next session in the protocol. However, depending on the time that has passed, a review session may be in order—where are we in the CPT protocol and where were we headed before the COTO occurred? A telephone contact reminding the patient briefly about the content of the last CPT session and the practice work that was assigned might prevent the need for a review session.

Previous research has shown that the availability of two crises sessions added to the CPT protocol did not negatively influence outcomes (Galovski et al., 2012). We also observed in the same clinical trial that a variable length of therapy (with number of sessions determined by patient progress) improved outcomes. Based on this and other studies, our current recommendations are to exercise caution in making too many modifications or too much modification in order to prevent the dilution of the effectiveness of the intervention.

Adjust length of CPT to address Criterion G of CPT as needed

CPT is currently conducted as a variable length therapy. The end of treatment is dictated by "patient improvement" and not by a standardized number of sessions. Patient improvement has heretofore been operationalized by symptom scores on standardized measures that reflect change on the core symptoms of PTSD. The case formulation (CF) approach to care expands the explicit target of therapy to include Criterion G of PTSD and, as such, the length of the therapy can also be altered to provide additional time to address COTOs, diverge and return to therapy, and/or to apply CPT techniques to address impairment in functioning.

Staying with Julie's example, imagine that she completes a successful course of CPT and no longer meets criteria for PTSD. In other words, CPT worked! But Julie remains quite terrified about her ability to raise two children on her own and the threat of her ex-husband continues to loom. She worries that she will not be able to love her kids as mothers should because they may look like her husband and remind her of him or they may act like him in some ways. This is a great example of continuing therapy even though she no longer meets PTSD criteria. The process is working and a few more sessions may really help Julie to alleviate her distress.

Research Support for Integrating a Case Formulation Approach into CPT: Dr. Nixon conducted a small-scale study with 23 PTSD positive trauma survivors to test the use of a case formulation approach to CPT (Nixon & Bralo, 2019) and continues to test this integrated approach in an ongoing clinical trial directly comparing CPT to CPT + CF. In both studies the case formulation approach specifically provides the therapist and patient to incorporate non-protocol sessions to target COTOs that emerge in treatment. Case formulation was used both in consultation and within session with clients with the overarching goal to increase patient engagement and better meet patient needs within the parameters of what justifies any deviation from the standard protocol.

Results of Nixon et al. studies indicated that certainly not all patients need to deviate from the CPT protocol. COTOs that warranted deviations included avoidance, affect dysregulation, maladaptive coping strategies to cope with affect, distress intolerance, and cognitive rigidity. Evidence-based deviations from the CPT protocol included motivational interviewing (Miller & Rollnick, 1991), distress tolerance training skills, and behavioral experiments. These results showed that (1) COTOs could be identified by repeated and consistent monitoring, and (2) patients who received CPT + CF and who were at risk of poor outcomes (because they were experiencing COTOs) were responsive to planned, well-conceptualized deviations that targeted issues interfering with standard delivery of CPT. Although preliminary, early analysis suggests that at-risk patients in the CPT + CF group had lower PTSD and depression severity at follow-up relative to those in the CPT alone group.

Summary

If the patient is engaging in CPT, then it must have been decided that PTSD is a clinical priority for the patient. Likely, the experience of PTSD is negatively influencing the patient's ability to function well and exacerbating other conditions and stressors in that patient's life. Removing PTSD from the patient's full plate is a priority and, as such, it makes sense to prioritize maintaining a course of CPT whenever possible, being thoughtful and intentional about modifications, and returning to the trauma-focused work as soon as possible. We hope that this framework and the information from the book in general helps you, the therapist, to make these clinical decisions wisely. Most importantly, the patient must never stop therapy thinking that, *although this works for so many others, this did not work for me. I am hopeless.* Anyone can change his or her mind, so the therapy should work. If it is not working, then the question must become what is getting in the way of recovery? We continue this theme in the next chapter.

References

American Psychological Association. (2013). *Diagnostic and statistical manual of mental disorders* (5th ed.). Washington, DC: American Psychiatric Publishing.

Bradley, R., et al. (2005). A multidimensional meta-analysis of psychotherapy for PTSD. *American Journal of Psychiatry, 162*, 214–227.

Chard, K. M., Kaysen, D., Galovski, T. E., Nixon, R. D. V., & Monson, C. M. (in press). Cognitive processing therapy. In D. Forbes, J. Bisson, C. Monson, & L. Berliner (Eds.), Effective treatments for PTSD: Practice guidelines from the International Society for Traumatic Stress studies (3rd ed.). New York: Guilford.

Cusack, K., et al. (2016). Psychological treatments for adults with posttraumatic stress disorder: a systematic review and meta-analysis. *Clinical Psychology Review, 43*, 128–141.

Ehring, T., et al. (2014). Meta-analysis of psychological treatments for posttraumatic stress disorder in adult survivors of childhood abuse. *Clinical Psychology Review, 34*(8), 645–657.

Falsetti, S. A., Erwin, B. A., Resnick, H. S., Davis, J., & Combs-Lane, A. M. (2003). Multiple channel exposure therapy of PTSD: impact on functioning and resources. *Journal of Cognitive Psychotherapy: An International Quarterly, 17*, 133–147.

Galovski, T. E., Blain, L., Mott, J., Elwood, L., & Houle, T. (2012). Manualized therapy for PTSD: flexing the structure of cognitive processing therapy. *Journal of Consulting and Clinical Psychology, 80*(6), 968–981. doi: 10.1037/a0030600.

Galovski, T. E., Harik, J. M., Blain, L. M., Farmer, C., Turner, D., & Houle, T. (2016). Identifying patterns and predictors of PTSD and depressive symptom change during cognitive processing therapy. *Cognitive Therapy and Research, 40*(5), 617–626. doi: 10.1007/s10608-016-9770-4.

Galovski, T. E., Monson, C. A., Bruce, S., & Resick, P. A. (2009). Does cognitive-behavioral therapy for PTSD improve perceived health? *Journal of Traumatic Stress, 22*(3), 197–204. doi: 10.1002/jts.20418.

Galovski, T. E., Sobel, A. A., Phipps, K. A., & Resick, P. A. (2005). Trauma recovery: beyond posttraumatic stress disorder and other Axis I symptom severity. In T. A. Corales (Ed.), *Trends in posttraumatic stress disorder research* (pp. 207–227). Hauppauge, NY: Nova Science Publishers, Inc..

Gutner, C. A., Galovski, T. E., Bovin, M. J., & Schnurr, P. P. (2016). Emergence of transdiagnostic treatments for PTSD and posttraumatic distress. *Current Psychiatry Report, 18*(10), 95. doi: 10.1007/s11920-016-0734-x.

Kehle-Forbes, S. M., Meis, L. A., Spoont, M. R., & Polusny, M. A. (2016). Treatment initiation and dropout from prolonged exposure and cognitive processing therapy in a VA outpatient clinic. *Psychology of Trauma, 8*, 107.

Miller, W. R., & Rollnick, S. (1991). *Motivational interviewing: Preparing people to change addictive behavior.* New York: The Guilford Press.

Niles, B. L., Polizzi, C. P., Voelkel, E., Weinstein, E. S., Smidt, K., & Fisher, L. M. (2018). Initiation, drop-out, and outcome from evidence-based psychotherapies in a VA PTSD outpatient clinic. *Psychological Sciences, 15*, 496–502.

Nishith, P., Resick, P. A., & Griffin, M. G. (2002). Pattern of change in prolonged exposure and cognitive-processing therapy for female rape victims with posttraumatic stress disorder. *Journal of Consulting and Clinical Psychology, 70*, 880–886. doi: 10.1037/0022-006X.70.4.880.

Nixon, R. D. V., & Bralo, D. (2019). Using explicit case formulation to improve cognitive processing therapy for PTSD. *Behavior Therapy, 50*, 155–164.

Persons, J., Roberts, N., Zalecki, C., & Brechwald, W. A. (2006). Naturalistic outcome of case formulation-driven cognitive-behavior therapy for anxious depressed outpatients. *Behaviour Research and Therapy, 44*, 1041–1051.

Powell, B. J., Proctor, E. K., & Glass, J. E. (2014). A systematic review of strategies for implementing empirically supported mental health interventions. *Research on Social Work Practice, 24*, 192–212.

Rosen, C. S., Matthieu, M. M., Stirman, S. W., Cook, J. M., Landes, S., Bernardy, N. C., ... & Hamblen, J. L. (2016). A review of studies on the system-wide implementation of evidence-based psychotherapies for posttraumatic stress disorder in the Veterans Health Administration. *Administration and Policy in Mental Health and Mental Health Services Research, 43*(6), 957–977.

Shalev, A. Y. (2000). Measuring outcomes in posttraumatic stress disorder. *Journal of Clinical Psychiatry, 61*, 33–42.

Steenkamp, M. M., Litz, B. T., Hoge, C. W., & Marmar, C. R. (2015). Psychotherapy for military-related PTSD: a review of randomized clinical trials. *Journal of the American Medical Association, 314*, 489–500.

Swift, J. K., & Greenberg, R. P. (2014). A treatment by disorder meta-analysis of dropout from psychotherapy. *Journal of Psychotherapy Integration, 24*, 193–207.

Weathers, F. W., Litz, B. T., Keane, T. M., Palmieri, P. A., Marx, B. P., & Schnurr, P. P. (2013). The PTSD checklist for DSM-5 (PCL-5). Scale available from the National Center for PTSD.

Chapter 6

Therapy is hard: Improving patient engagement and working through avoidance

Chapter outline

The cognitive processing therapy (CPT) manual contains all the information necessary to administer the therapy and is replete with excellent suggested scripts and examples. Over the years, the manual has grown to include examples of stuck points, completed example worksheets, alternative worksheets, handouts, and other psychoeducational aids. Training in CPT has been standardized to require the two-day workshop and the completion of two cases under consultation. The case consultation has been shown to be particularly effective in learning CPT and in administering the therapy with fidelity (Resick, Monson, Galovski, Chard, & Kattar, 2010; Rosen et al., 2016). Despite the advancements over the years in the quality of the manual, training, and consultation, no single therapy could ever address all of the universe of possible Challenges to Optimal Therapy Outcomes (COTOs) and the interaction of those challenges that we, as clinicians, will undoubtedly face during the course of administering CPT.

Flexible Applications of Cognitive Processing Therapy. http://dx.doi.org/10.1016/B978-0-12-816715-1.00006-6

Difficulty getting started: tenuous patient engagement

Our goals in becoming therapists likely did not include acquiring sales and marketing expertise. Yet, we may often find ourselves in the position of attempting to increase the "buy-in" of a potential CPT patient by "selling" the therapy. In many cases, increasing "buy-in" simply consists of offering some education about the overall effectiveness of the therapy and providing a solid overview of the protocol to educate the patient and demystify the process of change. However, during the pretreatment and early treatment phases, we may find ourselves pulled in the direction of trying to convince patients that CPT will be helpful. We may even teeter on the brink of working harder than our patient in getting CPT started and ultimately we may risk pulling (dragging?) a patient into trauma-focused work prematurely and embarking on an uphill struggle with ambivalence for the remainder of the protocol. The reality of trauma therapy is that a patient is rarely eager to jump into trauma-focused work. Remember, by definition, the avoidance inherent in posttraumatic stress disorder (PTSD) can be prohibitive in a patient agreeing to begin this process of engaging with the trauma memory—essentially recalling the worst thing that ever happened to him/her.

Patient ambivalence or concern about beginning CPT

Let's consider the typical scenario in which this issue of increasing patient "buy-in" might arise. Presumably, in most cases, at the outset of therapy, the patient would have offered the therapist some information suggesting that he/she was struggling with posttraumatic distress related to a traumatic event. The patient might have sought treatment specifically for this reason or perhaps the patient has been in therapy for some time and trauma-related distress is an emerging clinical issue. On the other hand, perhaps a loved one convinced the patient to seek therapy (or had even given the patient an ultimatum to get help) or perhaps the therapy was mandated by a judge or by an employer. However the information about the traumatic event and resultant PTSD diagnosis emerged, it is clear that something terrible happened and the patient is experiencing significant distress. It must also be clear that the distress is, indeed, PTSD and that the PTSD is the primary disorder. This latter point is important. We will discuss this in more detail throughout the book, but if there is a different clinical issue or diagnosis on the patient's plate that takes priority over PTSD, then the clinician should likely be focused elsewhere. Ultimately, if the therapist is offering CPT to the patient, then there should be consensus that a trauma has occurred that resulted in PTSD and that trauma-focused therapy is thus a treatment priority. Yet, we still might hear hesitation or even refusal by the patient around getting CPT started. Indicators of ambivalence include statements like: "I don't think this will work for me." "I'm not ready to talk about my trauma yet." "I'm not sure this is a good idea. Talking about my trauma will be re-traumatizing."

Given this clinical scenario, the question to the ambivalent or avoidant patient becomes, "why not get started in CPT?" You, the therapist, *genuinely* want to know! As therapists we need to ask, not assume, the reasons why someone might be hesitant to start therapy. Let's consider our three case examples. Patients' answers to this important question can be quite variable and will dictate the therapist's intervention.

Anna (our Army Veteran) may be very concerned about driving through the city to get to therapy appointments. The idea that she may be overwhelmed by PTSD therapy (and working through her avoidance of the trauma memory) and may experience a flashback or panic attack in city traffic might present a real deterrent for her to get started. Contrarily, she may be concerned that her partner (who perhaps does not know about her trauma) might find out about the sexual assault. Given her experiences growing up in a very conservative town, she may also have concerns about disclosing her sexual orientation and discomfort talking about her sexual assault with a therapist whom she does not know well.

Steve (our forklift operator) has been in therapy for some time addressing symptoms related to his car accident. However, he may be quite nervous about approaching the memory of his childhood trauma—an event that he has only recently disclosed. Steve's hesitancy to engage with his trauma memory may be a clear case of PTSD-related avoidance. On the other hand, Steve may be concerned that he will become quite upset if he talks through his childhood abuse and his job performance may worsen—potentially jeopardizing his employment.

Julie (our intimate partner violence survivor) has become more and more agoraphobic since filing for divorce and has reduced the number of times that she leaves the house. Adding therapy to her schedule may seem overwhelming. She is also dealing with major psychosocial stressors including ongoing litigation over child custody. Finally, given that her ex-husband is clearly dangerous, has threatened her in the past, and is currently stalking her, she may be understandably concerned for her safety. She may also be concerned that her mental illness and therapy records might be subpoenaed during the course of her child custody proceedings and could hurt her chances of getting custody of her daughter.

Strategies to increase engagement at the outset of therapy

Intervening with ambivalence would typically first be informed by the reason *why* a patient is hesitant to begin the very intervention that will alleviate the distress he or she is describing to the therapist. This is a critical part of the process because the reason why someone is avoiding (not engaged, etc.) directly informs your intervention. Intervening with the goal of improving engagement often includes one of the following strategies (again depending on the reason for avoidance): psychoeducation, problem-solving, or, last but not least, discovery and challenging of the relevant stuck point. Socratic dialogue is a useful tool for implementing any of these strategies!

- First, *psychoeducation* about the role of avoidance in maintaining PTSD can be very helpful.
  - *Case example*: If Steve, for example, can consider that while avoidance of the trauma memory might seem helpful in the short term, avoidance has not been effective in recovering from the traumatic event in the long term. Trying something else, such as intentionally approaching the trauma memory, might be very helpful. Having this psychoeducation about the role of avoidance in maintaining PTSD in his repertoire might help him challenge a related stuck point such as "I can't tolerate this therapy."
- Second, *problem-solving* might be very effective in targeting situational or logistical barriers that might contribute to hesitancy to begin CPT.
  - *Case example*: Julie's concern that she has a lot on her plate right now and that this might not be the right time to begin this therapy may, in truth, be quite well-founded. Problem solving around these issues can be helpful. For example, if Julie is in imminent danger from her ex-husband, she may need to prioritize case management services and/or additional support and resources. However, if her husband's behavior and the child custody battle are going to be more long-term and chronic, then the therapist might help the patient weigh whether recovery from PTSD through CPT in the immediate future might be quite beneficial in helping Julie cope with these more chronic stressors in the long term.
  - *Case example*: Similarly, Anna's concern that she may get into a car accident if triggered while driving through city traffic is a logical concern. Asking additional questions to understand the likelihood of an accident helps to evaluate if it might wise to ask a supportive friend to drive Anna to session or if public transportation might be an option in the short term. Triggers that are causing Anna's panic attacks and roadway fears will be addressed in therapy with the full expectation that soon she will be driving much more comfortably.
  - *Case example*: Steve's concerns about potentially losing his job if his distress levels increase warrant a similar conversation. If the risk is deemed to be high, problem-solving strategies might include the timing of appointments (i.e., Friday afternoons), taking leave from work for a period of time if necessary, or having a backup plan such as involving his wife in the therapy to provide additional support (not to participate in the CPT sessions).
- Third, *finding and challenging stuck points* is likely a very effective strategy. Often patients' fears and concerns about embarking on therapy for PTSD are driven by an underlying stuck point such as "I can't tolerate this therapy" or "Therapy will make me worse." If the therapist can help a patient articulate the stuck point underlying the avoidance of therapy, the process becomes much more straightforward. Remember, the patient has not even begun CPT or is only in the very early stages. So the patient may not be familiar with

the concept of stuck points and cognitive restructuring. Yet, the therapist can still weave this therapeutic technique into the session. Some of our favorite Socratic questions to challenge "fear of treatment stuck points" such as *I cannot tolerate this therapy* are listed below:

Possible Socratic question: *Which part of the therapy would be difficult*? Note how the question changes the wording a bit from *intolerable* to *difficult*. Even this wording change alone might help the patient to start thinking about the difficulty of beginning therapy in a different and less insidious way. This simple question asks the patient to break down a substantial and seemingly overwhelming fear of therapy into more specific and smaller parts. By virtue of breaking the fear down, the patient begins the process of considering (challenging) a stuck point along with all the relevant aspects of the therapy situation. The large looming thought of "therapy is too much" might start to seem a bit more manageable if broken down into parts.

Possible Socratic question: *What might be different about intentionally approaching the trauma memory as opposed to being triggered (blindsided) by the memory in daily life*? Many differences will be very apparent. The idea behind the question is that the patient will be able to identify differences between thinking about or approaching a trauma memory *intentionally* with the help and guidance of a therapist compared to *being blindsided* by PTSD symptoms in one's everyday life when unexpectedly reminded of the traumatic event (nightmares, trauma reminders, unexpected thoughts, etc.).

Augmenting CPT at the outset of therapy

In some circumstances, patient ambivalence may present barriers to accessing care or to fully benefiting from therapy. Motivational interviewing (MI) is an intervention that has been found to be successful in targeting patient ambivalence with demonstrable influence on increasing patients' readiness (or motivation) to change (Miller & Rollnick, 2012). The efficacy of MI has been demonstrated across a number of patient populations, with perhaps the preponderance of studies conducted with participants suffering from substance use disorders. Resick, Monson, and Rizvi (2008) identify patient ambivalence as a potential challenge to optimal outcomes in treating PTSD and Rooney et al. (2005) have shown that patients with PTSD certainly present with varying degrees of ambivalence. The challenges with patient engagement, compliance, and retention in the treatment of PTSD that we have been discussing here and that are observed in both clinical trials and clinical care settings led us to examine the utility of MI in the context of CPT. We tested the ability of three sessions of MI (based on Westra & Dozio, 2003) delivered prior to CPT to enhance patients' motivation to commence therapy and to optimize engagement in the therapeutic process once therapy begins. This small, uncontrolled pilot study (Blain & Galovski, Unpublished dissertation) was conducted with 17 female survivors of interpersonal violence. The results were a bit surprising. Over the course of the three sessions of MI, readiness to change, views of CPT and fear of beginning treatment did not change. This may be due to a number of reasons, including lack of effectiveness of MI in targeting these variables, lack of statistical power to detect change, or perhaps patients were not ambivalent at all (i.e., maybe avoidant, not ambivalent per se).

The MI techniques learned prior to CPT in this trial were also available throughout therapy to be utilized as needed during CPT. Utilization of MI techniques was variable across participants. On average, therapists used two applications of MI techniques during CPT across patients who completed at least nine sessions. Implementation of MI techniques was relatively short in duration (approximately 5 min or less) with some variability (one course of treatment included six applications of MI in total). The timing of the use of MI techniques also differed across courses of CPT with the most frequent use of MI occurring in Session 4 and coinciding with the trauma narrative. In sessions when MI was used, no improvement in readiness to change was observed. Thus, it is not clear that the MI intervention had the intended effect during the junctures in therapy at which therapists thought MI was most needed. Also of note, 8 out of 17 (47%) participants terminated therapy prematurely. Though none dropped out during MI, the addition of MI did not improve dropout rates relative to other studies. In fact, of the CPT trials conducted at the same location with very similar patient populations, this pilot trial ended with the highest dropout rates of all five trials. Further, 8 out of 17 MI + CPT participants that we intended to treat and 3 out of 9 treatment completers remained PTSD positive at the end of therapy. These rates of non-recovery are also exceptionally high compared to other trials at the same location.

While this is only one uncontrolled pilot study, it causes us to pause and consider *when* we would want to alter the CPT priority of breaking through avoidance and instead engage in a different intervention such as MI. We might consider whether we are facing true ambivalence (which might warrant MI) or facing avoidance (which is clearly covered by CPT). In this pilot study, these were treatment-seeking participants who, by definition, may have been "ready enough" to commence trauma-focused treatment, albeit with some hesitancy and trepidation. In fact, it is likely that there are very few patients with PTSD who are chomping at the bit to begin trauma-focused therapy. Delaying that process by adding MI prior to CPT (even with our best intentions) might have actually colluded with avoidance in some way. It may be quite important to strike while the iron is hot and get started in CPT as soon as possible. A controlled trial would be necessary to answer this question.

Following this line of thought, leveraging MI might be more appropriate and helpful in addressing ambivalence and readiness to change in a nontreatment seeking or reluctant patient population. For this reason, we instituted an MI arm of therapy in a jail diversion program for a population of participants suffering from comorbid severe mental illness, a high rate of comorbid substance use disorders, and a host of major psychosocial stressors including poverty and homelessness. In this program, individuals were diverted from jail to receive a range of mental health services including services for posttraumatic stress (Feingold, Fox, & Galovski, 2018). The 81 participants who were eligible for the trauma-focused portion of the program and whom we intended to treat could choose whether they would like to receive CPT, more general cognitive behavioral therapy, or MI for those who were ambivalent about (or simply not wanting to) commence therapy. Each therapy and the rationale for each therapy were described to patients. Of the 81 patients included, 11 patients chose MI. Of those 11, 5 switched over to another arm of the study. MI was successful in those five patients as the intervention theoretically helped increase readiness to change and paved the way for engagement in trauma-focused treatment. Six patients only received MI and, of those six, four dropped out and could not be retained in treatment at all. Only two patients were designated as treatment completers after finishing the MI arm. While again, the absence of an randomized, controlled design limits interpretation of these data, we found that the vast majority of participants (87%) chose a more diagnostic-specific treatment when given the choice, even when participants were not treatment-seeking. For those who did choose MI, the results are mixed on its helpfulness in increasing engagement in treatment. Less than half of the participants eventually made their way to a more targeted therapy specific to their disorder, a third dropped out altogether, and the remaining two participants gained enough benefit from MI alone that they were deemed treatment completers.

In summary, both studies sought to address poor engagement and increase motivation by incorporating MI techniques, with little success. However, these studies are limited by small sample size and an RCT is really required to understand the relative efficacy of augmenting CPT with another intervention method such as MI. As the clinicians on this study, our lesson learned was when administering the CPT protocol, trust the process of CPT and first rely on CPT tools to address avoidance. Our first goal should be to understand stuck points behind the perceived ambivalence, lack of motivation and readiness to change. When those CPT-specific tools are not effective, switching to a different technique (MI is a great choice!) with a clear plan to return to CPT may be effective (see Chapter 5 for specifics in applying this type of a case formulation approach to CPT).

Addressing CPT engagement during therapy: The brief session

For some patients who have a history of failing to engage, whether that manifests itself by coming late to session or not completing practice assignments or other tasks, one of us (RN) has occasionally used the "5-min session" approach with good success (see Waller et al., 2007, for details). This is only instigated *after* there has previously been: a clear discussion about the importance of commitment to therapy and associated tasks, *psychoeducation* including the rationales of therapy components have been revisited, *problem-solving* of barriers to therapy has occurred, and fear of therapy and other relevant *stuck points* have been identified and addressed. These discussions have thus culminated in a collaborative agreement about what is expected from the patient, with the shared goal of maximizing the effectiveness of therapy in which the importance of being engaged in therapy is made explicit. This sets the scene for the brief session as follows.

When such a discussion has been had, if a patient comes to the next session *without* undertaking practice assignments as agreed, or is 20 min late, etc., the therapist does not rehash the importance of engagement (remember, that conversation has already been had, and if we continue having the conversation we are unintentionally reinforcing avoidance!). Rather, the therapist gently explains that the work of today's session was predicated on these tasks having been completed, and, without that, the session cannot precede. The therapist briefly asks when the patient is likely to be able to complete the task, and then reschedules the appointment sometime after then. This "session" is only 5–10 min long. Remember, it is not a CPT session nor a non-protocol session of normal duration to address a genuine emergency. It is intended to communicate that therapy requires the patient's active participation and normal sessions cannot precede until that is occurring. It is critical to remember this is not intended to be a punitive strategy and therapists need to be aware of their motivation for instigating a brief session. The therapist remains empathetic and is clear they have every confidence that the patient is capable of undertaking the task(s). The prior work has been set up collaboratively with the patient, and the brief session is intended to help break a cycle of nonengagement or "presenteeism," in which there is a repetition of sessions in which failure to complete a task becomes the dominant conversation, but with little change in actual behavior. This also can help shape the patient's behavior of relying on the therapist to help them do the work only in session, and can keep therapists from inadvertently reinforcing a patient's stuck points around not being able to tolerate the work of CPT.

As noted by Waller and coworkers (and in RN's experience), although such an approach might be uncomfortable for therapists, it is more often than not associated with a patient returning to the next session with a clear understanding of what is needed to help themselves, and improved engagement in session and with future tasks. We emphasize that this is not the only way to manage issues of noncompliance and lack of engagement, and we discuss further strategies in the next chapter, as well as how to judge "how much is enough" when asking patients to complete practice assignments and other tasks during CPT. We now outline some examples of when we might (or might not) use the brief session approach.

Brief session scenarios

Imagine three patients (based on actual, recent patients of ours) who often come quite late to session, miss every other session over the course of over a year, and rarely or sporadically complete practice work. Patient 1 has extremely severe PTSD, is quite dissociative—in fact, she got into car accidents on two separate occasions coming to session due to dissociation, and was incredibly avoidant of thinking about the trauma. She did recognize that she "desperately" needed therapy for PTSD and kept trying to engage. Patient 2 has very little money and needs to rent her car out to get money to pay her rent. She also describes severe PTSD and is very engaged in session, but can only attend if her car is available (which she rarely knows ahead of time). She rarely does worksheets but really evidences cognitive change in session and her PTSD is improving. Patient 3 always attends session late and with a fresh cup of Starbucks coffee, she continually looks at her watch and is often off-topic, she has taken calls during session and overall seems quite ambivalent. She completes worksheets between sessions, but they are sparse and typically center around current life events despite feedback.

For Patient 1, we would consider using a brief session approach after we had exhausted other avenues of addressing engagement. For example, we would first address stuck points underlying the client's high level of avoidance, and, as we will detail in a later chapter, there may be alternative CPT delivery methods (e.g., intensive therapy conducted daily) that could help this client. It is important to remember that although reporting "she desperately needs therapy," recovery is unlikely if the patient is canceling every second session and doing little work outside of sessions, and this lack of progress in recovery is one of the conditions for considering instigating a brief session.

For Patient 2, although her attendance and out-of-session work are suboptimal, she is showing cognitive change in session and her symptoms are improving. There appear to be genuine barriers to her attendance (access to a car); however, despite that, we have good indicators of progress. Assuming the therapist believes there is real change occurring (indexed by resolution of stuck points seen in session, reduced symptoms on objective measures such as PTSD Checklist [PCL]), we would feel the client is doing their best in suboptimal circumstances and, importantly, is evidencing improvement. Thus, we would not introduce a brief session. Although it is likely more rapid improvement could occur if the patient was able to attend more regularly and was more systematic in her worksheets, we feel she is gaining enough benefit from therapy and reducing her PTSD to justify continuing along this track. We would still look out for ways to address the transport barrier, and we would continue to encourage her to practice out of session as much as possible!

Patient 3 is a more clear-cut example of where a brief session appears necessary. Remember, we would have had discussions about the rationale of therapy, engagement, and the importance of practice assignments. We also would have examined potential stuck points getting in the way of engagement. Conducting a brief session with this patient will likely result in one of two outcomes, both of which are beneficial. One, it kick-starts the patient to engage. This is a win for the patient. Or, the patient realizes that this is not the right time for them to be able to fully engage in PTSD treatment. As discussed in the next session, if the brief session strategy does result in the patient ceasing therapy at this time, it is discussed in a way that ensures the patient does not go away with the impression that they have "failed" therapy or are untreatable.

Finally, when to terminate therapy

We have all had patients who clearly do not want to engage in the process for any number of reasons (patient 3 in the case example earlier might be a good example of a less-engaged patient). Often we have waitlists of patients who would benefit from therapy. In these cases, it can be helpful to have a conversation with the patient about terminating therapy or switching to something else. Several points should be included in this conversation: (1) this might not be the right time for you (suggesting that another time might be better and keeping the door open for future care), (2) attesting to the fact that CPT was not conducted (in order to ensure that someone does not leave thinking that "trauma-focused therapy does not work for me" or "I am untreatable"), and (3) that it is your professional opinion that he/she would truly benefit from trauma-focused therapy in the future.

Therapist: *I understand that the time is not right for you at this point in your life to continue CPT* (insert reasons). *I appreciate the difficulty and commitment in delving into your trauma memory and sorting out your thoughts and emotions. I know* (insert factors that are interfering with recovery here) *has prevented you from engaging in the process, but I have every confidence that trauma-focused treatment will be very helpful in treating your PTSD in the future when the time is right.*

There is no hard and fast rule as to how many missed sessions is too many sessions, resulting in a decision to terminate therapy. That said, we find that two to three sessions of either missed appointments without good reason, or two or so sessions of marked lack of engagement in session or CPT tasks generally is a trigger for the conversation earlier. We emphasize that this is only done after the therapist has explored the reasons for nonengagement or resistance and has established that it is clear that therapy is not a priority for the patient at this time. Missed appointments and lack of engagement is not uncommon, and we need to ensure we are not prematurely "exiting" a patient out of therapy.

If, however, a decision is made to terminate therapy, it is useful to know that research has shown that patients who prematurely terminated CPT but returned at a later date (and received a full dose of therapy) had outcomes just as good as those who were able to complete therapy the first time around (Schumm, Pukay-Martin, & Gore, 2017). Communicating this to patients is likely to be helpful, underscoring our point earlier that while the timing might not be right for a patient at this time, they are not closing the door to recovery via CPT in the future.

The importance of language

In delivering this therapy to patients and training clinicians in CPT over time, it has become clear that we, as therapists, can always improve the therapeutic alliance and quality of our work simply by the language that we use in session. The way we introduce concepts and skills can influence the reception of these ideas by our patients. CPT is taught as a process of "collaborative empiricism." This means that we are always on the same team as our patients and, together, we are exploring and testing their cognitions in an effort to move toward recovery. It is never our intention to dictate instructions to our patients; we collaborate with them. Nor do we tell our patients that they are "thinking wrong"; we wonder with them or ask for further clarification through Socratic dialogue. This is intentional. We ultimately want the patient to become his or her own therapist and their agency in this process is critical to its success. Minor tweaks in therapy language may be quite helpful in achieving better outcomes. Perhaps one of the best examples of being mindful of the language that we choose in administering the CPT protocol is in our introduction of and discussion around practice work throughout therapy.

Tweaking language

No one likes to do homework. The very word elicits memories of cranky elementary school teachers assigning boring tasks. "Practice assignment" is better and this is the current language in the CPT manual. However, one could argue that a therapist "assigning" practice is not particularly collaborative. The word assignment suggests a job with a start and an end. Our CPT work is intended to be a process and the worksheets are intended to be a method of bringing the process into everyday life where patients need it the most. As such, we see practice assignments as really being an extension of therapy. As such, another choice of language in describing these assignments might be calling them "out-of-session therapy."

Introducing out-of-session therapy

We have heard time and again that patients can feel overwhelmed or even irritated by the worksheets. The way therapists introduce this part of the therapy can be very helpful in increasing the likelihood of patient buy-in to this part of the therapeutic process. Consider why therapists ask patients to continue therapy outside of the session. We know that there are 168 hours in the week and typically only one of those hours is spent in therapy. We ask our patients to take the skills, perspectives, and information learned in session into their lives where it really can make an impact. A good method for continuing therapy outside of the session is through continued practice on the worksheets. Communicating this basic concept to the patient is important! Too often we may introduce the out-of-session therapy as if the patient is completing worksheets for us: "I'd like you to complete 7 worksheets over the next week." When the patient comes back with completed worksheets, we sometimes thank him or her for doing the work. While very polite, this management of worksheets gives the impression that this is an assignment that the patient is completing for us, the therapists. This could not be further from the truth. Completion of the out-of-session work is fairly irrelevant to the therapist's well-being. It is very relevant to the patient's wellness. Think about the out-of-session therapy as an *opportunity*, not an assignment, to continue the work toward recovery. Consider introducing the out-of-session therapy this way: "We've developed some tools to help you move this process of sorting through your stuck points between sessions. These sheets provide you with the opportunity to move the therapy out of the session and into your life where it really matters."

Keep it real campaign

Consider taking a minute and *genuinely* thinking about why you are asking your patient to complete the out-of-session therapy and then personalizing the "assignment" to that individual. Perhaps introducing the work as such, "I believe that this next piece of the therapy is really going to be helpful in continuing your work outside of the session." Try to personalize the assignment as much as possible, answering the question—how is this work going to specifically propel *this* patient's recovery? Then share those thoughts with the patient when you introduce the next piece of the work. "The Impact Statement that you wrote for today's session really helped me to understand all of the reasons why you believe your trauma occurred and the ways that this event has affected your life. I think these ABC sheets that I am going to share with you next will be particularly helpful for you in taking your work today a step further." Increasing the patient's intrinsic motivation for completing out-of-session therapy will likely result in both increased quantity and quality of the out-of-session work and translate into better outcomes.

We continue to provide examples of such tweaks in language and the presentation of concepts that we have found to be helpful across each of the four cornerstones of therapy in the next chapter.

Other issues that impact engagement

Time management

One of the greatest challenges in implementing a manualized therapy (particularly the first few times a therapist administers the intervention) is managing time and being sure to fit all of the therapy elements into the session. We have often heard that time management is particularly difficult in Session 1 (psychoeducation) and in Sessions 4 and 5 (introduction of the Challenging Questions worksheet and Patterns of Problematic Patterns of Thinking worksheet). Time management difficulties can really emerge at any point in the therapy, particularly with a verbose or tangential patient or someone who is very avoidant. As therapists, we all know that there are 10,080 min in each week and we only get 50 for therapy (and only if our patient arrives on time!). We need to treat those minutes like liquid gold and take advantage of each and every one of them. We hope the following clinical hints for each of the therapist concerns help therapists manage time in CPT sessions more effectively.

I cannot fit all of the information into one session

As the CPT manual has evolved over the years, the number of aids, handouts, and paperwork has increased substantially. However, the core goals and elements (and the rationale for those elements) have remained consistent. The goals of each session are outlined in the manual. Prioritizing meeting those goals is critical for the patient to get the full dose of the therapy. Meeting those goals, however, might look different from patient to patient. For example, our first priority in Session 1 is to assure the patient that we understand PTSD, that we have seen it before, and that we are confident we can move through her story and distress and emerge at the end of the therapy in a better place. If the patient does not leave the session feeling supported, understood, and at least a bit hopeful, it is unlikely that the patient will return. Would you?

Seamless delivery of therapy

As therapists get more and more familiar with the protocol, the delivery of the intervention begins to become more seamless. Practice makes perfect! To hasten this acquisition of skills and develop a more natural, seamless delivery of the therapy, we advise clinicians to spend a bit of time reviewing the challenging questions prior to beginning the protocol and, again, just before delving into the Socratic questions. While we are not suggesting that the therapist introduces the Challenging Questions (CQ) worksheet earlier than directed by the manual, we have often found that opportunities arise as early as Sessions 2–4 to work in a challenging question or two as part of your Socratic questions.

Case example: Imagine that Julie (our intimate partner violence survivor) is telling herself that her abuse happened because she was a bad wife. Her therapist might ask her from whom she got that information and help Julie to see that her husband (who was abusing her) was probably not a credible source of information. Later, when the therapist introduces the challenging questions on the CQ worksheet, the question "Is the source of information for your stuck point reliable?" will look familiar to Julie and she will already be well on her way to mastering the independent cognitive restructuring portion of the therapy.

Reviewing the important elements of the session ahead of time can really help in time management. Too often we hear that a therapist was getting good traction with a stuck point and then had to move on to introduce the next piece of therapy. Leaving enough time to introduce the next worksheet is important, but the therapist can build on the good work being done in the session during the Socratic questions and continue that work via the next worksheet. In other words, integrate the two session elements to keep the process of cognitive restructuring fluid.

Case example: Let's use our case example of Steve. Steve has been very hesitant to talk about his childhood traumas. The therapist is a little over halfway into Session 5 and Steve finally begins to disclose the details of his childhood abuse. The therapist knows she has to introduce the CQs and recognizes that this can take some time, but she is also concerned that to shift gears might create a missed opportunity to help Steve engage with his trauma memory.

Steve: *... and the worst part of it was—I could not protect my brothers. I was bigger and stronger than them and I had to stand by and watch them get hurt. I should have protected them.*

Therapist: *That must have been so hard.* (Steve is looking down and wiping away tears. He nods.) *How old were you at this time?*

Steve: *I was seven. My brothers are younger than me.*

Therapist: *Seven years old. You guys were all pretty young?* (Steve nods). *I think it is important what you said a minute ago, "I should have protected them." I wonder if that might be one of these stuck points that we've been talking about.* (Steve shrugs.) *I think that this next piece of the therapy might be really helpful in thinking this stuck point through. I'm really interested in considering this stuck point a bit more closely.* (Therapist writes the stuck point down on a CQ worksheet and they continue the discussion and challenging of this thought together using a *combination* of the worksheet and supplemental Socratic questions).

Finding time for continuous assessment

As highlighted in the CPT manual, routine outcome monitoring with a PTSD symptom measure each week (such as the PCL) is a critical piece of CPT, and routine monitoring is considered good clinical practice in psychotherapy in general. Sometimes therapists or patients might question whether this needs to be done or done as frequently. We believe the value in such practice far outweighs the perceived burden. You would not want to see a physician who just asked you how you felt your blood pressure medications were working and never checked your blood pressure! But that is what we do as clinicians, when we just ask how our patient is feeling, and we do not regularly monitor symptom change. In terms of making this an efficient process as possible, we recommend having patients complete the questionnaire in the waiting room before the session, thus ensuring valuable therapy time is not taken up with its administration. This helps when patients might be a little slower than average in filling out measures. The value of routine monitoring of PTSD symptoms is several-fold. First, it provides therapist and patient with an index of progress that is more accurate than generic questions about how the past week was or relying solely on clinical observations in the session. Second, it can be quite motivating for patients to see scores reduce in key symptom areas as therapy progresses. Third, when progress is not as smooth as expected, or there are discrepancies between a patient's verbal report of adjustment and a measure like the PCL, having such a measure provides an excellent starting point to explore this further, to assist in addressing the relevant issue. It can also be used to help challenge stuck points about therapy components or progress.

Case example: For example, imagine that Julie is worried about getting "worse" during therapy and fears that her experience of PTSD could somehow be used against her in a custody dispute by her partner. There are potentially two, if not more, stuck points embedded in this concern. The therapist could examine Julie's scores up to this point of therapy, and through Socratic Dialogue explore the fact that despite Julie engaging in a trauma-focused therapy that has been at times quite emotionally challenging, her PTSD symptoms have started to lessen. This would pave the way for some challenging of Julie's *perception* that she is getting worse or not coping well with therapy, which in turn could also be used in relation to the belief about fitness to parent (especially in light of symptom improvement).

CPT concepts are too complex for my patient

We often get the question: how do we know it is ok to "move on" to the next therapy element? We realize that CPT is described as a building block therapy, meaning that each session builds on the last. Following that logic, it makes sense that therapists are concerned that if their patients do not understand the material in the current session, they may become lost in later sessions. Leaving your patient in the dust for no good reason, other than "because a manual says so," is a valid clinical concern! However, CPT was intentionally built to be less linear and more dynamic. The protocol is designed to circle back and provide additional time for review, practice, and discovery of stuck points and evidence against stuck points. For example, we collect stuck points as they emerge throughout therapy, not only during Sessions 1 and 2 when we introduce the stuck point log. Each worksheet not only builds on previous concepts, but also provides a new lens for a patient to examine and challenge stuck points. Each session then provides opportunities for patients to continue to learn and practice the skills introduced in the previous sessions while offering new tools and fresh material as well.

Patients are quite variable in terms of which element of the therapy seems to be the silver bullet for recovery. For some people, the Socratic questions are really the key to success and the worksheets are seemingly not as helpful; for others, the Problematic Patterns of Thought worksheets really seem to help with challenging stuck points. Still other patients use only the ABC sheets throughout therapy, as the longer worksheets may seem too comprehensive or complicated. The CPT therapist has quite a bit of choice and latitude in flexing the worksheets (there are many examples of modified worksheets in the CPT manual) and relying heavily on Socratic questions throughout the protocol. One word of caution—there is very little reason to insert sessions into the CPT protocol! We have watched videotaped sessions of many therapists delivering the protocol over the years. Adding sessions, even with the best of intentions, almost certainly stalls the therapy. Patients come to expect something new and fresh each session and it is the therapists' job to foster the sense of forward momentum in moving toward the goal of resolving PTSD. Stalling and repeating sessions has the effect of grinding the process of therapy to a halt and significantly increases risk for dropout.

That said, there are certainly instances in which it does make sense to alter course. If your patient comes to session 30 min late, it might make sense to use the remaining time in session to discuss engagement, avoidance, and the importance of getting a full dose of therapy, and then resume CPT the next session. Emergency sessions are a separate issue and we will outline the use of this therapy modification separately. As a rule of thumb, CPT is designed to provide lots of opportunities for examining stuck points with different lenses and ample time for practice to acquire skills. There is really no need to repeat sessions. Keep moving forward, maintain the momentum, and add sessions at the end (as described later in the book) if necessary. Try to trust the process!

The many faces of avoidance

Avoidance comes in many shapes and forms, ranging from the very overt (*I didn't come to my last appointment because I just didn't want to think about my trauma*) to the subtle (e.g., the patient who appears extremely socially skilled and interested in other people may engage in such behavior to avoid conversations becoming focused on themselves because if that occurred, other people would "see" what a damaged/hopeless person they were as a result of their trauma). We end this chapter by briefly discussing some general issues with avoidance, and continue this conversation in the next chapter with concrete suggestions around managing avoidance, whether that be around specific CPT tasks such as the impact statement or trauma account, or more general issues relevant to CPT as a whole (e.g., avoidance of practice assignments). Before discussing several types of avoidance that we might see in patients (and how to address them), we need to be mindful of our role as therapists in unwittingly (or sometimes wittingly!) colluding with patient avoidance.

For some therapists it can be uncomfortable to highlight or call out possible avoidance in a patient. However, failing to do so means that we are not addressing one of the factors critical to the maintenance of our patient's PTSD. In addition to addressing our own therapist stuck point and our fears around noting a patient's avoidance during session (are we worried it will be damaging to the therapeutic alliance? Are we concerned labeling avoidance might cause a patient to drop out?), we find it helpful to externalize avoidance right from the beginning of CPT, as seen in this dialogue in Session 1 with Julie, our intimate partner violence survivor.

Therapist: [having discussed the role of avoidance in maintaining PTSD symptoms]. *Something I'd highlight about avoidance, Julie, is that there might be a time during therapy that you feel like avoiding either a task or even a session. A part of our work together will be working out how to navigate and overcome that avoidance when it rears its head. So, when avoidance shows up, we'll work together to figure why that is happening, and most importantly, how we are going to deal with it. And it is important to know that there is always a way for us to move through avoidance, whether we have to go around it, over it, under it, or straight through it. So, you and I will need to keep an eye out for it. If I think that something you are doing or not doing might be a form of avoidance, I'm going to ask you about it. Equally, it's helpful for you to monitor your reactions to how therapy is going and the things we do, so that you can let me know if that avoidance is trying to creep up and get you off track.*

By talking about avoidance this way, the therapist is distinguishing the avoidance from something that is intrinsic to Julie. It is thus far less confronting for Julie when the therapist later wonders with Julie whether something might be an avoidance behavior. Even though the avoidance most often stems from the patient, externalizing it in this fashion minimizes the chance that a patient will feel personally criticized when a behavior is put under the "avoidance" spotlight. Rather, the patient and therapist can work together to better understand the cause and function of these behaviors, with the goal that these behaviors are nonjudgmentally discussed and addressed.

A wide range of behaviors by patients can be conceptualized as forms of avoidance. In their most severe form, they might require intervention in their own right (e.g., serious substance abuse), which we tackle in Chapter 10 when we discuss how to address comorbidities. In less severe forms, such behaviors can often be addressed within the standard CPT framework. For example, we see many patients engage in behaviors such as excessive drinking, binge eating, online gaming, internet pornography, frequent and/or risky sexual encounters, excessive or impulsive spending, to name a few. Exploring these behaviors often shows they serve several functions, commonly as ways to alleviate emotional pain or distress, as well as ways of distracting the patient from having to think or confront trauma memories and trauma-related stimuli.

Case example

Take our forklift driver Steve, for example. Although seemingly at odds with the inattentiveness he has shown at work, in the home environment he spends a large amount of time keeping track of the family's routine, knowing where his sons are at all times, and what activities they and his wife have in the upcoming weeks. Without context, and on the surface, we might misattribute this behavior as controlling due to malintent or a domineering personality. In Steve's case, however, this behavior reflects, amongst other stuck points, an intolerance of uncertainty. In an attempt to gain a sense of control (i.e., *if I know where everyone is at all times, that means they are safe*), Steve's behavior helps him avoid the distressing emotions associated with *not* always knowing what is happening with his family. Identifying this function will help both Steve and the therapist work on the underlying stuck points driving this avoidance, avoidance that ultimately is maintaining maladaptive behaviors around safety (and perhaps power or control), resulting in the persistence of his PTSD.

Sometimes avoidance is hidden within the appearance of tackling avoidance! Take for example a patient who brings back a trauma account not on the index event as discussed in the previous session, but of another event. Brief exploration of why they did this is important. While on some occasions the patient has genuinely and insightfully identified what is in fact their worst trauma (*I realized after our session last week that this is the trauma that bothers me the most and is the one I try hardest to forget*), we often find that when patients do this it is because when they sat down to write on the originally agreed event, they believed that it would be too difficult, or have convinced themselves that this other event was in fact the worst event. At this point, revisiting some of the advice outlined in the CPT manual in relation to identifying the index event can be helpful to discriminate between the two traumas and to decide which should be the focus of future writing. Challenging stuck points about fears of tackling the worst event is likely to be useful at this point, and one variant of these stuck points has been addressed earlier in this chapter (e.g., *I can't tolerate this therapy*), with other forms discussed further in the next chapter. It is still important to acknowledge to patients that they have made an important step in trying to reduce their avoidance of trauma memories, while reiterating the importance of addressing the memory that is resulting in the most distressing symptoms or having the most impact on their lives.

Summary

We have addressed in this chapter some of the barriers clinicians and patients might face when initiating CPT, especially in relation to concerns in engaging in a trauma-focused therapy, ambivalence and lack of engagement, practical barriers (e.g., time management within session), as well as an initial discussion of some of the avoidance behaviors that can interfere with progress and outcomes. Along this theme, we continue in the next chapter with possible solutions to issues that can arise in response to key components of CPT, namely out of session practice, eliciting emotion, and what to do when faced with stuck points that seem to want to remain "stuck."

References

Blain, L. (Unpublished dissertation). Motivational interviewing as an adjunctive therapy to CPT. T.E. Galovski, Chair.

Feingold, Z. R., Fox, A. B., & Galovski, T. E. (2018). Effectiveness of evidence-based psychotherapy for posttraumatic distress within a jail diversion program. *Psychological Services*, *15*(4), 409–418.

Miller, W. R., & Rollnick, S. (2012). *Motivational interviewing: Helping people change* (3rd ed.). New York, NY: Guilford Press.

Resick, P. A., Monson, C. M., Galovski, T. E., Chard, K., & Kattar, K. (2010). *Cognitive processing therapy veteran/military version: A consultant's manual* (2nd ed.). Boston, MA: Veterans Health Administration.

Resick, P. A., Monson, C. M., & Rizvi, S. L. (2008). Posttraumatic stress disorder. In D. H. Barlow (Ed.), *Clinical handbook of psychological disorders: A step-by-step treatment manual* (4th ed.). New York: The Guilford Press.

Rooney, K., Hunt, C., Humphreys, L., Harding, D., Mullen, M., & Kearney, J. (2005). A test of the assumptions of the transtheoretical model in a post-traumatic stress disorder population. *Clinical Psychology & Psychotherapy*, *12*, 97–111. doi: 10.1002/cpp.441.

Rosen, C. S., et al. (2016). A review of studies on the system-wide implementation of evidence-based psychotherapies for posttraumatic stress disorder in the Veterans Health Administration. *Administration and Policy in Mental Health and Mental Health Services Research*, *43*, 957–977.

Schumm, J. A., Pukay-Martin, N. D., & Gore, W. L. (2017). A Comparison of veterans who repeat versus who do not repeat a course of manualized, cognitive-behavioral therapy for posttraumatic stress disorder. *Behavior Therapy*, *48*, 870–882. doi: 10.1016/j.beth.2017.06.004.

Waller, G., Cordery, H., Corstorphine, E., Hinrichsen, H., Lawson, R., Mountford, V., …, & Russell, K. (2007). *Cognitive behavioral therapy for eating disorders: A comprehensive treatment guide*. Cambridge, MA: Cambridge University Press.

Westra, H. A., & Dozois, D. J. A. (2003). Motivational interviewing adapted for anxiety/depression (Unpublished treatment manual).

Chapter 7

Navigating rough waters: Managing common challenges across the four cornerstones of CPT

Chapter outline

Clearly, cognitive processing therapy (CPT) is a manualized intervention and fidelity to the manual ensures that the patient is receiving the proper content and dose. However, as all therapists know, sessions do not always transpire according to plan. No matter what therapy we are administering, we sometimes find ourselves seemingly down a rabbit hole with no clear exit plan to

Flexible Applications of Cognitive Processing Therapy. http://dx.doi.org/10.1016/B978-0-12-816715-1.00007-8

get back on track. In those therapy moments, it can be helpful to focus on the critical elements of the protocol and leverage them to get the process back on track. The CPT workshop has identified the critical elements of CPT (termed the four cornerstones of CPT in the training workshop) as (1) emphasis on practice work between sessions, (2) promotion of the expression of natural emotions, (3) prioritization of challenging assimilated (trauma-related) stuck points before over-accommodated (current and future) stuck points, and (4) the use of Socratic questions (SQs). These theorized active elements of therapy capture the spirit of the protocol and can really provide quite a bit of guidance when you are faced with clinical decisions throughout the therapy, particularly when *your* therapy is not looking quite like the process described in the manual!

Farmer, Mitchell, Parker-Guilbert, and Galovski (2016) conducted a study in which 550+ CPT therapy sessions were videotaped and then watched by CPT raters to assess the extent to which therapists in the studies *adhered* to the manual (i.e., did they do the things they were supposed to do according to the manual). Therapist *competence* (i.e., how good the therapists were at administering the different parts of CPT) was also evaluated. Therapist adherence and competence together provide us with an overall estimation of fidelity to the protocol. This study showed that overall these study therapists scored high rates of adherence—they administered the manual fairly closely to the way that it was written. Competence was a bit more variable—simply put, some therapists were more skilled than others in delivering the therapy. The unique and novel contribution of this study was that this was the first time anyone had really closely looked at how well these theorized four cornerstones of CPT were administered in actual therapy situations. Perhaps even more importantly, this was the first time that the contribution of these important therapy elements to recovery from posttraumatic stress disorder (PTSD) had been evaluated. In other words, we say that it is important to do these things in CPT (e.g., prioritize assimilation before over-accommodation, etc.), but how *critical* is each element in the success of the intervention in treating PTSD? Interestingly, we found that prioritizing assimilation before over-accommodation *and* the therapist skill in SQs significantly contributed to improvements in PTSD. Therapist emphasis on the expression of natural affect and attention to practice assignments were not related to improvement in CPT outcome.

It is important to keep in mind that we were not measuring the amount of affect that a patient exhibited (vs. emotional numbness, etc.); we were measuring the extent to which the therapist focused on affect (and the relationship of this therapist skill to outcomes). Likewise, we were not measuring the amount of practice work that a patient did; we were measuring how the therapist attended to the practice work in session. Our results suggest that it is critical to focus on those assimilated stuck points first. If you get distracted by more current stressors and over-accommodated stuck points, you are likely avoiding the trauma right along with the patient. Results also suggest that the SQs are the heart of the therapy and critical for success. Honing this skill is important. These two elements may have emerged as critical for success because of their influence on these other cornerstones. When you address assimilated stuck points first, you bring your patient closer to the memory of the trauma and the heart of PTSD. Likewise, your SQs bring the patient closer and closer to the details of the trauma and the pain of PTSD. Both cornerstones are likely to lead to the expression of emotion. And then encouraging the use of the practice work outside session just cements these accomplishments and gains as patients move through avoidance and toward recovery.

The following sections address a number of common challenges to following protocol that emerge over the course of CPT. Keeping these four critical elements of CPT front and foremost will help you maintain fidelity.

Cornerstone 1: Emphasis on practice work between sessions

The dog ate my homework and other sordid tales

Noncompliance: Difficulty with completing the out-of-session therapy can be caused by a number of reasons including feeling emotionally overwhelmed by the trauma memory, a belief about being "graded" on the work and failing, worrying about someone at home accessing written work and discovering trauma details, or simply struggling to find the time to fit in the work with busy schedules. The reason why your patient is hesitant about approaching the out-of-session work will dictate your intervention. So, first step—ask! One effective question is: "Which part of the engaging in the out-of-session therapy seems hard?" This is always a great SQ because it prompts the patient to begin dismantling the process and really thinking through what piece is particularly challenging about the work. If we can break a process down into pieces, it might seem less daunting and overwhelming. Consider some typical reasons for poor compliance with out-of-session therapy:

1. *Feeling overwhelmed by the thought of practice work*: Think about introducing the out-of-session therapy similarly every time—with confidence and enthusiasm. Begin with the assumption that the patient is on board with continuing the therapy outside of session. Avoid disheartening and ominous statements like: "People find this next assignment difficult," or "This is going to get worse before it gets better" (we have heard that said more than once—sounds a little scary and the truth is, we have no idea how hard any assignment will be for any given patient), or "This next worksheet can be really confusing." These statements might be well intentioned by the therapist, but they really start the assignment off on the wrong foot and are unduly alarmist and/or pessimistic. Most patients catch

on pretty easily to these concepts and worksheets and, if they struggle, we have many ways that we can make adjustments. There is plenty of time for practice and honing skills.

Next, the therapist might use SQs to challenge stuck points that are causing the patient's distress and avoidance of the practice work. Depending on where you are in the protocol, the therapist could also leverage the worksheets by adding "out-of-session therapy" to the A column and the related stuck points to the B column with feelings caused by the stuck point in the C column. The following is an example of SQs around Steve's practice work-related stuck points.

Steve: *I cannot handle thinking about this trauma. I will lose control.*

Therapist: *Which part of completing this work would be hard for you?*

Steve: *Thinking about the actual rapes. When I am reminded of my trauma, I have a panic attack. I need to be able to function at work, and while driving, and when I'm with my kids, etc.*

Therapist: *Definitely. It seems like these thoughts, when they intrude on you in these places and times when you don't want to be thinking about them, really can create havoc—like panic attacks. What might be different about a situation like sitting down to think through your thoughts about the rape on these worksheets?*

Steve: *Well, I could plan a time and a place where I have some privacy. But I still feel unsafe—I hate thinking about it—I thought I would die during one of the rapes.*

Therapist: *Yes—I think that makes a lot of sense—intentionally approaching the memory in the privacy of your home (instead of being blindsided by it at work or in the car) is very different. As far as being unsafe—I agree, during the rape you were in great danger. What is different about approaching the memory of the rape compared to being in that situation?*

Steve: *I can see that it is very different. There is no actual danger in thinking about it—it's over and done. I just hate thinking about it. But I understand that working so hard to avoid thinking about it is not working either—I still have PTSD.*

Therapist: *I agree—the rape is over and done and thinking about it as being in the past is a big step. You are no longer in danger from that rape. It also makes sense that thinking about it is very hard and that you hate it. But is this new thought different than the original thought that you cannot handle thinking about this trauma?*

Steve: *Yes, I can see what you are saying. I am anticipating that this will be very, very hard. But I believe I can handle it—even when the thoughts about the rape blindside me, I get through it.*

Therapist: *I just want to point out that you really did a remarkable job changing your mind about a pretty big stuck point. We began this session with you saying that you could not do this work. And in just thinking through that belief for a few minutes, you moved to the thought that although it will be very hard, you will be able to handle thinking about your trauma and these* *worksheets. I think this therapy is a really good fit for you—it's all about taking a minute and examining what you are telling yourself and leaving open the possibility of changing your mind.*

2. *Fears about being graded on worksheets and failing*: Some patients have not written an essay (like the Impact Statement) or completed worksheets in years. This written work can remind people of bad experiences in school, poor grades, and resultant embarrassment and shame. The concern becomes—am I doing this correctly? This might be particularly true for specific pieces of the therapy such as the Impact Statement, written in essay form. In an effort to allow the patient to really understand and articulate their beliefs about why the trauma has happened and the impact that it has had on his/her life, the instructions for the Impact Statement are intentionally broad and open-ended. As a result, the responses are quite variable. For example, it is not uncommon for patients to feel compelled to describe *what* happened before they delve into *why* they believe the event happened. In these cases, the Impact Statement can read much like a trauma narrative. Patients can also be abrupt or avoidant or very concrete. We have had long Impact Statements returned (the average across the Galovski trials was seven pages) and we have had one sentence Impact Statements returned as well (e.g., *I saw my friend die in combat because we were at war*).

Given that this is the first attempt at out-of-session therapy, patients can be anxious that they "get it right." In this first assignment, it is important to take whatever your patient brings in (even in the case of nothing) and build on it in session. Therapists may ask patients to talk through what they would have written if they had completed the assignment (or build on whatever they did bring back). Therapists can jot down bullet points to capture what was mentioned during the session. At the end of the session, it can be very helpful to make a copy of the outline of the Impact Statement captured during the conversation and give the notes to the patient. "This is really good work and this really helps me to understand your perspective on this event. I think we are off to a great start. If you are able, please take a look at what I've captured between now and the next session and add anything that I missed or any additional information that you might recall." If the patient simply needs to continue building on this good work, now the patient is back on track and involved in his/her own therapy—a success experience. By saving a copy of the Impact Statement outline, the therapist has an existing skeleton of the Impact Statement to read back to the patient at session 12 (in the event that the patient never completes the assignment).

Choosing your words wisely in introducing out-of-session therapy to patients concerned with performing poorly on written work can be very helpful in reducing anticipatory anxiety. Weave the introduction of the new worksheet into the session a bit earlier to allow for a little more exposure to the concepts behind the piece of therapy. Explain again why continued work at home is important to the therapy and recovery using nonthreatening, nonjudgmental words with a manageable timeline: "We don't often take the time to really think about what it is that we are telling ourselves. These sheets give you the **opportunity** to take a **minute** and sort out your thoughts. This will help us as we start to take the next step in deciding which thoughts are 100% accurate and which are **less than 100% accurate**. If thoughts are not wholly accurate and are causing you pain, it makes sense to change them! But first, we need to sort them out—so how about taking some of these home and spending **some time** on them and see what you come up with? **Play** around with them, **maybe one per day**, and it will get us off to a great start in next week's session."

3. *Fears about others reading through material*: This patient concern requires some behavioral planning around the timing of engaging in the out-of-session work and the storing of materials. We have had this issue emerge in cases of intimate partner violence, in cases in which roommates, parents, or older children are sharing the residence, in prisons, and in inpatient units. Deciding how best to maintain privacy and address concerns for safety is case specific. In some cases, we have offered time and space prior to the therapy session in our clinics and people have completed the work in-house and stored materials with us between sessions. Other patients have stored work in their car or at a location other than home. One patient was bilingual and wrote on her worksheets in a language that her roommate could not read. Be helpful, clever, and creative in meeting the spirit of CPT's critical element of encouraging compliance with out-of-session therapy to optimize patient's success in this part of the process.
4. *Finding the time to work on CPT outside of session*: Getting in the habit of asking the patient if he/she anticipates any difficulty getting the out-of-session therapy completed can be very helpful, as is proactively manage any barriers that might arise. Using motivational interviewing techniques to increase intrinsic motivation to squeeze the work into everyday life can also be theoretically helpful, though there are little data to demonstrate this added benefit. Differentiating real-life challenges from avoidance or ambivalence is important as well. If, in fact, there are real-time management barriers to getting the work done, then problem-solving is time well spent.

When the best intervention is not effective in increasing compliance with practice work

The CPT manual is clear about the overall session format and about refraining from inserting extra sessions or repeating sessions during the protocol. As suggested, administer the assessment instruments (PTSD Checklist [PCL], etc.) prior to session, start the session by asking the patient about out-of-session therapy and then use that material as content for the session. Leave time to introduce practice work with a good working example. This usually works quite well … until it does not! For example, this master plan can fall apart due to the heavy reliance on the completion of the out-of-session therapy and the clear variability in patient willingness and ability to complete practice work.

Given the heavy reliance on out-of-session therapy in the protocol, it could be argued that a patient who is not engaging in work outside of the session is truly not doing CPT and perhaps should try another type of therapy. In the case of obvious ambivalence, this may be true. However, what is "obvious ambivalence"? Operationalizing "obvious ambivalence" may be, in some cases, fairly straightforward and might include indicators such as the patient answering his/her phone during session, arriving late, seeming disinterested, being more concerned about other topics of discussion, etc. However, there are many other issues already outlined earlier in the chapter that might be preventing engagement in the process including PTSD avoidance, dissociation, affective dysregulation, PTSD-related cognitions. It is critically important NOT to terminate therapy with a patient simply due to noncompliance with practice work. In many cases, this would constitute kicking a patient out of therapy for PTSD for having PTSD symptoms.

Clearly a number of factors can interfere with the therapist's ability to follow the CPT session format including, but not limited to, patient characteristics and behaviors, patient noncompliance, patient tardiness or prolonged absence from therapy, patient crisis, or difficulty comprehending the material. Each of these challenges will be discussed in more detail throughout the book, but the take-home message with respect to out-of-session therapy is to keep moving ahead with the therapy and reassign practice work for the next session. Theoretically, you could be at session 7 and have a backlog of seven sessions' worth of practice work due to repeated noncompliance and subsequent reassignments. Should the therapist terminate therapy? Should the therapist become more creative and try to develop other avenues to move the work into the patient's life? Should the therapist just bank on the time in therapy and forego the out-of-session work? What circumstances should dictate the clinical decision?

The practice work logjam: For some patients, the worksheets are a perfect fit. Perceived helpfulness of the work is rated highly with maximum compliance. Most patients fall somewhere in an average range and do a fair amount of practice work with variability across assignments. Often some attention to noncompliance in the beginning of the protocol and all of the suggestions provide in this chapter can right a course of noncompliance early on in therapy. A fairly small number of patients never do any practice work and this noncompliance can clearly be attributed to disinterest, ambivalence, and is clearly related to little movement in recovery. Then there is this interesting group of patients who complete zero practice work but who make great strides in session. PTSD scores march down across the protocol, affect in session brightens, the therapist can hear the change in stuck points over time (self-blame is out the window), and the patient shows improvements in psychosocial functioning (socializing, applying for a job, etc.). In this case, there is no real rationale to keep insisting on the completion of practice work. Using session time for the cognitive work is clearly effective—why waste those minutes and argue about seven sessions' worth of old practice assignments that have not been completed? In this case, it may be time for the therapist to desist trying to get the old assignments completed. However, there is certainly value in introducing new worksheets and suggesting that the patient give them a try between sessions. In these cases, therapists might worry less that the out-of-session work is a critical element of therapy for this patient; but it is still worth giving worksheets for the patient to read given we do not currently know whether understanding the concepts laid out in the worksheets and having copies of them in the future to navigate stuck points that might arise down the road will be critical in maintenance of treatment gains.

Getting creative with out-of-session therapy: Our best bet in helping our patients to recover from PTSD is to administer the therapy in the way it was intended (e.g., use the worksheets). However, that is simply not always possible. Bass et al. (2013) conducted a clinical trial in the Democratic Republic of Congo. Patients had, on average, a year and a half of formal education and so the worksheets in their traditional form were not helpful. Dr. Kaysen reformulated the content of the worksheets to adapt to the needs of this population by substantially reducing the text on the sheets, including pictures, and training the treating clinicians in methods to help their patients memorize the content of the sheets and insert the task into their daily routines. The women in the groups also got together between sessions to help each other challenge their stuck points! This study is a great example of thinking outside the box and finding creative ways to move the therapy into individuals' lives, even when traditional methods like worksheets are not effective.

Feingold, Fox, and Galovski (2018) describe a study in which CPT was implemented in an urban community mental health setting with patients suffering from severe mental illness, burdened by significant psychosocial stressors such as homelessness and poverty, and high rates of illiteracy. When needed, we borrowed strategies from the Congo study and also offered space to patients in the facility to complete practice prior to session when completing worksheets outside of session was not possible. When individual patients present with any number of other barriers to out-of-session therapy, we have also encouraged using art and drawings to identify and challenge stuck points. We have used recording one's voice versus writing—this has been helpful with amputees or people suffering from chronic pain such as arthritis. We even had one tremendously resilient patient who suffered from severe dissociation create a website to track stuck points and challenging questions. In summary, the CPT protocol has clearly been demonstrated to be effective and most often can be administered in clinical care as written, but creativity can be very helpful in unusual cases.

Cornerstone 2: Promoting the expression of natural emotions

CPT is predominantly a cognitive therapy. This means that the therapist's focus is mainly on the patient's thoughts about why the trauma happened and more current and future beliefs about oneself, the world, and others. But the goal of cognitive therapy is not merely to change the wording of the thought and then call it mission accomplished. The goal in considering the meaning of the event quite carefully is to ultimately change the feelings associated with the thought. CPT's focus on thoughts is a marked departure from different types of therapies that predominantly target feelings (e.g., exposure therapies). Consistency in this approach across the entire CPT protocol is very important. The more that therapists can consistently approach a patient's distress or struggle by identifying the stuck point and assisting the patient in challenging it and restructuring it, the more this process will become engrained in the patient's repertoire and generalize to other traumas and other life problems. This does not mean that CPT therapists do not attend to emotion or that cognitive therapy does not elicit emotion. Instead, cognitive therapy elicits emotions by understanding the related thoughts. For a more in-depth discussion of these concepts, see Chapter 2 on the practical application of the theories underlying CPT.

Therapists often worry that a patient is emotionally numb and may begin to focus too heavily on trying to elicit affect in session. For example, questions such as "Where in your body are you holding this pain? Where do you feel it?" or continued check-ins such as "Are you feeling anything now? How about now?" can really shine a spotlight on the emotional numbness and elevate "feeling one's feelings" to the primary goal of therapy. This technique is not wrong and is effective in other therapies. However, CPT takes a different approach in trying to understand the meaning that a patient is making of the event and where that patient got stuck. In talking about why the trauma happened, the patient will access the pieces of the trauma that are associated with the pain and distress. In other words, the therapist's SQs will elicit more and more description of the trauma as well as stuck points, etc. The key is for the CPT therapist to allow the patient the space to move closer and closer to the heart of the trauma memory and the opportunity to feel his/her feelings around the parts of the trauma that, by definition of having a PTSD diagnosis, she/he has likely been avoiding. Engaging with the memory will yield natural affect. Identification of stuck points will reveal the associated manufactured emotion. The former will run its natural course and the latter will dissipate with the cognitive challenging and resolution of the stuck point.

Consider the case example of Steve. As you recall, he has been avoiding the memory and any discussion of his childhood trauma. He may appear very emotionally numb in session. He is numb because he is working very hard to suppress those memories and not feel as badly as he did during his trauma. CPT suggests that the therapist allows him to access his natural emotions associated with the event by giving him the opportunity to talk about his trauma in the safe therapy environment.

The trauma narrative

The trauma narrative was originally part of the CPT protocol, but is now optional. Resick et al. (2008) conducted a randomized clinical trial in which the full CPT protocol (at the time this included the trauma narrative) was compared to a written exposure only condition (WE) and to CPT without the narrative and purely cognitive restructuring (CPT-C). More detail on this study and its results are described in Chapter 3. Suffice it to say for these purposes that the written trauma narrative did not add anything to recovery from PTSD and depression over and above the effects realized by the cognitive therapy. Removing the narrative from the protocol allows more time to accomplish the cognitive work. However, therapists remain concerned that for some patients, the trauma narrative might be a critical ingredient in recovery and it is true that we simply do not know at this time for whom this is the silver bullet.

Theoretically, the trauma narrative appears to be the perfect tool to enable a patient to engage in the trauma memory and feel his/her natural feelings about the event. As discussed in Chapter 3, treatment outcome data have shown that CPT (without the trauma narrative) resulted in a faster reduction of symptoms and less dropout (Resick et al., 2008). There are important caveats—this finding is from one study and we do not know for which patients the narrative might really be helpful and for whom it is less helpful. We do know that CPT (without the narrative) is *not* a watered down version of CPT-A in eliciting natural emotions. Choosing the cognitive only version of the therapy (CPT) is not an "easier" route or a less intense therapy. Far from it, the CPT version can actually afford the therapist more time to really engage in the cognitive work and fully probe the meaning of the event. In fact, it has been our experience that patients who do choose the trauma narrative can run into the same problems that can occur with any practice work—they may avoid completing it or only provide scant details about the event, forget to bring it to session, or present with any number of typical difficulties with practice compliance. Thus, the time spent in introducing the trauma narrative assignment, discussing avoidance or noncompliance, and then trying to recreate it verbally in session and reassigning it for the next week might be better spent on using SQs to engage in the trauma memory.

Through SQs, a therapist can guide the patient right to the heart of the memory of the traumatic event and begin to sort out the evidence for and against the assimilated stuck points that are maintaining the PTSD. This evidence includes the trauma details that would have been captured in a trauma narrative. The patient experiences the natural affect associated with the trauma memory during the Socratic dialogue similarly to experiencing the natural emotions when writing and reading a well-written trauma narrative. So CPT (without the narrative) actually provides more time in session to flesh out the details around the traumatic event (engaging with the memory of the event and breaking through avoidance—the goals of the trauma narrative) *and* more time to identify and challenge the stuck points (goals of the cognitive work). However, for some patients, the process of sitting down and writing it all out in detail might truly be effective and therapeutic—particularly in cases where this piece of out-of-session therapy is well done. The difficulty for the therapist is knowing a priori for whom this portion of the therapy will be effective.

Conceptually, it seems that offering the option of the trauma narrative at the outset of therapy is optimal as it provides choice to the patient. Providing choices places the patient a bit more firmly in the driver seat and has the potential to increase ownership of one's own recovery and investment in the chosen course of action (the therapeutic process). Importantly, choosing one version over the other may improve the fit of the therapy to the patient's needs. Since we have determined that we simply do not know for whom the written narrative may be very effective, it makes sense to rely on the patient's opinion on goodness of fit.

Once the patient makes the choice (which should be made at session 1), the therapist should stick with that decision and implement CPT accordingly. That being said, it is not uncommon for the patient to make the choice to write the trauma narrative, the therapist to assign the narrative, and then the patient to avoid the actual writing. We are often asked by therapists if they should "switch" to CPT without the narrative in this case. The answer is probably not. In this scenario, the patient is likely avoiding the trauma narrative and so "switching" out of this part of the therapy might amount to colluding with the patient's avoidance. If the patient has specifically chosen to write his/her trauma narrative and then avoided it, the patient may finish the protocol thinking that she/he had gotten some benefit but never was able to accomplish that one part. Writing the trauma narrative might loom larger than is necessary. Instead, treat the noncompliance with writing the trauma narrative as you would with any other piece of out-of-session therapy: do the work in session verbally, talk through what got in the way of completion, and reassign. If the patient continues to avoid on the second writing, continue on course and reassign for a final time. If the patient avoids a third time, it may then be helpful to move on and minimize (accurately) the necessity of that part of the intervention for recovery.

Suggested script: *It sounds like it has been difficult to write this narrative between sessions, but I feel as if I've gotten a very good understanding of what happened during your trauma from your description in session. We also have excellent stuck points on our stuck point log. I suggest we continue on with the cognitive work and really explore these stuck points you've identified. If, at any time, you think it might be helpful to write down your story, feel free to do so. Some people find it helpful and others, not as helpful.*

Eliciting emotion with Socratic dialogue

As described, the trauma narrative may (or may not) be a tool to help patients engage in trauma memories and feel natural feelings. Socratic dialogue serves the function of eliciting natural affect as well. For example, asking the patient to provide evidence for and against a trauma-related (assimilated) stuck point requires the patient to consider the facts of the event, which requires engaging in the memory of the event. Consider our Army Veteran, Anna. Anna presents in session 1 with dark glasses and expresses little affect as she provides her 5-minute version of her trauma (being shot and witnessing the death of her fellow soldier and her ensuing sexual assault). She writes a very sparse impact statement at session 2 and her assimilated stuck points include "Brian (medic) was headed to help me when he was shot. It's my fault he died." Anna read her impact statement a bit like a police report. She told her therapist that she had to complete a similar type of report in the investigation after the attack. During session 3, the therapist gently challenges this stuck point and the patient logically agrees that she did not cause Brian's death, yet continued to show very little emotion.

Therapist: *I hear you say that you caused Brian's death? Can you tell me more about how he died that day?*

Anna: *Yes, we were preparing to head out and were loading into the vehicles as quickly as possible. We exited the building one by one and covered each other as we moved across the open space before jumping into the vehicle. Brian was right ahead of me and as he reached the Humvee, I started across.*

Therapist: *Did you cover him as he crossed the open space?*

Anna: *I did watch his back to the extent that I could, but the real coverage came from the Marines on the roof—they had the vantage point and were providing our cover as we were loading up and moving out.*

Therapist: *What happened next?*

Anna (with very little emotion): *Everything happened very fast. I was the first to get hit. At first I did not even realize what had happened. I never heard the shot, but Brian must have because he turned from getting in the car and started to run at me. I could tell from his face that something was wrong but it took me a minute to understand that it was me who was hit. I looked down and saw my arm covered in blood, but the pain did not really register at that time. I took a step back and sunk to my knee and tried to raise my weapon, but could not because of my injury. Brian was about two steps from me and then suddenly sort of flew at me and landed on top of me and died.* (Anna looks down.) Clinical hint when helping a patient to feel feelings, track both verbal report of event and body language. Anna suddenly ends her story with "he died" and simultaneously looks down. This might indicate that this is a "hot spot" of her event.

Therapist: *That must have been chaotic. One minute you were preparing to get out of the area and in the next moment, all hell broke loose. In a matter of seconds, you are shot, then under more fire, Brian tries to reach you and then he also takes fire with this horrible end. What happened then?*

Anna: *The Marines on the roof located the enemy fire and took them out. They pulled us into the vehicles and got us back to base.*

Therapist (keeping her there and not moving on to whatever happened back at base): *How long did it take to get the situation under control enough to evacuate you and Brian?*

Anna: *I don't know … 5 minutes before they could reach us. The Marines who had gone ahead of Brian were pinned down in the vehicle and everyone left in the building was on the roof or returning fire. It was just me and Brian in the entry-way of the building.*

Therapist: *Five minutes? That's a long time.*

Anna (long silence, looking down): *Yep.*

Therapist: Just lets her sits with this part of the memory. A minute goes by.

Anna: *I could not save him. I tried. He never spoke, he couldn't. But I think he knew I was there. I hope he knew I was there. He didn't deserve to die like that on a street in Iraq. He was better than that. He wouldn't have died there, in that way, if he hadn't come back for me. I felt his life leave him. He was just gone and that can never be changed.*

Through the course of Socratic dialogue, Anna stayed with her traumatic event, especially the parts that she worked hard to gloss over. By asking some questions, the therapist is able to help her remember the worst part of the event in significant detail. It is likely that Anna would be feeling emotions by this point as she pushes through the avoidance by remembering details of the trauma. Hopefully this example portrays the ways that SQs and dialogue can serve the same function as writing a trauma narrative in terms of helping the patient engage with the trauma memory.

In summary, emotions are an enormous part of any therapy. People come to therapy to *feel* better. CPT is no different than any other therapy in acknowledging the importance of emotions. There are many paths to Rome and CPT gets to Rome by helping people talk about the meaningfulness of their event(s). Through this process, we can identify inaccurate thoughts and correct them, but we also allow our patients the opportunity to lay down their burden and safely share the memories that truly haunt them. In this way we help our patients move through both the manufactured emotions (those directly caused by the stuck points) and the natural emotions.

Cornerstone 3: Prioritizing assimilated stuck points before over-accommodated stuck points

The first step in cognitive therapy is identifying what it is that people are telling themselves that is getting in the way of them living their best lives. As a predominantly cognitive therapy, CPT is no different with one very important distinction. The thoughts sought by the therapist and targeted throughout therapy are related to the traumatic event. This makes complete sense given that CPT is a trauma-focused therapy. The reasons for this are outlined in Chapter 2. Suffice it to say that trauma-related thoughts are precisely the culprits that keep people stuck in PTSD (hence the term stuck points!) and, as such, should be the primary focus if one wants to prioritize recovery from PTSD.

In review, assimilated stuck points are those beliefs about *why* the trauma happened. These most typically include self-blame, other-blame, or statements of undoing. Over-accommodated stuck points are more current and future focused. It might be helpful to think of these types of stuck points as beliefs about one's self, world, and others that were negatively (and inaccurately) influenced by the traumatic event. Assimilated stuck points must be prioritized in therapy, but can be elusive and difficult to detect. We can honestly say that we have never seen a patient who has his/her head around the traumatic event 100% accurately *and* has PTSD. Thus, the assimilated stuck points are there, even if not readily apparent.

Staying trauma-focused in CPT requires that one begins at the beginning of the patient's PTSD (the trauma) and progresses to the current and future beliefs. Beginning at the beginning means prioritizing assimilated stuck points. The order in which we challenge stuck points is critical in recovery. First, as discussed in the previous section, the assimilated stuck points are closely related to the trauma details. Engaging with the trauma memory and disentangling fact from assumptions, recalling important aspects of events that have been disregarded, and generally working through avoidance is the preponderance of the recovery process. Second, the assimilated (inaccurate) stuck points are often the evidence for the over-accommodated stuck points. When assimilated stuck points crumble through Socratic dialogue, the over-accommodated ones hold far less credibility and are much more easily challenged. Let's continue with Anna's case as an example. Imagine that we had not prioritized and successfully challenged the assimilated stuck point of "It is all my fault that Brian died on the streets of Iraq," and instead we started with "I am worthless." It would be very difficult to challenge the idea that Anna is worthless if her evidence for being worthless is her belief that she caused Brian's death. Now imagine that we had continued the dialogue earlier and challenged the assimilated stuck point first.

Therapist: *I agree. He didn't deserve to die there that day. But it also sounds like you did whatever you could to prevent that from happening? And the reality was that you couldn't do anything to stop it?*

Anna: *By the time he fell, I think it was over. I honestly don't think anyone could have saved him. But if I hadn't gotten shot, he never would have been in the line of fire. It's my fault he was shot at all.*

Therapist: *I hear what you are saying. You were in the line of fire and took a bullet. He turned back to help you. And the enemy continued to fire. Was there something else you could have done? Not come out of the building?*

Anna: *Well no—we needed to get out of there. Almost everyone had evacuated—there were just a few of us left. We were leaving because it was dangerous.*

Therapist: *Oh—I see. So you needed to get out of there. Were ordered to get out of there?* (Anna nods.) *And it makes sense to you that you were ordered to get out, that it was becoming increasingly dangerous?* (Anna nods again.) *What about Brian? Does it make sense that he took the actions that he took at that time?*

Anna bristles: *Yes! He was an excellent soldier—he did exactly what he supposed to do—he was trying to save me.*

Therapist: *I hear you. The whole unit was trying to get out of there because the threat level was increasing. And they were right—it was the right order to evacuate. And you were following that order, as was Brian. You were doing your job, and, when Brian turned back, as a Marine and a medic, he was doing his job as well. The only part that I am still not hearing is—how was this your* *fault? Looking back, was there anything that you could have done differently?* (Anna shakes her head no.) *Was there any reason for you to do anything differently?* (Again, Anna shakes her head no.) *When it comes right down to it, why do you think Brian died that day?*

Anna (after a long minute): *Because he was a Marine in Iraq and was fired on by the enemy during battle. And that can never change. He will never come back.*

Therapist (lets Anna sit with that emotion and sadness): *And that is true and very, very sad. But was Brian's death your fault?* (Anna shakes her head no.)

Moving through assimilated stuck points early in therapy often clears the path for the challenging of over-accommodated stuck points. Imagine down the road—at session 11—Anna begins challenging esteem-related stuck points. Perhaps she is telling herself, "I am worthless." If the therapist had not already helped Anna resolve the assimilated stuck point earlier, she likely would be considering the belief that she was to blame for Brian's death as evidence for the idea that she is now worthless. We have often found that successful challenging of these big assimilated stuck points at the heart of the PTSD can have the effect of dissipating over-accommodated beliefs—sometimes without ever having to even challenge them. For example, Anna might have said "I am worthless" in session 2 in her Impact Statement, but if the assimilated stuck points were largely resolved early in the therapy with excellent SQs, then she might have changed her mind on her own by session 11 when the theme of esteem is introduced.

In summary, the therapist's instinct to use session time early in the protocol to grapple with low-hanging fruit (over-accommodated stuck points) can present a conundrum. Any therapist would note that a statement like "I am worthless" is quite problematic and would want to help the patient change that belief about himself or herself. In CPT, however, that would be considered an over-accommodated thought and so would take a back seat to an assimilated thought.

In Anna's example, she is able to stay with the assimilated stuck point and begin to resolve it through SQs. Sometimes this process is not so straightforward. One of the challenges that can emerge is when the patient continues to focus on the current psychosocial stressors and over-accommodated stuck points and the therapist is in a position of continually trying to redirect back to the assimilated thoughts. This can often be conceptualized as avoidance. Patients might avoid talking about a trauma by focusing on psychosocial stressors (and related over-accommodated stuck points). The question becomes: how do we redirect (and stay trauma-focused) without being directive? The following clinical hints provide some strategies to stay focused on assimilated stuck points.

Leverage the worksheets

It can sometimes be helpful to ask the patient if he/she minds if you take a look at the worksheets together. If the pile of worksheets is in the therapists' hands, the therapist is able to give a nod to each worksheet but spend more time on the assimilated stuck points. This is a way to work around a patient who might "bury" the assimilated stuck points at the bottom of the worksheet pile.

Platform dive

We try very hard to avoid drawing a line in the sand with our patients during therapy sessions. CPT is a process of collaborative empiricism, meaning that the relationship is not hierarchical. It is collaborative. Yet, we need to exert some pressure at times during the protocol to help move through avoidance and stay trauma-focused. One way to do this is what we call the "platform dive." Imagine that current, significant over-accommodated stuck points are really grabbing your patient's attention. This might be due to avoidance or distraction (big psychosocial stressors can be very distracting!). It can be very helpful to choose a salient over-accommodated stuck point and use it as a platform to dive back into the waters of underlying, assimilated stuck points. Let's use Steve's case as an example. Imagine that Steve is at session 3 of CPT. The therapist and Steve identified the assimilated stuck point, "I should have protected myself" in session 2. Steve comes into session 3 feeling very agitated. He and his wife had gotten into a huge fight the night before and she was threatening to leave him. He was terrified that she would leave him and take his sons. The therapist knows that they need to prioritize the assimilated stuck point, but it is hard for Steve to focus on anything but this fight.

Steve: *Things cannot keep on this way. This therapy is making me worse. I am going to lose my family. Things were not great before I started therapy, but they were not this bad.*

Therapist: *Can you walk me through what happened?*

Steve: *I came home from work and my kids told me that they had been playing in the new neighbor's house all afternoon. I blew up. We don't know that family. My wife could not possibly watch them if they were in the house. Anything could have happened. I feel like I can't even go to work—look what happens when I am not home.*

Therapist: *What did happen when you weren't there?*

Steve: *My kids could have been danger and no one would have even known it. If I do not control everything, we are in danger. I can't even sleep at night.*

Therapist: *That's important what you just said right there: "If I do not control everything, we are in danger." How long have you had that belief?*

Steve: *Forever—since I was a child.*

Therapist: *I can understand that, given your assaults as a child. How did this belief play out during those assaults? I'm reminded of the thought that we had talked about last session—"I should have protected myself." The two thoughts seem a bit related to me?*

Steve: *I learned pretty quickly that if I didn't do everything perfectly as a child, I would be beaten ...*

Therapist: *I can see how being in control and danger are closely tied together based on these experiences. It seems like this belief really may have* *been born during your childhood and carried through to now. Let's walk through this together. It might be helpful in understanding this current situation with your kids' playdates* (begin SQs on assimilated stuck point).

Clock is ticking

We are often asked how a therapist should know when it is time to move on to over-accommodated stuck points. The simple answer is that the assimilation should always take priority over the over-accommodation. As we move into the latter part of the therapy, the modules are more geared toward addressing over-accommodated stuck points. However, the transition happens differently across patients. If the patient is still holding onto assimilated stuck points in the second half of therapy, the therapist should be thinking about *why* the patient has not successfully challenged the assimilated stuck points. There are a number of likely culprits that may be to blame. These will be outlined later in this chapter. Keep in mind in these situations that the modules are intentionally broad and overlapping. Think about the themes and the related questions and materials as different lenses upon which to examine stuck points. Considering stubborn assimilated stuck points with these different lenses may be helpful in cognitive restructuring. Similarly to Steve's example earlier, consider weaving the challenging of over-accommodated stuck points into challenging of those stubborn assimilated stuck points during the last five sessions. In summary, trust the process! Prioritize assimilation before over-accommodation and keep moving forward with the protocol. You can add sessions at the end if necessary.

Cornerstone 4: Socratic questions

As written in the CPT manual and taught in the CPT workshop, SQs are a key element of the intervention. As a brief review, Socratic questioning and the dialogue that evolves is the process of drawing forth the wisdom and knowledge about any given individual, his/her life experiences, and certainly information regarding the traumatic event through guided questions. This process of Socratic questioning appreciates that each individual is truly his/her own expert on the topic of him/herself. As such, the individual holds all of the relevant information and answers—it is there to be drawn forth with SQs. Through the process of SQs, information is elicited from our patients and our patients are able to consider real evidence based on their own experiences, and then reconsider inaccurate conclusions and beliefs that may be preventing them from recovering from their traumatic event and living their lives fully and well. Moving in the direction of accuracy and recovery based on changing one's own mind is quite empowering to the patient and is very different than the experience of "telling" or "convincing."

Our job as CPT therapists is to provide the space and opportunity for the individual to truly engage in our four-step process: (1) identifying precisely what it is that he/she has been telling herself/himself, (2) decide if the thought is inaccurate (a stuck point), (3) if it is a stuck point, begin the process of challenging it with real evidence (through SQs), and (4) change one's mind in favor of more accurate conclusions or beliefs (the alternative thought). Seems simple enough? And often the process is quite straightforward—we see those "light bulb moments" in session in which a patient suddenly realizes "I was just a child. This happened through no fault of my own. The problem was the perpetrator." However, the process of changing one's mind and moving through stuck points through SQs can also often be quite challenging. The following clinical hints highlight some of the likely culprits that might be slowing the process of recovery and offers guidance in addressing these difficulties.

Step 1: Identify the beliefs and Step 2: Decide if it is a stuck point

Honing the stuck point

In review, honing the stuck point and arriving at a thought that is inaccurate and challengeable are critical in the process of cognitive change. We must start the process of challenging the stuck point with a true stuck point or the process is destined to be very frustrating and ultimately unsuccessful. Stuck points *should* be clear and concise (e.g., it is my fault), *should not* include feelings (e.g., the world feels scary to me), *should not* be incontrovertible facts (e.g., I married someone who abused me), and *should not* be larger moralistic statements (e.g., people should protect their children). Importantly, the therapist must first judge the accuracy of the thought—we do not challenge accurate beliefs. That being said, accurate beliefs that are emotion-laden or very negative can offer clues about potential underlying stuck points. We think about this process as honing the stuck point.

Let's take the example of our army Veteran, Anna. Imagine that Anna states (in session or in her Impact Statement), *I always feel angry at the world and at myself. I'm the one who joined the army and got shot and then our medic died in my arms*. None of these statements in their current form can be challenged—they are not true stuck points (they are feelings and factual: Anna does feel angry, she did make the decision to join the Army, and the medic did die in her arms). But they provide us clues as to stuck points that might be lurking just below these types of statements and may be preventing Anna's recovery from PTSD. Helping Anna pull apart these thoughts should unearth stuck points. It can be very helpful to think about this in your CPT therapist head as an ABC sheet (or even pull out an ABC sheet and complete together in session) and engage in SQs accordingly.

Therapist: *From what you describe, your early days in the service were really rewarding and I remember you saying that you had planned to continue and make a career out of the military. Can you tell me a little bit more about when you started feeling angry at the world?*

Anna: *Every time I think about everything I lost—my confidence, my career, my mental health, I just get so enraged. I put just as much into this war and that unit as the Marines did and they betrayed me.*

Therapist (clarifying question): *Those Marines who assaulted you the night of the assault on your unit did betray you.* (Clinical hint—notice how the therapist did not identify the thought that the Marines betrayed her as a stuck point. This might come back up later, but likely the patient is referring to the men who specifically assaulted her as betraying her. This is a true statement and so not a stuck point. Instead, she leverages the word betrayal and continues accordingly.) *It makes a lot of sense that the memory of that betrayal brings up feelings of rage. Tell me more about the rage you describe currently "at the world"?*

Anna: *That experience taught me that men cannot be trusted—it just makes me want to scream out against the world.*

Therapist: *I think I understand what you are saying. "Men cannot be trusted" and when you think about this it makes you very angry. I can see a clear relationship between that thought and those feelings you describe. I wonder if this might be one of those stuck points that we had discussed? How about we add this to our stuck point log so we don't lose track of it and come back to this one. I'm also really interested in what might be driving the other part of what you had said earlier—where is the anger at yourself coming from?*

Anna (adds "All men cannot be trusted" to her stuck point log): *I am the one who put myself in this position. If I had not joined the army, this would not have happened. I put myself in this position. And I should have protected myself from those Marines that night—I was a trained soldier. I let that assault happen.*

Therapist: *Let's pull that apart a bit because there may be some more stuck points in there. First, let's think about you joining the army. I think I heard something along the lines of "I should never have joined the army (and then this wouldn't have happened). Is that right?* (Anna nods). *Let's add that to your stuck point log as well—"I should never have joined the army." It almost seems like you are saying that joining the army caused you getting shot and the medic's death? Let's talk through that one a little bit more. But first, I also want to be sure that we capture this other piece—I heard you say: "I should have protected myself from the Marines who assaulted me that night." When I hear these different statements that you are making—["I should not have joined the army," "My joining the army and being present that day caused my injury and the medic's death," and "I should have protected myself"], I hear you pointing the finger of blame for these events directly at yourself and it clarifies for me why you are experiencing the anger that you describe. But it also leaves me wondering if there may be other reasons that these bad events (the assault on your unit and the sexual assault) might have happened. For now, let's add these to your stuck point log and we will think about these a bit more in turn.*

The hunt for the elusive stuck point

Sometimes it is quite difficult to even find the slightest clue as to what the stuck point might be. We assert that all trauma survivors with PTSD have stuck points (both assimilated and over-accommodated). If someone were 100% accurate in their thinking about the traumatic event, they simply would not have PTSD.

However, stuck points can be quite elusive and the following provides hints for ways to uncover them in session.

Stuck points can be elusive for any number of reasons—sheer avoidance is a likely culprit. Avoidance can manifest in a number of ways. The most painful stuck points are often the ones that lie at the heart of the PTSD. Even speaking those words might seem overwhelming to the patient, so he/she may simply refuse to disclose in session. Sometimes the patient has not articulated the stuck point at all to himself/herself. If someone has been actively avoiding the whole memory of the traumatic event and pushing it away, then it is likely they have not had the opportunity to precisely examine their thoughts. The therapy session might be the first opportunity to engage in this metacognitive process (thinking about what you are thinking). In this case, the stuck points will not rise as easily to the surface, but they are there and can be revealed with SQs. When stuck points are elusive, it may take extra time to identify them. Therapists can get worried as the therapy clock ticks and they have not generated a "good" stuck point log yet. However, the hunt for stuck points is time well spent. Often times, this seemingly meandering path of identifying the stuck point also serves the function of uncovering lots of information that can be used to challenge the stuck point. We have found that by the time we actually identify the stuck point, the patient might be surprised that this is what he/she has been telling himself/herself and the challenging is much more straightforward. In other words, half the battle is just helping the patient to articulate what she has been telling herself.

Traumas that occurred during childhood might result in elusive stuck points because the patient has been thinking this way for a long time and not able to identify a time when the belief system changed. Very concrete thinkers ("my thinking is based entirely on fact") or less introspective thinkers also might not have engaged in the type of metacognitive exercise required in identifying stuck points. Let's consider Steve's example. If you recall, Steve had completed 10 sessions of CPT due to PTSD secondary to a car accident. He had made little progress and then disclosed a significant childhood history of assault. Although he is already at session 10, Steve and his therapist will have to begin identifying stuck points about his childhood trauma. This trauma happened about 30 years ago and Steve has worked very hard to not think about it at all. He and his therapist have been able to identify that the worst part of his childhood abuse was when his mother prostituted him to men for drug money. CPT does not have to begin at the beginning—no need to relearn all of the session 1–10 materials. However, refreshing the stuck point log and identifying relevant assimilated stuck points will be important. They can be challenged using the CBWs.

Therapist: *Your description of these assaults during your childhood and the fact that you have really avoided talking about them for a very long time suggest to me that we might want to start to find stuck points that might be related to this trauma. I agree with you that these childhood events really are likely linked to the PTSD symptoms that you are experiencing. I'm going to pull out a new* *stuck point log so that we can think through why you believe that this trauma happened to you and how these events have influenced the way you think about yourself and the world and others. Can we start with the first part? Why do you think that you were raped by those men during those years?*

Steve (stares at therapist): *Because my mother needed money for drugs.*

Therapist (realizing that her question was not helpful): *It makes sense that your mother needed money for drugs. Drug addictions can pose really difficult situations—do you know if there were any other options for her?*

Steve: *I have no idea. I was seven.*

Therapist (enlarging the context): *You are right—there is no way to know what options were available or even what her reasons were for choosing between options. I'm thinking a bit about you being seven. You would have been in first grade? Second?* (Therapist uses this softball question—how old were you to get the patient back in that frame of mind and engaged in the dialogue. Patient nods.) *When you went to school or hung out in your neighborhood, do you recall noticing if other kids seemed to be experiencing the same sort of everyday life as you were experiencing?* (Patient shrugs.) *How about looking back now, do you think this was a very different childhood? Even for kids who have parents with drug addictions?*

Steve: *I don't know. I never knew a normal childhood.* (Therapist waits.) *For as long as I can remember, my parents were clear that they didn't want us. They told us, and each other, as often as they could. Finally, my dad just took off and never came back—he was probably smart to get out. There was nothing for him there.*

Therapist: *You were there? Your brother was there?*

Steve: *That didn't matter—he told us he wished he didn't have us. I was actually relieved when I realized he was gone. I was hoping the beatings would stop. I could have tolerated my mom being high all the time. I would have taken care of Jeffrey.* (He pauses and stares down.) *But then the men started coming and it turns out I couldn't take care of much of anything.*

Therapist: *Do you think you should have been able to take care of things?*

Steve: *Prior to my dad leaving, I had taken care of a lot. I took most of the beatings for Jeffrey. I got him out of the house as much as I could. When the men started coming, I wanted to run away but I couldn't leave Jeffrey. I thought if I'd stayed then I would just take this too, for both of us. But this was different than my dad hitting me. And now look at me—I'm ruining my marriage and my kids' lives and might lose my job.*

Therapist: *The beatings sound awful. Tell me more about how surviving the rapes were different?*

Steve: *I guess I could take the beatings and could sometimes avoid them. I could figure out some ways at least sometimes to protect myself and I almost always protected Jeffrey. There was no getting away from these men. I didn't know when and I didn't know who. And the worst part about it was I tried to run one time but came back. While I was gone, the men used Jeffrey. I didn't protect myself and I didn't protect Jeffrey.*

Therapist: *Should you have?* (Steve nods and is very upset.) *I think what you just said right there is very important. I should have protected myself. I should have protected my brother.*

Enlarging the context

This case example illustrates a technique that we call "enlarging the context" to discover the elusive stuck point. Instead of stopping our search for stuck points at the point when the client says "This happened because my mom sold me for drugs" and coming to the conclusion that there are no stuck points (because this is a fact), we step back a bit further and ask more questions about the context of the situation. We build on what the patient has given us and follow the trail to the true stuck point. This patient might eventually disclose stuck points about internalizing the messages that he had gotten from his parents (worthless, unlovable). There are other hints in the dialogue that the patient might be blaming himself for "ruining" his marriage, kids' lives, etc. The idea that he and his brother were raped because he did not protect himself or his brother is a very good start. More SQs will continue to reveal more stuck points. On this meandering path to find the stuck point, the therapist has also accumulated a lot of information to aid in SQs. She now knows that he was only 7, that he actually did do everything humanly possible to protect his brother, that he did try to run away—but came back to save his brother, that his mother was addicted to drugs—essentially lots of information to support the idea that the problem clearly was not him.

Pulling at threads

In terms of finding elusive stuck points we might also use a strategy called pulling at threads. When stuck points are not readily apparent and you think you have exhausted all likely avenues and are feeling at lost for direction, you might consider building on some detail of the story that might seem relatively innocuous. The goal of this strategy is to explore new angles on the trauma memory and see if pulling at a new thread might loosen up elusive stuck points. Let's take Steve's example again. Imagine that your SQs and enlarging the context have not yielded any stuck points. When you asked about Steve's childhood, his thoughts were quite balanced, including several mentions of riding his bike. Because Steve mentioned riding his bike, you might take a leap and pull on that thread by perhaps just asking him to tell you more about hanging out with friends and bike riding. Think about this strategy as a way to build on what your patient is giving you, what seems to be important to him in his childhood recollections, and leveraging these memories as a way to get closer and closer to his trauma memory where you know that the stuck points are hiding. Pulling on this "new memory thread" helps you to take a new angle in session and avoid finding yourself in a SQ rut. Word of caution—this technique can be very helpful, but keep your eye on the prize. Do not go too far down a rabbit hole discussing irrelevant events. Instead, use this technique to get you closer to the trauma memory and the elusive stuck point.

Therapist: *Tell me more about riding your bike during you childhood—is this a good memory?*

Steve: *The only time I felt happy and free was when I was on my bike. I felt like all the other kids, normal. Like I could get away anytime—just ride away.*

Therapist (smiles): *That does sound normal. It must have been hard to get off the bike.*

Steve: *Yep—the other kids would keep laughing as they headed home. But I would feel like darkness was descending on me. Why couldn't that be my life? Why can't I keep laughing?*

Therapist: *Why do you think?*

Steve (looking at his hands): *I don't know—maybe they were right. Maybe I was garbage. What kind of kid can't even get his parents to love him?*

Therapist: *Is that what you think was the problem? That you weren't lovable?*

Steve: *Well, that's what they said was the problem. And my dad showed it to be true when he left us and never looked back. And my mom chose drugs over us. Seems pretty clear to me. If I had been lovable, they would have loved me instead of hurting and leaving me.*

Therapist: *That is very important what you just said right there—let's write that down because I really think it will be helpful to think that through together.*

Steve: *A stuck point?*

Therapist: *A big stuck point.*

Finally, it should be noted that, for any number of reasons, some patients continue to struggle identifying stuck points throughout the protocol. Continuing to figure out the reason for this difficulty and intervene accordingly remains important. But it is also important to continue with the protocol. Moving on and assigning new worksheets when the patient continues to struggle with identifying good stuck points can seem very challenging to therapists. We do not want our patients to get frustrated and find the new, more complex worksheets impossible simply because they are trying to challenge poorly constructed stuck points. In these instances, dividing the assigned worksheets in half and taking a minute to write down stuck points on *half* of the worksheets (e.g., in the B column of the CBWs) for the patients and leaving the other half of the worksheets blank can be a very effective strategy in moving the patient forward. Writing down critical stuck points before you send the sheets home ensures that the patient will engage in the process of challenging and continue to solidify that skill. Leaving half of the sheets blank ensures that the patient will still have the opportunity to practice the art of identifying new stuck points as they emerge throughout the protocol.

Step 3: Challenge the stuck point using Socratic questions

As we described, SQs involve asking, not telling. Asking the question invites the patient to weigh the evidence and then agree or disagree. Either way, the patient comes to his or her own conclusion and has a much higher likelihood of truly digesting and owning the new conclusion or alternative thought. A good rule of thumb for CPT therapists—never draw a line in the sand with your patient during the therapy session. Using warmth and compassion in your SQs allows you to stay on your patient's side and prevent tug of war experiences.

Using the words "challenging and restructuring" can evoke a bit of a hierarchical if not contentious relationship between the therapist and the patient. Therapists can be worried that their patients will feel affronted, insulted, or invalidated by the "challenging questions." We can understand this concern, especially if you are envisioning a CPT session to be reminiscent of a courtroom situation. ("Evidence for and against" might seem like stuck points are on trial.) Indeed, some therapists and patients resonate to the idea of whether the evidence behind a stuck point would stand up in court. If that is helpful, use that courtroom metaphor! As long as the therapist and patient are on the same team and relying on the patient's wisdom—any such metaphor is helpful.

Another option might be for the therapist to conceptualize the Socratic questioning process as a *CPT Dance*. The process really is a joining together (identifying a stuck point) and then gently moving apart (therapist wondering aloud about the stuck point or offering an SQ), joining together and agreeing on real evidence and shifts in thinking and so on. Joining a patient on his or her team and wondering about stuck points together and moving in the direction of recovery seems very validating. As CPT therapists, we always validate the patient, and we never validate stuck points. Why would we since they are inaccurate and harmful to the patient? Socratic dialogue, cognitive restructuring, and challenging stuck points can empower the patient to move himself/herself through PTSD to recovery—but only if we never draw a line in the sand and always maintain our warmth, regard, and respect for the patient.

There is little doubt that developing the art of SQs requires practice. There is, however, much comfort in knowing that, by definition, using the SQ technique means that you (the therapist) do NOT have to know all of the answers or provide solutions! All you have to do is ask the questions—which brings us to the challenges of posing SQs! Common therapist concerns and related solutions are highlighted in Table 7.1 Examples from our case vignettes will follow to further elaborate on honing your skill in shaping your SQs.

Honing your Socratic questioning skills

Arrow-down technique

Sometimes stuck points can be buried under other stuck points. Finding the most salient stuck point that is the biggest contributor to PTSD distress is very important. Using the arrow-down technique can be helpful in sifting through layers of stuck points that might reveal the "true stuck point" or a very significant stuck point that is keeping the patient stuck in PTSD. Imagine that our patient Steve is working on an over-accommodated stuck point. Each step in the following dialogue demonstrates how the therapist works with Steve to find the

TABLE 7.1 Common therapist concerns about patient progress during CPT and possible solutions.

Therapist concern	Solution
I feel like I am going in circles and not seeing any progress?	*Get specific*: In this case, you may be challenging generalities ("all my life ...," or "people are all ..."). Try to get specific. Ask the patient for an example. Particularly with over-accommodated stuck points, ask for an example of a time when this stuck point was relevant. If you stay too broad, your patient will always be able to find mountains of evidence for the stuck points and you will get lost there.
The same stuck point keeps popping up and it is like "rewind, repeat" as we challenge it over and over.	*Break the rewind, repeat cycle*: When a patient seems like he/she successfully challenges a stuck point, but the stuck point keeps resurfacing, the patient may be avoiding talking about other (more painful and salient) stuck points, because this one is easier. But really, you are just spinning your wheels. Try pointing out the pattern or identifying if there is another stuck point that we should be working on, but are avoiding.
I have tried everything. Nothing is working.	*Try something new*: This therapist concern sounds a bit like a therapist stuck point. Examine the process, see where it is broken and repair it. Remember the underlying premise of the therapy—people can change their minds! The question is what is preventing this patient from changing his/her mind. How can I, as the therapist, ask this differently or take a new angle?
My patient will not let go of a stuck point.	*Identify the underlying function of the stuck point*: If, despite all evidence to the contrary, the patient simply will not let go of a stuck point, then this stuck point is likely serving an important function for the patient. Identify the function that this stuck point serves, the underlying stuck point, and then challenge that stuck point.
Presumably "resolved" stuck point rears its head again.	*Mid-session refresher*: A spontaneous reemergence of a stuck point can happen, particularly with assimilated stuck points. Therapists can think that the stuck point ("it's all my fault") was largely resolved. Then, later in the protocol it rears its head again. This presents a great opportunity to turn the reins of the therapy over to the patient and allow the patient to recall how this stuck point had been challenged earlier in the therapy and an alternative belief generated. Often this process is just a brief refresher, but it is a good opportunity to show a patient how these old stuck points can be habitual. Recognizing them as old habits and not incontrovertible facts can be important in sustaining the benefits of patient's good work going forward.

most salient stuck point once realizing that he/she is on the wrong track with challenging an over-accommodated stuck point, "I am unworthy of love."

Significant time is spent on challenging this stuck point and Steve recognizes that he is a good father, husband, friend, and employee in many ways. Thus, there is not much evidence to support this stuck point and the therapist would have expected this to resolve fairly quickly. So we have an example of a belief that is (1) recognized by Steve as inaccurate and (2) causing him distress. Logically, it would seem that he would change his mind fairly easily, develop an alternative thought, and never look back. Why hold onto a belief that is wrong and painful? There are a number of reasons why SQs can be effective and help people gather evidence against their stuck points, but developing and digesting an alternative thought can remain challenging. We have often heard patients say, "I hear it in my head, but I don't feel it in my heart." There are a number of likely culprits preventing acceptance of the alternative thought. One example—you may be on the wrong stuck point. Using the arrow-down technique can help the therapist and patient get to the heart of the matter—the stuck point that may be driving the PTSD. The following is an example of how the therapist uses this technique to move from a stuck point that does not quite fit to helping the patient articulates the more salient beliefs (bolded throughout dialogue) contributing to PTSD.

*Steve struggles with challenging the stuck point: "***I am unworthy of love.***"*

Steve: *I understand that there are many ways that I am a good husband, father, etc. On paper, there are a lot of "good person" boxes checked off. It is just so hard for me to accept that I am worthy or even normal. So much of me was hidden for so long from everyone and most of me is still hidden from most people now. It's hard to imagine myself ever really feeling normal or fitting in.*

Therapist: *I know that most people do not know about your trauma history. Is there a difference between not disclosing parts of your past to everyone versus keeping your true self hidden from everyone? In other words, is it possible to truly know and value someone without knowing details about their past?*

Steve: *I think you can know people to an extent without knowing their past. But in my case,* ***if people knew about my childhood they would be disgusted****.*

Therapist: *I think that is important what you just said there. This sounds like a different, although related, stuck point. What part would people find disgusting?*

Steve: *Me—they would find the things I did disgusting.*

Therapist: *It's impossible to know, without asking, what other people might think, really, about anything. I can imagine people having all kinds of reactions to hearing about a child harmed in the way you were harmed. I noticed you said that people would think the things that* **you** *did were disgusting? Can you tell me more about that?*

Steve: *If people had all the facts, they would realize that* ***I am disgusting****. I participated. I did all kinds of things with these men. In fact, there were times I enjoyed it. What does that make me—disgusting.*

Therapist: *So,* ***because you enjoyed the sexual abuse by those men when you were a kid, you are disgusting now****? I'm trying to understand where you came to this belief of "I am disgusting".* (Steve is getting very upset and nods yes.) *I think this is really important—can we stay with this belief for a minute? I know this abuse happened over a long period of time. Were there times when the abuse was more tolerable? Tell me more about the word enjoy.*

Steve: *In my head I hated it. I hated them. But I must have enjoyed it. I was sexually aroused during the sex almost every time. What kind of person am I?*

Therapist: *OK—this sounds like this is a very important stuck point. If I am hearing you correctly, you are saying, "****Because I was aroused during my assaults, I must have wanted them to happen****." "****I am a disgusting person for wanting to be assaulted.****"* (Steve nods his agreement.)

The arrow-down technique moved the patient from the stuck point "If people knew about my childhood they would be disgusted," to the more nuanced (and hidden) stuck point, "Because I was aroused during my assaults, I must have wanted them to happen." Without getting to this stuck point, the SQs would look much different and not really propel recovery. The therapist can now go on to challenge the idea that Steve ever wanted this to happen and to help him sort out the idea that his sexual arousal has absolutely nothing to do with his complicity in the rape.

Clinical note

We use this example because this quite often is salient for sexual trauma survivors who experience arousal during the rape. We have seen that it is particularly true for males given that the arousal is more obvious in the case of an erection. It is important to keep this in mind as this can be a part of the trauma that is difficult for patients to disclose. Related stuck points: "I must have wanted this to happen." My body betrayed me." Or, "The abuser must have thought I wanted it to happen—I was complicit in this."

Silver platter technique

Staying with Steve's example, a very helpful line of SQs is the silver platter technique. Once the therapist and Steve have arrived at the core stuck point (I must have wanted this assault, therefore I am disgusting), the therapist already has contradicting information (provided by Steve in earlier sessions) that she can use to help Steve challenge this stuck point. In this case, the therapist has heard Steve say many times how awful the abuse was and Steve has provided many examples of everything he did to stop the abuse and to protect his brother from the horror of the abuse. Now she is hearing new information that contradicts previous information. Using Steve's own words and examples, it can be helpful to figuratively place the pieces of contradicting information side by side and hand them back to the patient on a silver platter. If a patient is able to take a step back and weigh his/her own information (evidence for and against), he/she might be able to more clearly evaluate the stuck point based on real facts.

Therapist: *I know we've talked a lot about how badly you were treated and how you even ran away at times to escape the situation.* (Steve nods.) *But then you came back to try to save your brother? I also remember how hard you worked and planned to do anything to save your brother from experiencing the assaults himself?* (Steve nods again.) *I understand that you were sexually aroused during the rape and you consider your arousal to be evidence for the idea that you must have wanted this assault to happen. Was there ever any other evidence for the idea that you enjoyed these assaults?*

Steve thinks for a long moment: *No. It was awful. I spent years pushing this away.*

Therapist: *Yes—it even took you many weeks to tell me about what had happened. It seems like the preponderance of the facts support the idea that you did NOT enjoy these assaults. Is enjoy the right word?*

Steve: *No—when I think about it, enjoy is entirely the wrong word. But what is wrong with me? It is disgusting to think that I could get an erection during these rapes. I must have wanted this, even in some small way.*

Therapist: *Is there any other reason that you might have gotten an erection during the rapes besides the fact that you "wanted" this to happen?* (Steven looks confused.) *Do boys sometimes get erections for very little reason except something might have stimulated them—like the wind? Is it possible that people can experience arousal and not want to have a sexual experience at all? When you think back, was there any part of this that you wanted?* (Steve takes a minute and then shakes his head no.) *So, who was disgusting in this situation?*

Steve: *The men who raped me and my mother for selling me to them. I was just a little kid.*

Therapist: *Yes, it sounds like the problem was them, not you.*

Grasping at straws

Let's switch to our patient, Julie. When challenging stuck points with Julie, her therapist often finds that she is very compliant and stuck points are fairly easily identified and challenged. However, another stuck point seems to resurface quite often and take its place. As a result, the therapist gets the sense that Julie really understands the process, but is not making much true progress in reducing PTSD symptoms. Again, when we find ourselves in this position as therapists, we have to take a step back and objectively understand where the process has broken down and what is preventing Julie's recovery. In this case, the problem seems to be that Julie's stuck points are like weeds—as soon as one is plucked, another takes its place. Prior to session 6, the therapist takes a minute and thinks about the road that the therapy has taken thus far. It almost seems that Julie is (almost desperately) "grasping at straws" to try to understand why this trauma has taken place. Understanding the function that this serves for the patient may help elicit an underlying or core stuck point. The therapist starts session 6 with a review of the path of therapy to date:

Therapist: *I wanted to spend a bit of time today thinking about where we've been and where we are going in therapy. You have done an excellent job thinking through your stuck points and you have really worked very hard challenging them in session and between sessions. Before session, I was thinking back through these stuck points and wanted to trace their course a bit.* (Therapist summarizes several assimilated stuck points and the challenging to date.) *I should have been a better wife.... I should never have married him ... I attract bad men ... I didn't protect my daughter ... I should have known this would happen .... I should have told someone that my piano teacher raped me.*

Each one of these assimilated stuck points seems like an excellent candidate to prioritize and challenge, but, as we noted, as soon as one stuck point is successfully challenged, another takes its place. In other words, the process is not generalizing well across beliefs and the therapist needs to identify the problem. Finding a common thread among these "straws" might help the patient discover and articulate the core stuck point.

Therapist: *As I think back through these stuck points that we've discussed over the last few sessions, I'm starting to see a bit of a theme emerge. For example, all of these stuck points have an element of assigning blame—are you seeing that as well?* (Julie nods.) *In which direction is the finger of blame pointing?*

Julie: *Yes, I see what you are saying—I'm blaming myself, but truly, if I hadn't done these things, I would not be where I am now.*

Therapist: *OK—I see what you are saying, although it is always hard to know what else may have occurred. Let's think a minute more about what did occur. During the time you were raped by your piano teacher and during the time that your husband was beating you, you seem to be taking a lot of blame.*

Julie: *Yes—when I look back—there are so many decisions that I could have made differently. I understand the concepts of hindsight bias and everything that we've talked about, but you can't deny that I could have changed my own destiny at any point.*

Therapist (CPT Dance: therapist joins with her and then dances away): *Yes, I hear what you are saying—going left instead of right on life's paths may have had a different outcome. And so your decision, however well-founded at the time, had a role in the outcome.* (Julie nods). *But even given that, is there anyone else at all that may to be blame in these events?*

Julie (thinks for a moment): *Well, I guess my piano teacher and my husband.* (Therapist waits.) *I mean that seems kind of obvious, but I'm the one who didn't tell anyone and then who married him.*

Therapist: *Yes, that's true and we've talked through all of the reasons why you could not do so at the time. What would it mean if these traumas were beyond your control?*

Julie (visibly crying): *If I can't figure out what I should have done differently to protect myself, then how am I ever going to protect my daughter. I have no one to trust and I certainly can't trust myself.*

Therapist: *It sounds like you are between a rock and a hard place. On one hand, you are trying really hard to figure out what you did wrong and on the other hand you know that you were not at fault for other people's crimes. I think I heard a stuck point in there somewhere—If these assaults weren't my fault then ... what?*

Julie: *Then it can happen again. And now I have my daughter to protect too. I can't trust myself.*

Therapist: *Those both sound like important stuck points to challenge.*

Sometimes the patient's avoidance of stuck points seems particularly profound and the therapist is left to wonder if CPT is perhaps not the right therapy for the patient. We tend to take a different stance on avoidance. The more the patient digs his/her heels in (in any number of ways), the likelier it is that we are getting closer and closer to the heart of PTSD—in other words, we are right on track. We just need to break through avoidance. This avoidance can manifest in a number of different ways. For example, a patient responding "I don't know" repeatedly to any question is a good example of avoidance. CPT therapists need to find ways to move through this inertia. Being patient, asking the question in a different way, responding with "Tell me what you think," or being comfortable with some silence during session can help gently prod the patient into opening up the dialogue.

Avoidance by trauma

Avoidance by trauma is another strategy that patients can use to avoid engaging with the memory of the index trauma. Avoidance by trauma becomes apparent when the patient responds to SQs by switching topics and discussing a second or third trauma. As a therapist, it can be difficult enough to track the traumas, much less the SQs. You may feel as if the therapy session is over and not too much was accomplished. Redirecting patients may seem particularly challenging because new trauma information is emerging and it can be difficult to be sure to hear all of the patient's story and not seem directive or appear to be minimizing one trauma over another. However, this shotgun approach is not helpful as the therapist and patient are never quite able to move through a stuck point from beginning to end. As a result, the patient will never be able to experience the process of the therapy and benefit from the results of the process. Because CPT is intended to be collaborative in nature, we recommend having this conversation with the patient. Point out that every time you both approach this part of the trauma, the conversation goes in a different direction. Every time you ask this question to challenge this specific stuck point, the topic of conversation changes again. Perhaps wonder with the patient how you two might manage this. In all reality, there is all the time in the world to get to any traumas that are contributing to PTSD. However, the process needs to start somewhere! Together the therapist and the patient can agree to stay focused on the index trauma today and maybe keep a list of other events that are relevant to talk about down the road. It has been our experience that when the therapy is successful with stuck points related to the index trauma and PTSD is reduced, there is rarely a need to process additional traumas.

Finally, we have all certainly observed patients *avoiding by intellectualization*. For example, engaging in philosophical or existential discussions, while extremely interesting and often fruitful, can also serve the function of avoiding the actual work at hand. For example, Anna might spend much time focusing on the larger messages received in military service, political debates over US ongoing involvement in post 9/11 wars, and the discrimination against women in the workplace. Each conversation is relevant and interesting, but if too much time is spent in discussing sociopolitical issues that cannot be changed in the 50-minute therapy session, then the opportunity to challenge and change one's mind on a stuck point is lost. One way to help patients move through intellectualization is by getting very specific—"Can you give me an example from this past week?" Move from generalities to specifics and keep the conversation relevant to the stuck point at hand!

Step 4: Generate an alternative thought

After the therapist and patient successfully identify and challenge the stuck point, it is usually a fairly straightforward process to generate an alternative thought. When a patient arrives at the alternative thought, it can be very helpful to review the process of cognitive change in a *brief recap*. This ensures that the patient understands the process of moving from stuck point to alternative thought (not just replacing one thought for another). This can be especially helpful in the beginning of therapy to help the patient get the gist of the processes to reach the goals of CPT. If the therapist can recap the resolution of a fairly straightforward stuck point quickly and easily, then the patient can apply the process of cognitive change to more salient and emotion-laden stuck points. For example, imagine the following situation. Anna comes into session 3 quite agitated because she is running a bit late and really prides herself on being on time. The traffic was quite heavy and driving on crowded streets is also a PTSD trigger for her. When exiting the highway, there was a line of cars on the exit ramp and the backup extended onto the highway bringing traffic to a halt. This situation contributed to her anxiety, which often manifests in anger.

The recap

Therapist (after Anna describes her trip to the clinic): *I'm glad you made it. That sounds very stressful.*

Anna (irate): *I've just about had it. People are such jerks—they drive like idiots and only care about themselves.*

Therapist (knowing it is important to get a little bit more specific in order to challenge with real evidence): *Was it bad driving that caused the slowdown?*

Anna: *No—just the time of day. But as I am sitting there in this long line of cars at the exit ramp thinking someone flying down the highway is going to* *crash into me from behind and stressed about not being here on time, this complete idiot whizzes by all of us on the shoulder of the highway in his Mercedes and cuts into the line. Because none of us have anywhere to be! He is clearly so important. I'm just tired of it—people are such jerks and drive like maniacs.*

Therapist (gives her a second to calm down): *It does seem like that driver was a jerk. I'd be angry too, if someone cut in line like that. What were all the other drivers doing?*

Anna: *We were all just sitting there waiting our turn. He just cut us all off. There's no way that he could have missed this long line—unbelievable. The whole world is just out of control and it is especially dangerous on the highway. It's like I don't even want to leave the house.*

Therapist: *That is important what you just said right—the whole world is out of control. People are jerks. Drivers are maniacs. Just thinking about today's experience, it seems like this long line of drivers were doing the right thing and there was 1 driver behaving badly? Sounds a little bit like the opposite—the vast majority of drivers were actually pretty responsible, even in a stressful traffic jam situation.*

Anna (laughing a little): *OK—yes—but it just takes one to cause an accident. And he was a complete jerk.*

Therapist (smiling): *Yes—you didn't hear me challenge that part! But if you stop and think about what just happened here* (**THE RECAP**), *you were pretty ticked off and upset and even thinking—"I'm not sure if it makes sense to even leave the house with the whole world out of control." But we spent just two minutes thinking it through and realized it is not the whole world—it was one person. And even though that one person was driving badly, you were not really in any danger from him?* (Anna nods.) *Sounds like the greater danger would have been from people crashing into you from behind?* (Anna nods again.) *But people approaching the traffic jam were slowing down accordingly, right?*

Anna: *Yes—I kind of made a mountain out of a molehill and got a little over the top. But you have to understand, driving in Iraq and coming to a standstill like that meant danger. I felt panicked and had a really hard time calming down while I was walking in here.*

Therapist: *I hear what your saying. Being on the highway here in that situation reminded you of being in Iraq and it felt dangerous. We will be spending a lot of time identifying and challenging related stuck points* (**CONTINUES THE RECAP**). *But I want to point out that I think this therapy will be really effective for you, because look what just happened. Just a few minutes ago, you started the session saying: "The world is out of control and people are jerks and dangerous on the roadways" and feeling very agitated as a result. Within minutes, just by talking it out and evaluating real evidence from this very driving situation, I heard, "OK—one guy was a jerk and the rest of the drivers drove very well and safely even in a stressful traffic jam situation." And then you laughed. That is CPT and I am excited to see how you apply this different way of thinking to other types of stuck points as we go forward.*

Challenges in generating alternative thoughts

Lip service

There are a couple of challenges that may occur at this stage of the process of recovery. First, sometimes patients generate an alternative thought according to what they think their therapists want to hear (vs. what they really think). It is important for therapists to monitor their own reactions as they observe the patient's process of challenging and resolving a stuck point. If it seems as if the patient is paying lip service to the alternative thought, or not 100% sold on this new way of thinking, the therapist can certainly ask additional questions. "This new thought is remarkably different from your stuck point—can you walk me through *how* you got there?" This type of question is not intended to question the veracity of the patient's report, but more to be sure that the process of change is fully developed.

Practice makes perfect

Second, patients may be very hesitant about embracing a new way of thinking. Sometimes this is because the alternative thought just does not seem comfortable yet. Moving from "The world is dangerous" to "There are many places where I am safe" represents a big shift in thinking. It can be helpful to complete a worksheet on the stuck point and suggest to the patient that he/she practice it a bit.

Breaking the habit

Some stuck points have been around for a long time. Patients can wonder whether they will be able to "break the habit" of a stuck point. The answer is yes! By definition, stuck points are inaccurate and cause pain. The alternative thought is more accurate and does not cause pain. So, with little reason to continue holding onto painful stuck points, they do tend to fall away in a far shorter period than anticipated. Sometimes patients can feel a bit nervous about letting go of a stuck point, "I've been thinking this way a long time—I'm not sure I can change." The amount of time one has been thinking an inaccurate and painful thought is not really a good reason for continuing to hold onto that thought. In fact, quite the contrary—why waste any more time thinking thoughts that prevent one from living their best life? We have used the analogy of continuing to walk into a wall to get to the other side. It is painful and often fruitless. If you discovered a door and could more easily get to the more desirable other side, would not you choose this much better solution? You would not continue to walk into the wall just because you had done so for years, right?

I hear what you are saying and it makes logical sense, but ... Finally, owning and digesting the alternative thought can be very difficult if the stuck point serves an important function for the patient. In some circumstances, preserving a stuck point, while painful, might be valuable to the patient in some way. If the stuck point is somehow important for the patient to preserve, then the patient is far less likely to generate an alternative thought, no matter how excellent the SQs. In this case, the therapist must identify the *function* that the stuck point serves and find a related (underlying) stuck point to challenge.

Take Anna's example of a stuck point related to her traumatic event during which the medic died. Anna and her therapist were working on the stuck point—"It is all my fault he died." Anna has responded to SQs very well and has realized that there is little to no evidence supporting this stuck point and lots of evidence against it. Anna is able to generate the alternative thought: "The medic died because we were soldiers under attack during a battle while at war. This is not my fault. This is bigger than me." However, Anna rates her belief in this alternative way of considering her role in the medic's death as very low (10%) and says she hears this logic in her head but does not feel it in her heart. The therapist discerns that somehow the stuck point, "It is my fault the medic died," is serving an important function for Anna and, while painful and clearly not accurate, it is hard to let go. The therapist needs to figure out why it is hard for her to accept the logic and digest the alternative thought.

Therapist (first briefly recaps the Socratic dialogue on this stuck point to be sure she and Anna are on the same page): *Let's back up. We began working on this idea: "It is my fault that Brian* (the medic) *died that day." You were able to identify a host of other reasons for Brian's death including the fact that the enemy was intentionally firing at all of you as you evacuated, that you were soldiers, that being in harm's way is part of your job, and that the United States is at war and this was a battle in that war. We talked about how your role in that evacuation from the building was to provide cover for those who went before you and that you did that successfully. All the men successfully made it to the trucks, including Brian. When your turn came to move across the open space, you were hit and it was at that point that Brian turned to come back. We talked about the fact that you did your job well, and, in turn, in coming back to help you, Brian did exactly what he was supposed to do. We could not identify any examples of mistakes made during this chaotic event. When we think about this stuck point, "It is my fault that Brian died," can you think of anything we missed? Is there any piece of the story that is evidence for the idea that this is your fault?*

Anna: *No. That's all correct. I guess it is just hard to explain to someone who wasn't there. We need to operate as a unit and we need to have everybody's back. If we don't, then people get hurt and die.*

Clinical Hint: Note that the therapist does not follow the thread that she "wasn't there and therefore cannot understand" or is not herself military or a Veteran. These are all facts and will be true for all trauma survivors' experiences irrespective of the traumatic event. We may share some commonalities and life experiences to different degrees with patients, but, in truth, each patient's experience is unique. The Socratic process lends itself well to providing the patient the opportunity to explain the unique situation and the context that surrounded the traumatic event. In "teaching" the therapist about her specific event in the context of her life experiences, Anna has an opportunity to sort through it herself. The therapist should keep Anna on point—unravel the stuck point and avoid diverging down the rabbit hole of whether she shares the patient's experience. We will never completely match with our patients in important ways (race, religion, gender, sexual orientation, shared experiences such as service in the military, being a police officer, etc.). Instead, we must provide the opportunity for our patients to teach us about their experiences. Then, our task is to help patients challenge their stuck points based on real evidence, their personal framework and life experience.

Therapist: *Brian died, so ...*

Anna (very upset): *So that means that someone did not do his/her job. I'm the one who got shot—a little flesh wound. Not worth his life. And now I sit here, and he never got to come home. He never got to see his little brother again. He never got to have a family. Everyone he loves never got to say goodbye to him.*

Therapist (pauses for a minute to allow patient to feel those feelings): *That is very true and a real tragedy. Brian really sounds like the epitome of a soldier and a really great guy.*

Anna: *He was the best. He deserved better than dying over there like that. He was there one minute—so alive and then he was just gone.*

Therapist: *I agree. In some ways, it must seem so hard to make sense of this. So sudden and so final* (pauses for a minute as they reflect) *I'm thinking back to something you said just a minute ago—something along the lines of ... "everyone has each others' backs. That's how we all come home. When someone doesn't come home, that must mean someone did not do her job." It must be hard to reconcile that idea with the facts of the situation that we've gone over and over—the facts suggest that you did your job very well and so did Brian. And still this terrible outcome happened.* (This is an example of pointing out the contradictory nature of two of the patient's thoughts, putting them on silver platter, and handing them back to the patient to sort through.) *How do you sort through these very different concepts: "It must have been my fault" versus "I can't figure out any ways that this was my fault?"*

Anna: *I just know that I came back and he didn't and that is not fair. I get to live and he doesn't.*

Therapist: *That is true and cannot be changed. What would it mean to you if all that you just said is true <u>and</u> you also believe that it wasn't your fault? What would be good/positive about waking up tomorrow and truly believing thats Brian's death was not your fault?*

Anna (a bit angrily): *Well according to you and this therapy, I wouldn't have PTSD anymore—I guess I would just be happy and carefree.*

Therapist (gently): *OK—what might be <u>hard</u> about waking up tomorrow and believing that Brian's death was not your fault?*

Anna: *Look—if I just let this go like you seem to want me to, then it's like it was no big deal. I just get to go on, end of story? Like it didn't matter?*

Therapist (reframing in a stuck point format): *I think I hear what you are saying. "If I believe that Brian's death is not my fault, then his death will cease to matter to me?"* (Anna slowly nods.) *If you think about that statement for a second, do you think that Brian's death not mattering to you is possible? Do you think that Brian will ever stop being incredibly important to you?*

Anna: *Absolutely not. I will hold onto his memory to the day I die.*

Therapist: *I believe that. Is blaming yourself for his death and staying in the pain of PTSD necessary for holding his memory dear?* (Anna is thoughtful.) *Is that the best way to honor his memory?* (Anna shakes her head no.) *I remember when you described Brian to me in an earlier session and talked about his infectious laugh. He really sounds like he was such a great guy. How do you think he'd want to be remembered?*

Anna: *Brian wouldn't want this. He wouldn't want me or anybody else to be so sad and lost.* (Anna smiles.) *He was a medic—he'd want this to be fixed.*

Therapist: *If the situation over there had been reversed and you were not the one to come home, what would you have wanted for Brian?*

Anna: *Not this. I would have wanted him to live his best life and, truly, I would have wanted him to be happy. I see what you are saying—it is very important for me to honor s Brian's memory. When I look at myself, holding onto this pain, this doesn't seem so honorable. I don't want to forget him. When I find myself feeling happy for a moment and "getting better"—it washes over me that he can't have this. Why him and not me? But I've asked and answered that question. And the answer is—I don't know. But the answer is not, "It should have been me" or "It was my fault."*

Therapist: *I agree. Nothing can change the tragedy of what happened, but getting the unfounded blame and guilt off the table leaves room to mourn him and feel the sadness of his loss. Sadness will come and then it will pass. It is natural to feel very sad about losing people like Brian. Allowing yourself to feel that sadness will eventually allow you to move past the gripping memory of his last moments and move much more into the warm memories of the person he was and the times that you shared. From what you've said, this is how he would want to be remembered and honored.*

Anna: *I see what you are saying—it's been really hard for me to let go of the idea that Brian's death is my fault, even though I know in my head that it wasn't. I just felt so guilty that I got to come home and he didn't. It is like holding onto that pain was payback and finding relief compounded the guilt. I get to come home and be happy? But you are right, holding onto the pain and guilt does nothing to bring him back and, most importantly, Brian would not want this. There are far better ways to honor his memory. I want to think about this some more …*

And that is CPT! Understanding the function that a stuck point is serving, identifying the underlying stuck points, and walking this path with your patient can be quite a powerful session.

References

Bass, J. K., Annan, J., McIvor Murray, S., Kaysen, D., Griffiths, S., Cetinoglu, T., & ... Bolton, P. A. (2013). Controlled trial of psychotherapy for Congolese survivors of sexual violence. *New England Journal of Medicine*, *368*, 2182–2191.

Farmer, C. C., Mitchell, K. S., Parker-Guilbert, K., & Galovski, T. E. (2016). Fidelity to the cognitive processing therapy protocol: evaluation of critical elements. *Behavior Therapy*, *48*(2), 195–206. doi: 10.1016/j.beth.2016.02.009.

Feingold, Z. R., Fox, A. B., & Galovski, T. E. (2018). Effectiveness of evidence-based psychotherapy for posttraumatic distress within a jail diversion program. *Psychological Services*, *15*(4), 409–418.

Resick, P. A., Galovski, T. E., Uhlmansiek, M. O., Scher, C. D., Clum, G. A., & Young-Xu, Y. (2008). A randomized clinical trial to dismantle components of cognitive processing therapy for posttraumatic stress disorder in female victims of interpersonal violence. *Journal of Consulting and Clinical Psychology*, *76*, 243–258.

Chapter 8

Complex trauma histories

Chapter outline

Complex trauma and complex PTSD

We are regularly asked by clinicians whether cognitive processing therapy (CPT) is appropriate for patients with complex trauma histories and how to manage the associated challenges. Often these conversations involve discussion of patients with "complex posttraumatic stress disorder (PTSD)." We put this term in quotes simply because complex PTSD was not a diagnosis formally recognized in a classification system until only recently in ICD-11. It is important, however, to make a distinction between complex trauma and complex PTSD. Although definitions of complex trauma vary considerably, the ICD-11 defines traumas that could potentially lead to complex PTSD as an "exposure to an event or series of events of an extremely threatening or horrific nature, most commonly prolonged or repetitive events from which escape is difficult or impossible (e.g., torture, slavery, genocide campaigns, prolonged domestic violence, repeated childhood sexual or physical abuse)." (ICD-11; World Health Organization, 2018).

It is important to remember that although exposure to prolonged and repetitive trauma likely increases the risk of developing complex PTSD, complex PTSD is not automatically diagnosed following such traumatic experiences (Brewin et al., 2017). Complex PTSD, according to the ICD-11, includes the

Flexible Applications of Cognitive Processing Therapy. http://dx.doi.org/10.1016/B978-0-12-816715-1.00008-X

core symptoms of PTSD (reexperiencing, avoidance, and persistent perceptions of heightened current threat [including hypervigilance]) *plus* problems in affect regulation, persistent negative cognitions of oneself, and difficulties in relationships and connection to others (it is worth noting several symptoms in the DSM-5 reflect the complex PTSD symptoms in ICD-11). Comorbidity associated with complex trauma (such as personality disorders) can also contribute to perceived difficulties in treating patients who have suffered through chronic traumatic events. As we make clinical choices in treating patients with complex trauma histories, it is important to note that a significant proportion of patients included in randomized trials of CPT and effectiveness studies in community settings have experienced complex trauma. Although these studies could not formally assess patients for complex PTSD (as they preceded the recently released ICD-11 criteria), based on these trauma histories it is highly probable a substantial number of patients would have met this criterion. It is also important to note that these types of symptoms and these types of trauma histories have never been an exclusion criterion for the clinical trials testing CPT.

Of note, the developers of CPT are clinicians first and foremost and, in researching and delivering CPT, have always been mindful of complex trauma issues. For example, as early as 2003, Resick and colleagues reanalyzed their data to check whether patients with child sexual abuse (CSA) histories differed in response to trauma-focused therapy including CPT (Resick, Nishith, & Griffin, 2003). Not surprisingly, participants with CSA histories had experienced significantly more trauma in both child and adulthood (including childhood physical abuse). However, they demonstrated reductions in PTSD severity and other domains associated with complex trauma, such as dissociation, of the same magnitude as those without such histories. Similar findings have been observed more recently, with Veterans who had experienced military sexual trauma (MST) showing good CPT treatment response regardless of CSA history; nor did CSA history influence the number of sessions attended or dropout (Holder, Holliday, & Surís, 2019). When taking into account multiple childhood trauma types, some studies have found attenuated response to CPT (Bosch et al., 2019) or that such history was associated with higher dropout from an evidence-based psychotherapy such as CPT and PE (Miles & Thompson, 2016). However, substantial PTSD reductions were still observed in Bosch et al., and that in this study, being a Veteran had a larger impact on outcome than childhood trauma history (Miles & Thompson did not report on treatment outcomes, unfortunately).

Brewin and colleagues make an important point when reviewing the constructs of PTSD and complex PTSD—"Given that we treat symptoms not *history*, it is important that diagnosis is only guided, and not constrained, by the latter" (Brewin et al., 2017, p. 8, emphasis added). We would reiterate our point earlier—complex trauma does not necessarily result in complex PTSD (nor borderline personality disorder; BPD). In sum, for clinicians using CPT, patients presenting with complex trauma histories and complex symptom presentations are the norm, not the exception, whether this be in research trials, effectiveness and dissemination projects, or in the routine clinical work that CPT therapists engage in every day. That said, we recognize the clinical challenges that arise in what can be quite complicated presentations, and drawing on our own experiences and CPT colleagues, address how to manage some of these in this chapter and the next.

Concerns, decision paths, and strategies

When faced with patients with complex trauma histories, therapists may ask themselves *Where do I start? Is the patient too fragile? How will we ever be able to get to all of the traumas? Am I retraumatizing my patients?* The CPT manual has a great section (pp. 74–78) that addresses these common concerns and it is important to remember that if adequate assessment has been conducted that rules out significant imminent threat, patients with complex trauma *are* able to tolerate CPT and make substantial gains in functioning and decrease their PTSD (Resick, Suvak, & Wells, 2014).

Safety of CPT

For those interested, there are further research findings on the safety of CPT, including symptom exacerbation. For example, when symptom exacerbation occurs, it is usually short-lived, resolving within 1.5 weeks on average, and not significantly associated with trauma history, including childhood abuse (Larsen, Wiltsey Stirman, Smith, & Resick, 2016). Interestingly in this paper the authors documented that approximately 15% of those receiving interventions (including CPT and PE) showed symptom exacerbation between assessment and session 2 (i.e., *before* a focus on the trauma memory in therapy). Of course, it is important to be on the lookout for deterioration in therapy (and weekly administering of the PCL helps us do that!), but it is just as important to remember transient spikes typically resolve, and if we have conducted a careful assessment of our patient's history, we will frequently find that symptom exacerbation has occurred when they were NOT in therapy—and often it is an increase in symptoms that has brought the patient into therapy. This is consistent with the observation of exacerbation being more common in patients in waitlist conditions than those receiving trauma-focused therapy (Ehlers et al., 2014; van den Berg et al., 2016). Discussing the meaningfulness of symptom exacerbation can be helpful when patients or family members express concern about the potential for deterioration.

"Retraumatizing" patients

We hear this phrase a lot by concerned clinicians, especially when patients have substantial and complex trauma histories. We hope that the literature cited throughout the book (and elsewhere) has demonstrated the considerable good that is achieved in addressing our patients' PTSD, including those with complex presentations. We also think the language in this phrase is problematic, as it says that undergoing therapy for one's PTSD is the same as being assaulted/raped/abused again. When patients use this phrase, typically it is in the context of wanting to avoid focusing on their trauma memory or related CPT practice assignments. Accordingly, we spend some time discriminating between the experience of the actual traumatic event(s) and addressing *memories* or the *thoughts and feelings associated* with the event. These important discriminations can take the form of Socratic questions in session and can include objective evaluation of:

- Actual life threat: The idea that patients are objectively safe in therapy but might not have been at the time of the trauma.
- Actual level of control: Comparisons of the lack of control during the trauma versus actual complete control of what they would like to tackle in therapy.
- Concept of choice: The ability to *choose* to engage in discussion around the trauma versus memories/intrusions blindsiding them in day-to-day life.
- Skill development: The emphasis in therapy on learning *skills* to manage the consequences of the trauma (vs. feeling devoid of skills at the time of the trauma).

Length of treatment and stabilization

When thinking of treating patients with complex trauma histories, we often hear overlapping concerns around whether a relatively brief approach such as CPT can be effective, whether such patients need a stabilization phase before embarking on trauma-focused work, and that structured, brief therapies such as CPT do not allow time for (or interfere with) rapport and therapeutic alliance. Although the majority of published CPT studies had used the original 12-session protocol, flexible-length CPT is now recommended based on the findings of Dr. Galovski in her variable-length CPT trial (Galovski, Blain, Mott, Elwood, & Houle, 2012). As seen in this and earlier chapters, CPT results in positive outcomes in samples with substantial trauma histories, thus a "brief" course of high-quality CPT over 12–18 sessions is often sufficient and highly effective. Like other CPT studies, this trial did not exclude patients with complex trauma histories or personality disorders such as BPD. In a follow-up study, Galovski et al. (2016) more closely examined predictors of patterns of symptom change. The results showed that the presence of a personality disorder did not result in poorer outcomes. In other words, those with a personality disorder (borderline) recovered from PTSD just as well as those who did not have a comorbid personality disorder and they did not differ on number of sessions that it took to recover. An important note is that those without a personality disorder may evidence more substantial decreases earlier in therapy. Those with more severe initial PTSD and depression and a comorbid personality disorder may show a more gradual decrease in symptoms over therapy. This is critical clinical information. Our take-home message is: if symptoms are trending down—stay the course. The patient will likely achieve the full benefit of the therapy. It might just take a bit longer.

From a stepped-care point of view, if a patient presents with PTSD/C-PTSD and comorbid BPD with serious ongoing suicidal behaviors necessitating intervention, we would always advocate suicidality (or other treatment priorities such as homicidality) be addressed first (Harned, Korslund, & Linehan, 2014). In these cases, stabilization is required. However, we find that many patients who have either had past histories of self-harm and/or BPD diagnosis, display BPD characteristics, or simply have very complicated and extensive trauma histories are frequently not offered CPT (or any trauma-focused therapy) due to the belief that they will not benefit from a short-term therapy. As detailed in the CPT Manual and discussed in Chapter 10, if we have that established patients are safe and not at imminent risk, there is no reason to withhold an evidence-based treatment such as CPT.

Therapeutic alliance

But what about rapport building and alliance? We know that therapist factors play a role in patient outcomes in CPT (Laska, Smith, Wislocki, Minami, & Wampold, 2013) and we believe strongly that nonspecific therapist skills such as genuineness, warmth, and empathy are critical when working with traumatized patients. However, a cookbook approach such as in a structured therapy like CPT could not possibly provide room for alliance, you say! First, a protocol or manualized therapy does not have to be inflexible, as seen throughout these chapters. The Socratic process of CPT is a powerful method of gaining rapport and building a strong working relationship while fostering patient empowerment. Curious, nonjudgmental, and open-ended questioning shows we are genuinely interested in what patients have to say. Second, we have data over a variety of studies and samples that shows working alliance during CPT is just as good when directly compared to patients receiving unstructured therapy for their PTSD (Chen et al., 2019; Forbes et al., 2012; Nixon et al., 2016). Interestingly, when CPT has been modified to include extra rapport-building sessions for complex trauma patients with borderline traits (Dittmann et al., 2017), independent ratings of therapeutic relationship appear very similar to ratings reported when CPT has been delivered in its standard form.

CPT therapists are no different from other therapists in wanting to help decrease patients' pain and suffering and restore functioning as thoroughly and quickly as possible. Delivering the content of the CPT protocol kindly, respectfully, and warmly not only creates an environment of compassion and regard, it also treats the PTSD at the same time. We care very much about our patients (all of us!) and we all want them to be well as soon as possible. The research studies, patient reports, and our clinical experiences show us that developing rapport and treating PTSD are not mutually exclusive and outcomes are most positive when they occur hand in hand. An extra week or month of living with PTSD is a week or month too many.

The practical stuff

Let's talk through some of the decisions we might have to make when seeing clients with complex trauma and consider possible solutions to the challenges we might face. We delve into the management of emotional dysregulation in the next chapter and comorbid presentations in Chapter 10. These chapters will provide further guidance on issues pertinent to those with complex trauma histories.

Choosing an index trauma to get started

The CPT Manual already provides good guidance on choosing the index trauma most responsible for a patient's PTSD (Resick et al., 2016). We have also discussed how to manage "avoidance by trauma" in Chapter 7 (when patients hop over to another trauma as soon as the therapist starts challenging assimilated stuck points associated with the "index" trauma). Challenges with choosing and sticking to an index trauma can also emerge when the patient and therapist choose to use CPT + A (which is CPT plus the written trauma narrative). For example, after writing the first trauma account, a patient may decide another trauma is the index trauma. It can be tricky to determine whether the new event is indeed the index trauma and should take priority or if this trauma switch is a form of avoidance. In the first instance, we would have the patient rewrite the original event on a second occasion, so that the patient experiences the processing of the first account. However, assuming the new event is also a Criteria A event, we would incorporate a brief chat about why the patient believes this other event is the more traumatic experience. We would look out for indications that this other event is truly the "worst" event, how intrusive it appears to be, how much the patient avoids thinking about it, and how much distress it causes when it springs to mind.

We would also be interested in the types of assimilated stuck points associated with this event; for example, are there high levels of inappropriate self-blame that appear stronger than those associated with the other event? We might have the patient complete a PCL on this event to compare its impact with the event initially selected. Irrespective of which trauma is the "true" index trauma, we can always integrate the new stuck points into the therapy, either by suggesting the patient may want to spend some time on them outside session or by taking some therapy time to address in session. Following these processes helps us determine if switching to this other event (or putting these stuck points on the back burner for the moment) will be helpful in moving the patient to recovery. We could ask the patient to write a second account on this new event (if it is indeed the index trauma). After several sessions on this new event, we should have a good sense of whether this was the right decision, in terms of symptoms beginning to reduce, especially intrusions and avoidance (of the memory).

On the other hand, if it appears that swapping to another trauma might be avoidance, we would gently raise that possibility and explore the likely stuck points underlying the desire to avoid. Typically, we find avoidance centers around patients' concerns about not being able to handle the emotions associated with the memory or that doing so will make them worse. We have outlined earlier how we might handle this when discussing patient engagement (Chapter 6).

Sometimes in the case of complex trauma histories, it may be particularly difficult to choose an index trauma. It seems that you could choose five different events and just randomly choose one and it would be just as serious and related to PTSD as the next. In these cases, it is helpful for you and the patient to just get started. We make the following suggestions:

- In the case of multiple episodes of chronic abuse where many blur into each other and no particular one stands out, choose an episode that seems to be a prototype for all the abuse.
- If a patient has written on one event twice before you decide to switch events, they often will ask if they should write it out a final time. Give patients the choice to write another event—was it helpful for you the first 2 times? Yes? Then sure, go for it!

So many traumas, so many stuck points

Patients with complex trauma histories have not only lots of trauma, but also at times a seemingly exponential number of related stuck points. This can be overwhelming in session, especially if we attempt to challenge the multiple stuck point statements that seem to effortlessly come from a patient in any given session. It is like chasing a swarm of butterflies and expecting to be able to catch a specific one. However, to hijack an old saying about a job worth doing … we say better to address one stuck point *well* than to try to simultaneously challenge multiple stuck points (badly). Letting the structure of CPT assist us can be helpful.

Chasing the butterfly

In the early sessions of CPT, assimilated stuck points should be the focus. Sometimes, however, patients jump from a self-blame stuck point stemming from one trauma to another great stuck point that is related to a different trauma (or another episode of the same type of trauma). As a therapist, we can help patients pin down what is likely the critical stuck point or, if applicable, identify what seems to be the common theme running through the variants of self-blame statements. This might involve some circling around to what the key stuck point is; however, this meandering is part of the process. For example, let's expand on this issue which we brought up in an earlier chapter (Chapter 7) when discussing Julie, our intimate partner violence survivor, who experienced repeated sexual assault as a child and repeated violence in her marriage. She blames herself for all these incidents, albeit maybe in a slightly different way according to the incident. As soon as the therapist begins to question the accuracy of one specific self-blame statement, Julie goes on to talk about what she should have done in another incident (and would jump to another self-blame statement in relation to another incident if allowed).

Julie: ... *and that is just when I was younger* (referring to when the piano teacher assaulted her). *With Ted, I should have known how this was going to go when he first attacked me, but I just kept on letting it happen ...*

Therapist: *Julie, I just want to jump in here, because I think I'm hearing a bit of a theme. So what I've heard is ...* (therapist repeats the three to four variants of self-blame stuck points). *What I'm trying to work out is whether there is a single statement we can write down that sums up all of these self-blame thoughts? I'm thinking if we can shift that common belief a bit, it might make a big difference to how you feel about yourself?*

Julie: *I don't know, because I could have done different things in the different situations, so that is why I keep blaming myself. I had so many chances to stop these things from happening.*

Therapist: *Yes, I can see why you think that, given all your experiences. How about we stop for a second, and rather than focusing on the specifics of each incident, tell me why you are so upset with yourself about these events? Is there one sentence that sums up this blame?*

Julie: *I guess it is like I said before, I always had a chance to stop them.*

Therapist: *I think you've summed that up nicely. And if you think you had a chance to stop them, it means ...?*

Julie: *That because I didn't stop bad things from happening, the traumas were all my fault. I guess it always comes back to that.*

Therapist: *Ok, so why don't we look at that belief more closely by applying it to one of the situations. Which incident do you think you blame yourself the most about? Is there one you are most convinced you should have stopped?*

Julie and the therapist go on to examine this self-blame stuck point with reference to the incident Julie identifies. You might notice that the therapist has asked if there were any incidents which Julie strongly believed she should have been able to stop (relative to others). Consistent with the general approach of CPT, the therapist is aiming to target the strongest self-blame belief—the heart of PTSD. The rationale here is that if this big belief can begin to shift, then others will too. We would also expect that as this belief changes, Julie will experience significant reductions in guilt and shame. There are further considerations to keep in mind. Despite the refocusing earlier, Julie might continue to drift to describing other incidents. The therapist will gently direct Julie back to the stuck point and the incident they have started to explore. As we said earlier, better to address one stuck point well versus many poorly. The therapist can always jot down the other stuck points/incidents that arise during the conversation on the stuck point log or a worksheet, for Julie to complete out of session. But within this session, the therapist will work on getting some traction on addressing the major self-blame stuck point identified in the earlier conversation.

Get specific

In the brief dialogue earlier, we can see that the therapist dances between generality and specificity. Ultimately, patients and therapists need to be specific about the situation and the stuck point for cognitive restructuring to be effective. Attempting to challenge a general stuck point about things always being Julie's fault when it comes to her traumas will likely be unsuccessful—the unhelpful belief is too broad, and there are too many pieces to multiple events. However, to distill the self-blame stuck point to a very specific statement and referenced to a specific incident, the therapist did need to start with a wide net to help Julie (and herself) gain a better understanding of what the critical self-blame stuck point might be. Sometimes with patients with chronic trauma histories and rigid beliefs, we might think they have successfully challenged a stuck point, only to see it rear it's head in a slightly different form. As discussed earlier, this might reflect a core belief, suggesting an underlying cognition has not yet been identified (review Chapter 7 for techniques on how to identify this).

What's different now?

It is also possible another stuck point (or, in the case of long trauma histories, a deeply entrenched core belief) is propping up the belief being challenged or getting in the way of the belief shifting. Sometimes it is helpful to turn this on its head slightly. For example, imagine that despite some good work by Julie and the therapist, self-blame thoughts persist. The therapist could seek out an underlying stuck point or core belief by asking Julie what would it mean to fully accept/believe the traumas were not her fault? What might be getting in the way of truly believing that? A patient might then say a number of things such as "If I accept that all of this trauma wasn't my fault, it means that there was nothing I could do to stop any of it and I have no control or way of protecting myself," or "It means that my whole life is just bad and I have no value." To challenge these underlying, common stuck points borne from a long history of trauma and abuse, it can be helpful to ask the question—*what is different now*? For example, we can explore with patients their levels of control and ability to protect themselves *now* compared with before/during the trauma(s). We can challenge the link between someone perpetrating trauma and the assumption that this means the victim "has no value." And we can review general differences between when the patient was traumatized (e.g., you were a child then and had little recourse; we were at war) and his/her current situation. Generally speaking, if we are engaging in this type of work, we are dealing with the situation where a patient intellectually is understanding the trauma might not have been their fault but is having trouble digesting or truly believing this information. Like a pesky prickle on a sock, another stuck point is hanging on, interfering with challenges to the original stuck point.

Keeping things on track

Many of our patients, especially those with complicated trauma histories, have stressful lives, with ongoing stressors that can interfere with therapy attendance and engagement. We have already talked about strategies to address this (cf. Chapter 6) and will talk about ways of managing serious clinical crises (self-harm, suicidality) in Chapter 10, with these methods applicable for patients who have experienced complex trauma. In terms of containment and reigning in chaos, we find agenda setting, a staple of CPT and many other therapies, a very useful tool but one that can be overlooked or used in only a cursory manner. Although "agenda" sounds very rigid and formal, in most cases it is simply (and briefly!) giving the patient a sense of what you had in mind for that session. However, for patients who are particularly avoidant and/or have a tendency to bring the crisis of the day to every therapy session (common in our complex trauma patients), this agenda can help provide some structure to the session while ensuring patients feel respected and that their concerns are being taken seriously.

Thus, at the beginning of the session we outline what we have planned in terms of CPT content and ask the patient whether there are any important matters they would like on the agenda. When patients have other matters that require attention, we can discuss where it needs to sit on the agenda. Note that we have used the word "important" to convey a sense that the session time is precious, and we want to ensure important issues receive the time they need in session (such as resolving our patient's PTSD). Although on some occasions patients will of course have genuinely important issues that do need to be prioritized for discussion at the beginning of session, which we discuss in a moment, we find that patients are usually quite happy for us to reserve 5 minutes or so toward the end of the session for that item. We then find that once we get to that item, either it is no longer a burning issue that requires discussion, or it can be discussed relatively briefly without it hijacking the entire session.

We invariably adopt a CPT stance when discussing these issues, and if the patient needs further time to consider relevant stuck points, we can often suggest working on the issue outside of session on a worksheet, even if not directly related to their trauma (e.g., working on stuck points that seem to arise when the in-laws come to visit, and challenging any unhelpful beliefs). If we notice that each week there is a new crisis to put on the agenda, we can talk to patients about this, and formulate with them what might be going on. This can be useful in deciding whether discussion about ongoing stressors is a form of avoidance or whether there is a sustained, ongoing problem that needs addressing. If it is the latter, this does not necessarily mean that CPT becomes derailed or is put on hold. Rather it may involve some problem-solving around how the patient might enlist help or resources to address that issue without their PTSD treatment taking the backseat (e.g., engaging with another service to assist with finding new housing). Chapter 6 provides suggestions as to how to navigate these types of ongoing psychosocial stressors.

It's a crisis

As shown by Dr. Galovski's flexible-length study, we can disrupt the CPT protocol with an "emergency or crisis session" without comprising outcomes (Galovski et al., 2012). When a patient reports a serious psychosocial stressor or emergency (e.g., family death, loss of job for primary breadwinner of the household), we can use that session to offer support around that issue. We still present this as a choice for the patient (patients do not always choose this option), while being clear that the plan is to return to CPT. We often will use CPT techniques to help the patient in these sessions. On average we would only use one to two of these types of sessions throughout the course of CPT. If genuine emergencies or crises continue, then we would discuss with patients whether additional support can be accessed elsewhere for these issues (in parallel to CPT), or in rare cases, whether CPT might need to be temporarily put on hold.

I do not have thoughts

Although not restricted to patients who have experienced complex trauma, we often find that such patients can readily identify feelings of distress but struggle to identify preceding cognitions including stuck points. We have outlined a number of strategies that can help tackle this challenge in the preceding chapter, and a standard CBT technique of working backwards from the feeling can help (i.e., *I wonder what you might be saying to yourself that makes you feel that way?*). We can take this one step further for patients with complex histories accompanied by somatic complaints, in which individuals may notice physical distress before they pick up on the emotions or thoughts. For example, we might have a patient who notices a stiff neck or shoulders as we are circling around a topic that causes distress due to muscle tension from anxiety. This provides the opportunity to move to the ABC model to trace back to emotions and ultimately what someone might be saying to themselves to cause these feelings and accompanying physical sensations.

Therapist contact between sessions

Some patients might engage with the therapist between sessions by frequent emails or other communication methods that involve either questions about the therapy, update on "insights" or crises, or just a running commentary on how they are feeling. In some cases, this could be a form of avoidance, where patients engage in this behavior but are sporadic in their attendance of actual sessions. We have already talked about some strategies of dealing with lack of engagement (e.g., the brief session approach). It is also important to inform patients about how you (and your service) operate at the beginning of therapy (e.g., what you will respond to, when, and under what circumstances). It is unfair to expect patients to follow rules or abide by boundaries if they have not been explained! That said, depending on the exact behavior, we can often channel oversteps of boundaries into productive behavior that hopefully will help the patient progress. For example, encouraging patients who email "insights" or "musings" to instead put those in a relevant worksheet. If they are struggling with an issue, it is likely there is a stuck point that could be tackled. Light-bulb moments can be documented on a worksheet and presented at the next session—we want to celebrate this breakthrough with our patients. If patients have questions that are not urgent, encourage them to write them down and bring them to the next session.

We always advocate commonsense in these interactions. If a patient is struggling with how to complete a new sheet introduced in the previous session, and has emailed their frustrations, a brief phone chat to clarify what is expected is quite reasonable and may prevent a patient from throwing in the towel. If this becomes a repeated behavior, then this might require discussion in session to determine whether there is a larger problem at hand. As much as possible, we communicate to patients that we want them to use their time (and ours) as effectively as possible in terms of helping them recover from PTSD.

Therapy room setup

As with any good therapy approach, patients need to feel as safe as possible in CPT, and those with complex histories might benefit from additional resources that can give a sense of safety and containment (e.g., weighted blankets, cushions), and which can assist with grounding. We discuss the latter in more detail in the following chapter.

Safety, the final frontier

For patients with complex trauma histories, multiple incidents may have contributed to strong beliefs about danger (e.g., men are dangerous, the world is dangerous, it is dangerous to get into relationships, my local shopping mall is dangerous …). In fact, these safety-related stuck points are often the final frontier of therapy. Unlike the other 19 symptoms of PTSD, it has been our experience that patients may not want to get rid of hypervigilance. Patients want to stop nightmares and flashbacks, want to feel positive emotions again, want to restore sleep. But patients sometimes struggle with the idea of giving up hypervigilance because their vigilance is perceived to be the only thing standing between them and danger. Let's consider Anna's example.

Anna (reports that she panicked on her way to session): *I was absolutely terrified. I had to pull over and would have turned around and gone home if I had not been so close.*

Therapist: *That sounds really frightening. What prompted your reaction?*

Anna: *I just hate driving on city streets. It reminds me of driving in Iraq. I know it is different here, but accidents happen all the time and people drive like idiots. It feels like I roll the dice every time I get in the car.*

Therapist: *OK—so even though I hear you recognizing that it is not the same as driving in Iraq, I'm also hearing you say that the roads seem pretty dangerous?*

Anna: *Yes, driving is completely unsafe.*

Therapist: *I think we have our stuck point. Let's challenge this a bit. How likely is it that you will be harmed on your way here?* (We know the probability challenging question is a great start to challenging safety related stuck points. This groundwork needs to be laid first).

Anna: *Probably pretty low—I've driven on these streets many times before I enlisted and after and I've never gotten into an accident. But honestly, I don't care how unlikely it is that I will get in an accident, if there is even the slightest risk, it is enough to really stress me out. And frankly, you would understand if you'd seen what I've seen. I'm a soldier. I was trained to be on guard and alert all the time. How am I supposed to just put that away?*

Therapist: *It sounds like you learned skills that were really important in keeping you safe during service. And you've described at least some of the situations that you were in where those skills were critical to your very survival. Were there times over in Iraq that you didn't need to exercise those skills? Or were you 100% on guard and alert 100% of the time.*

Anna: *No, of course not. I had to sleep and we were able to let off steam when we returned to base. We had to amp it up on patrols and particularly in known hot spots.*

Therapist: *Ok—so sounds like you were able to weigh the level of alertness and guardedness over there depending on information at hand. How about over here? Are you always 100% on guard or is there some variability?*

Anna: *It feels like I am always on guard, but I guess there is some variability. I'm calmer in here than I was driving in!*

Therapist: *Ok, good, so it sounds like there is information that amps up your alertness but also information that calms it down. Tell me what it is about driving that might amp you up?*

Anna: *It's honestly not just driving. It is public places, certainly crowds, but also when I am by myself. I am always looking over my shoulder and fearful. My fear in those situations keeps my guard up and keeps me safe.*

Therapist: *That's important—can you explain to me how your fear keeps you safe? Is your fear relevant to your safety?*

Anna: *Well yes—it is very relevant. When I feel fear, I am on guard.*

Therapist: *But does it protect you? During each of those events in Iraq that you've described, did you feel fear?* (Anna nods.) *And were you in danger?*

Anna: *Very much so.*

Therapist: *And other times, like today driving, did you feel fear?* (Anna nods again.) *And were you in danger?*

Anna: *No I guess not.*

Therapist: *So is your fear the best discriminator between safety and danger?* (Anna shakes her head no.) *But it already sounds like there is lots and lots of other information that you rely on that does help you to calm down fear and hypervigilance? I wonder if it would be more helpful (and more safe) to rely on this type of information more than feelings of fear as an early alert system.*

The therapist can go on to think through all of the things that Anna does to increase her safety—fasten her seat belt, check her surroundings, lock her doors, etc. All of these are reasonable tasks, particularly when one has survived the types of things our patients have survived. Their traumas and their survivals of those traumas are part of their learned history. It makes sense that they have altered their behaviors somewhat. Our job is to help them to weigh the facts and rein in their hypervigilance and fear accordingly.

One of us (TG) often uses the example of airport security. We have all heard the announcements about unattended bags—"see something, say something." Working with trauma survivors for so long has altered my learning history. My family calls me the baggage police because I will report an unattended bag faster than you can blink. That behavior and level of watchfulness may be further along the continuum than many of my fellow citizens. But once the baggage has been claimed and the situation resolved (new information), I am able to calm myself down and continue with my trip. Helping our PTSD patients to recognize that their fear (or hypervigilance) is not what is keeping them safe, but that they do have lots and lots of other information to make informed decisions about their safety, is a step toward decreasing the hypervigilance which really is prohibitive in fully engaging with the world.

Summary

Although we know patients who have experienced complex trauma can derive enormous benefit from CPT, the nature and chronicity of their traumatic experiences can pose challenges to the CPT process. We discuss strategies around managing emotional dysregulation in the next chapter and address other issues relevant to complex trauma such as therapy interfering behavior, clinical crises, and risk in subsequent chapters.

References

Bosch, J., Mackintosh, M. -A., Wells, S. Y., Wickramasinghe, I., Glassman, L. H., & Morland, L. A. (2019). PTSD treatment response and quality of life in women with childhood trauma histories. *Psychological Trauma: Theory, Research, Practice, and Policy*doi: 10.1037/tra0000468 (advance online publication).

Brewin, C. R., et al. (2017). A review of current evidence regarding the ICD-11 proposals for diagnosing PTSD and complex PTSD. *Clinical Psychology Review*, *58*, 1–15. doi: 10.1016/j.cpr.2017.09.001.

Chen, J. A., Fortney, J. C., Bergman, H. E., Browne, K. C., Grubbs, K. M., Hudson, T. J., …, & Raue, P. J. (2019). Therapeutic alliance across trauma-focused and non-trauma-focused psychotherapies among veterans with PTSD. *Psychological Services*doi: 10.1037/ser0000329 (advance online publication).

Dittmann, C., Müller-Engelmann, M., Resick, P., Gutermann, J., Stangier, U., Priebe, K., …, & Steil, R. (2017). Adherence rating scale for cognitive processing therapy—cognitive only: analysis of psychometric properties. *Behavioural and Cognitive Psychotherapy*, *45*, 661–670. doi: 10.1017/S1352465816000679.

Ehlers, A., Hackman, A., Grey, N., Wild, J., Liness, S., Albert, I., et al. (2014). A randomized controlled trial of 7-day intensive and standard weekly cognitive therapy for PTSD and emotion-focused supportive therapy. *American Journal of Psychiatry*, *171*, 294e304.

Forbes, D., Lloyd, D., Nixon, R. D., Elliott, P., Varker, T., Perry, D., …, & Creamer, M. (2012). A multisite randomized controlled effectiveness trial of cognitive processing therapy for military related posttraumatic stress disorder. *Journal of Anxiety Disorders*, *26*, 442–452.

Galovski, T. E., Blain, L. M., Mott, J. M., Elwood, L., & Houle, T. (2012). Manualized therapy for PTSD: flexing the structure of cognitive processing therapy. *Journal of Consulting and Clinical Psychology*, *80*, 968–981.

Galovski, T. E., Harik, J. M., Blain, L. M., Farmer, C., Turner, D., & Houle, T. (2016). Identifying patterns and predictors of PTSD and depressive symptom change during cognitive processing therapy. *Cognitive Therapy and Research*, *40*(5), 617–626. doi: 10.1007/s10608-016-9770-4.

Harned, M. S., Korslund, K. E., & Linehan, M. M. (2014). A pilot randomized controlled trial of dialectical behavior therapy with and without the Dialectical Behavior Therapy Prolonged Exposure protocol for suicidal and self-injuring women with borderline personality disorder and PTSD. *Behaviour Research and Therapy*, *55*, 7–17. doi: 10.1016/j.brat.2014.01.008.

Holder, N., Holliday, R., & Surís, A. (2019). The effect of childhood sexual assault history on outpatient cognitive processing therapy for military sexual trauma-related posttraumatic stress disorder: a preliminary investigation. *Stress and Health*, *35*, 98–103. doi: 10.1002/smi.2838.

Larsen, S. E., Wiltsey Stirman, S., Smith, B. N., & Resick, P. A. (2016). Symptom exacerbations in trauma-focused treatments: associations with treatment outcome and non-completion. *Behaviour Research and Therapy*, *77*, 68–77. doi: 10.1016/j.brat.2015.12.009.

Laska, K. M., Smith, T. L., Wislocki, A. P., Minami, T., & Wampold, B. E. (2013). Uniformity of evidence-based treatments in practice? Therapist effects in the delivery of cognitive processing therapy for PTSD. *Journal of Counseling Psychology*, *60*, 31–41. doi: 10.1037/a0031294.

Miles, S. R., & Thompson, K. E. (2016). Childhood trauma and posttraumatic stress disorder in a real-world veterans affairs clinic: examining treatment preferences and dropout. *Psychological Trauma: Theory, Research, Practice, and Policy*, *8*, 464–467. doi: 10.1037/tra0000132.

Nixon, R. D., Best, T., Wilksch, S. R., Angelakis, S., Beatty, L. J., & Weber, N. (2016). Cognitive processing therapy for the treatment of acute stress disorder following sexual assault: a randomised effectiveness study. *Behaviour Change*, *33*, 232–250. doi: 10.1017/bec.2017.2.

Resick, P. A., Monson, C. M., & Chard, K. M. (2016). *Cognitive processing therapy for PTSD: A comprehensive manual*. New York, NY: Guilford Press.

Resick, P. A., Nishith, P., & Griffin, M. G. (2003). How well does cognitive-behavioral therapy treat symptoms of complex PTSD? An examination of child sexual abuse survivors within a clinical trial. *CNS Spectrums*, *8*(5), 340–355.

Resick, P. A., Suvak, M. K., & Wells, S. Y. (2014). The impact of childhood abuse among women with assault-related PTSD receiving short-term cognitive-behavioral therapy. *Journal of Traumatic Stress*, *27*, 558–567. doi: 10.1002/jts.21951.

van den Berg, D. P. G., de Bont, P. A. J. M., van der Vleugel, B. M., de Roos, C., de Jongh, A., van Minnen, A., …, & van der Gaag, M (2016). Trauma-focused treatment in PTSD patients with psychosis: symptom exacerbation, adverse events, and revictimization. *Schizophrenia Bulletin*, *42*, 693–702. doi: 10.1093/schbul/sbv172.

World Health Organization. (2018). International statistical classification of diseases and related health problems (11th Revision). Available from: https://icd.who.int/browse11/l-m/en.

Chapter 9

Managing emotional dysregulation

Chapter outline

By definition of having PTSD, our patients are experiencing emotional suffering. PTSD symptoms can include significant distress and fear when reminded of one's trauma(s). Patients tell us about angry outbursts with complete strangers as well as with loved ones. Patients also tell us about being numb and disconnected, walking through the world as if wading through molasses and watching life go by as if through opaque glass. Some of our patients may experience only one end of this emotional spectrum, whereas others bounce from one emotional extreme to the other. In CPT, we distinguish between the natural emotions that we expect to dissipate if the patients allow themselves to feel them (e.g., distress triggered by memories of the trauma), and the manufactured emotions such as guilt that we know are caused by stuck points (e.g., *It was wrong of me to...*). A challenge in CPT is working out when we can let strong emotions (or lack thereof) run their course, knowing that these are within the "normal" range and will not interfere with therapy progress, and knowing when emotional dysregulation is going to be problematic and interfere with the patient deriving maximum benefit from CPT. The burning question—what to do when dysregulation is problematic? How much should we focus on emotional regulation in therapy before we run the risk of inadvertently derailing the CPT process or, even worse, colluding with avoidance? We address these issues over the course of this chapter.

Flexible Applications of Cognitive Processing Therapy. http://dx.doi.org/10.1016/B978-0-12-816715-1.00009-1

Optimal levels of emotional engagement

Before diving into understanding optimal levels of emotion during therapy for PTSD, we would highlight that as therapy progresses, we will get to know our patients better. As scientist-practitioners, this means accumulating evidence that helps us better understand the role and function of strong emotions in our patients. This is not to say that we need multiple non-CPT sessions to build up alliance in order to better understand the emotions, rather, it is a recognition that for some emotional regulation issues, an improved understanding of the role of emotion might develop as a result of multiple conversations as therapy progresses. Other times there will be quite discrete, "lightbulb" moments within a session that will help us understand the function of problematic regulation. Understanding the cause of the emotion and the function that it serves informs our therapeutic decisions in administering CPT.

An optimal level of emotion or arousal is needed to promote recovery during therapy. If patients are too engaged (e.g., overly distressed or angry) or not engaged enough (i.e., completely numbed out), their therapeutic outcomes are diminished. If a patient is overly distressed (or numb), he/she may not be absorbing what is said in session. For example, if we are absolutely furious about something, we probably are not open to a rational discussion about that issue while our blood is boiling. Not surprisingly, negative affect impacts day-to-day cognitive processes such as attentional control and working memory (Brose, Schmiedek, Lövdén, & Lindenberger, 2012), which are important when we are trying to comprehend new information or evaluate our thinking. Information processing models hold that in order to modify cognitive structures related to anxiety, some level of activation of the fear network is required (Foa, Huppert, Jonathan, & Cahill, 2006). This activation must be enough to (1) bring up the types of thoughts and feelings we are trying to modify and (2) for them to be in a modifiable state. Too much or too little activation will either not allow these structures to be modified or prevent them from being accessed in the first place.

In the treatment of depression, for example, good therapeutic gains were obtained when patients experienced strong emotions during a portion of their session (in this case about 25% of the session); however, higher and lower amounts of activation were associated with poorer outcomes (Carryer & Greenberg, 2010). In PTSD, high engagement with traumatic memories has been associated with good outcomes compared with those who showed lower levels of engagement (Foa et al., 1995; Jaycox et al., 1998). In an unpublished CPT study, we coded sessions for patients' level of emotional engagement and arousal (Angelakis, Weber, & Nixon, 2019). We found that patients who showed a range of emotional engagement that included expression of some distress had optimal outcomes, whereas those patients who showed either extremely high or very low levels of affect for the majority of the session had PTSD and depression symptoms that did not attenuate nearly as much. In summary, like the sweet spot of your favorite sporting equipment, whether it be a baseball or

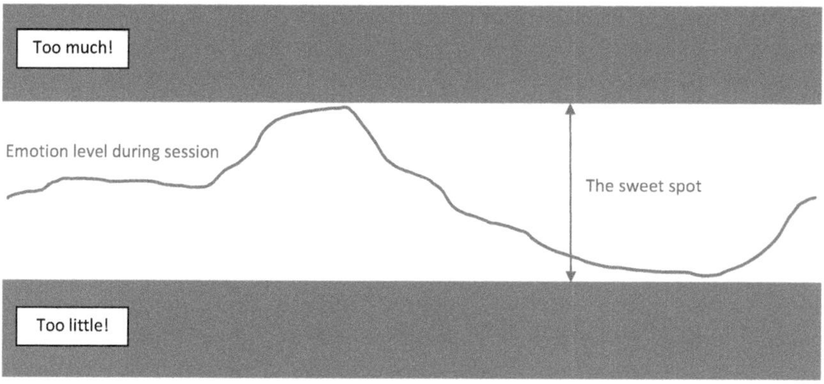

FIGURE 9.1 Optimal levels of engagement in session.

cricket bat, tennis racquet, or hockey stick, there is an optimal "sweet spot" of emotional engagement to promote recovery (see Fig. 9.1 as an example). The trick is to develop strategies to manage situations when patients' affect exceeds those levels in either direction.

Managing over-arousal and big emotion in session

Managing our own therapist beliefs and anxiety!

People generally go into the mental health field wanting to make people feel better. It makes sense then that when a patient sits in front of us, sobbing uncontrollably after describing the fear, shame, and impact of her/his traumas, a therapist's natural reaction is to rush in and try to help the patient feel better as quickly as possible—fix the problem. A common concern we hear from therapists in relation to administering trauma-focused therapies is that their patient is too fragile for this work and that the therapy itself will harm him/her. We have shown in earlier chapters that if we address and monitor real risks of harm (suicidality, homicidality) that therapies such as CPT are not only effective and safe, they actually reduce real risk of harm in the vast majority of cases. It is ironic that by trying not to hurt our patients, we may instead be withholding the very thing that can help them—evidence-based therapy for PTSD. Thus, we encourage therapists with such concerns to examine this idea of patient fragility just as we would address a stuck point with a patient to assess whether the concerns are grounded in real-world evidence, or whether they may not be entirely accurate.

Therapists who are anxious themselves are less likely to use evidence-based therapies or techniques that can provoke anxiety or distress in patients (Meyer et al., 2014; Waller & Turner, 2016). This makes sense—for those of us who are generally anxious, the client's anxiety is more likely to activate our own anxiety and our own stuck points. Even experienced CPT therapists can hold beliefs that make them reluctant to offer CPT to patients with certain presentations despite research that shows CPT is effective in such situations (Marques, Dixon, Valentine, Borba, Simon, & Wiltsey Stirman, 2016). Such "therapist stuck points" are associated with poorer fidelity of CPT delivery and lower numbers of patients being offered CPT (LoSavio, Dillon, Murphy, & Resick, 2019). In the face of strong emotion from patients, it is critically important that we are aware of our own beliefs and successfully adopt an accommodated stance that will allow us to deliver CPT in a way that maximizes that patient's chance of recovery.

All of us have at one time or another internally asked whether CPT is the right approach for a patient who is in significant distress and displaying dysregulated affect in session. We continually monitor our own stuck points such as *If I don't help her reduce this distress immediately, then I'm a bad therapist* and *Maybe this patient isn't ready for CPT*. But by evaluating real evidence around this belief, we have often persevered with CPT and have seen patients who initially showed extraordinarily labile affect go on to learn to process stuck points, ride out strong emotion, and to demonstrate, in many cases, quite remarkable outcomes. After all, if PTSD is causing the excessive distress or numbness, shouldn't we be relying on the very treatment that has perhaps the best chance of treating PTSD?

Anger as an example

Imagine Anna has arrived for session 5. As she walks in, the therapist senses there is some agitation.

Therapist: [setting the agenda] *Hi Anna, how did your Challenging Question Sheets go last week?*

Anna: [angrily] *I'd really like you to get some people off my back – you wouldn't believe what I've had to put up with this week.*

Therapist: *Can you briefly tell me what's happened?* [Note, it is a good idea to get a sense of the issue so that decisions can be made as to whether what has happened to Anna could be addressed with typical CPT techniques, what level of priority is needed for the issue, and not to assume it is either a minor or major issue without more information. The therapist has deliberately used the word 'briefly' to set some containment here].

Anna: [still sounding angry]. *Well my friend said she'd help me move some furniture out of my place. She knows I'm getting help for my PTSD and how it is important for me to get better. I don't have the time for this nonsense. Then, at the last minute she cancels on me....* [voice getting louder, looking upset as well as angry].... *And now I don't know if I should even bother with being here today because if don't get this sorted I don't know when I can...and.....* [voice getting louder and angrier].

Therapist: [gently interrupting] *Anna, I can see that this is really upsetting you and I want to find out more about this, but can we take sec to take a breath, then talk it through?* [therapist is trying interrupt an escalation of Anna's affect before it gets to a point it is difficult for Anna to benefit from verbal help].

Anna: [still angry] *So you don't think this is a big deal? You don't know what it is like having people let you down, especially when you are trying to get better!*

Therapist: *I definitely see this is really bothering you, and I want to help you with that, but like we've talked about previously, when our emotions go into over-drive, it is sometimes a bit hard to come up with solutions easily. I'm also thinking this situation sounds like some of those you've told me about before, when you've gotten very angry at people and said or done things you really regretted. I know you want to change that, and I'm wondering if we could pull out a sheet to work out a good way forward?*

Anna: [curt nod, and still looking angry] *Ok.*

Therapist: *Ok, we can do that now, but I also want to check with you whether you think this issue is important enough for us to spend time on right now, as I'm mindful that we've talked before about past experiences when anger has been used as a kind of avoidance so you didn't have to think about what was really bothering you. And I know from last week you were going to specifically focus on some of your self-blame stuck points for your practice assignments. I just want to make sure we are using our time together well to talk about the things that will reduce your PTSD and get the best outcome for you.*

Anna: [sounding slightly calmer] *Yeah, I know what you are saying. Moving this furniture is pretty important but maybe we can talk about it later in session. I did do some sheets that really stirred me up, maybe we should be talking about those first.*

Therapist: *Great, that sounds like a plan. Let's pull those out but I'll make sure we have time in today's session to touch back on the furniture moving.*

Throughout this interaction, the therapist is juggling a few options and having to think quickly. A primary goal was to downshift Anna's escalating anger, which the therapist felt was approaching a point of no return. This is not to say that strong emotion in session is bad—far from it—anger is frequently a quite appropriate and helpful emotion in certain situations. However as discussed earlier, too much affect likely impedes patients' ability to process information, and in Anna's case, prevented her from helping herself work through the underlying issues or stuck points. In this dialogue, the therapist was doing a lot of talking. This was deliberate, as the therapist was adjusting his tone and rate of speech to counteract Anna's heightened tone. The therapist was also cognizant that for Anna, anger has been used as a form of avoidance, thus gently explored this possibility when trying to determine whether this item needed to be prioritized in session.

Using the CPT framework

The therapist also attempted to bring the structure that CPT offers to address the issue bothering Anna. This serves a dual purpose. Getting the issue down on paper will help Anna direct her attention to a concrete task, one that ultimately will help her process the stuck point and the accompanying emotion. This technique might help modulate the anger compared with a free-wheeling discussion of the issue which would run the risk of simply reinforcing her angry response. It is also a nice way of ensuring a collaborative working relationship. Anna can see the therapist is taking her seriously and is interested in working through the concern to better understand why it is an issue, and to assist her in addressing it. We also find that re-directing a patient's attention to the CPT framework (in this case a worksheet) is a helpful way of interrupting an escalating emotional situation. We do not have to rely just on paper sheets for this—standing up together and working on a whiteboard (if available) can be a handy strategy. The physical movement of getting up and temporarily shifting focus is sometimes enough to take the edge off what might have turned into an uncontrolled rant.

Other possible strategies

The above example with Anna illustrates one method that can be used in session to manage big emotions. Patients are, of course, going to need repeated practice to learn how to better manage emotional dysregulation. Part of that skill-building comes from CPT itself – getting into the habit of using sheets to address the stuck point underlying the strong emotion is a regulation strategy in and of itself. Although in *extreme* cases when it is clear a patient has become so dysregulated they are not able to pay attention to what a therapist is saying, we might have a mini-break in session, to stand up, "shake it off," or go for a little walk to disrupt the escalating emotion. A key point when interrupting the session is to be explicit with the patient of the purpose of this and that the mini-break is *not* to avoid emotions nor to say that the patient cannot handle them.

CPT "as normal" is an effective strategy

As we become more skilled in using the CPT techniques and materials (Socratic dialogue, worksheets), we become more expert in managing these high affect situations using our CPT skills without diverging from the protocol. For example, in the face of significant emotional arousal in session, the therapist could briefly reiterate psycho-education around the fight/flight/freeze (or anger) response to help focus the patient on the link between the emotion currently being experienced and then use a CPT relevant technique (e.g., challenging questions) or module (e.g., on safety) that could be used to better understand that emotional response. This is relevant when we might conceptualize a patient's big emotions to be reflecting a perceived threat (i.e., an amygdala-type response), and thus we use the cognitive framework as a means of bring the prefrontal cortex online, so to speak.

Another strategy, useful in the early sessions of CPT when we are getting to know our patient better, is to proceed through the session as normal. It is possible the high affect will de-escalate of its own accord. The experience of moving though big emotion and emerging unscathed on the other side provides a useful model (and evidence for) the idea that that strong emotion can be tolerated, not only by the patient but also for the therapist! When this experience of tolerating emotion occurs in session, it is important to point this out to patients who may not have consciously observed that they have weathered the emotional storm by simply focusing their attention on the work happening in the session. It is also important to note that using the skills of CPT, through the worksheets and through the process of Socratic dialogue, teaches emotion regulation skills, even if we are not overtly focusing on developing these skills. In analyses of mediators of therapeutic change from one of our clinical trials, increases in distress tolerance predicted improvements in PTSD symptoms (Kaysen, Bedard-Gilligan, Huh, Smartlowit-Briggs, & Pearson, 2017).

A final comment on anger

With respect to anger, we often observe that what initially appears to be an outwardly focused emotion in fact represents the outcome of a more internalized stuck point. For example,

- A statement from our patient Steve who expresses anger and disgust at people who "don't do the right thing" might lead to detection of a just world type of belief (*It isn't fair that my brother and I were abused*).
- Julie's anger at herself for not leaving her husband earlier in the relationship might be partly driven by beliefs of worthlessness or incompetence (*I'm no good, I can't do anything right*).
- Anna's anger at the situation that resulted in a comrade's death might be the veneer that covers a strong sense of vulnerability or lack of control (*No matter what I do, something will still hurt me*).

Sweet spot conversation

Occasionally, we have patients who benefit from brief strategies and skills that can be used in session to help manage strong affect. For example, one of us supervised a case where the patient spent large portions of the early sessions sobbing almost uncontrollably, limiting her ability to make any progress during session (as reflected in a lack of change in PCL scores). The therapist discussed with the patient how too much emotion sometimes interferes with our learning (i.e., the "sweet spot" conversation) and together they brainstormed simple "calming" strategies that could be useful during the session. The therapist was then able to prompt the patient to use her skills in subsequent sessions when distress began to escalate to a tipping point. The patient was also given materials on distress tolerance and self-soothing skills to read at home and to practice outside of therapy. Over the remainder of therapy, the patient used these strategies in conjunction with typical CPT methods (e.g., challenging beliefs about dangerousness of emotions) to increase engagement in session. Consistent with the message earlier in the chapter, the purpose of the addition of simple affect management strategies was to help the patient to focus on the content of the session. The therapist is always careful to normalize the experience of emotions, noting that the strategies are not intended to avoid feelings or be used because such feelings were "bad." It is worth noting that the calming strategies adopted by patients can be very simple (in the case discussed earlier, taking 20 s to remind herself she was ok, to slightly slow her breathing) and really do not interfere with the structure of the CPT session.

We always spend the minimum amount of time necessary to help patients with these skills to guard against the trap of relaying the message to our patients that they need extensive help with anxiety management techniques or are unable to handle strong emotions. Remember that the CPT task of considering stuck points and thinking through real evidence serves the function of not only changing problematic thoughts, but also decreasing natural emotion as our frontal lobe comes more and more online. Preserving as many therapy minutes for CPT work is the active ingredient that moves our patients toward recovery. Supplementing with simple and brief affect management strategies can be helpful in the handful of cases in which affect dysregulation prohibits the cognitive process.

Summary tips when faced with extremely strong emotion in session:

- Work through a worksheet to help patient focus on the cognitive task at hand.
- Identify the underlying stuck point. Use the CPT process to discuss.
- Consider whether the observed emotion is excessive and needs to be managed. Natural emotions will dissipate naturally.
- In extreme cases, brief strategies to help patients manage strong emotions can supplement CPT.

My patient is just numb—managing lack of emotion in session

Although therapists often are most concerned about high levels of affect, the opposite end of the spectrum—when patients appear to be very disconnected with their feelings is also very common and just as challenging. We frequently hear patients describe this symptom of PTSD as feeling "numb." Sometimes emotional numbness might also be further complicated by a comorbid depressive disorder or can present as depression, but not always. Given the emphasis of CPT on encouraging patients to feel their feelings, we sometimes hear therapists worry about an apparent lack of emotional expression. Therapists may worry about progressing to the next stage of CPT (We can't move on until she is feeling her feelings). We would suggest in most cases that it is a good idea to proceed with CPT as planned, allowing the natural course of CPT to help you and the patient better understand what might be driving emotional numbness, and ultimately employ CPT strategies to address this. Even in the case of comorbid depressive symptoms, we fully anticipate that the symptoms of depression will improve alongside PTSD (as seen in almost all trials of CPT).

Helping patients identify their feelings

A first step in managing emotional numbness is to understand whether a patient can feel *any* feelings and the degree to which the patient may have deficits in identifying and describing those feelings. More often than not, we typically find that patients *are* able to feel feelings—by definition a number of PTSD symptoms require an emotional response (e.g., distress when reminded of the trauma)—but that they are not particularly good at labeling them, or are very good at keeping a lid on these (we'll address this soon, and also discuss alexithymia later in the chapter).

In the early sessions of CPT, we provide psycho-education around emotions and the range of their intensity. It is easy to underestimate how useful good psycho-education can be for patients, especially for those for whom identifying or labeling emotions is a real struggle! For some patients, all experiences of negative affect may fit under the umbrella of "I felt bad." One strategy that can be useful in these early CPT sessions, as patients are completing ABC sheets, is to ask patients who are struggling to identify their feelings to monitor very closely how the emotions they write in the "C" column are felt. Do they notice they "sit" in a particular part of the body? Was there any part of the day that they felt different from "numb"—what was different about this feeling, how would they distinguish it from the "numbness" they are used to? For patients who tell us they don't know what they are feeling, it can be incredibly helpful to pull out the Identifying Emotions Handout and use this visual guide to assist. We find that patients usually can pick out an emotion from this sheet. Using these strategies, we are trying to help patients become more adept at noticing and distinguishing their emotions. As therapy progresses, patients get better at differentiating emotions, increasing their ability to identify and label these feelings. And with more practice, they can learn to distinguish not just between different emotions but also to notice the intensity of the emotional experience and label it. This goes hand in hand with identifying and addressing stuck points—being able to label a feeling as "shame" versus "I just feel sad" can help patient and therapist specify the underlying cognition.

Avoidance by numbing

Most often, in the context of PTSD, we find the numbness might serve as an avoidance strategy, one that has become an automatic, habitual pattern of dampening down unpleasant or distressing emotions. We saw in an earlier chapter that the therapist elicits emotion via Socratic dialogue when addressing self-blame with Anna (whose fellow soldier died in her arms after being shot). Although Anna has demonstrated emotional liability (e.g., anger) in session, like many patients, we might also see examples of the opposite. Imagine in a later session Anna presents as "numbed out" as she and her therapist look at a worksheet on which Anna has written *I'm worthless.*

Therapist (holding worksheet): *Anna, I notice you've put "nothing" for the emotion for this stuck point. Can you tell me what you mean by that?*

Anna (appearing very flat): *Well, I just didn't feel anything, there is…just, no feeling.*

Therapist: *Ok, and when you think about that thought now, what kind of emotion are you feeling?* [therapist trying to work out if there was no emotion at the time Anna wrote the sheet versus not having feelings currently].

Anna: *Just the same, there isn't anything there.*

Therapist: *Does that statement "I'm worthless" bother you? I guess I'm curious because normally something negative like that comes along with negative feelings.*

Anna: *Well, I don't like thinking that about myself, so I try not to be bothered by it.*

Therapist: *Ok, so it sounds like it does kind of bother you from what I'm hearing. Is "bothered" the emotion that you feel when you say that to yourself, or is there another feeling?* [therapist suspects a stronger emotion is more likely, but for the moment is trying to help Anna identify any emotional response to the stuck point].

Anna (still sounding flat): *I just don't want to have any feelings about it.*

Therapist: *Ok, what would it mean if you had a feeling about it or put a feeling down on the sheet?*

Anna (quietly): *I'd feel the feeling.*

Therapist: Stays silent.

Anna: *And if I let myself feel it, then it is going to bring all the other feelings that come with it, and I just don't want to feel like that. It's better to just numb it out.*

From this point in session, it is likely that Anna and the therapist will identify a specific feeling or feelings associated with the stuck point. Thus, although initially Anna reported not experiencing any feelings, we see that this isn't the case. Really, Anna was avoiding having feelings because they are so truly unpleasant. Again, avoidance seems like a good strategy on paper, but Anna's idea that it does not hurt (or bother) her to believe that she is worthless really doesn't hold water—irrespective of how much she tries to tell herself otherwise. It is our job as CPT therapists to push forward a bit and identify the stuck point that is likely underlying the emotional numbness. This line of Socratic questioning sets the scene for Anna and the therapist to explore what Anna is afraid might happen if she experiences her feelings. For instance, she may be worried that she will not be able to tolerate the feelings (e.g., *If I feel my feelings, I will lose control*). Anna might believe that big feelings are evidence that the belief is true (emotional reasoning: e.g., *Because this feels so bad, it must be true*). Contrarily, Anna's "numbness" may be a way of simply avoiding painful feelings (e.g., *Feeling my feelings is the same as experiencing the trauma*). Subsequent challenging of unhelpful stuck points will likely reduce this avoidance and allow Anna to feel more comfortable with experiencing emotions of all valence. Sometimes patients come across as very rational or logical in their manner with little emotion. This might be a form of "avoiding by intellectualization" that we have previously discussed and provided possible solutions (see Chapter 7).

Lack of emotion in a trauma account

We sometimes see patients reading trauma narratives as if they are akin to a "police report"—that is, just reciting the "facts" of the trauma, with an apparent complete lack of emotion. In these situations, it is worth checking whether there is indeed emotion being experienced *internally* (not all patients may outwardly express their distress—there might be a stuck point for addressing later—i.e., *If I show my emotions outwardly, then....*). If patients are in fact experiencing strong affect but not showing it, we are less concerned than if a patient is not feeling emotions at all. With the latter, having the patient read the account more slowly, and asking him/her to pause at what are likely the "hotspots" of the trauma and to sit with feelings for several minutes can be helpful. This reduces the likelihood a patient will read the account quickly, skipping through the difficult parts, and provides some reflective time in which the emotions can "catch up," as it were, with what has just been read. When asking the patient to read the account for the first time in session, we are very explicit in our instructions to read it slowly to minimize the risk of avoiding emotion.

Of course, reminding patients of the rationale of feeling their feelings is important too. Sometimes patients might not have experienced strong emotions at the time of the trauma (e.g., if they dissociated or were "in shock"), and thus may not have emotions to write about in their account on the first occasion. However, when we ask patients to write the account for the second time, we ask them to write further thoughts and feelings, especially those they are experiencing *now*. This provides an opportunity for the current emotions to be written about (and experienced) in session and at home when reading as part of their practice assignment. It is important to remember that Socratic questions can help patients open up about the particularly difficult parts of their trauma. For example, we saw in Chapter 7 the therapist assisted Anna to stay on topic during discussion of her fellow soldier's death. Often patients can appear numb, simply because they are not accessing the parts of events that hurt the most. Discussions such as these therefore allow the feelings to be experienced and patients to learn these feelings are manageable. We can complement this also by helping patients address stuck points that lead to their avoidance of emotion and by assisting with restricted affect to ensure smoother progression throughout therapy.

The role of alexithymia

The relationship between alexithymia and trauma is still poorly understood (e.g., whether alexithymia is a risk factor for PTSD, a consequence of trauma, and/or overlaps with the numbing features of PTSD; Eichhorn, Brähler, Franz, Fridrich, & Glaesmer, 2014), although we do know it correlates strongly with PTSD (Frewen, Dozois, Neufeld, & Lanius, 2008). In the absence of firm data to guide how to best determine which difficulties with emotions are due to alexithymia versus numbing in the context of PTSD, we would suggest following the CPT protocol. Research has shown that symptoms of alexithymia improve following CPT (Monson et al., 2006), which is consistent with reviews that indicate psychological interventions can result in significant changes in alexithymia (Cameron & Ogrodniczuk, 2014; Norman, Marzano, Coulson, & Oskis, 2019). As we would do for other issues that might pose residual problems following successful PTSD treatment (e.g., sleep, depression), it might be useful to implement other strategies to address alexithymia if it remains problematic after CPT concludes. In this case, the reviews cited earlier suggest both CBT and mindfulness-based approaches could be considered.

Summary tips when faced with difficulties experiencing emotion:

- Discern between lack of emotion or avoidance of emotion.
- Have patients pay close attention to their emotions when they are felt, how are they experienced.
- Draw out and focus on the feelings via worksheets, sitting with "hotspots" in trauma account.

Managing dissociation in and out of session

Dissociation is a broad term that is sometimes used loosely in the context of trauma and PTSD treatment when in reality it is likely to be a multi-faceted construct (see Bryant, 2007, and Carlson, Dalenberg, & McDade-Montez, 2012, for clinically oriented discussion). We discuss dissociation further in the context of a state of disconnection with the self and environment that reflects the experiences of our clients such as depersonalization, derealization, and a failure to remain grounded in the present time. Although clinically we would conceptualize the dissociation we see in session as a response to overwhelming anxiety, fear, or over-arousal, we do not subscribe to the view that dissociation is a unique causal consequence of trauma alone (see Dutra & Wolf, 2017, for relevant discussion). Regardless of the etiology, most therapists agree that when dissociation becomes an automatic response to distress or reminders of a trauma, it is maladaptive and may increase risk of patients' exposure to additional trauma (e.g., they might appear vulnerable to potential perpetrators, may not assess potentially dangerous situations as effectively as possible). Extreme, outwardly obvious dissociation might display itself in session such as a flashback; however, at times, dissociation might initially be more subtle. We see patients who on the surface may simply appear to be becoming withdrawn or disengaged in session, but actually are sliding into a less obvious state of dissociation—one that might not mimic the dramatic picture of someone vividly being "back in the trauma" but nonetheless results in a patient not being fully present in our session.

As seen in Chapter 4, CPT is often associated with improvements in dissociation without needing dedicated sessions or interventions to address this issue. A therapeutic approach that provides psychoeducation about dissociation being a learned avoidance behavior, coupled with a calm matter-of-fact response by the therapist to reported or observed dissociative behaviors can be quite helpful. At times therapists may inadvertently reinforce dissociation by immediately retreating from trauma content, adding sessions, or discontinuing a trauma therapy. That said, when dissociation is more severe, we find that simple grounding techniques both in and out of session can be helpful. In session, the therapist must be attuned to the patient's presentation and signs that dissociation maybe occurring (e.g., not appearing "present" in the room, content of speech suggesting the patient is "back" at the time of the trauma). Basic grounding strategies include asking the patient orienting type questions (e.g., tell me your name, how old are you, where are you) and using tactile reminders to improve a sense of awareness of time and place (e.g., asking patient's to rub their hand on the arms of the chair, notice and report on the feeling of their feet on the ground). Having patients make observations based on the five senses can be helpful (tell me what you can see… feel….hear…, etc.). Alternatively, ask them to perform a task that requires concentration and is incompatible with being drawn into the trauma in a dissociative state. For example, having the patient try to stand on one leg while describing the effort of balancing. We stress that the purpose of this grounding is to address dissociation, not to distract a patient from strong emotions per se. The latter could unwittingly promote avoidance and unhelpful beliefs about not being able to handle strong emotions. In these cases, we would want patients to feel their feelings, and, with Socratic dialogue and challenging, learn they have the capacity to experience strong emotions without an inevitable negative outcome (e.g., a "breakdown").

Patients can obviously have dissociative experiences outside of session. When there is a possibility of this occurring around practice assignments (e.g., writing or re-reading the trauma account, addressing a stuck point that is strongly associated with a particularly difficult aspect of the patient's trauma(s)), CPT therapists have long suggested that patients keep some type of timer with an alarm next to them. Initially, the patient can set the timer for a relatively brief interval (e.g., 30 s). The patient begins writing (or re-reading) their account, with the ring of the timer used to interrupt any slipping into a dissociative state and serves as a reminder of where the patient is and what they are doing. The patient then re-sets the timer and continues reading. As therapy progresses, the intervals on the timer are set to be longer, with the patient learning to stay engaged in the account for longer periods without needing as frequent interruptions. When we started out as therapists, we would suggest patients use an oven timer for this—of course now with phones and other mobile devices ubiquitous, the need for such antiques is much diminished! Other therapists have had patients use smelling salts or essential oils to assist with grounding, soft but spiky balls that can be held or pressed between themselves and the chair, fidget spinners, and handling smooth rocks.

As previously discussed, patients' dissociative symptoms reduce as their PTSD resolves. Although the finding needs to be replicated, Resick and colleagues observed that patients with high levels of dissociation tended to have faster reductions of PTSD when asked to write a trauma account as part of their therapy versus those who did CPT without an account (Resick, Suvak, Johnides, Mitchell, & Iverson, 2012). Research and our clinical experiences suggest that dissociation is not a contra-indication for CPT. In fact, for many patients a dissociative response to trauma reminders can be conceptualized as a coping response, albeit a maladaptive one, similar to any other type of coping response. It is possible that writing a trauma account gives patients a structure with which to organize their memories of their experience, possibly maximizing the benefits of the subsequent cognitive restructuring component of CPT (e.g., addressing stuck points about dangerousness of strong emotion as well as other trauma-specific negative beliefs). As patients gain experience with challenging maladaptive thoughts, the automatic need to "check out" is reduced as they have learned more effective coping strategies. We sometimes are asked about how we manage patients with very severe dissociation such as seen in Dissociative Identity Disorder (DID). We highlight that such cases are extremely rare. We are aware of cases where CPT has been used with patients with DID but strongly recommend getting consultation from experienced CPT practitioners for these rare presentations.

In summary, dissociation in CPT is managed at several levels with varying techniques. This includes assisting patients to better identify and discriminate between their emotions, which helps patients detect early indicators of increasing arousal, reducing the perception that these are coming out of the blue. Challenging unhelpful beliefs about the strong emotion reduces the likelihood patients will engage in avoidant type coping, with better tolerance for strong affect allowing patients to "ride out" these feelings, possibly leading to reduced tendency of more automatic avoidance coping processes (such as dissociation) occurring. Finally, simple but effective grounding techniques can be employed both in and out of session to complement the therapy. Combining these methods, we have found that even highly dissociative patients benefit from CPT.

Summary tips when faced with dissociation:

- Identify patient's preferred grounding strategies for use in and out of session.
- Assist patients in identifying early warning signs.
- Use CPT techniques and materials to address the precursors to dissociation (e.g., escalating arousal).
- Consider using Trauma Account for dissociative patients.

Dysregulation into regulation

We began this chapter by highlighting that for patients to obtain maximum benefit from therapy they do need to be optimally engaged, neither overly aroused nor completely numb. These latter states likely interfere with a patient being able to take in information and to emotionally process their experiences—ultimately this interferes with learning new ways to recover from their PTSD. We spoke about ways to manage dysregulated emotion, typically incorporating the framework and skills that CPT teaches patients in the usual course of treatment, but also spoke about other strategies that are not necessarily specific to CPT (e.g., grounding techniques for disassociation). Throughout we emphasized the importance of obtaining a good understanding of the dysregulated emotion. Do we conceptualize its function as a form of avoidance and/or an expression of poor coping? Is it in part driven by underlying stuck points, the addressing of which might be able to be resolved through our traditional CPT techniques? We hope that we have been able to show that when managing dysregulated emotion, the CPT therapist will ultimately assist patients in gaining self-efficacy in their ability to manage emotions at both extremes of the continuum, turning dysregulation into regulation. We continue from this theme into the next chapter, where we address the challenges that arise from specific comorbidities that commonly arise with PTSD, and outline, where they exist, the modified protocols developed to address PTSD in the context of these comorbidities.

References

Angelakis, S., Weber, N., & Nixon, R.D.V. (2019). Does emotional engagement influence outcomes for treatment of comorbid posttraumatic stress disorder and major depressive disorder? Manuscript in preparation.

Brose, A., Schmiedek, F., Lövdén, M., & Lindenberger, U. (2012). Daily variability in working memory is coupled with negative affect: the role of attention and motivation. *Emotion, 12*, 605–617.

Bryant, R. A. (2007). Does dissociation further our understanding of PTSD? *Journal of Anxiety Disorders, 21*, 183–191. doi: 10.1016/j.janxdis.2006.09.012.

Cameron, K., Ogrodniczuk, J., & Hadjipavlou, G. (2014). Changes in alexithymia following psychological intervention: a review. *Harvard Review of Psychiatry, 22*, 162–178. doi: 10.1097/HRP.0000000000000036.

Carlson, E. B., Dalenberg, C., & McDade-Montez, E. (2012). Dissociation in posttraumatic stress disorder Part 1: definitions and review of research": correction to Carlson, Dalenberg, and McDade-Montez (2012). *Psychological Trauma: Theory, Research, Practice, and Policy, 4*(5), 489. doi: 10.1037/a0030230.

Carryer, J. R., & Greenberg, L. S. (2010). Optimal levels of emotional arousal in experiential therapy of depression. *Journal of Consulting and Clinical Psychology, 78*(2), 190–199. doi: 10.1037/a0018401.

Eichhorn, A., Brähler, E., Franz, M., Fridrich, M., & Glaesmer, H. (2014). Traumatic experiences, alexithymia, and posttraumatic symptomatology: a cross sectional population-based study in Germany. *European Journal of Psychotraumatology, 5*, 1. doi: 10.3402/ejpt.v5.23870.

Dutra, S. J., & Wolf, E. J. (2017). Perspectives on the conceptualization of the dissociative subtype of PTSD and implications for treatment. *Current Opinion in Psychology, 14*, 35–39. doi: 10.1016/j.copsyc.2016.10.003.

Foa, E. B., Huppert, J. D., & Cahill, S. P. (2006). Emotional processing theory: an update. In B. O. Rothbaum (Ed.), *Pathological anxiety: emotional processing in etiology and treatment* (pp. 3–24). New York: Guilford Press.

Foa, E. B., Riggs, D. S., Massie, E. D., & Yarvzower, M. (1995). The impact of fear activation and anger on the efficacy of exposure treatment for posttraumatic stress disorder. *Behavior Therapy*, *26*(3), 487–499. doi: 10.1016/S0005-7894(05)80096-6.

Frewen, P. A., Dozois, D. J., Neufeld, R. W., & Lanius, R. A. (2008). Metaanalysis of alexithymia in posttraumatic stress disorder. *Journal of Traumatic Stress*, *21*, 243–246. doi: 10.1002/jts.20320.

Jaycox, L. H., Foa, E. B., & Morral, A. R. (1998). Influence of emotional engagement and habituation on exposure therapy for PTSD. *Journal of Consulting and Clinical Psychology*, *66*(1), 185–192. doi: 10.1037/0022-006X.66.1.185.

Kaysen, D., Bedard-Gilligan, M., Huh, D., Smartlowit-Briggs, L., & Pearson, C. (2017). *Mechanisms of change in cognitive processing therapy among American Indian women.* In: C. Monson (chair). Assessment and Treatment of Culturally Diverse Trauma-Exposed Groups in Low-Resource Settings. Symposium at the 33rd Annual Convention of the International Society for Traumatic Stress Studies, November 9–11, Chicago, IL.

LoSavio, S. T., Dillon, K. H., Robert A. Murphy, R. A., & Resick, P. A. (2019). Therapist stuck points during training in cognitive processing therapy: changes over time and associations with training outcomes. *Professional Psychology: Research and Practice, 50,* 255–263, doi:10.1037/pro0000224.

Marques, L., Dixon, L., Valentine, S. E., Borba, C. P. C., Simon, N. M., & Wiltsey Stirman, S. (2016). Providers' perspectives of factors influencing implementation of evidence-based treatments in a community mental health setting: a qualitative investigation of the training-practice gap. *Psychological Services*, *13*, 322–331. doi: 10.1037/ser0000087.

Monson, C. M., Schnurr, P. P., Resick, P. A., Friedman, M. J., Young-Xu, Y., & Stevens, S. P. (2006). Cognitive processing therapy for veterans with military-related posttraumatic stress disorder. *Journal of Consulting and Clinical Psychology*, *74*(5), 898–907.

Meyer, J. M., Farrell, N. R., Kemp, J. J., Blakey, S. M., & Deacon, B. J. (2014). Why do clinicians exclude anxious patients from exposure therapy? *Behaviour Research and Therapy*, *54*, 49–53.

Norman, H., Marzano, L., Coulson, M., & Oskis, A. (2019). Effects of mindfulness-based interventions on alexithymia: a systematic review. *Evidence-Based Mental Health*, *22*, 36–43. doi: 10.1136/ebmental-2018-300029.

Resick, P. A., Suvak, M. K., Johnides, B. D., Mitchell, K. S., & Iverson, K. M. (2012). The impact of dissociation on PTSD treatment with cognitive processing therapy. *Depression and Anxiety*, *29*(8), 718–730. doi: 10.1002/da.21938.

Waller, G., & Turner, H. (2016). Therapist drift redux: why well-meaning clinicians fail to deliver evidence-based therapy, and how to get back on track. *Behaviour Research and Therapy*, *77*, 129–137. doi: 10.1016/j.brat.2015.12.005.

Chapter 10

Addressing comorbid disorders and conditions

Chapter outline

"I would like a simple, straightforward case, with no comorbidities, to learn CPT." New cognitive processing therapy (CPT) therapists often hope to find relatively straightforward cases while learning CPT. However, if we wait for that client to show up, we would be waiting a long time! Posttraumatic stress disorder (PTSD) is highly comorbid with other psychiatric disorders and medical conditions (Kessler, Chiu, Demler, & Walters, 2005; Pietrzak, Goldstein, Southwick, & Grant, 2012). Two-thirds of people with PTSD have at least two other disorders (Keane, Marshall, & Taft, 2006). CPT therefore has to perform well for individuals with multiple comorbid diagnoses or the intervention would not be useful as a PTSD treatment for the majority of patients. That being said, it is not always easy for clinicians to know how to address the complications of a patient with potentially many comorbid conditions—when to rely on the skills of CPT to address comorbid concerns? When should therapists bring in other treatment approaches? When should they choose another treatment altogether? This chapter will provide a detailed, hands-on look at CPT and ways of managing the comorbidity complications.

Flexible Applications of Cognitive Processing Therapy. http://dx.doi.org/10.1016/B978-0-12-816715-1.00010-8

The importance of a good history and good case conceptualization

Although we will be talking in a more detailed way about how to respond to each of the specific comorbidities, it can be helpful to have a general framework when thinking about addressing PTSD in the context of multiple problems. Several issues and considerations cut across the various presentations that we discuss later. Creating a good CPT case conceptualization prior to beginning therapy is particularly important (Nixon & Bralo, 2019). This includes getting a sense of the order of onset of the disorders as well as how the disorders may fit together.

Order of onset: Understanding the order of onset may help dictate a case conceptualization and treatment plan.

- If the comorbid condition predated the trauma and PTSD, the comorbidity could have increased vulnerability to developing PTSD. The comorbid condition may also be less likely to improve as the PTSD improves. This *may* suggest a sequenced format to treatment.
- If the comorbid condition came after the PTSD, it might have been a response to the PTSD or an additional response to experiencing the trauma. Treating the PTSD could help address the comorbid condition as well.

A functional analysis of symptoms: Conducting a functional analysis of how the symptoms of PTSD and of the comorbid condition influence each other can also help guide case conceptualization and treatment planning.

- Looking at short-term reinforcers and long-term consequences can help determine whether to use CPT.
- If avoidance behaviors appear to be maintaining PTSD symptoms and the comorbid condition, treating the PTSD will likely be effective with both disorders.
- If there are overlapping stuck points, then the skills of CPT are likely to be helpful for remediating symptoms associated with both disorders.
- If the symptoms of the comorbid condition appear to vary independently of the PTSD, you may be less likely to see changes in the comorbid condition with CPT. However, this does not necessarily mean you should prioritize treating the comorbid condition first.

An analysis of the impact of symptoms on the course of CPT: In general, the most important consideration in treatment planning is whether the comorbid condition is so severe that it impacts patient safety or gravely impacts the patient's ability to engage in CPT.

- Assess a patient's history of impulsivity, suicidality, and nonsuicidal self-injury, as these are concerns that can influence decisions of whether and when to start CPT.
- If a comorbid disorder is so severe that a patient is not going to show up for sessions regularly, the comorbid condition may need to be managed first.

Thinking about these general guidelines can help guide you in creating a good treatment plan for whether and how to implement CPT. There are many comorbid disorders and conditions that we could address over the course of this book. We chose to touch on those with the highest rates of comorbidity and those which seem to present the most clinical challenges. It is also noteworthy that there is not much available literature guiding us in treating a host of other disorders that can, and do, co-occur with PTSD (e.g., OCD, GAD). For other disorders, there is guidance, but no large-scale, randomized clinical trials to support our suppositions around flexing the CPT manual to best treat the comorbidities (e.g., eating disorders Trim et al., 2017 and psychotic disorders Feingold et al., 2018). For each of the disorders we review later, there are strong, evidence-based interventions. It is beyond the scope of this book to review all possible treatments. If in generating your case formulation earlier, you determine that the comorbid disorder is your primary clinical concern, consider using a different treatment to address the primary disorder, and then reassess the need for CPT. This chapter details how to address comorbidity, when PTSD is primary, using the tools of CPT.

CPT for individuals with comorbid mood disorders

PTSD is more likely to show up with a comorbid mood disorder than any other pattern of comorbidity (Rytwinski, Scur, Feeny, & Youngstrom, 2013). There are multiple theories explaining the co-occurrence of depression and PTSD including the idea that the comorbidity represents a shared vulnerability and that depression increases risk of trauma exposure or of PTSD (Angelakis & Nixon, 2015). There are multiple shared cognitive and memory processes implicated in the development of the two disorders as outlined in cognitive theory (see Chapter 2, see also Kleim & Ehlers, 2008; Nixon, Resick, & Nishith, 2004).

Avoidance is also implicated in both disorders. Depression is thought to develop when there is a loss of positive reinforcement and where depression is maintained as patients engage in avoidance behavior to escape negative emotions (Carvalho & Hopko, 2011; Trew, 2011). Rumination, a key feature of depression, sometimes operates as an avoidance behavior, and it may increase the likelihood to think repetitively about the trauma, which in turn may maintain PTSD (Cribb, Moulds, & Carter, 2006; Kubota, Nixon, & Chen, 2015).

Can we address depression in CPT? In the clinical trials of CPT, as reviewed in Chapter 3, approximately 40%–70% have had a comorbid diagnosis of depression, with substantial reductions in depression observed without modifying CPT. We also have not found that adding a depression-focused therapy before beginning CPT to be essential. When we examined what happened when we added sessions of Behavioral Activation (BA) to CPT for a group of patients who all had PTSD and depression (Angelakis, Weber, & Nixon, 2019), we were somewhat surprised by the results. For two groups, we added five sessions of BA either before starting CPT, or after CPT had finished; a third group received CPT only. Although the modest sample size meant observed differences were not significant, those who had CPT *first* followed by BA demonstrated larger pre-posttreatment effect sizes for PTSD severity and depression (effect size differences ~1.0), and we saw higher dropout in BA + CPT. Our conclusion from this study is that in the presence of comorbid depression, delaying CPT is not helpful, and our present recommendation is that using BA can be effective, but is better introduced to "mop up" residual depressive symptoms at the end of CPT. Indeed, adding interventions prior to CPT for a depressed patient may just slow down the rate of progress. This may be because depression treatment is, in many ways, already baked into the DNA of CPT.

Let's talk about some of the ways in which depression can create challenges in CPT and consider possible solutions to those challenges. Other helpful strategies can be found in Chapter 9 (managing emotional dysregulation).

Motivation and engagement challenges: Depression is often associated with a lack of motivation, feeling overwhelmed, and with hopelessness, all of which may in turn affect treatment engagement. These can be hard to manage if you feel like you are having to drag your patient through CPT. And for the patient, it makes sense. It is hard to keep going when you truly do not believe things will change! There are a number of CPT-consistent and effective strategies that the therapist can rely on to increase motivation and engagement that are compromised by the added burden of depression.

First, we suggest that the therapist works with the patient to *identify and challenge depression specific stuck points* that are interfering with the patient's progress or engagement in CPT. For example, the common belief that "I have to *feel* like doing something to be *able* to do it" *is* a stuck point and can be challenged. Most of us do not "feel like" doing our taxes or cleaning our toilets, but we push through these tasks to avoid a fine or to keep our toilet clean. Other depression-related stuck points include "This effort is not worth it." or "This will never change." or "I'm not worth it." These stuck points can clearly interfere with practice assignments for patients with depressive symptoms. Although we know that challenging assimilated stuck points first is very important in CPT, this might be an example of a time to break this rule. Prioritizing challenging the idea that the therapy is not worth it or that the patient is incurable might prevent drop out or a stagnant therapy situation. A patient who begins to believe that change might be possible will be more likely to engage in the therapy process and ultimately achieve recovery.

A second helpful strategy to increase motivation and engagement includes *breaking down the out-of-session work*. For some patients who are overwhelmed about adding the practice to their daily lives, detailed planning around how to approach the practice assignments and breaking them down into manageable bites can be helpful. Even though there might be a pull to cut a client a break and dramatically reduce the assignment, the therapist's job is to reinforce the patient for moving forward and to not collude with the avoidance.

A third strategy to help increase patient motivation is the *addition of out-of-session contact with one's therapist*. Out-of-session therapist contact such as text messages, an ultra-brief phone call, or an email to help encourage approach behaviors can be effective in increasing motivation. This could involve having the patient briefly contact the therapist after completing the practice. Practice assignment completion is then reinforced by the therapist's further encouragement and support. The therapist might want to arrange a plan to call and follow up if the patient does not call and leave a message that the practice happened. Occasionally, for patients who are really having a very difficult time getting any between-session practice accomplished, the therapist can ask for fewer worksheets with the goal of increasing practice work over therapy. Keep in mind this is the rare exception rather than the more common approach to PTSD with depression!

Rumination challenges: When our patients are spinning their wheels and just thinking about a problem but not actively working on it, it is often avoidance. Patients might spend hours fantasizing about how the traumatic event could have been avoided or worrying about keeping their loved ones safe. It can even look like problem solving but if they are thinking about the same topic for more than 20 minutes without making any progress it is probably rumination. Identifying what situation prompted the rumination and working with the patient to identify and challenge the underlying stuck point can help break through the rumination and continue progress toward recovery. For example, a patient might be ruminating over an upcoming situation. They are thinking "I need to attend an upcoming family event and I don't know what is going to happen. I'm worried it might go badly." The underlying stuck point may be "If I don't know what's coming, something bad will happen. I have to be in control." The patient is spinning his/her wheels, thinking of everything that could happen! By identifying the underlying stuck point (which is challengeable), the therapist can then use Socratic questions to tug at that need to control the outcomes or the belief that not being completely in control is always dangerous. By reducing those beliefs, rumination should decrease. Another strategy to wrangle rumination is to put a time limit on it. This helps it from becoming a never-ending avoidance cycle.

Cognitive rigidity challenges: Depression can be associated with cognitive rigidity which can create quite a challenge in CPT. This can be particularly true when you hit core depressive beliefs such as "I am unlovable" or "I am unworthy." When these beliefs show up early in CPT, as they often do, remember these are over-accommodated beliefs and are not what you want to spend early sessions on in CPT. Even later in CPT, it can be tempting when you find these extremely rigid cognitions to try "convince" your patient and to deviate from that air of gentle curiosity that is the core of good Socratic dialogue. For this type of cognitive rigidity, the therapist should look for any shift in the belief. It can be helpful to ask what it would be like if the belief changed or what would it be like to be someone who did not have that belief. This is also a time to explore if there is a stuck point lurking under the stuck point that is not shifting, to see if you are missing something critical.

Steve: *I am a failure. I'm a wreck. I can't function. I scare my kids.*

Therapist: *I hear a couple of stuck points in that list. What do you think?*

Steve: *I guess "I am a failure" is a stuck point. I tried to work on that but I failed at that too.*

Therapist: *Where did you get to with it?*

Steve: *I couldn't change it at all. I can barely function at work. I can't drive. I didn't protect my brother. And I can't get off these pain pills.*

Therapist: *You are really good at naming the things that you don't think you do well. Anything you have done well?*

Steve: *There are some things. I've never hurt my kids. I have a good marriage … although I don't know why she puts up with me. But I still think I've failed.*

Therapist: *Hmm. That one really is stuck. What would it be like if you were someone who didn't think they were a failure? How would that shift things?*

Steve (silence): *I would have to accept that I didn't have the ability to protect my brother* (sobs).

Therapist: *Mmmm. How does that feel different?*

Steve: *It's hard. It's hard to accept that I didn't have that power. But I also did what I could.*

Therapist: *And that stuck point now about being a failure?*

Steve: *It's a little less stuck. I have kept my boys from being hurt. I've hung onto my job despite the accident. I'm not a complete failure.*

Positive affect building challenges: The inability to feel pleasure is found in both PTSD and depression. For some patients blunted positivity means that they do not experience pleasure even after things have gone well. Helping patients target and identify positive emotions, not just decrease negative ones might be particularly important for treatment of depression (Dunn, 2012; Werner-Seidler, Banks, Dunn, & Moulds, 2013). Using the ABC sheets or later CBW's to identify and target positive events is one way to address this in CPT. When doing so, make sure to target stuck points that inhibit the experience of positive emotions (Dunn, 2012) such as "I don't deserve happiness" "If I feel good, something bad will happen." For patients who have trouble noticing the positive emotions, the emotion sheet may be helpful to increase their awareness of their experiences. Attending to the behavioral activities later in CPT can also help in addressing the reward mechanisms in both PTSD and depression. Both the pleasant activity scheduling and giving compliments activities reengage the reward mechanisms affected by PTSD and depression. The activities may not initially feel enjoyable, especially for patients who are more depressed. In this case work with the patient to have them notice the extent to which they were truly attending to the task. Were they physically present but their thoughts were somewhere else? If so, identify this and work on what pulled them out of the moment and, if there are stuck points, help them work on those.

Reasons to not do CPT or to prioritize the mood disorder

If the depression is so severe that it would be prohibitive to achieving any recovery from PTSD, such as with patients who are not able to engage in activities of daily living or who are not able to get out of bed, then getting the depression under control would be paramount. These patients are relatively rare though! For a patient who is currently manic, they need to be stabilized. In both the cases of severe depression and with mania, working on those disorders does not mean that CPT could not be provided later, after the patient's depression or mania was adequately treated.

Suicidality challenges: Suicidality is another potential reason to prioritize other treatment strategies before starting CPT. However, untreated PTSD is also associated with suicidality, as PTSD confers the same degree of risk of suicidal ideation and attempts as depression (Cougle, Resnick, & Kilpatrick, 2009). Thus, there are risks to *not* addressing the PTSD as well. When thinking about suicidality, consider past suicidal behavior, coping resources, current intent, access to means, and other risk factors like substance use, social supports, and family history of suicidality. If a patient is endorsing intent, safety will always be the first priority. It is little more tricky with patients who might fall in between. Chronic suicidal ideation can often be addressed within CPT and has been found to decrease in CPT (Bryan et al., 2016). CPT also has not been found to increase preexisting suicidal ideation. Suicidal thoughts are frequently stuck points and can be addressed using the tools of CPT (e.g., "I will never get better." and "Everyone would be better off with me gone.") With chronic suicidal ideation you also are less likely to have this turn into an imminent crisis.

Use appropriate clinical common sense when considering starting CPT with a patient who has a history of suicidality and impulsivity, or a history of attempts, especially if those attempts involved more lethal means. An excellent tool for assessing suicidal risk is the Collaborative Assessment and Management of Suicidality protocol, which is both an assessment and intervention tool for suicidal behavior (Jobes, 2015; Jobes, Lento, & Brazaitis, 2012). For a therapist that might feel more uncertain about assessing or responding clinically to suicidal behavior, this provides an excellent framework. As part of the process of determining whether to provide CPT or to provide a suicide stabilization treatment, in addition to the careful assessment discussed earlier, listen carefully to the patient's level of motivation to change and commitment to staying safe. A patient who says "I want the PTSD to get better so I don't feel so desperate" is very different from the patient who says "If you make me talk about it, I'll get suicidal." In the case of the second patient, there may be an underlying stuck point to challenge, as well as some decisions to make about their safety and likelihood to benefit from CPT.

In sum, the heart of CPT is well integrated with core features of treatments for depression. Although there is some data that depression may affect PTSD treatment outcomes, there is no consistent data that suggest that augmenting CPT with other treatments improves PTSD or depression outcomes. Instead, use the tools of CPT to thoughtfully address beliefs and behaviors that likely maintain both disorders.

CPT with comorbid panic disorder

The risk of having a panic disorder for someone who has PTSD is about 3.9 times higher compared to people without PTSD (Michael, Zetsche, & Margraf, 2007), although studies of treatment-seeking individuals with PTSD have found rates of panic attacks ranging from approximately 50%–70% (Cougle, Timpano, Sachs-Ericsson, Keough, & Riccardi, 2010; Teng et al., 2013). PTSD and panic may share a common vulnerability (Berenz et al., 2019). People who are more likely to have panic responses are also more likely to have had those reactions during a traumatic event, which may lead to those responses becoming PTSD cues (Falsetti, Resnick, Dansky, Lydiard, & Kilpatrick, 1995). Then catastrophic beliefs about the experiences of panic like "I am going crazy," "Other people will notice I'm shaking", and focusing on physiological reactions that could signal panic responses help maintain the panic disorder (Hinton, Hofmann, Pitman, Pollack, & Barlow, 2008). As patients focus more and more on avoiding those sensations of panic, the avoidance maintains both the PTSD and the panic disorder.

Can we address panic disorder in CPT? In the clinical trials of CPT (Chapter 3), comorbid panic attacks or panic disorder have never been an exclusion criterion. Around 10% of the participants in the trials met criteria for panic disorder, although some studies did not report on the rates of panic disorder. In a recent review of PTSD treatment literature, not specific to CPT, a little over half of the people with PTSD/panic disorder did not meet criteria for panic disorder following PTSD treatment (Teng et al., 2013). That suggests that for many people with PTSD and panic disorder, treating the PTSD is a good approach.

By its very nature, panic disorder can be associated with catastrophic assessments of the risks of having a panic attack. Thus, completing a careful assessment of the realistic nature of these concerns is important. In some cases, this may also include consulting with a physician for patients with complicated medical presentations to ensure patient safety.

The anxiety sensitivity challenge: Anxiety sensitivity or the tendency to interpret the experiences that go along with anxiety in catastrophic ways is seen in both PTSD and panic disorder (Lang, Kennedy, & Stein, 2002; Vujanovic, Zvolensky, & Bernstein, 2008). Anxiety sensitivity includes interpreting the physical sensations that go along with anxiety, like your heart racing, flushing, or sweating, as signs of illness or danger, loss of control, or social catastrophe (*People are going to think I'm crazy!*). In CPT, patients may be scared about what reactions they are going to have in treatment or that treatment will hurt them (e.g., a panic attack in session). This can impact engagement in session as well as result in avoiding practice exercises or in completing them halfheartedly.

Sometimes we as clinicians also get scared that CPT is going to cause a panic attack, make our patient worse, or cause them to dropout. This may cause us to dilute the therapy in some way or not provide the full dose. However, drop out rates for various therapies for panic and PTSD treatments are fairly similar (Swift & Greenberg, 2014). This suggests that PTSD treatments are not inherently more aversive than panic treatments. In addition, in the studies of CPT drop out, panic has not emerged as a predictor of failing to complete CPT or having PTSD symptoms worsen while in CPT (Larsen, Stirman, Smith, & Resick, 2016).

Targeting panic attacks in the context of CPT

Psychoeducation: Some of the issues for PTSD/panic disorder can be addressed through the psychoeducation elements of CPT that can easily incorporate information about fear responses, especially as we talk about the fight-flight-freeze response. Providing some education about how panic may develop following a trauma, and how these are learned associations (and can therefore be unlearned), can be helpful in and of itself. We can also build in just a little more information about panic attacks. The physiological responses of anxiety are normal and common. It's our body doing what it is hard wired to do. Panic itself is also common and, although unpleasant, panic attacks are not dangerous. That also means that anxiety triggered by the work of CPT also is not dangerous.

Socratic questions: The bedrock skill of CPT, Socratic dialogue, and the stuck point log are helpful in addressing the anxiety sensitivity that underlies both disorders. Panic-related stuck points to address might include "Fear means I'm going to die," "If I remember the event, I'll lose control," or may be more consistent with cognitions central to the panic disorder itself ("This means I'm going crazy," "My heart racing means I'm having a heart attack"). Regardless, the cognitive tools of CPT can help your patient look at the beliefs from a different perspective. Through this cognitive processing, our patients sit with the emotions and the physiological reactions that go along with them. To address panic attacks that occur out of the blue we find that working on the cognitions about the *meaning* of the reactions or the anticipated consequences is a good way to handle those situations. Research in panic disorder has found that cognitive therapy is equally as effective in addressing panic frequency, daily anxiety levels, and psychopathology complaints as is interoceptive exposure (exposure to the physical sensations of anxiety) (Arntz, 2002), which again supports the use of CPT as a way of addressing those fears without having to build in new components. As the CPT therapist, if you address the beliefs about the panic, and the avoidance, the physiological arousal should come down.

Managing panic attacks in session: It can be helpful to work through your own therapist beliefs and potential stuck points about managing a panic attack during session. An in-session panic attack will provide the chance to identify the patient's cues and cognitions in real time, and challenge any stuck points. Further, by remaining calm, the therapist normalizes the experience as an experience of distress and not a life-threatening event. The situation itself becomes evidence against future panic sensations being life threatening, etc.

Incorporating non-CPT techniques: Several panic treatments include techniques such as relaxation or mindfulness. In CPT we teach people to feel their feelings and challenge related stuck points. Relaxation may inadvertently teach the opposite—that the patient cannot tolerate the emotions without escaping. Only in rare cases would relaxation be incorporated, such as when the patient's level of physiological arousal is so high that you are concerned he/she may dropout of treatment. You might then add a few minutes of relaxation at the end of the first few sessions. This serves to prevent relaxation from becoming a method of avoiding the trauma content. Remember, the closing structure of each CPT session is designed to be calming; generally adding relaxation is not really needed.

In sum, the jury is still out on whether PTSD/panic disorder requires an integrated treatment. Unless the panic disorder seems primary, using CPT, while also attending to panic-specific cognitions and avoidance seems equally likely to be helpful for both disorders. Should panic symptoms persist following CPT, at that time provide more panic specific intervention strategies.

CPT with comorbid substance use disorders

Trauma exposure, PTSD, and substance use disorders (SUDs) frequently co-occur. Around 21%–43% of individuals with PTSD have a comorbid alcohol use disorder or SUD (Simpson, Rise, Browne, Lehavot, & Kaysen, 2019). About one-third of those with PTSD and a past history of an alcohol or SUD (PTSD/SUD for this chapter) have met criteria for the SUD over the past year. Although there are several theories about PTSD and comorbid SUDs, the most widely accepted one is self-medication. Individuals start using substances to avoid PTSD-related distress. Over time, this usage can lead to an SUD.

Can we address PTSD/SUD with CPT? Conventional wisdom used to dictate that you treat the SUD first and then you treat the PTSD. However, having PTSD can prevent optimal progress in SUD treatment, so this treatment plan may not really work (Read, Brown, & Kahler, 2004). We have an emerging literature on the use of CPT with PTSD/SUD. Among Veterans receiving care at a VA clinic, PTSD/SUD was associated with higher initial PTSD symptoms than PTSD only, but had the same level of PTSD improvement, dropout, and treatment engagement as those without SUD (Kaysen et al., 2014). In three separate randomized clinical trials of CPT among PTSD/SUD patient populations, CPT has been associated with improvements in PTSD and substance use outcomes

(Haller et al., 2016; Kaysen, Simpson, Fleming, Jaffe, & Rhew, 2019; Pearson et al., 2019). CPT was not associated with increased risk of relapse or with poorer substance use outcomes (Kaysen et al., 2019). This new and emerging literature on the use of CPT for individuals with PTSD/SUD shows very strong preliminary findings on the safety and effectiveness of CPT for PTSD/SUD. If we do not offer a treatment like CPT because of unfounded fears of elevated risks of dropout or relapse, we run the risk of leaving untreated the very disorder maintaining the substance problems.

Comorbid SUD can present a variety of challenges to the delivery of CPT. Patients may come to sessions high or intoxicated, not complete practice assignments, and miss or repeatedly cancel sessions. Substance misuse can create problems with the process of CPT by blocking emotional processing, interfering with retention and learning, and reinforcing avoidance. Substance use also brings unique challenges to the table including managing relapses, withdrawal symptoms, and cravings. Individuals with PTSD/SUD experience more psychiatric and social impairment than those with PTSD alone, such as being below the poverty line, being homeless, having experienced incarceration, and being unemployed (Simpson et al., 2019). If these challenges are on your patient's plate, managing these logistical issues (transportation, safe place to complete practice work in the clinic) prior to getting started with CPT makes a lot of sense.

Managing in-session intoxication: We also recommend a clearly stated policy of what you will do if a patient is high or intoxicated when they come into session and that this be discussed prior to starting CPT. If the patient does show up intoxicated or high, you can briefly meet with them to problem solve around their use, remind them of the treatment rationale, and encourage them to use the cognitive skills to work on the triggers for using before the next session. However, we generally do not complete a CPT session and we tend to keep that session as a brief check-in. Clearly ensure they have a safe way to get back home! If they drove, you may need to call them a cab or help them arrange for transportation.

CPT process challenges: Patients are often using substances specifically to avoid PTSD-related cues or symptoms. However, that very reason for using also maintains both PTSD and SUD. Using Socratic dialogue is a great way of delving into the topic area of how the substance use may get in the way of CPT and to highlight the short-term gains but longer-term consequences associated with use. *Has it really been working all that well to keep trauma symptoms away? Does it work long term? What about after the substance is out of your system? What's the cost?*

Setting goals around outside of session use: Laying out clear goals around the substance use during CPT is important. In general, we ask patients to reduce or minimize their use. Ideally, we would like people to stop using entirely through the duration of treatment, but our goal may not be consistent with some patients' own substance use goals. If abstinence is not a substance use goal for your patient, one option is to contract around use in a way that it does not interfere with CPT, such as avoiding using immediately before or after sessions or practice assignments. Providing a rationale for decreasing usage is one way to build this commitment with a patient. For example, reiterating that the patient's hard work with emotional processing and learning new skills might be compromised with substance use can be helpful. If a patient is struggling to reduce use, ask about times or previous situations they have successfully coped without using. Is there a setting where they would never use? This can be helpful evidence to challenge beliefs that they cannot cope without using.

SUD relapse during CPT: Fear of causing a lapse or a relapse can also create a challenge in treating PTSD/SUD. Relapses are fairly common with SUDs, regardless of the type of treatment and, as we mentioned earlier, untreated PTSD can also cause relapses. First, we suggest weekly monitoring of substance use and cravings. This can be as simple as asking for quantity and frequency of use over the week and a numerical rating of craving intensity. This allows you to track change in use and gives you the opportunity to head off an increase before it becomes a problem. If cravings escalate, it's time to have a conversation about what might be driving urges/use with your patient. Specifically look for substance use-related stuck points, and remind patients about use of substances as an avoidance strategy.

It is also helpful to distinguish between a lapse, which is a brief resumption of use, and a relapse, which is returning to their old levels and patterns of use (Marlatt & Donovan, 2005). When faced with a lapse, keep an eye out for "the abstinence violation" effect—when the person lapses, they feel like the whole process is a waste and this can precipitate a larger relapse. Think about the last time you tried to change a habit like exercising more regularly. You skip a workout day. Do you go back to working out regularly or do you give up? The person who abandons a whole exercise regimen due to a lapse may be experiencing the abstinence violation response. There are clear associated stuck points ("I can't get this under control. I'm weak," etc.). Shame following a lapse is likely related to a stuck point as well. The cognitive tools of CPT can be extremely helpful following a lapse, as they can be used both to address the initial triggers for the lapse and the beliefs around the lapse, as well as the accompanying negative emotions.

Managing triggers and cravings can be tough when addressing PTSD/SUD and seem overwhelming for a therapist. Often triggers are PTSD-related, but could also be unrelated to PTSD like getting good news and feeling like celebrating or walking by a bar on payday and thinking "I can just go in. I don't have to drink." The cognitive restructuring skills of CPT are quite useful in response to substance use cues without modifying CPT. Beliefs about substance use can also go on the stuck point log and can be challenged using Socratic dialogue. Some common SUD-related stuck points are "I can't cope without a drink," "I'm garbage because of the things I've done when I was high," "Alcohol helps me handle the PTSD," or "I deserve this." In an ultra-brief treatment inspired by CPT, we found that using CPT cognitive restructuring skills to address these types of beliefs significantly reduced alcohol consumption and increased abstinence in a community sample with chronic PTSD/SUD (Stappenbeck et al., 2015). We illustrate some of these points with Anna, our Veteran who has struggled with alcohol previously.

Therapist: *So Anna, tell me what your drinking has been like this week?*

Anna: *The cravings have been pretty intense. I have to admit, I had a few drinks. It's no big deal. I know I wanted to change but it was really strong. I couldn't cope without it. I just had to get a break. And hell! I deserve it. I've worked hard in here.*

Therapist: *I'm hearing a couple of stuck points in there. First let's step back though. Tell me a little about the drinks. When was that?*

Anna: *Two days ago. I had a really bad day and couldn't sleep at all the night before. I felt like I was at my wit's end.* (Therapist nods.)

Anna: *It was payday. I had a little extra money on me and I needed to go grocery shopping anyway. While I was there I picked up a bottle of wine. I know we had agreed I wouldn't keep it in the house but I figured, one time couldn't hurt. I got home and started drinking while I made dinner. Next thing I knew I had finished the bottle.*

Therapist: *And what's your drinking been like since then?*

Anna: *I haven't had any more but it's been tough.*

Therapist: *I'm really glad you brought all this up so we could talk about it! As we've talked about, a slip like this doesn't necessarily mean you're going to go back to that old pattern. So let's take a minute and look at one of these stuck points. When you think about that wanting to drink, which thought really seems to be pushing you that direction?*

Anna: *I feel like a failure because I drank again. And I also don't feel like I can cope with this CPT stuff without it.*

Therapist: *Hmmmm. We'll definitely work on both of those. What do you think of us starting with that belief that you can't cope with working on the trauma without the alcohol onboard? I'm curious, have there been times you've been doing the CPT work and not been drinking?*

Anna: *Well yeah. A lot. I haven't had a drink in weeks.*

Therapist: *OK. And has that always been awful?*

Anna: *No. Most of the time it's been tolerable. And it had been getting easier. I just had had a really crappy day.*

Therapist: *So it had been getting easier but that day you felt like you were at the end of your rope. Have you had other times where you felt that way and you <u>didn't</u> have a drink? What was that like?*

Anna: *Now that you bring it up, yes. There have been days where I didn't drink even though I felt bad. After a while it gets a little easier.*

Therapist: *OK. So then is it accurate that you can't cope without a drink?*

Anna: *No. I guess not. I can cope. Sometimes it's just hard.*

Anna and the therapist work to find the places where the belief is just not true. You might notice that the therapist is highlighting all the times that Anna is coping and that there is a difference between something being difficult and being *impossible*. You will also notice that the therapist is careful not to reinforce Anna's belief that the lapse makes her a failure (and will likely target that next) but is also careful not to buy into that belief that she should just give up.

Leveraging scheduling pleasant activities: Another place to address substance use in the context of CPT is around the pleasant activities scheduling in Session 10. One challenge for some patients with severe PTSD/SUD is generating pleasant activities that are not substance-related. Social activities and friendships may be strongly wrapped up in the substance use or they may be socially isolated due to the time their SUD has taken up. In these cases, you may need to get more active and creative in helping patients identify things they could enjoy that do not involve substance use and begin to develop more healthy social networks.

Reasons to not do CPT or prioritize the SUD

For those individuals for whom the substance use is more severe and there are safety concerns, it makes sense to start detox first and to prioritize addressing the substance use. We also do not have much information about the impact of the *type* of substance on outcomes, as most studies lump together all SUDs and polysubstance use as well (Simpson et al., 2019). However, it seems likely that some substances may be more difficult for people to stop using without enhanced support. For example, medication-assisted treatment can be very effective for addressing opiate dependence and would likely need to be an adjunctive treatment for someone with comorbid PTSD and opiate dependence (Saunders et al., 2015). If the SUD predates the PTSD and is largely unrelated, patients may theoretically also benefit from the broader set of skills found in substance use treatment programs. However, for patients where the PTSD symptoms trigger use and much of the use seems coping motivated, a treatment like CPT may indeed prove beneficial.

Safety issues: Risks of overdose and of withdrawal are concerns with PTSD/SUD. It is up to the therapist to conduct a thorough assessment of the use prior to starting CPT. Screening around quantity and frequency of the use, risk of overdose, and symptoms of physiological dependence is essential. The Alcohol and Drug Abuse Institute has a helpful library of assessment tools that contains a searchable index that can be a helpful jumping off point (http://lib.adai.washington.edu/instruments/).

In sum, there is a good reason to think that in many cases CPT is a reasonable approach for treating PTSD/SUD, especially for those patients who identify the PTSD and trauma as the driver for their substance use.

Managing characterological features during CPT

In epidemiological studies, PTSD has been associated with increased odds of personality disorders, including narcissistic, borderline, and schizotypal personality disorders (Pagura et al., 2010; Pietrzak, Goldstein, Southwick, &

Grant, 2011). As management of what are called the Cluster B personality disorders (i.e., antisocial, borderline, histrionic, and narcissistic) are among the most challenging for clinicians, we have focused this chapter on addressing clinical challenges associated with this constellation of Personality Disorder. We have focused this chapter in particular on managing the most difficult challenges including suicidality, self-harm, anger, and crisis behavior. For more detailed information on how to address Personality Disorders more broadly we would encourage readers to specifically seek out some of the excellent treatment manuals in that domain (Beck, Davis, & Freeman, 2015; Linehan, 2018).

an we address symptoms of Personality Disorders in CPT? It is important to note that Personality Disorders have not been exclusion criteria in any of the existing CPT research trials. At the same time, individuals who were engaging in serious nonsuicidal self-injurious behaviors or suicidality were excluded from these studies, which makes good clinical sense! The tricky part for clinicians is to know where in the gray area between "good to go" and "STOP" is the spot where we can provide CPT for patients with PTSD and Personality Disorders. As discussed briefly in Chapter 8, we do have some data to guide us. Much of the existing research has focused specifically on borderline personality disorder (BPD). In looking at combined data from the original CPT and PE comparison trial (Resick, Nishith, Weaver, Astin, & Feuer, 2002), women with higher BPD traits did not drop out from treatment more than women who were lower in those traits (Clarke, Rizvi, & Resick, 2008). Higher BPD traits predicted higher initial PTSD symptoms but did not predict poorer treatment outcomes. Intriguingly, BPD traits also appeared to improve with PTSD treatment, highlighting the potential benefits of CPT for those with comorbid BPD. Similarly, in a reanalysis of data from a study on military sexual trauma, BPD did not predict treatment completion or the number of sessions attended and, although BPD was associated with higher PTSD at the beginning of treatment, it did not affect rate of improvement over time (Holder, Holliday, Pai, & Surís, 2017). And characterological features were not been associated with needing a longer course of CPT in using flexible length treatment (Galovski et al., 2016b). This is all good news in suggesting CPT may be helpful for those with PTSD and Personality Disorders presentations even as a stand-alone treatment!

There are a number of ways in which symptoms of comorbid Personality Disorders can add challenges to CPT. Several of these are addressed in other chapters such as dissociation (Chapter 9), emotion over-engagement and under-engagement (Chapter 9), therapeutic alliance (Chapter 8), complex trauma histories (Chapter 8), and treatment noncompliance (Chapter 7). We have focused this chapter on challenges that are outside the scope of those prior chapters—specifically how to manage suicidal behavior and nonsuicidal self-injury and what to do with intense emotional responses like shame or self-hatred and experiences of invalidation (Harned, 2013).

Managing intentional self-injury: When thinking about the impact of BPD specifically, and of other types of Personality Disorders, on the course of CPT, therapists are often concerned about how to establish basic safety, both in terms of managing nonsuicidal self-injury and suicidal behavior. Intentional self-injury can serve a variety of functions, including tension relief, a way of addressing emotional numbing, self-punishment, and an attempt to block out trauma-related cues (Harned, Rizvi, & Linehan, 2010). Thus, intentional self-harm behavior serves as avoidance around trauma-related emotions and stuck points. Fear of worsening these symptoms by working directly on the traumatic event keeps many therapists from trying a treatment like CPT with their patients with BPD disorders.

In the dialectical behavior therapy (DBT) literature there are a couple of key concepts that may be helpful in thinking about how to address intentional self-injurious behaviors in relation to CPT (Linehan, 2018). It's important to note that these are only concepts and really, at the end of the day, we defer to the clinician in the room for determining level of safety and treatment priorities. In the hierarchy of DBT targets, imminently therapy destroying behaviors would be targeting first, followed by life-threatening behaviors; actual behavior is prioritized over urges, and more severe behaviors are prioritized over less severe behaviors. Only after these are addressed are quality of life-interfering behaviors addressed. In this framework, PTSD is seen as a quality of life-interfering behavior.

From a CPT perspective, a patient who presents for an initial session with more serious life-threatening behaviors, such as nonsuicidal self-injury requiring medical attention and clear suicidal behavior, might benefit from using stabilizing approaches to ensure that the client can keep themselves safe throughout treatment. This is particularly true for a patient with more chronic or severe intentional self-injurious behaviors. Ideally, this is caught prior to starting CPT but sometimes it may have been hidden or a patient's level of stability changes and becomes a crisis. Thoughts that lead to self-harm behaviors are likely stuck points and can be challenged using the skills of CPT. This includes the immediate thoughts such as "I can't cope with this," "I hate myself" or may be fueled by thoughts earlier in the cognitive chain. Slowing down and addressing these can defuse suicidality and nonsuicidal self-injury. The patient's belief that this is the only way or the best way to manage the distress is also another stuck point to challenge!

Use of the crisis session: Often the experience of a life crisis can prompt suicidality or self-harm behaviors. Assuming it is not an imminent crisis necessitating hospitalization, the use of a crisis session is one option in how to address this. In general, the use of a crisis session is intended to apply CPT skills to manage the crisis at hand. The insertion of a crisis session has not been found to diminish clinical outcomes with CPT (Galovski, Blain, Mott, Elwood, & Houle, 2012). The therapist must first make a clinical decision about whether the situation is indeed a crisis. Determining factors include evaluating emergency versus an ongoing stressor, acute or chronic situation, or whether this was driven by PTSD. Some examples of emergencies have been: patient finds out he/she or a loved one has a life-threatening illness, the dog died the night before, the person in the news last night who shot a police officer was the patient's grandson, the patient has been raped again, the patient has been sentenced to jail time, or had children removed from home. You can easily see that all of these situations constitute emergencies. We expanded more on handling ongoing psychosocial stressors in Chapter 7. If, in your clinical opinion, you determine that this is indeed an emergency warranting specific therapeutic attention, then offer the patient the choice of whether or not to use a crisis session. It is important to have this be the patient's choice. When given that option, patients actually refocus back on the trauma-related work about 50% of the time (e.g., "I just wanted to let you know what was going on, but I understand the importance of staying trauma-focused")! We can still use the CPT tools and worksheets to address the issue if helpful (and if there are indeed stuck points—sometimes a patient just needs support). Using sheets to identify and challenge stuck points also helps with generalization of the skills to address the crises that life can throw at us. There should also be an a priori plan of when the therapist and patient will return to CPT. After the crisis session(s) are held, return back to the CPT protocol. If we think of our patient Julie who is pregnant with her perpetrator's child, dealing with stalking and involved in a custody battle, we can see her presenting to session in an extremely distressed state, even as being slightly suicidal. A crisis session as just described could be used to navigate these issues.

If it appears that the use of a crisis session is not likely to suffice due to the clinical severity of the patient's symptoms (i.e., more severe suicidality or nonsuicidal self-injury, therapy interfering affect regulation difficulties, escalating other self-harm or risky behavior), then it may be a situation where the addition of crisis tolerance skills is indicated. It is helpful to remember what a crisis is—it is something that is a short-term situation where the client is experiencing a serious and unsolvable problem. By definition, if it is a long-standing situation, that is no longer a crisis but is the norm for that patient. Crisis tolerance skills are used to help get someone through that immediate crisis and are not intended to be long-term coping strategies. Indeed, some of them are intentional avoidance and may even be seen as reinforcing PTSD in the long term. Although a detailed description of the DBT crisis tolerance skills exceeds the scope of this book, in general they focus on distraction, soothing, trying to improve the immediate situation as much as possible, and review of the pros and cons of tolerating the situation versus coping in ways that make it worse. Readers are encouraged to review the DBT skills manual and other materials should they need to incorporate these skills (Linehan, 2018).

Managing intense emotions and responses: The level of chaos and affect that can accompany many of the Personality Disorders can be like a whirlpool, sucking the therapist into its vortex and before you know it, you have abandoned all your good CPT therapist behaviors! However, in coping with this chaos, the structure and predictability of CPT can be your friend. First of all, laying out for the client what the expectations are and the underlying rationale for therapist behaviors can create a safer and more predictable space for someone who might need that containment. Using the agenda to create a collaborative road map for the session also allows the therapist to not lose control of the session. Using worksheets can create a model for wrangling emotions and for organizing one's thoughts. Using the structure of CPT as a framework also helps us as clinicians to not inadvertently reinforce unhelpful behaviors from the patient.

CPT is well situated as a therapy to address some of the more difficult emotions associated with BPD in particular, but also with other Personality Disorders. Shame, guilt, and self-hatred all lend themselves well to cognitive strategies. And the activity of discussing the reason for feeling ashamed with a warm and accepting therapist can serve in and of itself as evidence against some of the beliefs. In addition, our experience has been that some patients with characterological traits may experience a flurry of related stuck points. Watching them all spill out, you can understand how the patient got to this level of intense emotion. Learning how to slow down and tease these beliefs apart can be a way of learning affect tolerance and regulation skills.

The nuances of Socratic dialogue: One challenge in working with patients with characterological traits is that they may perceive Socratic dialogue as invalidating. In some ways, that's true. We are telling them that their belief or perception might not be 100% accurate! For someone with a history of being invalidated, that can feel pretty bad, even when it is done in a caring way and out of intentions to help the patient. Let's use the Challenging Questions worksheet as an example. The questions "What is the evidence for your belief" and "Is the source of information reliable" can be puzzling when the patient is the source of information. Are we asking if they are unreliable? Are we saying their evidence does not count? Such questions can feel intensely invalidating. We suggest preemptively stating that this particular challenging question means that it is *possible* that *sometimes* all of us are not *always* a good source of information because of our current mood or because something has happened to make us look at things with blinders. Reminding the patient of the rationale behind challenging questions can also be helpful. We are not poking at them, we are poking at *beliefs* that keep the PTSD going and the PTSD feels awful. Keeping that air of curiosity is also essential, as is staying away from trying to guide them to a specific answer. We are just trying to understand. We actually do not know the answers and rely on them to share their expertise about what they have experienced and the meaningfulness of those experiences.

Managing anger and big reactions: It can be hard for us to tolerate big reactions from patients—particularly when they are reacting to us. It's easy to feel defensive, flustered, or upset. It's also easy for us to back off and retreat. Try to think about the function that the patient's anger or reactive behavior is serving. Oftentimes, patients' behaviors have been reinforced in some way in their everyday lives. For example, a patient's angry outbursts or big accusations (e.g., "You don't care about me. No one cares about me. You're making me worse") may serve the function of either keeping people at a distance in everyday life or, contrarily, ensuring that people will stick around to care for him/her. For example, Anna, our Veteran, may lash out at people. Her anger serves the function of maintaining a wall between her and others. If she maintains her perimeter, she would not get hurt. On the other hand, Julie might use a big reaction to be sure that people continue to help her and prevent people from abandoning her. The anger might present similarly in both patients, but understanding the different functions that it serves will guide your intervention. How to intervene? Do the opposite of what everyone in your patient's life is doing. Stop reinforcing the behavior. In Anna's example, calmly continue forward, pull out a worksheet, and find the stuck point. Understand the anger to be related to a stuck point, not to you. There is so much pain behind the anger; it is just a matter of getting around it. It is also appropriate to be candid and honest about how the patient's response is affecting you (i.e., therapy interfering behavior) and your concerns about this dynamic affecting both of your ability to do the work. Therapists do not need to tolerate abusive behavior from patients and setting limits to big reactions makes sense for both of you.

In sum, with patients with Personality Disorders, including BPD, and PTSD, as long as there is not severe or acute intentional self-harm behavior, CPT is a reasonable approach and there is no data suggesting phase-based interventions are superior.

CPT with medical comorbidities

PTSD is associated with a variety of physical health complications and medical comorbidities, including increased risk of various chronic medical conditions including cardiovascular disease, arthritis, chronic pain, diabetes, and gastrointestinal disorders (Pacella, Hruska, & Delahanty, 2013). Further, PTSD-related distress can amplify the experience of normal everyday physical maladies (headache, stomach ache, etc.). Injuries incurred during the traumatic event (traumatic brain injury [TBI], scarring, soft tissue damage, etc.) can further disrupt functioning in important ways as well as present reminders of the traumatic event that can cue PTSD symptoms. Any of the symptoms associated with these medical comorbidities (or concerns about these symptoms) can affect CPT treatment. Patients may miss sessions due to conflicting doctor's appointments or may have so many doctor's visits that it's hard for them to find the time to do their practice. They may have trouble with medication side effects impacting their concentration or making them drowsy. Physical symptoms may make it harder to be emotionally present in session. The bidirectional relationship between physical and mental health is quite obvious. Galovski, Monson, Bruce, and Resick (2009) showed clear decreases in health-related concerns and in sleep impairment as people recovered from PTSD and depression. Considering the effects of medical conditions, pain and injury are critical in holistic recovery. We are often asked about several physical health comorbidities that can have a meaningful impact on the delivery of CPT—TBI, sleep disorders, and chronic pain. We now discuss how to address each with CPT.

CPT for traumatic brain injury

Many of the types of events that can lead to PTSD, such as combat, motor vehicle accidents (MVAs), physical assaults, and intimate partner violence, also can cause TBI (Laker, 2011; Stein & McAllister, 2009). There is overlap between symptoms of TBI and PTSD (Walter, Kiefer, & Chard, 2012), as well as the behaviors and comorbidities associated with both disorders, such as lability, numbing, concentration problems, suicidality, sleep disturbance depression, and anxiety (Tanev, Pentel, Kredlow, & Charney, 2014).

Can we use CPT for patients with TBI? In general, there is limited research on what to do for those with PTSD and TBI. Two uncontrolled studies conducted in a Veterans Health Administration residential treatment program used CPT embedded within a larger comprehensive treatment program and found PTSD and depression improved over the course of treatment (Chard, Schumm, McIlvain, Bailey, & Parkinson, 2011; Walter et al., 2012). In addition, symptoms associated with TBI also improved along with the PTSD (Walter et al., 2012). However, it is important to note that CPT was delivered within a program of comprehensive rehabilitation rather than as a stand-alone intervention. This does give us some evidence that TBI is not necessarily a reason to exclude someone from CPT.

It is important to acknowledge that TBI and post-concussive syndrome is a big umbrella and patients vary in terms of both level and type of cognitive impairment. Thus, the strategies we use to treat those with PTSD/TBI need to be individualized. Remember that the patient is the expert on his or her own cognitive impairments. It can be helpful to spend a session, prior to starting CPT, talking to the patient about where their impairments lie and what strategies have been helpful for them in the past to manage them. The vast majority of TBIs (~85%) are mild and likely more easily treated with a straightforward course of CPT.

Several aspects of CPT are already optimal for patients with TBI (Gallagher, McLeod, & McMillan, 2019). The therapy includes a fair amount of repetition. Skills build on each other and there is lots of opportunity to practice. There is written information that accompanies the verbal content in session, with handouts that consolidate key teaching points, and handouts that act as a reminder about what the practice is (Kneebone & Hull, 2009). The therapy builds in modeling practice completion by starting practice in session, which is another strategy found to be helpful in adapting CBTs for TBI (Hsieh at al., 2012; Kneebone & Jeffries, 2013). So, for many patients with TBI it might not be necessary to modify the therapy, or you may only need to modify some aspects of treatment delivery and context but not the therapy itself.

Attentional challenges: TBI can be associated with problems in attention and processing speed (Ponsford et al., 2014). As the therapist, you can help with attention and retention by slowing down. You can even ask patients to raise their hand if they are feeling overwhelmed or are having trouble keeping up. Ensure your office is quiet and free from distractions. Pause and ask the patient to provide periodic summaries of what you both just discussed. This can help check for retention and for memory consolidation. The periodic use of summaries is particularly useful during the more didactic parts of CPT but mini-summaries are also useful after periods of Socratic dialogue. That way you can make sure that what you think you are saying is what's actually being heard! To help with memory, it is fine to have the patient take notes in the session to help retain content, or to record the session to listen to later and to consolidate learning (Kneebone & Jeffries, 2013).

There are also strategies useful for addressing issues with attention and memory with CPT practice assignments. Similar to setting up your clinical space to minimize distractions, work with your patients in addressing how to approach the CPT practice (Ponsford et al., 2014). For someone who is struggling with attentional fatigue, it can be helpful to use a timer (like we discussed in addressing dissociation in Chapter 9). In this case, the patient would use the timer to take "brain breaks" every 20 minutes or so (depending on what works for that patient). The break can be quite brief, think a minute or two, with the lights off and no talking, to give them a chance to take a break and come back to the practice.

Addressing challenges with organization and initiation: Organization and initiation can also be impaired with TBI, which can in turn affect practice compliance. This can look like a lack of engagement or motivation. However, it may be that the patient was simply struggling with issues like mentally scheduling time to do the practice, or getting started. Sometimes this is indeed PTSD-related avoidance but at other times it actually is a function of the neurological damage. To address this, it can help to sit down with the patient and their phone and schedule specific times to do the practice, along with reminders. For daily practice tasks, like ABC sheets, you can have the patient pair the task with daily activities such as brushing their teeth or taking their medications, to help with the initiation piece. And if you have tried all of these things without success, and the patient is supportive of this, you can involve an adult family member to help with participation. They may be helpful with prompts or reminders about doing CPT practice or with helping with organization.

For some individuals with TBI you may find that the worksheets themselves create challenges. In some cases, the layout is the problem. The worksheets can involve some visual spatial organizational skills in moving between columns. One strategy is to list each step out as a sequential list—first you do the A column, then B, then C .... It takes more paper but otherwise is a pretty minimal modification. As an aside, this is also a really useful modification for older adults where that text on the challenging beliefs worksheet gets pretty small! If the issue is more that the worksheets seem overwhelming, it may be useful to use simplified versions of the worksheets. This can be particularly true with the challenging beliefs worksheet. Remember the goal of the worksheet is to help the patient challenge their stuck point, not to help the patient fill out a perfect challenging belief worksheet. You can, if it is clinically necessary, reduce the number of challenging questions down to four or five and reduce down the patterns of problematic thinking as well.

Working on the memory of the event: One issue that can come up for therapists is about how to handle the memory of the traumatic event with patients with TBI. PTSD can develop even for patients where there is no encoded memory of the trauma (Glaesser, Neuner, Lütgehetmann, Schmidt, & Elbert, 2004; Klein, Caspi, & Gil, 2003). Often individuals with TBI and a loss of consciousness cannot remember the event, although they may have memories of what other people told them about the event. This does not mean that they might not have assimilation-related stuck points about the event ("If only I hadn't gone out that night, the accident wouldn't have happened"). They may also have stuck points about the lack of memory ("If only I could remember what happened, I could figure out what went wrong"). At times clinicians have asked whether they can do an impact statement if there is no memory of the trauma. The answer is—of course! The impact statement is all about the meaning of the event, and those beliefs are present even if there is no memory. And, as you can see from the example earlier, sometimes there are stuck points about the lack of memory in and of itself. There also may be stuck points about the degree of impairment or the meaning of the impairment. These are all also legitimate targets for CPT!

CPT for PTSD and sleep disorders

Given that disturbed sleep and nightmares are both symptoms of PTSD, it is perhaps not surprising that PTSD is associated with increased risk of a host of sleep disorders. Approximately 70%–90% of those with PTSD report disordered sleep, including insomnia, nightmares, and obstructive sleep apnea (Krakow, Ulibarri, Moore, & McIver, 2015). For many patients disordered sleep can be one of the most difficult symptoms to cope with. Disordered sleep is associated with increased irritability, fatigue, depression, substance use, and suicide risk (Colvonen et al., 2015). Sleep helps with emotion regulation (Walker & van der Helm, 2009), is associated with learning and memory consolidation, and disturbances in sleep may interfere with extinction learning (Pace-Schott, Germain, & Milad, 2015). For therapists this can present a bit of a puzzle—do I treat the sleep disorder first or do I treat the PTSD and see if sleep improves?

Can we use CPT to also address sleep disorders? We have found that sleep improves following CPT (Galovski et al., 2016a, 2009; Gutner, Casement, Gilbert, & Resick, 2013; Pruiksma et al., 2016). However, despite these improvements found in sleep duration or quality and insomnia symptoms, sleep difficulties can persist at clinical levels even after completing CPT (Galovski et al., 2009; Gutner et al., 2013; Pruiksma et al., 2016).

One study assessed whether providing a sleep intervention prior to CPT could be helpful (Galovski et al., 2016a). In this study, individuals either received three sessions of sleep-directed hypnosis or received CPT after a period of sleep and symptom monitoring. The hypnosis was effective, as compared to the control, in improving sleep outcomes like sleep latency, impairment, global sleep, and insomnia. However, the hypnosis + CPT group did not show greater improvements in PTSD than the CPT only group, although it was helpful for them in addressing depression. What's more, the CPT-only group showed similar improvements in sleep, with the exception of sleep latency, as the CPT + hypnosis group. So, what's the take-home message? Similar to our findings in treating PTSD + depression, treat the PTSD first with CPT and tackle residual sleep impairment with a treatment for insomnia if the sleep disturbance does not remit. If the patient is so sleep-deprived that he/she cannot stay awake in session or is having difficulty functioning (e.g., driving), then it may be helpful to target sleep first with any number of strategies including sleep-directed hypnosis, cognitive-behavioral therapy for insomnia (CBT-I; Edinger & Carney, 2014), or imagery rehearsal if the sleep is specifically disrupted by nightmares (Krakow, & Zadra, 2006, 2010). Finally, it should be noted that there are many non-PTSD medical conditions that can interfere with sleep. If the sleep impairment is caused by something else, then this condition (e.g., sleep apnea) should be managed outside of CPT.

CPT with chronic pain

Chronic pain is defined as pain that lasts for more than 3 months or that lasts beyond the scope of the original injury (Merskey & Bogduk, 1994). Once seen as purely a physical phenomenon, we know it is much more complex. Chronic pain is a multidimensional and subjective experience that involves not only sensory components, but also psychological components (Asmundson & Katz, 2009). PTSD and chronic pain often go hand in hand—of those presenting for PTSD treatment in community settings around 30% also report chronic pain (Asmundson, Coons, Taylor, & Katz, 2002; Otis, Keane, & Kerns, 2003). Pain and PTSD may co-occur because severe injuries or more severe initial pain can cause both PTSD and pain (Brennstuhl, Tarquinio, & Montel, 2015). Pain itself can become a trauma-related cue. Avoidance may maintain both PTSD and can lead to deconditioning, which maintains pain (Morasco et al., 2013). It also may be that the emotional and cognitive resources necessary to cope with both PTSD and chronic pain leave little leftover for generating other strategies or behaviors, which then maintains both disorders.

Can I address chronic pain in CPT? Research on treatment of PTSD and chronic pain has lagged behind many of the other topics covered in this chapter (Goldstein et al., 2019). We are aware of one case study that applied unmodified CPT for treatment of PTSD and chronic pain following a severe MVA (Galovski & Resick, 2008) and another study that blended CPT with cognitive behavioral techniques for pain with three cases (Otis, Keane, Kerns, Monson, & Scioli, 2009). This included pacing of activities, interoceptive exposure, and pleasant event scheduling. Both studies showed promising results but clearly more research is required.

Ways to address pain as part of CPT: Given that we do not have much from the research literature to guide us, it can be helpful to think about how to integrate addressing chronic pain into CPT. It may indeed be helpful, if the pain is a core part of the PTSD, to either have the patient include that in their impact statement or, if they have the bandwidth, to write a second impact statement on the pain itself. Working on stuck points about the pain (e.g., "These memories will never leave me." "The pain will always be a reminder of what happened to me." "I can't cope with the pain," "I shouldn't do anything since it could make my pain worse") can be integrated into the regular work of CPT. Intentionally planning to engage in the CPT practice at a reasonable pace can be helpful, particularly when discussing pleasant event scheduling. Consider the time of day that might work best in approaching the practice and how to break the practice up, when possible, into smaller tasks. The use of strategies like relaxation certainly can be included but should be used at the end of sessions. Remember Steve, who had chronic back pain following his MVA (and who had experienced childhood abuse)? Initially he found it difficult to separate the distress caused from this injury from the emotional distress caused by his PTSD. It is also possible they fed off each other. However, pacing his day-to-day activities with CPT practice and targeted work on both pain and abuse-related stuck points allowed CPT to address both issues without his pain completely derailing efforts to recover from PTSD.

Summary

We have a plethora of data that illustrate CPT is flexible enough to address a range of comorbid presentations. In the majority of situations, the therapy can be used with minimal adaptation in a transdiagnostic fashion. This keeps the patient and therapist from having to learn and apply too many skills in the course of treatment. It also helps to keep the patient and therapist from drifting too far afield from the treatment target of trauma-related symptoms. That being said, there are some situations where adaptation may be necessary to help CPT better fit the patient. These cases should be guided by patient behavior and case conceptualization rather than a "cookie cutter" decision based on a patient's comorbid diagnoses.

References

Angelakis, S., & Nixon, R. D. (2015). The comorbidity of PTSD and MDD: implications for clinical practice and future research. *Behaviour Change*, *32*(1), 1–25.

Angelakis, S., Weber, N., & Nixon, R. D. V. (2019). Comorbid posttraumatic stress disorder and major depressive disorder: the usefulness of a sequential treatment approach within a randomised design. Manuscript submitted for publication.

Arntz, A. (2002). Cognitive therapy versus interoceptive exposure as treatment of panic disorder without agoraphobia. *Behaviour Research and Therapy*, *40*(3), 325–341.

Asmundson, G. J., & Katz, J. (2009). Understanding the co-occurrence of anxiety disorders and chronic pain: state-of-the-art. *Depression and Anxiety*, *26*(10), 888–901.

Asmundson, G. J., Coons, M. J., Taylor, S., & Katz, J. (2002). PTSD and the experience of pain: research and clinical implications of shared vulnerability and mutual maintenance models. *The Canadian Journal of Psychiatry*, *47*(10), 930–937.

Beck, A. T., Davis, D. D., & Freeman, A. (Eds.). (2015). *Cognitive therapy of personality disorders*. New York: Guilford Publications.

Berenz, E. C., York, T. P., Bing-Canar, H., Amstadter, A. B., Mezuk, B., Gardner, C. O., & Roberson-Nay, R. (2019). Time course of panic disorder and posttraumatic stress disorder onsets. *Social Psychiatry and Psychiatric Epidemiology*, *54*(5), 639–647.

Brennstuhl, M. J., Tarquinio, C., & Montel, S. (2015). Chronic pain and PTSD: evolving views on their comorbidity. *Perspectives in Psychiatric Care*, *51*(4), 295–304.

Bryan, C. J., Clemans, T. A., Hernandez, A. M., Mintz, J., Peterson, A. L., Yarvis, J. S., … & STRONG STAR Consortium. (2016). Evaluating potential iatrogenic suicide risk in trauma-focused group cognitive behavioral therapy for the treatment of PTSD in active duty military personnel. *Depression and Anxiety*, *33*(6), 549–557.

Carvalho, J. P., & Hopko, D. R. (2011). Behavioral theory of depression: reinforcement as a mediating variable between avoidance and depression. *Journal of Behavior Therapy and Experimental Psychiatry*, *42*(2), 154–162.

Chard, K. M., Schumm, J. A., McIlvain, S. M., Bailey, G. W., & Parkinson, R. B. (2011). Exploring the efficacy of a residential treatment program incorporating cognitive processing therapy-cognitive for veterans with PTSD and traumatic brain injury. *Journal of Traumatic Stress*, *24*(3), 347–351.

Clarke, S. B., Rizvi, S. L., & Resick, P. A. (2008). Borderline personality characteristics and treatment outcome in cognitive-behavioral treatments for PTSD in female rape victims. *Behavior Therapy*, *39*(1), 72–78.

Colvonen, P. J., Masino, T., Drummond, S. P., Myers, U. S., Angkaw, A. C., & Norman, S. B. (2015). Obstructive sleep apnea and posttraumatic stress disorder among OEF/OIF/OND veterans. *Journal of Clinical Sleep Medicine*, *11*(5), 513–518.

Cougle, J. R., Resnick, H., & Kilpatrick, D. G. (2009). PTSD, depression, and their comorbidity in relation to suicidality: cross-sectional and prospective analyses of a national probability sample of women. *Depression and Anxiety*, *26*(12), 1151–1157.

Cougle, J. R., Timpano, K. R., Sachs-Ericsson, N., Keough, M. E., & Riccardi, C. J. (2010). Examining the unique relationships between anxiety disorders and childhood physical and sexual abuse in the National Comorbidity Survey-Replication. *Psychiatry Research*, *177*(1–2), 150–155.

Cribb, G., Moulds, M. L., & Carter, S. (2006). Rumination and experiential avoidance in depression. *Behaviour Change*, *23*(3), 165–176.

Dunn, B. D. (2012). Helping depressed clients reconnect to positive emotion experience: current insights and future directions. *Clinical Psychology & Psychotherapy*, *19*(4), 326–340.

Edinger, J. D., & Carney, C. E. (2014). *Overcoming insomnia: A cognitive-behavioral therapy approach, therapist guide*. Oxford University Press.

Falsetti, S. A., Resnick, H. S., Dansky, B. S., Lydiard, R. B., & Kilpatrick, D. G. (1995). The relationship of stress to panic disorder: cause or effect? In C. M. Mazure (Ed.), Progress in psychiatry, No. 46. Does stress cause psychiatric illness? (pp. 111–147). Washington, DC: American Psychiatric Association.

Feingold, Z. R., Fox, A. B., & Galovski, T. E. (2018). Effectiveness of evidence-based psychotherapy for posttraumatic distress within a jail diversion program. *Psychological Services, 15*(4), 409–418.

Gallagher, M., McLeod, H. J., & McMillan, T. M. (2019). A systematic review of recommended modifications of CBT for people with cognitive impairments following brain injury. *Neuropsychological Rehabilitation, 29*(1), 1–21.

Galovski, T. E., & Resick, P. A. (2008). Cognitive processing therapy for posttraumatic stress disorder secondary to a motor vehicle accident: a single-subject report. *Cognitive and Behavioral Practice, 15*(3), 287–295.

Galovski, T. E., Blain, L. M., Mott, J. M., Elwood, L., & Houle, T. (2012). Manualized therapy for PTSD: flexing the structure of cognitive processing therapy. *Journal of Consulting and Clinical Psychology, 80*, 968–981.

Galovski, T. E., Harik, J. M., Blain, L. M., Elwood, L., Gloth, C., & Fletcher, T. D. (2016a). Augmenting cognitive processing therapy to improve sleep impairment in PTSD: a randomized controlled trial. *Journal of Consulting and Clinical Psychology, 84*(2), 167.

Galovski, T. E., Harik, J. M., Blain, L. M., Farmer, C., Turner, D., & Houle, T. (2016b). Identifying patterns and predictors of PTSD and depressive symptom change during cognitive processing therapy. *Cognitive Therapy and Research, 40*(5), 617–626. doi: 10.1007/s10608-016-9770-4.

Galovski, T. E., Monson, C., Bruce, S. E., & Resick, P. A. (2009). Does cognitive–behavioral therapy for PTSD improve perceived health and sleep impairment? *Journal of Traumatic Stress: Official Publication of the International Society for Traumatic Stress Studies, 22*(3), 197–204.

Glaesser, J., Neuner, F., Lütgehetmann, R., Schmidt, R., & Elbert, T. (2004). Posttraumatic stress disorder in patients with traumatic brain injury. *BMC Psychiatry, 4*(1), 5.

Goldstein, E., McDonnell, C., Atchley, R., Dorado, K., Bedford, C., Brown, R. L., & Zgierska, A. E. (2019). The impact of psychological interventions on posttraumatic stress disorder and pain symptoms. *The Clinical Journal of Pain, 35*(8), 703–712.

Gutner, C. A., Casement, M. D., Gilbert, K. S., & Resick, P. A. (2013). Change in sleep symptoms across cognitive processing therapy and prolonged exposure: a longitudinal perspective. *Behaviour Research and Therapy, 51*(12), 817–822.

Haller, M., Norman, S. B., Cummins, K., Trim, R. S., Xu, X., Cui, R., ... & Tate, S. R. (2016). Integrated cognitive behavioral therapy versus cognitive processing therapy for adults with depression, substance use disorder, and trauma. *Journal of Substance Abuse Treatment, 62*, 38–48.

Harned, M. S. (2013). Treatment of posttraumatic stress disorder and comorbid borderline personality disorder. In E. A. Storch & D. McKay (Eds.), Handbook of treating variants and complications in anxiety disorders (pp. 203–221). New York, NY: Springer.

Harned, M. S., Rizvi, S. L., & Linehan, M. M. (2010). Impact of co-occurring posttraumatic stress disorder on suicidal women with borderline personality disorder. *American Journal of Psychiatry, 167*(10), 1210–1217.

Hinton, D. E., Hofmann, S. G., Pitman, R. K., Pollack, M. H., & Barlow, D. H. (2008). The panic attack–posttraumatic stress disorder model: applicability to orthostatic panic among Cambodian refugees. *Cognitive Behaviour Therapy, 37*(2), 101–116.

Holder, N., Holliday, R., Pai, A., & Surís, A. (2017). Role of borderline personality disorder in the treatment of military sexual trauma-related posttraumatic stress disorder with cognitive processing therapy. *Behavioral Medicine, 43*(3), 184–190.

Hsieh, M. Y., Ponsford, J., Wong, D., & McKay, A. (2012). Exploring variables associated with change in cognitive behaviour therapy (CBT) for anxiety following traumatic brain injury. *Disability and Rehabilitation,* 34(5), 408–415.

Jobes, D. A. (2015). The CAMS approach to suicide risk: philosophy and clinical procedures. *Suicidology*, *14*(1), 3–7.

Jobes, D. A., Lento, R., & Brazaitis, K. (2012). An evidence-based clinical approach to suicide prevention in the department of defense: the collaborative assessment and management of suicidality (CAMS). *Military Psychology*, *24*(6), 604–623.

Kaysen, D., Schumm, J., Pedersen, E. R., Seim, R. W., Bedard-Gilligan, M., & Chard, K. (2014). Cognitive processing therapy for veterans with comorbid PTSD and alcohol use disorders. *Addictive Behaviors*, *39*(2), 420–427.

Kaysen, D., Simpson, T., Fleming, C., Jaffe, A., & Rhew, I. (2019). Cognitive processing therapy and relapse prevention in the treatment of PTSD and comorbid alcohol use disorders. In D., Kaysen, (chair), Trauma-focused therapies in the treatment of comorbid PTSD and substance use disorders. Symposium at the 16th European Society for Traumatic Stress Studies Conference, *Rotterdam*, The Netherlands.

Keane, T. M., Marshall, A. D., & Taft, C. T. (2006). Posttraumatic stress disorder: etiology, epidemiology, and treatment outcome. *Annual Review of Clinical Psychology*, *2*, 161–197.

Kessler, R. C., Chiu, W. T., Demler, O., & Walters, E. E. (2005). Prevalence, severity, and comorbidity of 12-month DSM-IV disorders in the National Comorbidity Survey Replication. *Archives of General Psychiatry*, *62*(6), 617–627.

Kleim, B., & Ehlers, A. (2008). Reduced autobiographical memory specificity predicts depression and posttraumatic stress disorder after recent trauma. *Journal of Consulting and Clinical Psychology*, *76*, 231–242.

Klein, E., Caspi, Y., & Gil, S. (2003). The relation between memory of the traumatic event and PTSD: evidence from studies of traumatic brain injury. *The Canadian Journal of Psychiatry*, *48*(1), 28–33.

Kneebone, I. I., & Hull, S. L. (2009). Cognitive behaviour therapy for post-traumatic stress symptoms in the context of hydrocephalus: a single case. *Neuropsychological Rehabilitation*, *19*(1), 86–97.

Kneebone, I. I., & Jeffries, F. W. (2013). Treating anxiety after stroke using cognitive-behaviour therapy: two cases. *Neuropsychological Rehabilitation*, *23*(6), 798–810.

Krakow, B. J., Ulibarri, V. A., Moore, B. A., & McIver, N. D. (2015). Posttraumatic stress disorder and sleep-disordered breathing: a review of comorbidity research. *Sleep Medicine Reviews*, *24*, 37–45.

Krakow, B., & Zadra, A. (2006). Clinical management of chronic nightmares: imagery rehearsal therapy. *Behavioral Sleep Medicine*, *4*(1), 45–70.

Krakow, B., & Zadra, A. (2010). Imagery rehearsal therapy: principles and practice. *Sleep Medicine Clinics*, *5*(2), 289–298.

Kubota, R., Nixon, R. D. V., & Chen, J. (2015). Trauma-related rumination mediates the effect of naturally occurring depressive symptoms but not momentary low mood on trauma intrusions. *Australian Journal of Psychology*, *67*, 75–86. doi: 10.1111/ajpy.12074.

Laker, S. R. (2011). Epidemiology of concussion and mild traumatic brain injury. *PM&R*, *3*, S354–S358.

Lang, A. J., Kennedy, C. M., & Stein, M. B. (2002). Anxiety sensitivity and PTSD among female victims of intimate partner violence. *Depression and Anxiety*, *16*(2), 77–83.

Larsen, S. E., Stirman, S. W., Smith, B. N., & Resick, P. A. (2016). Symptom exacerbations in trauma-focused treatments: associations with treatment outcome and non-completion. *Behaviour Research and Therapy*, *77*, 68–77.

Linehan, M. (2018). *Cognitive-behavioral treatment of borderline personality disorder*. New York: Guilford Publications.

Marlatt, G. A., & Donovan, D. M. (Eds.). (2005). Relapse prevention: Maintenance strategies in the treatment of addictive behaviors. New York: Guilford Press.

Merskey, H., & Bogduk, N. (1994). Classification of chronic pain, IASP Task Force on Taxonomy. Seattle, WA: International Association for the Study of Pain Press. Available from: www.iasp-painorg.

Michael, T., Zetsche, U., & Margraf, J. (2007). Epidemiology of anxiety disorders. *Psychiatry*, *6*(4), 136–142.

Morasco, B. J., Lovejoy, T. I., Lu, M., Turk, D. C., Lewis, L., & Dobscha, S. K. (2013). The relationship between PTSD and chronic pain: mediating role of coping strategies and depression. *Pain*, *154*(4), 609–616.

Nixon, R. D., & Bralo, D. (2019). Using explicit case formulation to improve cognitive processing therapy for PTSD. *Behavior Therapy*, *50*(1), 155–164.

Nixon, R. D. V., Resick, P. A., & Nishith, P. (2004). An exploration of comorbid depression among female victims of intimate partner violence with posttraumatic stress disorder. *Journal of Affective Disorders*, *82*, 315–320.

Otis, J. D., Keane, T. M., & Kerns, R. D. (2003). An examination of the relationship between chronic pain and post-traumatic stress disorder. *Journal of Rehabilitation Research and Development*, *40*(5), 397–406.

Otis, J. D., Keane, T. M., Kerns, R. D., Monson, C., & Scioli, E. (2009). The development of an integrated treatment for veterans with comorbid chronic pain and posttraumatic stress disorder. *Pain Medicine*, *10*(7), 1300–1311.

Pace-Schott, E. F., Germain, A., & Milad, M. R. (2015). Effects of sleep on memory for conditioned fear and fear extinction. *Psychological Bulletin*, *141*(4), 835.

Pacella, M. L., Hruska, B., & Delahanty, D. L. (2013). The physical health consequences of PTSD and PTSD symptoms: a meta-analytic review. *Journal of Anxiety Disorders*, *27*(1), 33–46.

Pagura, J., Stein, M. B., Bolton, J. M., Cox, B. J., Grant, B., & Sareen, J. (2010). Comorbidity of borderline personality disorder and posttraumatic stress disorder in the US population. *Journal of Psychiatric Research*, *44*(16), 1190–1198.

Pearson, C. R., Kaysen, D., Huh, D., & Bedard-Gilligan, M. (2019). Randomized control trial of culturally adapted cognitive processing therapy for PTSD substance misuse and HIV sexual risk behavior for native American women. *AIDS and Behavior, 23*(3), 695–706.

Pietrzak, R. H., Goldstein, R. B., Southwick, S. M., & Grant, B. F. (2011). Personality disorders associated with full and partial posttraumatic stress disorder in the US population: results from Wave 2 of the National Epidemiologic Survey on Alcohol and Related Conditions. *Journal of Psychiatric Research*, *45*(5), 678–686.

Pietrzak, R. H., Goldstein, R. B., Southwick, S. M., & Grant, B. F. (2012). Psychiatric comorbidity of full and partial posttraumatic stress disorder among older adults in the United States: results from wave 2 of the National Epidemiologic Survey on Alcohol and Related Conditions. *The American Journal of Geriatric Psychiatry*, *20*(5), 380–390.

Ponsford, J., Bayley, M., Wiseman-Hakes, C., Togher, L., Velikonja, D., McIntyre, A., Janzen, S., & Tate, R. (2014). INCOG recommendations for management of cognition following traumatic brain injury, part II: attention and information processing speed. *The Journal of Head Trauma Rehabilitation*, *29*(4), 321–337.

Pruiksma, K. E., Taylor, D. J., Wachen, J. S., Mintz, J., Young-McCaughan, S., Peterson, A. L., ..., & Hembree, E. A. (2016). Residual sleep disturbances following PTSD treatment in active duty military personnel. *Psychological Trauma: Theory, Research, Practice, and Policy*, *8*(6), 697.

Read, J. P., Brown, P. J., & Kahler, C. W. (2004). Substance use and posttraumatic stress disorders: symptom interplay and effects on outcome. *Addictive Behaviors, 29*(8), 1665–1672.

Resick, P. A., Nishith, P., Weaver, T. L., Astin, M. C., & Feuer, C. A. (2002). A comparison of cognitive-processing therapy with prolonged exposure and a waiting condition for the treatment of chronic posttraumatic stress disorder in female rape victims. *Journal of Consulting and Clinical Psychology*, *70*(4), 867.

Rytwinski, N. K., Scur, M. D., Feeny, N. C., & Youngstrom, E. A. (2013). The co-occurrence of major depressive disorder among individuals with posttraumatic stress disorder: a meta-analysis. *Journal of Traumatic Stress*, *26*(3), 299–309.

Saunders, E. C., McGovern, M. P., Lambert-Harris, C., Meier, A., McLeman, B., & Xie, H. (2015). The impact of addiction medications on treatment outcomes for persons with co-occurring PTSD and opioid use disorders. *The American Journal on Addictions*, *24*(8), 722–731.

Simpson, T. L., Rise, P., Browne, K. C., Lehavot, K., & Kaysen, D. (2019). Clinical presentations, social functioning, and treatment receipt among individuals with comorbid life-time PTSD and alcohol use disorders versus drug use disorders: findings from NESARC-III. *Addiction*, *114*(6), 983–993.

Stappenbeck, C. A., Luterek, J. A., Kaysen, D., Rosenthal, C. F., Gurrad, B., & Simpson, T. L. (2015). A controlled examination of two coping skills for daily alcohol use and PTSD symptom severity among dually diagnosed individuals. *Behaviour Research and Therapy, 66,* 8–17.

Stein, M. B., & McAllister, T. W. (2009). Exploring the convergence of posttraumatic stress disorder and mild traumatic brain injury. *American Journal of Psychiatry*, *166*(7), 768–776.

Swift, J. K., & Greenberg, R. P. (2014). A treatment by disorder meta-analysis of dropout from psychotherapy. *Journal of Psychotherapy Integration*, *24*(3), 193–207.

Tanev, K. S., Pentel, K. Z., Kredlow, M. A., & Charney, M. E. (2014). PTSD and TBI co-morbidity: scope, clinical presentation and treatment options. *Brain Injury*, *28*(3), 261–270.

Teng, E. J., Hiatt, E. L., McClair, V., Kunik, M. E., Frueh, B. C., & Stanley, M. A. (2013). Efficacy of posttraumatic stress disorder treatment for comorbid panic disorder: a critical review and future directions for treatment research. *Clinical Psychology: Science and Practice*, *20*(3), 268–284.

Trew, J. L. (2011). Exploring the roles of approach and avoidance in depression: an integrative model. *Clinical Psychology Review*, *31*(7), 1156–1168.

Trim, J. G., Galovski, T. E., Wagner, A., & Brewerton, T. (2017). Treating ED-PTSD patients: a synthesis of the literature and new treatment directions. In L. K. Anderson, S. B. Murray, & W. H. Kaye (Eds.), *Clinical handbook of complex and atypical eating disorders* (pp. 40–59). New York, NY: Oxford University Press.

Vujanovic, A. A., Zvolensky, M. J., & Bernstein, A. (2008). Posttraumatic stress and panic psychopathology: clinical import, research advances, and future directions—introduction to the special issue. *Cognitive Behaviour Therapy*, *37*(2), 63–65.

Walker, M. P., & van Der Helm, E. (2009). Overnight therapy? The role of sleep in emotional brain processing. *Psychological Bulletin*, *135*(5), 731.

Walter, K. H., Kiefer, S. L., & Chard, K. M. (2012). Relationship between posttraumatic stress disorder and postconcussive symptom improvement after completion of a posttraumatic stress disorder/traumatic brain injury residential treatment program. *Rehabilitation Psychology*, *57*(1), 13.

Werner-Seidler, A., Banks, R., Dunn, B. D., & Moulds, M. L. (2013). An investigation of the relationship between positive affect regulation and depression. *Behaviour Research and Therapy*, *51*(1), 46–56.

Part III

Dissemination and Implementation of CPT

Chapter 11

Applications of CPT in diverse populations and across cultures

Chapter outline

Applications of CPT in diverse populations and across cultures

Cognitive processing therapy (CPT) was originally developed and tested in the United States, a Western, largely educated, industrialized, and democratic country (Henrich, Heine, & Norenzayan, 2010). However, these characteristics are not true for the majority of the people in the world! In this chapter, we focus on the use of CPT with communities that vary from those that the treatment was developed with in terms of their personal characteristics such as race, ethnicity, sexual orientation or gender identity, or geography. However, the term culture is broader than this and is used to apply to other aspects of culture such as religion, socioeconomic status, and organizational or occupational community. All of these aspects of our context and identity are important and also can shape our worldviews and how we respond to a treatment. For the purpose of this chapter, we are predominantly focusing on aspects of culture most implicated in health disparities (e.g., race, ethnicity, sexual orientation or gender identity, and geography). CPT was originally developed and tested in a more diverse population than many EBP's. It has been adapted and applied for use with a wide range of

Flexible Applications of Cognitive Processing Therapy. http://dx.doi.org/10.1016/B978-0-12-816715-1.00011-X

patient populations, both locally and internationally. The core principles of CPT, as described throughout this book, emphasize flexibility, respect, and humility to the patient's experiences. These core principles have made CPT a particularly robust intervention for a wide range of patient groups.

Culture and evidence-based therapies

All interpersonal interactions occur within a multicultural context (APA, 2003). Both patients and therapists bring their cultural lens to viewing the treatment process (Schulz, Huber, & Resick 2006). Awareness of this fact and informing oneself about the client's culture and background are essential for effective therapeutic work (Bemak & Chung, 2000). There is increasing evidence that evidence-based practice and cultural competency are quite complementary (Huey & Polo, 2008; Whaley & Davis, 2007). That doesn't mean that you ignore culture or use a "one size fits all" approach. The reality is that therapies like CPT have very strong evidence that they work, yet in general there is a gap in access to these interventions for ethnically and culturally diverse clients and individuals in low and middle income countries (Kohn, Saxena, Levav, & Saraceno, 2004; Prince et al., 2007). There are several potential models for how to adapt evidence-based interventions for diverse populations (Griner & Smith, 2006). Adaptations that are most useful are those that maintain the evidence-based intervention's core while incorporating culturally responsive elements into the intervention (Huey & Polo, 2008).

As we discuss applications of CPT to diverse groups, it is helpful to remember that these groupings we discuss are rough at best. There are subgroups within categories and individuals may differ widely in terms of their own level of acculturation or their own identity and lived experiences. There is also the impact of intersectionality—people may not fit just in one category but may have multiple identities that all impact what they bring into the therapy. Knowing someone's demographics or geography tells you one thing about them but their story tells you so much more.

The impact of gender, race, and ethnicity on CPT outcomes in the United States

There are a few studies looking at the impact of race and gender on CPT outcomes. A recent paper reviewed the medical records for 750 veterans who received CPT or PE to look at the impact of race, ethnicity, and gender on treatment outcomes in standard VA clinical practice (Rutt, Oehlert, Krieshok, & Lichtenberg, 2018). To be able to adequately address questions about race, the researchers intentionally included specific Veterans Integrated Service Networks known to be high in diversity. The study included 125 women (16%). Of those veterans who received CPT, 47 were African American (6%) and 71 were Latino (10%) while 225 were White (30%). The study found no gender differences in PTSD improvements over time, nor were there gender differences in number of sessions completed. Similarly, there were no differences in treatment effects based on race nor ethnicity between the Caucasian, African American, and Latino veterans or differences in the number of sessions they completed. In other words, both men and women, within a diverse patient population, were quite comparable in terms of symptom reduction and dropout rates.

In delivery of group CPT, both the racial makeup of the group and the match of therapist and group members may influence CPT outcomes (Mackintosh, Cha, Willis, & Morland, 2019). A diverse sample of 114 male veterans (18% Asian, 7% African American, 54% White, 9% Latino, 1% Native American/ Alaska Native, and 15% Native Hawaiian/Pacific Islander) was seen across 26 CPT groups. The study found that groups that were more diverse had better PTSD treatment outcomes than those with lower levels of diversity. For each participant a mismatch between the therapist race and patient race predicted a poorer treatment outcome. It is impossible to say whether this reflected differing skill level in CPT across therapists, higher comfort with a therapist of one's own race or ethnicity, or that these therapists were able to be more culturally attuned in applying CPT to that particular group member. It is important to note that the finding, an average of an 8-point difference in post-treatment CAPS-IV scores, is not a clinically significant and it is important to note that these veterans still experienced significant improvements in PTSD with CPT, regardless of racial matching.

In contrast, one of the earliest papers to examine the impact of race on CPT outcomes reanalyzed the clinical trials data to see if there were differential outcomes for women who were White versus those who were African American (Lester, Artz, Resick, & Young-Xu, 2010). The study included 94 African American and 214 Caucasian victims of interpersonal violence who received CPT or prolonged exposure across two clinical trials. The results of this reanalysis of the data were quite interesting. African American women had the same degree of improvement from CPT as White women, however the rate of dropout for African Americans was much higher (45% vs. 73%). What's more, the African Americans who dropped out were doing better in terms of PTSD improvement than the White patients who dropped out and the African Americans had higher expectancies overall that therapy would be beneficial. It may be that the African American patients dropped out because they were feeling better and had gotten what they needed from treatment. They may have come primed for treatment and once they had met their goals, they left (Lester et al., 2010). The authors also suggested that clinicians consider modifying PTSD treatment for African-American clients to address potential factors involved in premature dropout such as mental health stigma.

There are gender differences in risk of PTSD and in the types of traumatic events men and women are exposed to (Galovski, Mott, Young-Xu, & Resick, 2011). The first study to look at gender differences on CPT outcomes

(Galovski, Blain, Chappuis, & Fletcher, 2013) consisted of a reanalysis of the modified flexible dosing version of CPT. The study included 22 men and 47 women who had all experience interpersonal assault. Overall the study found relatively few differences by gender. Both men and women completed treatment at the same rates and needed similar numbers of sessions to reach good end-state functioning on PTSD and depression. In terms of some of the secondary outcomes, women had more rapid treatment gains with guilt, anger, and dissociation than men. In contrast, an effectiveness study of 481 veterans presenting at a residential treatment program looked at the impact of both military sexual trauma and gender on treatment outcomes and did find gender differences in outcomes (Voelkel, Pukay-Martin, Walter, & Chard, 2015). More specifically the study found that women had a larger decrease in PTSD than men, although both women and men improved significantly.

In sum, in studies that have looked at the use of CPT within diverse communities within the United States, we have generally found that unadapted CPT works well for men and women, and for ethnic and cultural minorities. The data are inconclusive around whether there is differential dropout for some ethnic minority groups, and the impact that may have on clinical outcomes. Although there are some differences by gender, race, and ethnicity, in general the effect sizes are small, and individuals across groups benefit from treatment.

Use of adapted CPT within the United States

Use of CPT with Bosnian refugees

There have been two studies looking at adapting CPT to address unique needs of specific ethnocultural groups within the United States. One focused on Bosnian refugees and the other focused on the needs of inner city, predominantly Latino patients. In the study delivering CPT with Bosnian refugees in a community setting the degree of improvement in PTSD from the beginning to end of treatment was comparable with those in well-controlled RCTs of CPT (Schulz, Resick, Huber, & Griffin, 2006). There were specific factors in the Bosnian refugee community that led to thoughtful adaptations to the CPT protocol. The community had high rates of panic symptoms, somatic concerns, and agoraphobia. Changes in the treatment included conducting additional and longer sessions (i.e., a mean of 17 sessions at 1.5–2 hours each instead of the typical 12 sessions for 1 hour), including a relaxation component, and meeting with patients in their homes for sessions when necessary (Schulz, Huber, & Resick, 2006).

Adaptation of CPT with Latinos

As a slightly different model on approaching the adaptation process, one study used formative evaluation to assess relations between iterative cultural adaption (for Spanish-speaking Latino clients) and implementation outcomes (appropriateness and acceptability) for CPT (Valentine et al., 2017). Treatment was implemented in a diverse, urban low resource community clinic where a large proportion of the patient population was Latino. The investigator's approached adaptation of CPT in a systematic way as part of a larger clinical implementation trial. Educational differences, a lack of familiarity with Western psychological concepts, culturally specific idioms of distress, and cultural differences in values were all issues they considered in making the adaptations (e.g., familism, spirituality, trust) (Alamilla, Kim, & Lam, 2010). The final adaptation incorporated cultural values into the CPT rationale. It included more relevant trauma vignettes, included more local stuck points, and emphasized that trauma isn't always in the past. It also included new terms that were seen as a better fit for the Spanish dialects spoken by their patients. Feedback was solicited by Spanish-speaking providers and researchers on terminology in the manual. Based on results of the larger clinical trial, including both the Latino and non-Latino patients, clinical results were in the same range as larger randomized clinical trials of CPT (Marques et al., 2019). In general, in looking at the stuck points between the Latino and non-Latino patients, there were more similarities than differences in the beliefs although the ways in which patients arrived at those stuck points may have differed. In coded impact statements, the Latino patients more often emphasized family relationships, exposure to repeated experiences of violence, religion, poverty, and family culture influencing their beliefs about self, other, and the world (Marques et al., 2016). Safety beliefs were quite similar across the groups. Power and control stuck points were not endorsed by Spanish-speaking Latino patients, suggesting that module may resonate less culturally with that group.

Adaptation of CPT with Native Americans

In a study working with a Pacific Northwest tribe to adapt CPT researchers used an ecological approach for adaptation of health promotion interventions (Bartholomew et al., 2011). The clinical and research partners were invited into the community to work collaboratively with them to address trauma (Pearson et al., 2019b). Prior to starting the adaptation process the team formed a community advisory board to help guide the process, while also soliciting feedback from local clinicians, elders of tribal traditions, language, and values, and potential clients to review the CPT materials and protocol. CPT was adapted to include content on the role of historical trauma on mental health. CPT vignettes and session content were adapted to include language around spirituality, to emphasize the importance of extended family, and to address differences in aspects of how death is viewed within the community. For example, one challenge that came up was around challenging assimilation beliefs when an elder had perpetrated the traumatic event, given cultural beliefs about the importance and reverence for elders. After the team consulted with the community advisory board, we worked with therapists around reframing a difference between elders, as someone who is wise and revered, versus someone who is just old.

Cultural stories and metaphors were integrated into the manual. In addition, some language was changed to be more congruent with core cultural beliefs. For example, the term “challenging” was seen as confrontational and instead was changed to “balancing” questions. The CPT handout materials were adapted to include imagery meaningful to the local community. Some other adaptations including allowing for longer sessions and allowing clinicians to offer patients, if the patient wanted, the option to engage in prayer or smudging prior to starting the session to create a “safe space” to do the work. Content was included in the manual on how to keep this option contained so as not to cut into session time or reinforce avoidance. Given that patients had various levels of identification with their community, engaging in these practices was always left in the patient’s hands. Despite these changes the core elements of CPT remained intact. In the randomized clinical trial, comparing the adapted CPT to a waitlist control, CPT was effective in improving PTSD, as well as addressing high-risk sexual behavior and alcohol use (Pearson et al., 2019a). At the same time dropout rates in the study were quite high with only about 30% of the patients completing at least nine sessions. It is impossible to know whether this was a function in CPT not being an acceptable treatment or being too long for the community, the high rates of poverty and stress in the community, or the impact of comorbid substance use on treatment engagement.

Adaptation of CPT for sexual and gender minorities

Research on the use of CPT with patients who are lesbian, bisexual, or gay and with patients who are transgender or gender nonconforming has lagged behind the research on CPT for other diverse communities. There has been one case study describing the use of CPT with a gay man following a bias-based physical assault (Kaysen, Lostutter, & Goines, 2005). Although CPT was not adapted, treatment did include addressing internalized heterosexist beliefs, while also being sensitive to the real experiences of discrimination faced by the patient. The patient reported lower acute stress disorder and symptoms of depression at post-treatment and 3-month follow-up, as well as improvements in PTSD-related cognitions and internalized heterosexism. A CPT informed intervention, addressing HIV risk in men who have sex with men, with histories of childhood sexual abuse was found to reduce PTSD overall and avoidance symptoms as compared to HIV counseling and testing (O’Cleirigh, et al., 2019). The CPT informed intervention also improved high-risk sexual behavior. However, improvements in PTSD were not maintained at follow-up visits.

Given the paucity of data on addressing PTSD among sexual and gender minorities there are some general issues to consider in using CPT with LGBTQ patients. In providing psychoeducation, it may be helpful to also incorporate information on the impact of societal bias on mental health and to provide information on the impact of minority stress (Kaysen, Lehavot, & Dworkin, 2019; Shipherd, Valentine, & Woulfe, 2019). For example, in a longitudinal study of young lesbian and bisexual women, experiences of discrimination independently increased risk of developing PTSD, over and above trauma exposure per se (Dworkin et al., 2018). Experiences of discrimination also increased trauma-related cognitions, which then predicted risk of PTSD.

So what does this mean clinically? When engaging in Socratic dialogue in CPT, clinicians should keep an eye out for stuck points around minority stress. These could include esteem beliefs around oneself or about other sexual minority individuals rooted in internalized negative societal messages. Assimilation beliefs may also include that one's sexual or gender identity "caused" the event. This also can lead to overaccommodated beliefs that because of one's identity, one will never be safe. These are all stuck points and are fair game in CPT. At the same time, it is important to listen to one's patient as they are the expert in their own experience. Their assessment of safety or risk could also be quite accurate (and not a PTSD symptom) given the high rates of violence exposure for many sexual and gender minorities (Roberts, Austin, Corliss, Vandermorris, & Koenen, 2010; Shipherd, Maguen, Skidmore, & Abramovitz, 2011). Ongoing experiences of discrimination and threats of safety exist and can keep hypervigilance high.

Anna: *I'll never be safe.*

Therapist: *That's a nice clear stuck point for us to work on together Anna. And I see that this belief leaves you feeling quite scared and angry. What evidence do you have that the stuck point is true?*

Anna: *I'm always going to be gay. They knew this and this is why they attacked me. So I'll never be safe.*

Therapist: *I can definitely see why you're feeling stuck. Are you hearing any stuck points? Especially one that might be driving those fear and anger emotions?*

Anna: *That they picked me because of who I am. I can't change that.*

Therapist: *That is true, that you can't change who you are or who you love. But let's look at whether that's the reason you were assaulted, and whether that means you will definitely be assaulted again. Are there other reasons you could have been picked? Are straight women ever assaulted in the military?*

Anna: *That's true. There are straight women and men who get assaulted.*

Therapist: *Ok. So it may have played a role but it looks like sexual orientation isn't the only factor. So let's go back and look at how that fits with your stuck point "because I'm gay, I'll never be safe." Is it your sexual orientation that makes you unsafe?*

Anna: *Kind of. People do target you.*

Therapist: *That is absolutely true. People do. All people?*

Anna *No just some. There are definitely some people who've got my back.*

Therapist: *And is it all the time?*

Anna: *No. It's definitely not all the time. There are some situations where I have to be careful. But there are places where I don't have to be on guard.*

Therapist: *That sounds a little different.*

Take-home message: In sum, across a wide range of studies within the United States, ranging from newer immigrants to historically discriminated populations, we have found that adapted CPT can be acceptable and feasible within these groups. As we work with the local communities and get to know the needs of the patient population, we can listen and learn from them about where CPT may need to be adjusted and where it is a natural fit. Across these studies CPT has worked remarkably well. In addition, although we do see within group differences in some of the types of stuck points, far more stuck points are common across cultures and ethnicities than are different. What this may mean in your own practice is that while you may need to make some adjustments to meet the needs of a particular patient population, generally they should be small, and the core of CPT can remain the same. The process of Socratic dialogue—listening respectfully and being curious, remains the same. The other take-home message, again true to the heart of CPT, is don't assume you know what is true (or not true!) for that patient—be curious enough to inquire.

CPT hits the road: Applications of CPT outside of the United States

There have been CPT trials conducted in a variety of high-income countries including Australia, Canada, Germany, and Japan (Butollo, Karl, König, & Rosner, 2016; Forbes et al., 2012; Ito et al., 2017; Nixon, 2012) and CPT is being used in Germany, Denmark, Iceland, Hong Kong, Israel, and Japan (Resick, Monson, & Chard, 2016). In these settings the major adaptation has been translation of the materials and manual. Including more examples in the homework assignments, simplifying some of the language, or including drawings or pictures are other changes that have been made in some settings. In general modifications have been modest and the core of CPT has remained the same.

To adapt CPT for low- and middle-income countries, the therapy also needed to be adapted for settings with few trained mental health providers (Group, 2007). CPT has been tested in Northern and Southern Iraq for torture survivors and in the Democratic Republic of Congo (DRC) for female sexual assault survivors (Bass et al., 2013; Bolton et al., 2014; Weiss et al., 2015). Detailed description of the adaptations is published elsewhere (Bass et al., 2013 supplemental materials; Kaysen et al., 2013). CPT implemented in DRC was quite effective, demonstrating large and sustained reductions in PTSD, depression and improvements in functioning (Bass et al., 2013). CPT was also associated with improvements in perceived stigma posttreatment (Murray et al., 2018). In Northern Iraq CPT was associated with significant improvements in PTSD, functioning, and anxiety with mixed results on its effects on depression (Bolton et al., 2014). In Southern Iraq, CPT demonstrated significant improvements in PTSD and depression symptoms but did not improve functioning significantly over controls (Weiss et al., 2015).

In these settings changes in CPT needed to reflect the local context, culture, and use of paraprofessionals as providers. Despite the challenge in using paraprofessionals, this is seen as a preferable option to using non-local staff or ex-patriots to deliver therapy. Training local clinicians ensures that after the project end, the knowledge stays in those communities. It also ensures that the people delivering the care are aware of the local culture and language. In working to develop CPT in all three of these settings, there was first a pre-adaptation process, where the manual was simplified and professional jargon was removed. The adaptation process is described elsewhere (Kaysen et al., 2013) but used an iterative process throughout with high stakeholder engagement and feedback. Aspects of the content of the therapy were adapted to best fit the local context and culture.

For Iraq CPT needed to be modified to address issues of literacy as in the more rural areas, and for female patients, levels of literacy were low. Although we discuss these modifications in relation to Iraq and DRC, these are modifications could be used with clients of lower levels of literacy in high-income settings as well. Modifications to address literacy in Iraq, where we were providing CPT individually, included use of pictures on materials to act as visual cues for the skills, use of mobile phones to record practice assignments, linking completion of practice assignments to things that occurred daily like the call to prayer (*after afternoon prayer, do your practice*), or doing the practice in session with the clinician. In DRC CPT was delivered as a group intervention. Thus CPT was adapted so that all of the skills could be memorized. This included reducing the number of challenging questions to four and removing the patterns of problematic thinking. Similar to what was done in Iraq, the women in DRC were encouraged to link CPT practice to other daily practices such as walking to the fields or sweeping their homes. Women in the CPT groups also would meet at times between group sessions to help each other with the practice. Longer writing assignments, like the impact statement, were either done verbally in session or recorded (Northern and Southern Iraq) or were done in smaller portions and shared with the group (DRC).

In CPT, if the terminology or language is getting in the way, change the terminology but keep the core concept intact. In all of these settings there were concepts or words that were difficult to translate, either linguistically or culturally. For example, in Northern Iraq the concept of esteem could not be translated to Kurdish. The trainers worked with the clinicians and described both the behaviors and symptoms associated with esteem related stuck points. Based on this discussion the group settled on the term "respect" as the best proxy for esteem. In Southern Iraq, "why" questions were seen as harsh and disrespectful. Instead clinicians would get at the concept by asking "how do you think…." In DRC, in some of the local languages (CPT has been delivered in DRC in over six different local languages) there were difficulties differentiating between thoughts and feelings. We worked on thoughts coming from the head and feelings from the heart and helped therapists find the best words to explain these concepts in each local language. This principle of adaptation in CPT is true elsewhere including in work with diverse communities in the United States (Marques et al., 2016).

One difference in working in Iraq in particular that is worth highlighting was in how to incorporate family members. This was a setting where cross-gender therapy relationships could be forbidden, depending on how traditional the patient's family was. Due to the lack of number of providers, it was not always feasible to find a clinician of the same gender as the client. Ignoring these issues would not only have been culturally insensitive but it would have potential to put both the patient and the therapist at risk. In these cases we gave the patient the option to choose a family member to sit in the room with them. By having it be their choice we allowed them to have some degree of control over whether to do this and who to invite into the therapeutic space. It had the added benefit of at times giving them a supportive coach in addition to the therapist. Questions come up in the United States as well about whether it is appropriate to include family members in CPT, and if so, how to do so. The work in Iraq demonstrates that this is possible as long as it is in the patient's hands; patient safety is protected, which is necessary to provide the treatment. Be more cautious if the impetus seems to be more related to avoidance and less around respecting cultural norms.

Despite these types of changes, the core of CPT remained the same. In all of these settings therapists worked on assimilation stuck points about why the traumatic events occurred. Many of these were quite similar to the stuck points you might hear across many other settings (*"It happened because I went out that night." "If I had come home earlier my wife wouldn't have been taken." I should have fought back."*). Most of the CPT practice remained the same with the exception of modifications for simplifying language, simplifying to accommodate differing levels of literacy, and reducing the number of challenging questions. Generally the modules remained quite similar while including examples of culturally specific stuck points (*"Because I was raped I do not have a voice in my house." "My community did not respect my sacrifice.")* that fit for the various modules.

One challenge across these settings, but in particular in Southern Iraq and DRC was how to deliver CPT in contexts with ongoing conflict and violence. Providers are often worried that PTSD cannot be treated or should not be treated in settings where there is an active risk of danger. Indeed—the treatment guidelines provided by the World Health Organization states that trauma-focused interventions "should be considered when the person is within a safe environment, that is, there are no ongoing traumatic events and the person is not at imminent risk of further exposure to traumatic events" (World Health Organization and United Nations High Commissioner for Refugees, 2013, p. 10). We examined the data from DRC to see whether there were differences in CPT outcomes between the communities where there were high levels of ongoing violence, defined as the degree of ongoing presence or threat of presence of armed groups and incidents of violence at the site, as compared with sites with lower levels of ongoing violence (Kaysen et al., 2019). We found that although women in more dangerous communities had higher initial PTSD symptoms they had similar improvements over time as the women in the less dangerous communities. This has implications broadly, because we frequently have questions from therapists about what to do to treat PTSD for individuals living in communities with high rates of community violence and these findings suggest that treating their PTSD is possible and likely effective. That being said, working in these settings has several challenges including making it more difficult for supervisors to get to sites and, in Iraq, making it difficult at times for therapists and patients to meet. Overall though, these findings challenged our own stuck points about where we can treat PTSD!

Take-home message: Although the communities included in these projects are different than the places many of us live, there are ways we can use these findings to help all of us. First of all, these findings suggest that there is a wide range of patients who can benefit from CPT, despite differences in their level of literacy, religion, language, economic resources, or even level of safety in their community. Sometimes you may have to think on your feet to figure out how to teach the core skill but that doesn't mean that the skill should be scrapped. And some of these modifications, such as building CPT practice into a daily routine, are helpful broadly for many of the patients we work with. In DRC the therapists we taught renamed CPT as "Heart and Mind Therapy" and perhaps that is something else we can all take with us as the core of CPT.

CPT's core features appear culturally robust

As can be seen in the earlier review of CPT's applications to various communities and to various settings, the core features of CPT appear to remain largely intact. The treatment remains trauma-focused and time limited. It tends to jump into the trauma quickly, within the first 1–2 sessions, and it uses Socratic dialogue as a core therapeutic tool to shift trauma-related stuck points. The worksheets may be done in varying ways (using pictures, memorized, done verbally in session) but typically there is practice between sessions to help with generalization.

There are aspects of CPT that may help its applicability to diverse communities. The therapy length, although originally set up as a 12-session treatment, can be made longer or shorter, depending on the patient's need, which can be quite helpful in adapting the therapy to different communities. Although CPT is trauma-focused it also has the flexibility to accommodate day-to-day stressors, which again can be helpful. Perhaps the aspect of CPT that most readily enables its applicability to diverse communities lies in the central tenets of Socratic dialogue. This includes approaching the dialogue from a place of genuine respect for the patient and the idea that it is the patient, not the therapist who supplies the answers. The job of the therapist is not to create the new thought or convince the patient the old thought is wrong. The therapist may not be correct in his/her analysis of the patient's experiences or environment and invariably the patient understands his/her own world better than the therapist possibly can. The job of the CPT therapist is to ask curious questions to help draw forth a new understanding that is accurate and balanced. This is entirely congruent with approaching therapy from a place of cultural humility.

References

Alamilla, S. G., Kim, B. S., & Lam, N. A. (2010). Acculturation, enculturation, perceived racism, minority status stressors, and psychological symptomatology among Latino/as. *Hispanic Journal of Behavioral Sciences*, *32*(1), 55–76.

American Psychological Association (2003). Guidelines for multicultural education, training, research, practice, and organizational change for psychologists. *American Psychologist*, *58*, 377–402.

Bartholomew, L. K., Leerlooijer, J., James, S., Reinders, J., Mullen, P. D., Parcel, G., ..., & Fernandez, M. (2011). Using intervention mapping to adapt evidence-based programs to new settings and populations. *Planning health promotion programs: an intervention mapping approach*, *553*, 632.

Bass, J. K., Annan, J., McIvor Murray, S., Kaysen, D., Griffiths, S., Cetinoglu, T., Wachter, K., Murray, L. K., & Bolton, P. A. (2013). Controlled trial of psychotherapy for Congolese survivors of sexual violence. *New England Journal of Medicine*, *368*(23), 2182–2191.

Bemak, F. P., & Chung, R. C. Y. (2000). Psychological intervention with immigrants and refugees. In J. F. Aponte, & J. Wohl (Eds.), *Psychological intervention and cultural diversity* (pp. 200–213). Boston: Allyn & Bacon.

Bolton, P., Bass, J. K., Zangana, G. A. S., Kamal, T., Murray, S. M., Kaysen, D., Lejuez, C. W., Lindgren, K., Pagoto, S., Murray, L. K., & Van Wyk, S. S. (2014). A randomized controlled trial of mental health interventions for survivors of systematic violence in Kurdistan. *Northern Iraq. BMC psychiatry*, *14*(1), 360.

Butollo, W., Karl, R., König, J., & Rosner, R. (2016). A randomized controlled clinical trial of dialogical exposure therapy versus cognitive processing therapy for adult outpatients suffering from PTSD after type I trauma in adulthood. *Psychotherapy and psychosomatics*, *85*(1), 16–26.

Dworkin, E. R., Bedard-Gilligan, M., Gilmore, A., Lehavot, K., Guttmannova, K., & Kaysen, D. (2018). Predicting PTSD severity from experiences of trauma and heterosexism in lesbian and bisexual women: a longitudinal study of cognitive mediators. *Journal of Counseling Psychology*, *65*, 324–333.

Dworkin, E. R., Gilmore, A. K., Bedard-Gilligan, M., Lehavot, K., Guttmannova, K., & Kaysen, D. (2018). Predicting PTSD severity from experiences of trauma and heterosexism in lesbian and bisexual women: a longitudinal study of cognitive mediators. *Journal of counseling psychology*, *65*(3), 324.

Forbes, D., Lloyd, D., Nixon, R. D. V., Elliott, P., Varker, T., Perry, D., Bryant, R. A., & Creamer, M. (2012). A multisite randomized controlled effectiveness trial of cognitive processing therapy for military-related posttraumatic stress disorder. *Journal of Anxiety Disorders*, *26*(3), 442–452.

Galovski, T. E., Blain, L. M., Chappuis, C., & Fletcher, T. (2013). Sex differences in recovery from PTSD in male and female interpersonal assault survivors. *Behaviour research and therapy*, *51*(6), 247–255.

Galovski, T. E., Mott, J., Young-Xu, Y., & Resick, P. A. (2011). Gender differences in the clinical presentation of PTSD and its concomitants in survivors of interpersonal assault. *Journal of Interpersonal Violence*, *26*(4), 789–806.

Griner, D., & Smith, T. B. (2006). Culturally adapted mental health intervention: a meta-analytic review. *Psychotherapy: theory, research, practice, training*, *43*(4), 531–548.

Group, L. G. M. H. (2007). Scale up services for mental disorders: a call for action. *The Lancet, 370*(9594), 1241–1252.

Henrich, J., Heine, S. J., & Norenzayan, A. (2010). Most people are not WEIRD. *Nature, 466*(7302), 29.

Huey, S. J., Jr., & Polo, A. J. (2008). Evidence-based psychosocial treatments for ethnic minority youth. *Journal of Clinical Child & Adolescent Psychology, 37*(1), 262–301.

Ito, M., Horikoshi, M., Resick, P. A., Katayanagi, A., Miyamae, M., Takagishi, Y., Takebayashi, Y., Kanie, A., Hirabayashi, N., & Furukawa, T. A. (2017). Study protocol for a randomised controlled trial of cognitive processing therapy for post-traumatic stress disorder among Japanese patients: the safety, power, intimacy, esteem trust (SPINET) study. *BMJ Open, 7*(6), e014292.

Kaysen, D., Lehavot, L., & Dworkin, E. (2019). Application of evidence-based practices for trauma-related disorders among sexual minority women. In J. E. Pachankis, & S. A. Safren (Eds.), *Handbook of evidence-based mental health practice with sexual and gender minorities* (pp. 244–267). USA: Oxford University Press.

Kaysen, D., Lindgren, K., Sabir Zangana, G. A., Murray, L., Bass, J., & Bolton, P. (2013). Adaptation of cognitive processing therapy for treatment of torture victims: experience in Kurdistan, Iraq. *Psychological Trauma: Theory, Research, Practice and Policy, 5*(2), 184–192.

Kaysen, D., Lostutter, T. W., & Goines, M. A. (2005). Cognitive processing therapy for acute stress disorder resulting from an anti-gay assault. *Cognitive and behavioral practice, 12*(3), 278–289.

Kaysen, D., Stappenbeck, C. A., Carroll, H., Fukunaga, R., Robinette, K., Dworkin, E. R., ..., & Bass, J. (in press). Impact of setting insecurity on cognitive processing therapy implementation and outcomes in eastern democratic Republic of the Congo. European Journal of Psychotraumatology..

Kohn, R., Saxena, S., Levav, I., & Saraceno, B. (2004). The treatment gap in mental health care. *Bulletin of the World Health Organization, 82*, 858–866.

Lester, K., Artz, C., Resick, P. A., & Young-Xu, Y. (2010). Impact of race on early treatment termination and outcomes in posttraumatic stress disorder treatment. *Journal of Consulting and Clinical Psychology, 78*(4), 480.

Margaret-Anne Mackintosh, M., Cha, N., Willis, E. A., & Morland, L. A. (2019). How does racial diversity affect PTSD treatment outcomes in group cognitive processing therapy? Manuscript under review.

Marques, L., Eustis, E. H., Dixon, L., Valentine, S. E., Borba, C. P., Simon, N., Kaysen, D., & Wiltsey-Stirman, S. (2016). Delivering cognitive processing therapy in a community health setting: the influence of Latino culture and community violence on posttraumatic cognitions. *Psychological Trauma: Theory, Research, Practice, and Policy, 8*(1), 98.

Marques, L., Valentine, S. E., Kaysen, D., Mackintosh, M. A., De Silva, D., Louise, E., & Wiltsey-Stirman, S. (2019). Provider fidelity and modifications to cognitive processing therapy in a diverse community health clinic: associations with clinical change. *Journal of Consulting and Clinical Psychology, 87*(4), 357–369.

Murray, S. M., Augustinavicius, J., Kaysen, D., Rao, D., Murray, L. K., Wachter, K., Annan, J., Falb, K., Bolton, P., & Bass, J. K. (2018). The impact of cognitive processing therapy on stigma among survivors of sexual violence in eastern democratic republic of congo: results from a cluster randomized controlled trial. *Conflict and Health, 12*(1), 1.

Nixon, R. D. (2012). Cognitive processing therapy versus supportive counseling for acute stress disorder following assault: a randomized pilot trial. *Behavior Therapy, 43*(4), 825–836.

O'Cleirigh, C., Safren, S. A., Taylor, S. W., Goshe, B. M., Bedoya, C. A., Marquez, S. M., Boroughs, M. S., & Shipherd, J. C. (2019). Cognitive behavioral therapy for trauma and self-care (CBT-TSC) in men who have sex with men with a history of childhood sexual abuse: a randomized controlled trial. *AIDS and Behavior, 23*, 2421–2431.

Pearson, C. R., Kaysen, D., Huh, D., & Bedard-Gilligan, M. (2019a). Randomized control trial of culturally adapted cognitive processing therapy for PTSD substance misuse and HIV sexual risk behavior for native american women. *AIDS and Behavior*, *23*(3), 695–706.

Pearson, C. R., Smartlowit-Briggs, L., Belcourt, A., Bedard-Gilligan, M., & Kaysen, D. (2019b). Building a tribal–academic partnership to address PTSD, substance misuse, and HIV among American Indian women. *Health Promotion Practice*, *20*(1), 48–56.

Prince, M., Patel, V., Saxena, S., Maj, M., Maselko, J., Phillips, M. R., & Rahman, A. (2007). No health without mental health. *The Lancet*, *370*(9590), 859–877.

Resick, P. A., Monson, C. M., & Chard, K. M. (2016). *Cognitive processing therapy for PTSD: A comprehensive manual*. New York, NY: Guilford Publications.

Roberts, A. L., Austin, S. B., Corliss, H. L., Vandermorris, A. K., & Koenen, K. C. (2010). Pervasive trauma exposure among US sexual orientation minority adults and risk of posttraumatic stress disorder. *American Journal of Public Health*, *100*(12), 2433–2441.

Rutt, B. T., Oehlert, M. E., Krieshok, T. S., & Lichtenberg, J. W. (2018). Effectiveness of cognitive processing therapy and prolonged exposure in the Department of Veterans Affairs. *Psychological Reports*, *121*(2), 282–302.

Schulz, P. M., Huber, L. C., & Resick, P. A. (2006). Practical adaptations of cognitive processing therapy with Bosnian refugees: implications for adapting practice to a multicultural clientele. *Cognitive and Behavioral Practice*, *13*(4), 310–321.

Schulz, P. M., Resick, P. A., Huber, L. C., & Griffin, M. G. (2006). The effectiveness of cognitive processing therapy for PTSD with refugees in a community setting. *Cognitive and Behavioral Practice*, *13*(4), 322–331.

Shipherd, J. C., Maguen, S., Skidmore, W. C., & Abramovitz, S. M. (2011). Potentially traumatic events in a transgender sample: frequency and associated symptoms. *Traumatology*, *17*(2), 56–67.

Shipherd, J., Valentine, S. E., & Woulfe, J. (2019). An evidence-based approach to conceptualizing trauma responses among transgender and gender nonconforming adults. In J. E. Pachankis, & S. A. Safren (Eds.), *Handbook of Evidence-Based Mental Health Practice with Sexual and Gender Minorities* (pp. 268–290). USA: Oxford University Press.

Valentine, S. E., Borba, C. P., Dixon, L., Vaewsorn, A. S., Guajardo, J. G., Resick, P. A., Wiltsey Stirman, S., & Marques, L. (2017). Cognitive processing therapy for Spanish-speaking latinos: a formative study of a model-driven cultural adaptation of the manual to enhance implementation in a usual care setting. *Journal of Clinical Psychology*, *73*(3), 239–256.

Voelkel, E., Pukay-Martin, N. D., Walter, K. H., & Chard, K. M. (2015). Effectiveness of cognitive processing therapy for male and female US veterans with and without military sexual trauma. *Journal of Traumatic Stress*, *28*(3), 174–182.

Weiss, W. M., Murray, L. K., Zangana, G. A. S., Mahmooth, Z., Kaysen, D., Dorsey, S., Lindgren, K., Gross, A., Murray, S. M., Bass, J. K., & Bolton, P. (2015). Community-based mental health treatments for survivors of torture and militant attacks in Southern Iraq: a randomized control trial. *BMC Psychiatry*, *15*(1), 249.

Whaley, A. L., & Davis, K. E. (2007). Cultural competence and evidence-based practice in mental health services: a complementary perspective. *American Psychologist*, *62*(6), 563.

World Health Organization and United Nations High Commissioner for Refugees. (2013). Assessment and management of conditions specifically related to stress: mhGAP Intervention Guide Module (version 1.0). Geneva: WHO, pp. 1–273.

Chapter 12

Administering CPT across health care systems and clinical settings

Chapter outline

Strategies in disseminating and implementing CPT across systems

CPT has been widely disseminated in a variety of settings and healthcare systems to address PTSD (Chard et al., 2012). Within the United States Veterans Administration, CPT was the first evidence-based psychotherapy to be rolled out (Karlin & Cross, 2014; Rosen et al., 2016). In the time since the roll out began, CPT has also been implemented, as discussed in Chapter 4, in a wide variety of settings including in public and private mental health agencies (LoSavio et al., 2019), within the Australian and Canadian Veterans Administration Health system (Dalton et al., 2018; Forbes et al., 2012), within United States Department of Defense Clinics (Borah et al., 2013), primary care settings (Fortney et al., 2015), community mental health settings (Marques et al., 2016), tribal clinics (Pearson et al., 2019), rape crisis clinics (Beck, 2017; Nixon et al., 2016), and in correctional facilities/jail diversion programs (Ahrens & Rexford, 2002; Feingold, Fox, & Galovski, 2018) among other places! This wide range of settings within which CPT has been tried has provided a natural laboratory to understand implementation of CPT in real world settings. The settings discussed above are only a snapshot of the multitude of the places where CPT has been used. If CPT hasn't been delivered in a particular context that is relevant to your work, we are confident that the challenges and solutions described in many of these projects will be helpful in your own endeavors. With judicious planning, CPT can likely work well for your situation.

Flexible Applications of Cognitive Processing Therapy. http://dx.doi.org/10.1016/B978-0-12-816715-1.00012-1

Setting matters

The setting we are in can shape how successfully CPT is used and whether the therapy is able to grow and thrive or whether it dies out (Stirman, Gutner, Langdon, & Graham, 2016). The organizational climate around the administration of CPT can make a large difference in whether or not a clinic or program is able to implement CPT (Hundt et al., 2018). We discuss how to address a few of the challenges further.

Delivering an effective schedule of CPT

At some sites there may be factors that make it difficult to provide weekly CPT, such as policies around only providing monthly care or packed clinic schedules. This is important because when CPT sessions are spaced out more than weekly, they are associated with higher dropout and poorer treatment outcomes (Gutner et al., 2016). So what can you do? Certainly the information about dropout and outcomes can help you make a case for weekly therapy. Another potential strategy is to highlight for decision-makers at a site that monthly sessions still equals 12 visits, so it is the same number of visits, only delivered in a more effective schedule. This was the strategy we used during the rollout of CPT within the Veterans Administration to help shift clinic policies. If moving the organization culture isn't an option, another strategy is to compromise by scheduling the first five sessions weekly and then space the rest out to every other week. This will get the patient through the bulk of the assimilation work of CPT and will get momentum going.

To address packed clinic schedules, it can be helpful to schedule patients out for several sessions in a row. That way you have a lower risk of someone else taking your CPT slot or your patient getting confused about the day or time for their appointment.

Coping with a high clinical caseload

High caseload requirements can prevent clinicians from taking the time necessary to train in CPT or participate in consultation (Borah et al., 2013). It can also make it hard to find the time to prepare for sessions and hard to find time to fit in all those CPT sessions weekly. There are a couple of strategies that can help with reducing high caseloads.

Reducing long-term cases is one way to make space to provide CPT. First, you can try to graduate patients who have finished CPT rather than to keep them as long-term patients. In settings where there is a culture of long-term psychotherapy this is a shift! Another option is to move to spaced out booster sessions every few months or on an as needed basis, rather than weekly sessions for patients who have finished CPT but need more ongoing care as a way to free up more of your clinical time. Lastly, in some settings patients have been moved to groups for ongoing CPT support, to provide them with ongoing care while still making room for new patients in need of services.

Efficiency can also help as a way to address high caseloads. It isn't always possible, but when it is, it can be helpful to have several patients all at the same stage of CPT. You will have to review fewer sessions while getting prepared. This is especially helpful while you are learning CPT.

Difficulties in getting treatment to the patient

There may be other barriers to attending weekly CPT sessions. For example, in rural settings the distances involved can be difficult to manage coming in weekly. In other cases, factors such as poverty, transportation, or just a busy and inflexible work schedule can make it hard for patients to manage weekly sessions. Seeing the patient more frequently than weekly – such as the work done on providing CPT daily, may be helpful. It may be easier for some patients to carve out a week or two to do therapy, than to space it out over months.

Another option is to bring therapy closer to the patient. For example, we are providing CPT delivered in rural primary clinics via telehealth, even though the providers are many hours away. This can save patients' gas money, travel time, and make it more likely they will show up for the session. In another project, we've found that with really busy patients, telehealth sessions delivered in their homes is incredibly helpful in getting them care. Although use of telehealth is beyond the scope of this book, we would encourage you, if you use this method of care delivery, to research the ethical and legal issues around telehealth.

We have also done work bringing the therapy itself closer to the patients through the use of mobile therapists. In Iraq, CPT was delivered in community health settings but also in libraries or community centers. In ongoing work in DRC, the local NGO is using therapists on motorcycles to travel from community to community to provide CPT. CPT was provided in patient homes to get CPT to the Bosnian refugees (Schulz et al., 2006). Having providers closer to the patients they serve can work wonders in increasing accessibility.

Managing limited privacy

Some clinical settings have unique challenges to CPT. For example, in settings like correctional facilities or refugee camps, there can be challenges around privacy, either around who is attending CPT or around keeping CPT practice materials safe. This can also be an issue with intimate partner violence, where a partner may be stalking a patient or looking through her things.

To address issues around the privacy of attending CPT sessions, it can be helpful to have a generic name for the clinic or the treatment. When possible, it is better to have multiple reasons someone could be seeing that provider or be seen at that clinic. Calling CPT a wellness group rather than a CPT group can go a long way toward protecting privacy in settings where individuals have close proximity to each other and limited privacy. For example, in a refugee camp the intervention, although geared toward addressing intimate partner violence, was called "Strength" and was presented as a more general psychosocial program to protect the women's privacy and safety (Greene et al., 2019).

For some patients, even the materials of CPT can create risk for them. In these settings, there may be some advantage in allowing the patient time to work on practice after the CPT session in a separate space and then leave the materials in the clinic. You can also problem solve with them around whether there are safe places outside of the clinic to do the practice or to leave their materials. You can simplify the materials and have the patient memorize them, as we did in DRC for women who were illiterate (Chapter 11). Worst-case scenario, you can still provide CPT without the practice assignments. This may be less ideal but certainly is better than withholding treatment.

In sum, for a provider who wants to deliver CPT in a way where it is likely to be effective, it can be hard to push up against all of these organizational barriers. But it is doable! Effective dissemination efforts can involve either a push—"top down" approach or a pull "bottom up" approach (Karlin & Cross, 2014). We have found that laying out the data around the positive outcomes associated with CPT and tying those outcomes in with the organization's goals, can be one way to build organizational support from a "pull" perspective. Think about what aspects of administering CPT might be helpful for that organization's priorities. The priorities could include enrolling more unique patients, keeping medical utilization costs down, or demonstrating to funders the increased numbers of patients you can see with an efficient therapy like CPT, among others. This book has provided you with information that can be helpful for making the case for providing CPT to organizational leaders and key stakeholders. Brief, effective, time-limited interventions not only are more effective for our patients, but also when considered at scale, are clearly cost-effective for our organizations and agencies. Knowing where and how CPT can be flexible to adapt to the setting is also essential (Foa, Gillihan, & Bryant, 2013).

Training and support make a difference

Implementation of CPT takes money, time, and resources for training and consultation. One of the biggest barriers in adopting evidence-based therapies are the high costs associated with effective dissemination strategies (Foa, Gillihan, & Bryant, 2013). For example, one of the main barriers noted by rape crisis clinics in adopting CPT is that they do not have adequate operating budgets for training and supervision (Edmond, Voth Schrag, & Bender, 2019). Although it required persistence and advocacy within the service, we have all been involved in programs where staff made the case to those who manage the budget that the costs of training and supervision paid for themselves in terms of better outcomes for their patients (e.g., think of the savings of reducing re-hospitalizations).

Of course, the cheapest training model is to buy the treatment manual and give it a go! Manuals, like the CPT manual and like this book, that contain information on how to apply the therapy in real clinical settings, that include information on how to adapt the therapy to your setting, and that include applied practical information are more likely to lead to therapists picking up the skills and running with them than are traditional clinical treatment manuals (Kendall & Beidas, 2007). So this is a great step toward using CPT well. However, you are better off with more than just the manual.

In the early years of training CPT, it was fairly cursory. You might attend a half-day workshop at a conference or attend a lecture or two. The roll-out of CPT within the United States Veterans Administration was one of the largest psychotherapy dissemination projects ever conducted and really helped us evaluate and refine how best to train CPT. Over the years of trying things, learning from them, and tweaking the training model, we developed a program that has been largely effective in training providers in CPT and helping them use it. The current VA training model has individuals read the manual, attend a two-day training workshop, and then attend CPT consultation while they apply the therapy in their clinics (Chard et al., 2012). There is also a web-based refresher course to help you if you get rusty (https://cpt.musc.edu/). Case consultation is typically provided as a 60-minute, small-group telephone session, over a 4–8 month period, with an expert CPT clinician and several other trainees (Rosen, Ruzek, & Karlin, 2017). Consultation works both to enhance CPT skills mastery, and to help trouble-shoot around local implementation challenges. As of 2016, 5880 VA clinicians had attended CPT workshops and 2685 had completed case consultation (Rosen et al., 2016). This model, although developed for the VA, has now trickled down and informed how we generally train CPT across many settings.

The question often comes up then—how can I get this going in my site? There are often CPT mini-workshops at professional meetings or conferences. Another option is to look at the CPT website (https://cptforptsd.com/workshop/) for scheduled workshops and for consultation. For individuals and for smaller sites, this can be a cost-effective way to learn CPT. For larger sites, sometimes it makes more sense to schedule a CPT workshop specifically for your agency.

In many settings, consultation can be hard to schedule in or to justify. It is time out of busy clinic days and time out of caring for patients. *Consultation does make a difference in acquiring CPT skills.* In a novel research study, attending the CPT workshop only was compared to two kinds of follow-up consultation, one that included audio review of cases and the other, involved discussion and consultation of cases without the audio review (all therapy was recorded). Although patients' PTSD improved in all three conditions, the patients of the consultation therapists had significantly greater improvement (Monson et al., 2018).

Another option for really learning CPT is the learning collaborative. The goal of the learning collaborative is not only to train clinicians, but also to ensure that the intervention is sustainable (Nadeem et al., 2013). Learning collaboratives are a team-based learning approach that involves use of multiple face-to-face learning sessions mixed in with applied practice, and includes expert assistance in implementing the intervention. The difference between the VA rollout model and the learning collaborative model is that the learning collaborative model breaks up the face-to-face learning into smaller pieces, which allows learners to share their collective learning experiences and the learning collaboratives emphasize sustained learning across multiple settings. There is also an emphasis on training leaders who can help with organizational change. In a year-long learning collaborative of CPT, 60 clinicians across 18 agencies attended three in-person learning sessions, received weekly consultation, and submitted audio recordings of their therapy for feedback and evaluation (LoSavio et al., 2019). Patients treated by these providers demonstrated significant improvements in PTSD and depression. Six months after completion of the learning collaborative, 95% of the clinicians and 100% of the agencies were still providing CPT, suggesting that this model helps with sustained adoption of the therapy. Although this model appears highly effective in helping organizations adopt a therapy like CPT and improve patient outcomes, they take buy-in from various groups, can be expensive to use as a model, and are generally less easy to find than the typical CPT workshop + consultation model. There are occasional learning collaborative-style trainings that are listed on the cptforptsd.com website. This is also something that larger organizations can implement as a learning model to help ensure they don't just train clinicians but that the organizations are able to keep it going.

Another way to increase sustainability of CPT, and way of providing applied support in learning CPT is the Teaching-Family Model (Wolf, Kirigin, Fixsen, Blasé, & Braukmann, 1995). In this model, staff members at a site are taught how to train, coach, evaluate, and support implementation of a treatment. Each site basically develops its own in-house expertise and gradually reduces its reliance on more distant experts. The VA's move away from using National Trainers toward more local and regional trainers could be seen as an example of this model. The move toward local trainers has not demonstrated any loss in training or clinical outcomes in CPT (Rosen et al., 2016). In some settings providers may do this more informally by setting peer consultation groups. That way everyone can support each other in figuring out how to apply CPT in their setting. Finally, in some settings, periodic buying in of CPT expertise makes sense. Having an expert CPT trainer providing training every couple of years is helpful as a refresher for already trained staff and provides training for new staff. Combined with additional supervision for the latter, a relatively small outlay every few years can keep that service up to date in CPT despite staff turnover. Although the intervals are longer, this is analogous to getting your new car (CPT) serviced regularly.

In sum, the best way to learn CPT is to combine didactic teaching with applying the skills with some type of support. It's the difference between reading a cookbook, watching a cooking show, or cooking with a mentor who can help you master the skills. They all might get you supper, but you'll be able to master something more complex with more support during the hands-on learning process. All of these learning strategies have flexibility to match your needs, prior training, and budget.

Fidelity with flexibility

In implementing therapies in real world clinics, there is a totally understandable tendency to adapt the therapy to fit the local context, to address differences between the research setting where the therapy was designed and the one in which you are using it (Lundgren, Amodeo, Cohen, Chassler, & Horowitz, (2011). The modifications can range from slight changes in language to be a better fit for the clinical population to removing core components or adding in other elements. Some of these changes are done intentionally, but some of these changes happen organically over time. There can be tension in the decision of whether or not to modify the therapy. Some changes improve the treatment fit for the local setting, but others make the treatment less effective (Stirman, Miller, Toder, & Calloway, 2013).

Types of modifications to CPT can be categorized into delivery and content modifications. First, consider CPT delivery modifications. CPT has been extremely robust to changes in delivery. For example, CPT when delivered by a native speaker versus delivered via a translator has shown comparable outcomes and similar results to other clinical trials (Schulz et al., 2006). Similarly, CPT works equally well when delivered in person as compared to when the treatment is delivered via telehealth (Morland et al., 2015). So with delivery modifications, you are on pretty safe ground.

Changes in therapy *content* have more potential to dilute treatment effects, especially if clinicians are not mindful of what are core elements of the treatment. Sometimes we as therapists want to avoid the parts of the therapy that feel most difficult to us. However, those may be the most important pieces of treatment to include. Three studies have directly looked at the impact of fidelity to CPT outcomes. In a re-analysis of a clinical trial of CPT to treat military sexual trauma, two of the four therapists were found to have significantly poorer fidelity (Holder et al., 2018). The patients of these therapists also had poorer clinical outcomes. However, we do not know the ways in which these therapists were struggling with using CPT or what changes they were making to the protocol. Therefore, we don't know what specific therapist difficulties were leading to poorer clinical outcomes.

In a separate study, high therapist competence at Socratic Dialog and prioritizing assimilation stuck points was associated with better clinical outcomes (Farmer, Mitchell, Parker-Guilbert, & Galovski, 2017). Therapists varied more widely on attending to practice work during the sessions, although this was not associated with clinical improvement, nor was therapist skill in eliciting patients' emotional processing (i.e., focusing on having patients' feeling their feelings). That doesn't mean these elements aren't important! But they may be less related to therapist skill.

In a study of providers in a diverse, primarily Latino, community clinic, how well providers delivered CPT, whether they modified the treatment, and outcomes were all examined (Marques et al., 2019). This study looked at different types of modification, those that do not change core CPT elements, like lengthening session time or including culturally specific language, versus CPT inconsistent changes, like dropping out parts of the therapy or adding in new things. The study found that doing CPT competently and "by the book" was associated with improvements in depression and PTSD. Making changes that were consistent with core elements of CPT, but might have increased patient fit, also led to improvements in PTSD and depression. This suggests that personalizing the therapy by making the language accessible or using metaphors that resonate with your patient, doesn't hurt the therapy and may make it more effective.

New and shiny technique

So why does all of this matter? Often there is a tendency for clinicians (including us!) to drift. We learn something new and it is exciting and shiny. Should we add it into CPT? It might fit the patient we have. As we have discussed throughout this book, unless there is an overwhelming clinical need, it is likely that this will dilute the effects of CPT. Session time is precious. If you add in something new, it is likely that you won't have as much time for the active ingredients such as Socratic dialogue and chipping away at those assimilation stuck points.

Reliance on previous techniques

We also have a tendency to rely on what we know and what has been easy and comfortable. If CPT is new to you, there may be a tendency over time to switch to treatments you've used previously and are most comfortable with. This can lead to a "bleed over" of old strategies that are comfortable to you, into CPT. We've seen this with therapists who were previously trained in exposure therapies who feel uncomfortable leaving out the in vivo exposures and want to add them in or with therapists trained in mindfulness previously who want to add that in. Remember, in general we've found that adding more in doesn't help improve CPT.

But they don't get it yet

There is a tendency as well to overcorrect if a patient doesn't seem to be "getting it," especially if you are newer to CPT. This can manifest by repeating sessions early or in the middle of CPT until they get it. The problem is, this prevents patients from progressing to the stage of "owning" the CPT skills and really becoming their own therapists. In CPT they don't have to master one skill to learn the next as CPT has practice baked into the therapy structure. The other problem with repeating sessions is that it can inadvertently reinforce avoidance. By not moving forward with the treatment because "they aren't ready" we actually keep reinforcing both the message that they can't do it, and we may be reinforcing the avoidance itself.

Another issue that can come up is extending CPT longer than intended because the therapist doesn't think the patient has "gotten it" yet. As we have discussed, if you are not seeing symptom change, adding sessions in for additional practice is helpful. However, if this is continuing for months, the patient very likely needs to try a different therapy or it may be that there is something else getting in the way of their improvement.

All of these ways we can drift can dilute the effectiveness of CPT, reinforce therapist and patient avoidance, and can confuse the patient about the rationale or undermine it.

How to get CPT into my service and make it work?

We provide some websites at the end of the book to assist in accessing CPT training and to provide further information on the ways to keep up to date with CPT. Beyond the processes outlined above about optimal methods of being trained in CPT and the broad factors that influence its use in clinical settings, it is important to remember there is now an international CPT community. This means there are a number of CPT practitioners around the world who have come up against (and solved) the very challenges you might face in your own clinical setting when trying to introduce CPT. Make contact with this community, whether it be through the listed websites or chasing down the authors of the literature we have cited that is most relevant to your service. If we can help point you in the right direction to get this help, we are happy to do so!

Summary

CPT has been used in a wide variety of clinical settings, and with a wide variety of patient populations. To learn it well, it requires the use of multi-modal learning. In fact, we hope this book can be part of that process! It is also helpful to be aware of the organizational constraints that can be a help or hinderance in using CPT. Finally, although modifications to CPT to fit your setting and your patient are not bad and may even at times be helpful, it is essential to make those modifications in ways that do not alter the core elements of the treatment unless there is an overwhelming clinical reason to do so.

References

Ahrens, J., & Rexford, L. (2002). Cognitive processing therapy for incarcerated adolescents with PTSD. *Journal of Aggression, Maltreatment and Trauma*, *6*(1), 201–216.

Beck, J.G. (2017). Training cognitive processing therapy: application to the shelby County Rape Crisis Center. Available from: jgbeck@memphis.edu.

Borah, E. V., Wright, E. C., Donahue, D. A., Cedillos, E. M., Riggs, D. S., Isler, W. C., …, & Peterson, A. L. (2013). Implementation outcomes of military provider training in cognitive processing therapy and prolonged exposure therapy for post-traumatic stress disorder. *Military Medicine*, *178*(9), 939–944.

Chard, K. M., Ricksecker, E. G., Healy, E. T., Karlin, B. E., & Resick, P. A. (2012). Dissemination and experience with cognitive processing therapy. *Journal of Rehabilitation Research and Development*, *49*(5), 667–678.

Dalton, J. E., Thomas, E. W. S., Melton, H. A., Eastwood, A. J., & Harden, M. (2018). The provision of services in the UK for UK armed forces veterans with PTSD: a rapid evidence synthesis. *Health Services and Delivery Research*, 2050–4357.

Edmond, T. E., Voth Schrag, R. J., & Bender, A. K. (2019). Opening the black box: identifying common practice approaches in urban and rural rape crisis centers. *Violence Against Women* pp. 1–22. doi: 1077801219832903 advance online publication.

Farmer, C. C., Mitchell, K. S., Parker-Guilbert, K., & Galovski, T. E. (2017). Fidelity to the cognitive processing therapy protocol: evaluation of critical elements. *Behavior Therapy*, *48*(2), 195–206.

Feingold, Z. R., Fox, A. B., & Galovski, T. E. (2017). Effectiveness of evidence-based psychotherapy for posttraumatic distress within a jail diversion program. *Psychological Services*, *14*(4), 543–548 Advance online publication.

Foa, E. B., Gillihan, S. J., & Bryant, R. A. (2013). Challenges and successes in dissemination of evidence-based treatments for posttraumatic stress: lessons learned from prolonged exposure therapy for PTSD. *Psychological Science in the Public Interest*, *14*(2), 65–111.

Forbes, D., Lloyd, D., Nixon, R. D. V., Elliott, P., Varker, T., Perry, D., …, Bryant, R. A., & Creamer, M. (2012). A multisite randomized controlled effectiveness trial of cognitive processing therapy for military-related posttraumatic stress disorder. *Journal of Anxiety Disorders*, *26*(3), 442–452.

Fortney, J. C., Pyne, J. M., Kimbrell, T. A., Hudson, T. J., Robinson, D. E., Schneider, R., …, Moore, W. M., Custer, P. J., Grubbs, K. M., & Schnurr, P. P. (2015). Telemedicine-based collaborative care for posttraumatic stress disorder: a randomized clinical trial. *JAMA Psychiatry*, *72*(1), 58–67.

Greene, M. C., Rees, S., Likindikoki, S., Bonz, A. G., Joscelyne, A., Kaysen, D., …, Nixon, R. D., Njau, T., Tankink, M. T., Tiwari, A., & Ventevogel, P. (2019). Developing an integrated intervention to address intimate partner violence and psychological distress in Congolese refugee women in Tanzania. *Conflict and Health*, *13*(1), 1–16.

Gutner, C. A., Suvak, M. K., Sloan, D. M., & Resick, P. A. (2016). Does timing matter? Examining the impact of session timing on outcome. *Journal of Consulting and Clinical Psychology*, *84*(12), 1108–1115.

Holder, N., Holliday, R., Williams, R., Mullen, K., & Surís, A. (2018). A preliminary examination of the role of psychotherapist fidelity on outcomes of cognitive processing therapy during an RCT for military sexual trauma-related PTSD. *Cognitive Behaviour Therapy*, *47*(1), 76–89.

Hundt, N. E., Harik, J. M., Thompson, K. E., Barrera, T. L., & Miles, S. R. (2018). Increased utilization of prolonged exposure and cognitive processing therapy over time: a case example from a large Veterans Affairs posttraumatic stress disorder clinic. *Psychological Services*, *15*(4), 429–436.

Karlin, B. E., & Cross, G. (2014). From the laboratory to the therapy room: national dissemination and implementation of evidence-based psychotherapies in the US Department of Veterans Affairs Health Care System. *American Psychologist*, *69*(1), 19–33.

Kendall, P. C., & Beidas, R. S. (2007). Smoothing the trail for dissemination of evidence based practices for youth: flexibility within fidelity. *Professional Psychology: Research and Practice*, *38*, 13–20.

LoSavio, S. T., Dillon, K. H., Murphy, R. A., Goetz, K., Houston, F., & Resick, P. A. (2019). Using a learning collaborative model to disseminate cognitive processing therapy to community-based agencies. *Behavior Therapy*, *50*(1), 36–49.

Lundgren, L., Amodeo, M., Cohen, A., Chassler, D., & Horowitz, A. (2011). Modifications of evidence-based practices in community-based addiction treatment organizations: a qualitative research study. *Addictive Behaviors*, *36*(6), 630–635.

Marques, L., Dixon, L., Valentine, S. E., Borba, C. P., Simon, N. M., & Wiltsey Stirman, S. (2016). Providers' perspectives of factors influencing implementation of evidence-based treatments in a community mental health setting: a qualitative investigation of the training–practice gap. *Psychological Services*, *13*(3), 322–331.

Marques, L., Valentine, S. E., Kaysen, D., Mackintosh, M. A., De Silva, D., Louise, E., …, Ahles, E. M., Youn, S. J., Shtasel, D. L., Simon, N. M., & Wiltsey-Stirman, S. (2019). Provider fidelity and modifications to cognitive processing therapy in a diverse community health clinic: associations with clinical change. *Journal of Consulting and Clinical Psychology*, *87*(4), 357–369.

Monson, C. M., Shields, N., Suvak, M. K., Lane, J. E., Shnaider, P., Landy, M. S., …, Wagner, A. C., Sijercic, I., Masina, T., Wanklyn, S. G., & Stirman, S. W. (2018). A randomized controlled effectiveness trial of training strategies in cognitive processing therapy for posttraumatic stress disorder: impact on patient outcomes. *Behaviour Research and Therapy*, *110*, 31–40.

Morland, L. A., Mackintosh, M. A., Rosen, C. S., Willis, E., Resick, P., Chard, K., …, & Frueh, B. C. (2015). Telemedicine versus in person delivery of cognitive processing therapy for women with posttraumatic stress disorder: a randomized noninferiority trial. *Depression and Anxiety*, *32*(11), 811–820.

Nadeem, E., Olin, S. S., Hill, L. C., Hoagwood, K. E., & Horwitz, S. M. (2013). Understanding the components of quality improvement collaboratives: a systematic literature review. *The Milbank Quarterly*, *91*(2), 354–394.

Nixon, R. D., Best, T., Wilksch, S. R., Angelakis, S., Beatty, L. J., & Weber, N. (2016). Cognitive processing therapy for the treatment of acute stress disorder following sexual assault: a randomised effectiveness study. *Behaviour Change*, *33*(4), 232–250.

Pearson, C. R., Kaysen, D., Huh, D., & Bedard-Gilligan, M. (2019). Randomized control trial of culturally adapted cognitive processing therapy for PTSD substance misuse and HIV sexual risk behavior for Native American women. *AIDS and Behavior*, *23*(3), 695–706.

Rosen, C. S., Matthieu, M. M., Stirman, S. W., Cook, J. M., Landes, S., Bernardy, N. C., …, Chard, K. M., Crowley, J., Eftekhari, A., Finley, E. P., & Hamblen, J. L. (2016). A review of studies on the system-wide implementation of evidence-based psychotherapies for posttraumatic stress disorder in the Veterans Health Administration. *Administration and Policy in Mental Health and Mental Health Services Research*, *43*(6), 957–977.

Rosen, R. C., Ruzek, J. I., & Karlin, B. E. (2017). Evidence-based training in the era of evidence-based practice: challenges and opportunities for training of PTSD providers. *Behaviour Research and Therapy*, *88*, 37–48.

Schulz, P. M., Resick, P. A., Huber, L. C., & Griffin, M. G. (2006). The effectiveness of cognitive processing therapy for PTSD with refugees in a community setting. *Cognitive and Behavioral Practice*, *13*(4), 322–331.

Stirman, S. W., Gutner, C. A., Langdon, K., & Graham, J. R. (2016). Bridging the gap between research and practice in mental health service settings: an overview of developments in implementation theory and research. *Behavior Therapy*, *47*(6), 920–936.

Stirman, S. W., Miller, C. J., Toder, K., & Calloway, A. (2013). Development of a framework and coding system for modifications and adaptations of evidence-based interventions. *Implementation Science*, *8*(1), 8–65.

Wolf, M. M., Kirigin, K. A., Fixsen, D. L., Blase, K. A., & Braukmann, C. J. (1995). The Teaching-Family Model: a case study in data-based program development and refinement (and dragon wrestling). *Journal of Organizational Behavior Management*, *15*(1–2), 11–68.

Chapter 13

Future frontiers

Chapter outline

Where to now?

We hope we have shown throughout the book that CPT is a versatile and effective treatment for PTSD, even in the face of clinical complexity and challenges. Although CPT and other EBPs for PTSD help a substantial proportion of the patients we see, we know that not everyone derives equally positive outcomes. Accordingly, the field as a whole is trying to improve its understanding of why some patients engage easily and readily in therapy and others do not (Browne et al., 2019) and what factors influence treatment response. Ultimately, a more nuanced and individualized understanding of what works better for whom is required for therapists to more quickly and accurately determine when a patient is on the right course for successful versus unsuccessful outcomes (Sripada, Ready, Ganoczy, Astin, & Rauch, 2019). Unlike other domains of mental health (e.g., mood disorders), we do not have a standardized definition of what constitutes a treatment non-responder in the world of PTSD. A clear definition is critical if we are to advance our understanding of nonresponse as we continue to try to determine whether "non-responders" are truly in need of adaptations of current treatments or new treatments altogether.

Substantial efforts have been made to expand training opportunities for treatments such as CPT and to disseminate these therapies widely throughout healthcare services (Borah, Holder, & Chen, 2017). Despite these large-scale (and expensive) initiatives, we know that EBPs such as CPT are not being as widely used in routine clinical care as hoped (Maguen et al., 2019) and that the majority of patients who could likely benefit from a therapy like CPT cannot access it. Accordingly, dissemination and implementation research continues to

Flexible Applications of Cognitive Processing Therapy. http://dx.doi.org/10.1016/B978-0-12-816715-1.00013-3

not only improve the uptake of these therapies by therapists, but to ensure such efforts are sustainable in face of staff changes, organizational restructures, etc (Charney et al., 2019; LoSavio et al., 2019a). In this final chapter, we outline some of the endeavors that are underway (and some emerging findings) that relate to these challenges—endeavors that we believe will make important inroads to improving our care of those suffering from posttraumatic stress disorder.

Treatment engagement, patient choice, and matching

Like any therapy, those who do not initiate or engage with CPT are unlikely to experience its benefits. Ongoing research efforts will help us address these issues. For example, in contrast to some clinical lore, at least one study has observed that offering preparatory sessions before engaging in trauma-focused therapy such as CPT did not improve engagement or influence outcomes in those with comorbid substance problems (Wiedeman, Hannan, Maieritsch, Robinson, & Bartoszek, 2018). When patients are given a choice or receive their preferred PTSD treatment, not surprisingly, they tend to have better outcomes (Zoellner, Roy-Byrne, Mavissakalian, & Feeny, 2019). However, this research has focused on choices between psychotherapy (but not CPT) and medication, thus we do not know whether this impacts CPT outcomes (although in one study CPT was a preferred therapy over other psychotherapies; Schumm, Walter, Bartone, & Chard, 2015). Similarly, the use of decision aids to assist patients in choosing from a range of treatments that work for PTSD is likely to be helpful, but evaluation of the benefits of choice is still in its infancy (Harik, 2018). The idea of choice sounds good on paper—who wouldn't want excellent choices? But too many choices can give the impression that dabbling in one therapy and trying it on for size is an adequate and/or efficient strategy. After all, with many other options available if CPT (or any other therapy) doesn't quite fit, patients could operate under the impression that they can just easily try on another type of treatment. However, the underlying problem may really be avoidance—dabbling and choosing could be a form of avoiding getting fully engaged in *any* of the evidence-based therapies. It is thus critical to talk to patients about receiving a proper dose of therapy and considering changing to something else after at least 3–4 sessions are completed. Immediate gains do not happen for everyone and should not be the expectation. Prematurely discontinuing therapy obviously prevents the patient from receiving the proper dose of therapy and realizing the benefits of the intervention. The jury is still out on the benefits of choice. We maintain that providing recommendations for patients to engage in evidence-based therapy (essentially, the best we've got) optimizes their chances for recovery.

A key goal of current research is to better match patients to their optimal therapy. Researching such precision-medicine based approaches has only recently begun in the PTSD field, and again, has limited utility at present for the frontline clinician. Progress is being made, however. For example, efforts are underway to understand what characteristics of patients might make them better suited to CPT versus PE (and vice versa, see Keefe et al., 2018). We have applied sophisticated machine-learning approaches to better predict early in therapy who is likely to respond to CPT with the goal of developing guidelines for when and when not to pursue other treatment approaches (Nixon et al., 2019). Entering this mix is the hope that in the near future, psychobiological and genetic information can be used to complement predictions of outcome and optimal therapies. With advances in technology (e.g., allowing for big data collection) and increasingly sophisticated statistical methods, we anticipate that what has historically been a somewhat challenging area to research will become increasingly easier.

CPT and future innovations

A number of studies around the world are underway that aim to either improve CPT's efficacy, flexibility, or reach, and to better understand response/nonresponse. Here we provide a snapshot of just a few that we think might be of interest. For those interested in learning more about ongoing CPT trials, a search of clinical trial websites (e.g., clinicaltrials.gov, apps.who.int/trialsearch, anzctr.org.au) illustrates the substantial number of ongoing projects involving CPT.

Increasing flexibility and personalization

A modular form of CPT (CPT-M), which allows therapists to more flexibly administer the essential elements of CPT, is showing promise in terms of acceptability by therapists and positive outcomes with patients (LoSavio, Murphy, Wiltsey Stirman, & Resick, 2019c). In this modular version of CPT, sessions targeting assimilation are considered essential (especially the content of early CPT sessions) however therapists have choice about the dose of those sessions as well as which over-accommodation modules (e.g., safety, trust, etc.) they use. Building on the work cited earlier in the book (Nixon & Bralo, 2019), Dr. Nixon is testing the use of explicit case formulation with CPT (CPT-CF) in a veteran and first responder sample. It is hoped this extended protocol (up to 25 sessions) will better target complexities that interfere with optimal engagement in CPT as it allows for planned deviation from CPT for a discrete number of sessions where needed.

Stepped down models of care

Dr. Galovski is collaborating with Dr. Kehle-Forbes on her development of a therapist-assisted self-management intervention to assist CPT completers in stepping down from care. This was prompted by the observation that in the United States, Veterans who complete CPT report ongoing mental health needs and continue to engage in mental health services (Hundt, Barrera, Arney, & Stanley, 2017; Meyers et al., 2013). Part of this continued engagement seems to be due to low self-efficacy for building on treatment gains without the support of their therapists and a fear of relapse without ongoing mental health services

(Kehle-Forbes, Polusny, Galovski, & Possemato, 2019). The self-management program being trialed aims to increase patients' self-efficacy for managing their PTSD, enable the maintenance or building upon gains made in CPT through the continued application of and generalization of CPT skills, and to encourage engagement in meaningful life activities. Early results suggest that the intervention increases Veterans' self-efficacy for independently applying CPT skills. Although veteran focused, this project has implications for other trauma groups who are not immune to the same concerns regarding treatment cessation.

Adapting dose and delivery methods

We have previously discussed research that indicates CPT can be delivered intensively over short intervals (e.g., 2 weeks), with a recent case study detailing delivery over a single week (Held et al., 2019). Dr. Galovski is currently piloting the delivery of 12 sessions of CPT in 5 days (the work week) in a small sample of survivors of intimate partner violence with and without traumatic brain injuries. Six women have completed the 1-week version and six women are in the process of completing the comparison condition (12-week version of CPT). While still ongoing, none of the six women in the 1-week version dropped out of therapy and all six women evidenced quite substantial drops in PTSD severity. Imaging data will be available to detect changes in brain functioning (and potential group differences). Of interest, the therapists (national CPT experts) who treated the patients in the 1-week condition were astounded at the progress and all concluded that they "would only treat PTSD in a one-week format going forward if they had the chance." Finally, Dr. Galovski is also collaborating with Dr. Wachen on her large-scale RCT with active duty service members. This study is in its early stages and is comparing a combined individual and group CPT conducted in 1 week to individual CPT conducted in the traditional fashion (once or twice a week). Results will certainly provide much guidance about the benefits of this method of therapy delivery.

A very brief, CPT-informed, prevention intervention has been developed and is currently being tested for women following sexual assault to prevent PTSD and high-risk drinking. This intervention is one session, followed by four brief coaching calls (Bedard-Gilligan et al., 2019). A small open trial has been completed that found that the intervention was perceived as helpful and was associated with a large decrease in PTSD and a small decrease in alcohol use. A small randomized clinical trial is underway.

We know that CPT can be delivered effectively via telehealth and efforts are underway to improve CPT's reach further. Dr. Fortney and Dr. Kaysen have a trial that is in the last stages of completion testing CPT delivered via telehealth in rural, predominantly low income, primary care settings to see whether this treatment format extends access and reach of CPT and how this method of service delivery compares to a collaborative care approach (Fortney et al., 2019). To extend reach further, Dr. Monson and colleagues have developed a therapist-assisted, internet-delivered cognitive therapy for PTSD based on CPT (Monson, Fitzpatrick, & Wagner, 2017). Therapists assist clients in engaging in the intervention and troubleshoot any issues in its delivery through secure messaging. Program evaluation data are currently being collected on this approach.

Following a stepped-care model, Dr. Nixon is trialing delivery of online, guided self-help for PTSD where patients receive brief weekly support from a therapist as they work through trauma-focused CBT materials. This assistance can become more intensive if needed (e.g., the patient does not show a response), in which case patients are stepped up to standard CPT (also delivered via online telehealth). Once piloting is complete, this stepped-care approach will be tested against routine CPT in a randomized design.

Combination, adjunctive, and novel therapy approaches

As seen with other PTSD treatments, we anticipate the coming years will see further evaluations of how to maximize the effectiveness of CPT. For example, although the benefits of novel approaches such as repetitive Transcranial Magnetic Stimulation (rTMS) for PTSD are debated (see Shekelle et al., 2018, for review), a recent and well powered randomized trial showed large treatment effects were achieved when CPT was preceded by a course of rTMS relative to sham rTMS (Kozel et al., 2018). At this point in time we do not have rigorous data on whether the effects of CPT can be improved when combined simultaneously with standard psychopharmacology (e.g., antidepressants), or whether there are advantages to ordering the interventions (i.e., CPT first, followed by medication or vice versa). Similarly, there are novel approaches where psychopharmacology is used just before session to enhance memory re-activation and consolidation (Brunet, Saumier, Liu, Streiner, Tremblay, & Pitman, 2018); whether variants of such approaches are helpful for CPT remains to be seen. Of course, nonpharmacological methods of improving CPT may exist and will likely be researched in the years to come. As indicated by a search on the clinical trial websites mentioned earlier, clinical researchers are involved in a number of new tests of CPT, including comparing CPT against medication for those with PTSD and comorbid substance problems, combining CPT with a smoking cessation intervention, or enhancing CPT with executive functioning training (to name just a few!).

Future clinical research

The number of potentially fruitful avenues for further work is endless! By no means exhaustive, we now list several other areas that we believe require further study. For example, there needs to be more systematic research into patients' use of technology for helping with PTSD issues, especially mobile applications, including evaluating their effectiveness for which we still have only limited research (see Gould et al., 2019; Owen et al., 2018, for reviews). Relatedly, patients' day-to-day symptoms and functioning can now be easily reported several times a day on smart phones. Combining technology and advances in analysis of this type of data means this information may lead to more nuanced and personalized understanding of the subtle relationships within symptom types, the environment and the person's mood (Bourla, Mouchabac, El Hage, & Fereri, 2018). Ultimately, we envisage this information could guide what are the most effective components of CPT at an individualized level.

In terms of current CPT practice, although we know that those who make significant gains at the end of treatment tend to maintain those gains in the long-term, we know less about those who may be at risk of relapse. For example, we have very little research as to the value of strategies to ensure skills are consolidated, nor whether additional relapse prevention or booster sessions may be of benefit, although as highlighted earlier, work is now beginning in this area with respect to CPT. As also mentioned previously, we need to better understand the individual differences that might explain why some people do not respond to CPT. Although the field has high hopes regarding the eventual identification of psychobiological or epigenetic markers, to date, results have not quite eventuated (Schmidt & Vermetten, 2018), and this remains an ongoing line of research. One candidate variable we think deserves attention is belief inflexibility or rigidity. Modifying unhelpful beliefs is the heart of CPT and when they change, patients improve. Beliefs or attitudes that are resistant to change are seen not only in clinical disorders but more broadly in the general population (e.g., skepticism of the science underlying climate change forecasts or vaccinations). The trauma field may be assisted by drawing on work done in other domains of psychology such as cognitive and social psychology to improve our understanding of not only what make beliefs resistant to change, but also to help us develop new strategies designed to modify them.

Although the active ingredients of CPT have been studied in dismantling designs (Resick et al., 2008), understanding the therapists' role in CPT outcomes has only just begun (Farmer, Mitchell, Parker-Guilbert, & Galovski, 2016; LoSavio, Dillon, Murphy, & Resick, 2019b). Are there specific characteristics of therapists or specific skills that we can fine-tune for therapists that will further improve their effectiveness? Answers to these questions go hand in hand with the need to better understand how best to disseminate and implement CPT in routine care. As highlighted at the beginning of this chapter, there have been substantial dissemination and implementation initiatives that have certainly led to the increased reach of CPT, however a great deal remains to be done to ensure such initiatives are sustainable and maintain the effectiveness of the therapy.

As discussed earlier, there is a large gap between patients globally who could benefit from CPT and the number of trained therapists. Our models of training, use of workshops, followed by consultation, are expensive to scale. In many settings, this creates an insurmountable barrier to adopting or expanding CPT access. In addition, we do not know that current strategies and practices are the best or most efficient ways to train therapists, especially in the micro skills of CPT like Socratic Dialogue. Future research should examine whether there are more efficient and cost-effective ways to train therapists. In relation to CPT, alternative training methods that include blended online learning are underway which will be evaluated to examine their impact on training outcomes. In other areas of mental health highly innovative work is being conducted that uses automated intelligent tutoring systems to train therapists in behavioral therapy techniques (Aisenberg & Popović, 2019). However, as this study is underway, we do not know yet if it is effective, nor has it been applied to cognitive interventions at this stage. Similarly, there are studies that have used machine learning and signal processing to provide automated feedback to therapists regarding therapy quality. This has been used previously with Motivational Interviewing and is now being tested for cognitive behavioral therapy for depression. This strategy has not yet been applied to CPT but would have great promise in helping with scaling up therapist skills (for those interested in this area, see Hirsch et al., 2018; Imel, Caperton, Tanana, & Atkins, 2017; Xiao, Imel, Georgiou, Atkins, & Narayanan, 2016).

Conclusion

We hope that this book has been helpful in providing guidance in making CPT work for the patient sitting across from you in session. Although a protocol-based therapy, it has been our aim to show that "protocol" does not equal "inflexible." This book is a combination of our almost 60 years of collective experience with CPT, 2 decades of research, and the countless years of experience of colleagues and fellow CPT practitioners—the result of which we hope has provided you with useful tips and recommendations for delivering CPT effectively in the face of the complexities your patients bring to the table. We have provided some useful links over the page to enable you to stay up to date with all things related to CPT and PTSD and wish you the best with your clinical endeavors.

Resources

https://cptforptsd.com/—Official Website of CPT hosted by the creator of CPT (Dr Resick) and co-authors of the latest CPT Manual (Drs Monson and Chard).

www.cpt.musc.edu—Online CPT web-based learning course developed in collaboration with the CPT creators.

www.cognitiveprocessingtherapy.org.au—CPT website for Australian Clinicians.

www.ptsd.va.gov—Contains extensive information about PTSD, including CPT. You can sign up for three electronic publication alerts to keep updated on general findings in the trauma field (search for 'Clinician's Trauma Update Online', 'PTSD Research Quarterly', and 'PTSD Monthly Update'). Online training courses also available.

www.phoenixaustralia.org—Contains information about PTSD for clinicians and the general public (Australian focus).

www.istss.org—Website for the International Society for Traumatic Stress Studies. Disseminates latest findings on the effects and treatment of trauma and has public resources and policy recommendations. ISTSS also publishes guidelines on the prevention and treatment of posttraumatic stress disorders.

www.nctsn.org—US-based organization with a focus on children, adolescents and families that provides information and resources including online training.

References

Aisenberg, G., & Popović, Z. (2019). Remote training in evidence-based practices for clinicians who work with migrant workers. Available from: www.uwalacrity.org/current-projects/building-capacity/.

Bedard-Gilligan, M., Masters, N. T., Ojalehto, H., Simpson, T., Stappenbeck, C., & Kaysen, D. (2019). Refinement and pilot testing of a brief, early intervention for PTSD and alcohol use following sexual assault. Manuscript submitted for publication.

Borah, E. V., Holder, N., & Chen, K. (2017). Providers' use of evidence-based treatments for posttraumatic stress disorder: the influence of training, attitudes, and barriers in military and private treatment settings. *Best Practices in Mental Health: An International Journal*, *13*, 34–46.

Bourla, A., Mouchabac, S., El Hage, W., & Ferreri, F. (2018). e-PTSD: an overview on how new technologies can improve prediction and assessment of Posttraumatic Stress Disorder (PTSD). *European Journal of Psychotraumatology*, *9*, 1424448. doi: 10.1080/20008198.2018.1424448.

Browne, K. C., Chen, J. A., Hundt, N. E., Hudson, T. J., Grubbs, K. M., & Fortney, J. C. (2019). Veterans self-reported reasons for non-attendance in psychotherapy for posttraumatic stress disorder. *Psychological Services*doi: 10.1037/ser0000375.

Brunet, A., Saumier, D., Liu, A., Streiner, D. L., Tremblay, J., & Pitman, R. K. (2018). Reduction of PTSD symptoms with pre-reactivation propranolol therapy: a randomized controlled trial. *American Journal of Psychiatry*, *175*, 427–433. doi: 10.1176/appi.ajp.2017.17050481.

Charney, M. E., Chow, L., Jakubovic, R. F., Federico, L. E., Goetter, E. M., Baier, A. L., …, & Simon, N. M. (2019). Training community providers in evidence-based treatment for PTSD: Outcomes of a novel consultation program. *Psychological Trauma: Theory, Research, Practice, and Policy.*, *11*, 793–801. doi: 10.1037/tra0000427.

Farmer, C. C., Mitchell, K. S., Parker-Guilbert, & Galovski, T. E. (2016). Fidelity to the cognitive processing therapy protocol: evaluation of critical elements. *Behavior Therapy*, *48*, 195–206. doi: 10.1016/j.beth.2016.02.009.

Fortney, J. C., Heagerty, P. J., Bauer, A. M., Cerimele, J. M., Kaysen, D., Pfeiffer, P. N., … Unützer, J. (2019). Study to promote innovation in rural integrated telepsychiatry (SPIRIT): rationale and design of a randomized comparative effectiveness trial of managing complex psychiatric disorders in rural primary care clinics. Manuscript submitted for publication.

Gould, C. E., Kok, B. C., Ma, V. K., Zapata, A. M. L., Owen, J. E., & Kuhn, E. (2019). Veterans affairs and the department of defense mental health apps: a systematic literature review. *Psychological Services*, *16*, 196–207 doi: 0.1037/ser0000289.

Harik, J. (2018). Shared decision-making for PTSD. *PTSD Research Quarterly*, *29*, 1–9.

Held, P., Klassen, B. J., Small, C. F., Brennan, M. B., Van Horn, R., Karnik, N. S., Pollack, M. H., & Zalta, A. K. (2019). A Case report of cognitive processing therapy delivered over a single week. *Cognitive and Behavioral Practice*doi: 10.1016/j.cbpra.2019.07.006.

Hirsch, T., Soma, C., Merced, K., Kuo, P., Dembe, A., Caperton, D. D., ..., & Imel, Z. E. (2018). It's hard to argue with a computer: investigating psychotherapists' attitudes towards automated evaluation. In Proceedings of the 2018 Designing Interactive Systems Conference (pp. 559–571). ACM.

Hundt, N. E., Barrera, T. L., Arney, J., & Stanley, M. A. (2017). It's worth it in the end": veterans' experiences in prolonged exposure and cognitive processing therapy. *Cognitive and Behavioral Practice*, *24*, 50–57. doi: 10.1016/j.cbpra.2016.02.003.

Keefe, J. R., Wiltsey Stirman, S., Cohen, Z. D., DeRubeis, R. J., Smith, B. N., & Resick, P. A. (2018). In rape trauma PTSD, patient characteristics indicate which trauma-focused treatment they are most likely to complete. *Depression and Anxiety*, *35*, 330–338. doi: 10.1002/da.22731.

Kehle-Forbes, S. M., Polusny, M. A., Galovski, T., & Possemato, K. (2019). Mental health service engagement following completion of evidence-based psychotherapy for PTSD. Poster presented to the 35th Annual Meeting of the International Society for Traumatic Stress Studies, Boston, MA.

Kozel, F. A., Motes, M. A., Didehbani, N., DeLaRosa, B., Bass, C., Schraufnagel, C. D., …, & Hart, J. (2018). Repetitive TMS to augment cognitive processing therapy in combat veterans of recent conflicts with PTSD: a randomized clinical trial. *Journal of Affective Disorders*, *229*, 506–514. doi: 10.1016/j.jad.2017.12.046.

LoSavio, S. T., Dillon, K. H., Murphy, R. A., Goetz, K., Houston, F., & Resick, P. A. (2019a). Using a learning collaborative model to disseminate cognitive processing therapy to community-based agencies. *Behavior Therapy*, *50*, 36–49. doi: 10.1016/j.beth.2018.03.007 2.

LoSavio, S. T., Dillon, K. H., Murphy, R. A., & Resick, P. A. (2019b). Therapist stuck points during training in cognitive processing therapy: changes over time and associations with training outcomes. *Professional Psychology: Research and Practice*, *50*, 255–263. doi: 10.1037/pro0000224.

LoSavio, S. T., Murphy, R. A., Wiltsey Stirman, S., & Patricia P. A. (2019c). Making evidence-based treatment compatible with provider preferences: pilot of a modular version of cognitive processing therapy with community providers. Manuscript in preparation.

Imel, Z. E., Caperton, D. D., Tanana, M., & Atkins, D. C. (2017). Technology-enhanced human interaction in psychotherapy. *Journal of Counseling Psychology*, *64*, 385–393. doi: 10.1037/cou0000213.

Maguen, S., Li, Y., Madden, E., Seal, K. H., Neylan, T. C., Patterson, O. V., DuVall, S. L., Lujan, C., & Shiner, B. (2019). Factors associated with completing evidence-based psychotherapy for PTSD among veterans in a national healthcare system. *Psychiatry Research*, *274*, 112–128. doi: 10.1016/j.psychres.2019.02.027.

Meyers, L. L., Strom, T. Q., Leskela, J., Thuras, P., Kehle-Forbes, S. M., & Curry, K. T. (2013). Service utilization following participation in cognitive processing therapy or prolonged exposure therapy for post-traumatic stress disorder. *Military Medicine*, *178*, 95–99.

Monson, C. M., Fitzpatrick, S., & Wagner, A. (2017). Therapist-assisted cognitive therapy for post-traumatic stress disorder. Toronto, ON: Beacon Digital Therapy.

Nixon, R. D. V., & Bralo, D. (2019). Using explicit case formulation to improve cognitive processing therapy for PTSD. *Behavior Therapy*, *150*, 155–164. doi: 10.1016/j.beth.2018.04.003.

Nixon, R. D. V., King, M., Smith, B., Gradus, J., Resick, P. A., & Galovski, T. E. (2019). Predicting response to cognitive processing therapy for PTSD: a machine-learning approach. Manuscript in preparation.

Owen, J. E., Kuhn, E., Jaworski, B. K., McGee-Vincent, P., Juhasz, K., Hoffman, J. E., …, & Rosen, C. (2018). VA mobile apps for PTSD and related problems: public health resources for veterans and those who care for them. *MHealth*, *4*, 28–128. doi: 10.21037/mhealth.2018.05.07.

Resick, P. A., Galovski, T. E., Uhlmansiek, M. O., Scher, C. D., Clum, G. A., & Young-Xu, Y. (2008). A randomized clinical trial to dismantle components of cognitive processing therapy for posttraumatic stress disorder in female victims of interpersonal violence. *Journal of Consulting and Clinical Psychology*, *76*, 243–258. doi: 10.1037/0022-006X.76.2.243.

Shekelle, P. G., Cook, I., Miake-Lye, I. M., Mak, S., Booth, M. S., Shanman, R., & Beroes J. M. (2018). The effectiveness and risks of cranial electrical stimulation for the treatment of pain, depression, anxiety, ptsd, and insomnia: a systematic review [Internet]. Washington (DC): Department of Veterans Affairs (US); 2018 Feb. Available from: https://www.ncbi.nlm.nih.gov/books/NBK493132/.

Schumm, J. A., Walter, K. H., Bartone, A. S., & Chard, K. M. (2015). Veteran satisfaction and treatment preferences in response to a posttraumatic stress disorder specialty clinic orientation group. *Behaviour Research and Therapy*, *69*, 75–82. doi: 10.1016/j.brat.2015.04.006.

Schmidt, U., & Vermetten, E. (2018). Integrating NIMH research domain criteria (RDoC) into PTSD research. In E. Vermetten, D. Baker, & V. Risbrough (Eds.), *Behavioral Neurobiology of PTSD. Current Topics in Behavioral Neurosciences* (pp. 69–92.). (vol. 38). Cham, Switzerland: Springerdoi: 10.1007/7854_2017_1.

Sripada, R. K., Ready, D. J., Ganoczy, D., Astin, M. C., & Rauch, S. A. M. (2019). When to change the treatment plan: An analysis of diminishing returns in VA patients undergoing Prolonged Exposure and Cognitive Processing Therapy. *Behavior Therapy*doi: 10.1016/j.beth.2019.05.003.

Wiedeman, L. D., Hannan, S. M., Maieritsch, K. P., Robinson, C., & Bartoszek, G. (2018). Treatment choice among veterans with PTSD symptoms and substance-related problems: examining the role of preparatory treatments in trauma-focused therapy. *Psychological Services*doi: 10.1037/ser0000313.

Xiao, B., Imel, Z. E., Georgiou, P., Atkins, D. C., & Narayanan, S. S. (2016). Computational analysis and simulation of empathic behaviors: a survey of empathy modeling with behavioral signal processing framework. *Current Psychiatry Reports*, *18*(5), 49. doi: 10.1007/s11920-016-0682-5.

Zoellner, L. A., Roy-Byrne, P. P., Mavissakalian, M., & Feeny, N. C. (2019). Doubly randomized preference trial of prolonged exposure versus sertraline for treatment of PTSD. *American Journal of Psychiatry*, *176*, 287–296. doi: 10.1176/appi.ajp.2018.17090995.

Index

Note: Page numbers followed by "f" indicate figures, "t" indicate tables.

D

U

V

W

Kolibri 360 GmbH
Ferdinand-Jühlke-Straße 7
99095 Erfurt, Deutschland
produktsicherheit@kolibri360.de